DEMOCRACY
in the
EUROPEAN UNION

Dimitris N. Chryssochoou

I.B.Tauris *Publishers*
LONDON • NEW YORK

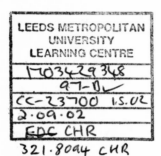
Paperback edition published in 2000 by I.B.Tauris & Co Ltd
Victoria House, Bloomsbury Square, London WC1B 4DZ
175 Fifth Avenue, New York NY 10010
website: http://www.ibtauris.com

In the United States of America and in Canada distributed by
St Martin's Press, 175 Fifth Avenue, New York NY 10010

First published in 1998 by Tauris Academic Studies,
an imprint of I.B.Tauris & Co Ltd

Copyright © Dimitris N. Chryssochoou, 1998, 2000

ISBN 1 86064 598 4

A full CIP record for this book is available from the British Library
A full CIP record for this book is available from the Library of Congress

Library of Congress catalog card: available

Typeset in Baskerville by Dexter Haven, London
Printed and bound in Great Britain by WBC Ltd, Bridgend, Mid Glamorgan

Contents

To my mother,

Karolina

Preface

This book is an exercise in theory-building. It aims to capture the dominant character of the relationship between democracy and the European Union by drawing on a rich spectrum of theories of democracy, regional international integration and comparative government. In so doing, it offers an account of alternative explanatory theses on the origins and development of what has become known as the 'democratic deficit' of the Union. The overall conclusion to be drawn is that the current democratic pathology of the larger polity stems as much from the inadequacy of existing institutional arrangements to meet the requirements of democratic shared rule as it does from the absence of a transnational *demos*: a self-conscious and politically active European citizen body capable of directing its democratic claims to, and via, the central institutions. This observation is crucial, for it addresses the question not only of 'Who Governs?', but also of 'Who is Governed?', suggesting that democracy, national or transnational, cannot exist without a *demos* conscious of its political identity.

Another premise on which this book heavily rests is that the more the Union approximates to a politically organised *Gemeinschaft*, the greater the possibilities for developing democracy within its structures. The crucial point here is that what is absolutely essential for the democratisation and legitimation of the larger polity is the development of 'a sense of community' among the constituent peoples. However, the present Union approximates a new type of collective entity, summed up in the concept of 'Confederal Consociation'. The latter, by resting on the properties of consensus elite government, compromises the principle of responsible government in the name of decisional efficiency and inter-elite accommodation. In this context, the crucial question is whether the democratic innovations of the Treaty on European Union and its recent revision in Amsterdam are capable of taking the transnational system beyond executive elite dominance, and closer to a European *Gemeinschaft*, thus allowing for the qualitative transformation of the Union from *democracies* to *democracy*.

Acknowledgements

Every intellectual journey has its own rewards, of which the greatest I find is being blessed with those who have made the journey worth taking. Difficult as it may be to impress feelings on words, what follows aims at no less. My primary debt is to my mother Karolina for providing the motivation to complete this study. It is to her that this book is dedicated. I am also indebted to Dimitris K. Vardas for his unreserved support over the years, and to Professor Percy Allum (formerly at The University of Reading) for generously offering his intellectual insights during the preparation of the PhD thesis which forms the basis of this book. My debt extends to my father Nikistratos to whom this book means so much. I am also grateful to Alexandra Moschonidou for her love and personal sacrifices; to my grandmothers Maria Anoni and Chyssoula Chryssochoou for their continuous encouragement; to my grandfather Alexandros K. Anonis who, although I have no memories of him, provided all the necessary financial support for making this study possible; and my grandfather Dimitrios K. Chryssochoos who would have been so proud of this publication. I am indebted to Professor Michael J. Tsinisizelis (University of Athens) for his notorious wake-up calls, sincere frienship and valuable academic advice, as I am to Dr Stelios S. Stavridis (The University of Reading) for his equally unreserved encouragement and support. I am particularly grateful to Professor Paul Taylor (London School of Economics and Political Science) whose recent work on European integration provided the intellectual stimuli for my research. For their valuable comments on various themes related to this study I would like to thank Dr Vincent Wright (University of Oxford), Professor Clive H. Church (University of Kent at Canterbury), Dr Hussein Kassim (Birkbeck College, London), Professor Richard Gillespie (University of Portsmouth), Professor Fulvio Attiná (University of Catania) and Professor Evangelos G. Raftopoulos (Panteion University, Athens). I feel equally indebted to all those who were kind enough to assist me with my primary source research and to my colleagues at the University of Exeter for their warm welcome into their academic family. Finally, I wholeheartedly wish to express my gratitude to Panagia Gorgoepikoos for answering my prayers.

Dimitris N. Chryssochoou
University of Exeter

PART I

Preliminary Considerations

CHAPTER 1

Setting the Framework for Analysis

ABOUT THE STUDY

It seems fair to suggest that Puchala's celebrated linking of the European Community (EC), now the European Union (EU), with the story of the elephant and the blind men has lost nothing from its original topicality in the early 1970s.[1] True, the 'elephant' is some 25 years older now, but so is the debate of conceptualising the conditions and dynamics of Union governance during these years. As then, students of integration find themselves engaged in a process of inventing concepts, comparing familiar models of governance and patterns of political behaviour, as well as elaborating on classical and novel ideas on joint decision-making, ranging from the unitary state model to dynamic conceptions of federalism and confederalism. Lying somewhere in the midst of an analytical spectrum whose two poles are represented by theories of international relations and approaches to comparative politics, the search for a clear model of Union governance seems somewhat interminable. This is perhaps why the various academic endeavours involved in the process of theorising about European integration have produced so far many promising departures but achieved few concrete arrivals. In that context, this study claims that the concept of 'confederal consociation' is a promising analogy for capturing the relationship between the Union and its component state/citizen parts. The central thesis advanced here is that the constituent polities are bound together in some form of 'union' to further certain common ends without losing their individual sovereignty to a higher central authority.

Equally striking is the fact that much scholarly writing has taken place within the framework of identifying a plethora of inherent paradoxes, succinctly summarised by Scharpf as 'frustration without disintegration and resilience without progress'.[2] Our analysis, by taking an active interest in revealing the primary causes motivating these trends, adds yet another paradox to the integrative process: although the Union possesses considerable state-like qualities in regulating the relations among peoples and states, it has failed to transform itself from democracies to democracy.

More specifically, the notion of a 'democratic deficit' in its structures has been almost exclusively confined to the inadequacy of current institutional arrangements to bestow the larger entity a parliamentary base of its own, somewhat similar to those found within its substructures. From this view, such a 'deficit' takes the form either of an institutional/parliamentary deficit, or of a federal/constitutional one, or even of a combination of the two. Crucial as it may be for elucidating the structural parameters of large-scale democratic shortfalls, this line of interpretation leaves unsaid their equally important socio-psychological dimension: the absence of a self-conscious, civic-minded and politically active 'transnational *demos*', whose members have developed a sense of 'belonging to' a European 'political community', and a sound determination to direct their democratic claims to, and via, the central institutions. The conclusion to be drawn is that the democratic pathology of the Union can only be remedied by paying attention simultaneously to the implications of further constitutional reform (concerned with the *form* of EU-level democracy), and to those resulting from the process of 'transnational *demos*-formation' (concerned with the political *identity* of the European citizen body). Accordingly, this book aims not only to address the oft-raised question of 'who governs?' but also 'who is governed?' Put another way, upon which popular, rather than merely institutional, infrastructure are transnational democratic arrangements expected to apply in order to bridge the long-standing gap between the worlds of interstate and intrastate democracy?

SOME PRELIMINARY NOTES

It is commonplace among students of integration that, although the Union has been constantly in search of an efficient response to the challenges of complex interdependence, all EU partners have sought to promote those tasks which seemed to be serving their domestic needs best, thus postponing or even excluding others that might put their respective integrities at stake. This partly explains the appearance in the relevant literature of a series of neologisms such as graduated integration, multi-speed Europe, variable geometry, *Europe à la carte* and, more recently, flexible integration, as instruments for bringing about different visions of Europe.

A perfect illustration of such a differentiated attitude towards extending the jurisdiction of the Union can be found in Taylor's sceptical academic analysis of 1983 on the influence of intergovernmentalism in the decisional context of the larger polity. Having stressed the limits imposed by the states in the integration process, he draws the conclusion that 'the challenges to sovereignty were successfully resisted and the central institutions failed to obtain the qualities of supranationalism'.[3] It is noteworthy that this comment was made at a time when Webb was criticising the member states for failing to respond 'to any kind of "Community spirit"',[4] and only a year after Wallace's observation that the EC was 'stuck between sovereignty and integration',[5] both confirming the Euro-pessimist mood of the early 1980s. But even before, as well as after, this 'intergovernmental' stage of integration, a number of equally discouraged statements have been reported, classifying the course of the shared undertaking into some identifiable phases according to the willingness shown by national governments to slow, freeze or further advance the pace of the transnational process.[6]

And yet, despite the intensity of national governmental retrogressions to established goals and commitments, such an attentive behaviour towards furthering the 'scope' (range) and 'level' (depth) of the regional arrangements,[7] has not always been strong enough to suppress the highest objective of integration, as set out in the preamble to the Treaty of Rome: the accomplishment of an 'ever closer union among the peoples of Europe'. In particular, the idea of a 'political' Europe, as opposed to a European free-trade area, has exhibited over time a remarkable dynamism of its own, allowing it to develop independently of intra-Community conflicts.

Equally, the force of multilateral collaboration, albeit a carefully-negotiated one, has demonstrated its ability to recover its strength and rediscover its faith even under the most unfavourable circumstances, when the prospects for creating a European political community looked particularly bleak, if not an elusive, utopian chimera. Although such an entity has yet to emerge, at least as Haas has originally envisaged it,[8] there are still signs of optimism for moving the larger unit closer to a community based on widely-shared assumptions about its political organisation. More importantly, both leaders and led have gradually come to recognise that its capacity to act in a democratically accountable and legitimate way should be augmented.

In retrospect, the vagueness of this treaty-based mandate offered a convenient framework from which a plurality of forces committed to a variety of outcomes, ranging 'from loose confederation to tight federation',[9] could eventually co-exist with each other without jeopardising the whole integrative experiment. The term 'union', for all its apparent political obscurity, provided for the general direction of integration, leaving the organisational aspects of the task to be decided in an incrementalist, 'step-by-step' fashion. On the other hand it has often led to political disagreements and conceptual misinterpretations over the 'terminal state' of integration, which have not allowed the 'quasi-constitutional' blueprint of the Rome Treaty to clearly indicate the means by which previously independent entities would be brought together in a larger unit 'rooted', in Tassin's words, 'in a common experience and tradition of thought and history that reside equally in all the peoples of Europe'.[10]

The transformation of the preamble of the Rome Treaty into a concrete operational method for large-scale community-building raises a number of distinct, yet interrelated, questions about our understanding of the current central arrangements. To that end, the governance of the European polity will have to be evaluated in terms of both national and transnational politics, territorial and non-territorial perspectives. For it is this distinctive duality in the character of the Union which so profoundly continues to excite the interest of political analysts all over the world to this very day.

TRANSCENDING THE BOUNDARIES OF THE 'POLITICAL'

Attempts to elucidate the basic properties and functions of the Union have produced a sense of renewed theoretical excitement in the study of international co-operation and integration. As Laffan notes, although 'both [processes] involve states in collective action... the latter can be distinguished from the former by the intensity of relations between the participating states and the manner in which those relations are organised and managed'.[11] Whereas co-operation is 'not intended to impinge greatly on national sovereignty' since it remains under the control of states,[12] integration, defined by Deutsch as a process of transforming 'previously separate units into components of a coherent system,'[13] has been portrayed by those stressing the 'totality' of the nation-state as a homogenising force capable of eroding cultural diversity, reducing territorial autonomy, and leading towards a superordinate political authority.

But it would be false to assume that the setting up of transnational institutions signalled the end of the European states system in a region which first gave birth to it several centuries ago. Instead, these institutions, accompanied by joint decision-making practices in areas of common concern, have challenged the 'classical' conception of sovereignty which perceives the state as 'the ultimate source of authority, law and legitimate force within its boundaries'.[14] For European institution-building has certainly not given birth to a supra- or post-national entity with a monopoly of law-making and law-enforcing powers. Rather, it has questioned the established perception of the nation-state as the only compelling reality of political organisation, offering to the participating units a unique opportunity to discover new ways of mutually beneficial co-operation across pre-established frontiers.

In many respects, the genesis of the Community constituted a by-product of a creative marriage between political idealism and economic rationalism. As Hallstein summarised the historical causes of unification, 'it took the boundless excesses of nationalistic policy in the Second World War and the equally total disaster they caused, to make obvious that in politics, and in economics also, the countries of Europe must sink or swim together'.[15] Post-war Europe was to be unified on the basis of nation-states willing to transcend the boundaries of the 'political' by means of pooling their sovereignty at a higher level for specific purposes. As Kolinsky put it: 'the real issue was not surrendering political sovereignty but ascertaining common goals and finding methods of working together'.[16] Indeed, far from losing their sovereignty to an uncontrollable European Leviathan, the member states sought to bolster their collective strength by means of participating in a transnational system of governance based on various combinations of self-rule and shared management.

The mere recognition by the states themselves of the limitations inherent in the exercise of sovereignty does not imply that sovereignty itself has been shifted upwards to a new 'centre'. As Taylor put it: 'what is changed is the wish of national legislatures and governments to do certain things in common, rather than their legal or constitutional right or capacity to do them'.[17] This implies that the traditional dogma of absolute sovereignty has been replaced by a more pragmatic interpretation of the sovereignty principle. By 'pragmatic' is meant that systems of collective management can form the basis of an acceptable political option which, by highlighting a unique sharing of national governmental functions, confirms Kirchner's contention that 'what might be lost individually is gained collectively through a common stand or policy'.[18] Or alternatively, 'giving up an outmoded condition of sovereignty came to be seen as necessary in order to preserve sovereignty'.[19]

Accordingly, a cluster of democratic nation-states decided to involve their respective political authorities in a larger co-operative system in which all partners to it − irrespective of differences in size, constitutional traditions, cultural identities, and levels of economic development − would perform a constructive role. This was achieved through a nexus of consensual and majoritarian modes of collective decision-making that were to operate in an 'extranational' fashion, 'neither above or below the nation-state, but "alongside"'.[20] Such an approach renders any 'zero-sum' conception of national and EU politics as analytically improper, implying instead that they can be mutually reinforcing (see below).

Finally, it was believed that Community membership would embody in the broader public a consciousness somehow distinct from territorially defined feelings of 'we-ness', perceived at the time as the primary source of the old rivalries. At most, it was hoped that the flowering of this politically new type of collective consciousness out of a rich spectrum of established identities would be capable of transcending a plethora of existing sentiments of selfish nationhood. At least, it was anticipated that strong feelings of 'Europeanness' could harmoniously co-exist with nationally inspired forms of fellowship. In any case, no clash between them was envisaged whatsoever.

SOME FURTHER DEMOCRATIC CONCERNS

From the very beginning, however, there seemed to be a missing piece in the jigsaw for the completion of the new polity: the role of citizens and their relation with the central institutions remained somewhat unclear. In particular, what would the position of the European public be in the integration process? Which set of principles, values and ideas were to guide the governance of the new collective entity? Also, how could citizen participation be adequately ensured in the shaping of common policies and taking of joint decisions? Oddly enough, questions relating to the establishment of concrete channels of communication between those involved in transnational decision-making and those whose lives were to be directly affected by these decisions were ultimately left unanswered.

Without doubt, European integration has come to resemble more a 'top-down' than a 'bottom-up' process driven by the grandiloquent aspirations of national governmental elites and accompanied by a utilitarian, rather than affective-identitive, support of the European public, otherwise known as 'permissive consensus'.[21] Such a consensus, however, has not extended 'beyond expected payoffs' to strengthening *horizontal* interaction among the constituent *demoi*, nor to generating any substantive levels of identification with one another and with the central institutions. For it is mainly the constituent governments, enjoying the backing of various administrative bodies, that play the key role in both setting the integrative agenda and taking the major decisions in an increasingly opaque way. In Laffan's words: 'Major decisions affecting the lives of individual citizens are now taken in forums far removed from "the man of the street"'.[22] As a result, the pursuit of 'ever closer union' has become a prisoner of its own vagueness and hence ever-more diluted, whilst the gap between the forces pressing towards further 'formal' integration and popular political sentiments is widening alarmingly (see chapter 8).[23]

Although a variety of conflicting ideas have always been at the very heart of the debate about the future direction of the Union, the quest for increased openness and transparency in its legislative process, for effective parliamentary control over its executive branches, and for extensive citizen involvement in the setting of its political agenda are but relatively recent manifestations of transnational democratic concerns. Despite the fact that national leaders have stressed the benefits of unity, as opposed to the ill-effects of fragmentation, it is difficult to ignore the fact that in the formative years of integration they were not particularly preoccupied with the task of embodying in the workings of the larger polity the democratic functions of government; to the extent that one can wonder whether the Union was ever intended to be democratic at all.

For instance, although the original treaties sought to establish some kind of parliamentary control over transnational activities, both the European Parliamentary Assembly of the European Coal and Steel Community (ECSC), and its successor European Parliament (EP) of the then European Economic Community (EEC), were primarily consultative bodies, possessing limited controlling and supervisory powers, as compared to those that the member legislatures had acquired through time. Instead, the preferred pattern of institutional development became one of convenience for national executives to exercise their transnational duties in a highly unaccountable environment. These conditions, unacceptable by liberal-democratic standards, have often pushed the Union closer to the traditional international relations model, and further away from the requirements of the democratic process.

It soon became evident, however, that a number of problems consequent on citizens' remoteness, political apathy and alienation from the central political system would have to be appropriately addressed if what had already been achieved was not to be undermined. But how was the increasing distance between leaders and led to be effectively narrowed? Under what conditions would it be possible for the peoples of Europe to engage themselves actively in the process of union? And also, would it be possible at all to envisage a terminal democratic state of European integration?

Without wishing to answer at this stage of analysis these preliminary questions, it is sufficient to note that as the regional system grew in importance, its members were eventually forced to look inwards and examine the strengths of whatever democratic properties it possessed, something which did not seem to be of cardinal importance when the 'Original Six' first set in motion the process of integration, despite the early warnings of the academic community. In particular, Brugmans, as early as in 1970, had warned that the Community was sacrificing its democratic principles on the altar of its integration.[24] Or, as Hallstein alternatively put it a few years later, 'the decisions that have been taken lag far behind public opinion in Europe'.[25] Similarly, Averyt noted that wider public participation might have been an obstacle to the creation of the Community itself.[26]

In retrospect, as the pace of union was advancing, the quest for democratising the Community was gaining an autonomous momentum of its own; to the extent that the notion of a 'democratic deficit' – the growing gap between the essential requirements of modern democratic government and the actual conditions upon which the governance of the Union is largely based – became one of the polity's most celebrated deficiencies. As a result, the emphasis gradually shifted from economic to democratic considerations, suggesting that concepts like responsible government, decisional efficiency and multinational shared rule are not incompatible with each other. As a result, the quest for a more democratic process of union, far from being an ephemeral political demand, has been elevated to a strong point of reference for those seeking to change a number of established rules about the conduct of EU politics.

THE 'DEMOCRATIC DEFICIT' AND BEYOND

As previously noted, the creative co-existence between different levels of authority within the Union points towards a multilogical system of governance which is neither national nor international in character, but one in which a multiplicity of institutional settings act and interact with each other in a 'positive-sum' manner. This implies that the Union and the states are bound together in a symbiotic and, hence, mutually dependent and reinforcing relationship: dependent in that no decision can be taken and no common action be successfully deployed unless all interested parties have a stake in it; and reinforcing in that the joint exercising of merged sovereignties rests on the idea of a balance of costs and advantages for all the 'uniting' parts.[27]

It is important at this point to stress that this study heavily rests on the premise that the emergence of such a symbiotic arrangement between national and regional political life, far from resembling a process leading towards a hierarchical, unitary European superstate, counterposes the dynamic enmeshing of different layers of government across a wide range of policy areas in the pursuit of consensually predetermined objectives. For symbiosis – a term used synonymously with 'mutualism' – first and foremost implies a harmonious association of different entities which eventually benefit from their interactive relations. In other words, it points towards a state of affairs whereby more than two actors learn to live with each other, test their strengths for co-operative behaviour and, where necessary, reconcile a variety of distinct interests in a mutually advantageous manner via joint endeavour.

In this sense, integration is not an 'all-or-nothing' process based on a 'winner-takes-all' governing ethos. To some extent, this moderate vision of the process reflects the 1975 Tindemans Report on European Union calling the member states 'to exercise their sovereignty in a progressively convergent manner'.[28] The gradualist process of integration provides the member states with a wide range of possibilities to resist any developments of the Union of which they disapprove. What is interesting, however, is that even the most reluctant of them prefer to go further down the road to integration for fear of being left outside the realm of influencing transnational politics. In other words, the driving force of integration is neither the maximisation of purely territorial interests nor, conversely, of a single recognised 'common interest'. Rather, it is a balancing act between the two, carefully orchestrated within the confines of common structures. It is a compromise which takes the form of a creative synthesis between the forces pressing towards a federal-type organisation and those preferring a more or less favourable version of intergovernmentalism as a means of promoting unification.

However, as this study will also try to illustrate, this vigorous inter-mingling of national and European political actors has greatly facilitated the consolidation of a process leading towards the 'recentralisation' of national political power in favour of 'executive-centred elites' and, inevitably, at the expense of traditional representative institutions.[29] As Williams put it: 'One of the unforeseen consequences of the Community... is the weakening of national parliaments *vis-à-vis* their own executives, even in those areas that lie outside Community competence at the present time'.[30]

This development has significant implications for EU democracy-building: it provides an encouragement for national governments to evade parliamentary control over their transnational activities. At the same time, by creating strong tendencies towards the 'interlocking' of national and European bureaucracies, it undermines the ability of the individual citizen to identify which level of government is ultimately responsible for specific decisions. It also suggests that the move towards 'ever closer union' is proving to be a slow and uneven process: slow, since the pace of integration is largely controlled by the executive branches of the constituent polities; and uneven, since it tends to promote a pattern of political interaction which undermines the ability of national parliaments to be effectively involved in EU legislative processes.

However lamentable, the roles and functions of both national parliaments and the European Parliament have remained marginal in comparison to those exercised by national executive and administrative agents. As a result, a significant widening of the scope of joint decision-making has been determined *in camera* at various ministerial meetings, decreasing the possibilities for executive responsibility to parliamentary institutions. Moreover, it brings to the surface serious considerations about the democratic legitimacy of the Union itself. For in a system of representative democracy, legitimacy ultimately rests on a 'public process of interaction' in which the *demos* exercises control, although indirectly, over the activities of those who are entitled to commit the polity as a whole.[31] This hardly corresponds to the actual conditions of European decision-making which, instead, seem to justify the fears about an ever problematic relationship between 'democratic practice in theory and in reality in the EC'.[32]

These 'realist' assumptions suggest that the evolution of the Union, instead of circumscribing the sovereignty of states, has led to a different kind of enfeeblement: the erosion of the democratic ethos in the conduct of transnational relations. In fact, one may parallel the process of integration with a contemporary *deus ex machina* for the participating governments to reassert their authority domestically, and even rediscover themselves as the principal actors of the national governing process. In the same vein, if the increasing role of national governmental elites in determining the range and depth of the regional process is not counterbalanced by a corresponding effort to enhance the levels of citizen participation in its structures, it may well result in the emergence of the most dangerous of all political cleavages, political elites vs the people, with unforeseen consequences for the political viability of the Union.[33]

PREMISES, THEORIES AND PROPOSITIONS

Although the preceding discussion might lead to the assumption that a 'democratic deficit' does exist in European structures, it is essential that its very origins, nature, and the means toward its elimination be cautiously explored. In addition, this study will attempt to elucidate the wider debate concerning the democratic legitimacy of the major central institutions, the search for a new interinstitutional balance of interests and power at the larger level, and the prospects for a more symmetrical relationship between territorial and non-territorial instruments of government. The main reason for reflecting upon these themes springs from a wider concern for promoting democracy in the Union, that of defending a certain spiritual heritage of European civilisation.

But how can one define the democratic deficit of the Union? How did it emerge in its institutional apparatus? Is it a mere extension of national parliamentary decline and, hence, a mirror-image of subsequent democratic shortfalls and/or dysfunctions of post-1945 Western European parliamentarism, or does it rather emanate from the absence of a formal constitutional settlement at the regional level? Should it be entirely equated with the European Parliament's quest for enhancing its formal role and powers in the central legislative process, as often appears to be the case in the relevant literature, or is there a deeper concern about extending citizen participation in the affairs of the Union? Furthermore, is there an optimal way for moving away from the dominant practices of 'conventional' intergovernmentalism, such as horse-trading, log-rolling, pay-offs, side-payments and the like, and towards non-bargaining issues based on the principal values, norms and conditions of democratic shared rule? And finally, what are the practical consequences of the deficit in question for the future institutional evolution and popular legitimation of the transnational polity?

Although one might justifiably assert that any attempt to account for these issues involves a number of value judgements, not least because of the inevitability of defining inherently debatable concepts that belong to various academic disciplines, such a task will nevertheless provide the theoretical stimulus of this study. Equally, to argue that because democratic perfection is practically unattainable little can be done to enhance the democratic ethos of transnational politics would simply amount to a convenient but no less irresponsible apology for inaction. For democracy, West and East, is the ultimate organising mechanism of civic association, the highest merit of which lies in its inherent ability to adequately guaranteeing the participation of the *demos* in the shaping of its political environment, thus creating a continuous and intimate relationship of mutual dependence between those possessing political authority and those subject to it. In this sense, democracy survives as the fundamental principle of political organisation, bringing the process of government closer to the citizen, whilst providing the necessary means to bridge the gap between 'decision-makers' and 'decision-receivers' not only within but also across borders.

At a more general level, although much analytical effort is being concentrated on exploring the 'individuality' and/or *sui generis* character of the regional system, fashioning political concepts to suit its distinctive properties and inventing new analogies to put its political evolution in some definable order, a number of issues continue to escape the focus of contemporary scholarship. Of these, the most crucial are the problems that European integration generates for both democratic theory and practice. Although the latter sphere has only recently started to be systematically explored, especially after the first formal constitutional amendment to the Rome Treaty in the mid-1980s, the former has hardly been investigated by the *acquis académique*.

Moreover, despite the fact that a number of diagnoses and prescriptions are offered as alternative means towards the elimination of the deficit concerned, little attention has been paid towards connecting the democratic pathology of the Union with what we understand today by the term 'democracy'. In Bowler and Farrell's words: 'There may be many proposals and counter-proposals for *solving* the "democratic deficit", but there appears to be little consideration given to outlining what *is* the problem'.[34] Or, as Neunreither put it: 'While almost everyone seems to agree that a democratic deficit exists, it is far from certain that there is a general understanding of what is meant by it'.[35] Thus, one of the primary aims of this study, and a largely unexplored analytical path, is to link any discussion on the dialectics of democratic rule with the *problematique* at issue.

This critical observation aims to address one of the greatest challenges to contemporary democratic thinking: the need to establish the missing link between domestic political life and the realm of transnational relations, and between the currently fragmented European citizen body and a transnational *demos* conscious of its political identity. In other words, the object is to transcend the current European *Gesellschaft* (society) by means of establishing a politically organised *Gemeinschaft* (community) as the necessary socio-psychological infrastructure upon which the third transformation of democracy, following the democratisation of the city-state and then of the nation-state,[36] be practically achieved (see chapter 4).

This historically new experiment in democratic self-transcendence refers to the process through which the Union will be transformed from a system of democratic governments into a democratic system of government. In the minds of some, it may be somewhat presumptuous to speak of an end result, in the form of a transnational *demos*, or even a contradiction in terms, in that it may lead towards the emergence of a new European 'political nation' as a prelude to the development of new forms of (supra)nationalism. Likewise, others may perceive the process of transnational *demos*-formation as totally undesirable and even necessarily detrimental to the preservation of high levels of segmental cultural distinctiveness and civic autonomy within a 'union of diversities' such as the Union of today.

Our response to these concerns is that if there is indeed a democratic deficit in the Union, it is as much a structural deficit, reflecting both the current asymmetry in the allocation of power among its major institutions and the loss of democratic autonomy by national legislatures, as it is a socio-psychological deficit, reflecting an apparent lack of 'a sense of community' among the member publics. From this view, the Union is closer to the model of confederation, albeit of a dynamic kind, since it manifests itself as 'a unity constituted by *states*',[37] as distinct from being a 'close unity' emanating from the united will of a European *demos*.

The argument advanced in this study is that if the Union is to evolve into a political system to deserve the title 'democracy', such a qualitative leap is not to be achieved merely either by granting the European Parliament full co-decision powers with the Council of Ministers, or by the enactment of central legislation concerning the polity's democratic (re)orientation, or even by further constitutional amendments to the original treaties. However essential, these lines of democratic pursuit will fall short of bearing the expected fruits if they are not accompanied by the development of fellow-feelings among the constituent *demoi* and the transformation of the latter into a civic-minded and politically-responsible *demos*. This requires the existence of a transnational 'public sphere' for democratic principles to be made operative, rather than a document (or a set of documents) signed by 'The High Contracting Parties', confirming yet again their common determination to furthering the democratic cause. Such a determination should be shown by its anonymous citizens themselves.

For democracy, according to a revealing point made by Schattschneider, 'has much to do with what people think, what they think about themselves, who they think they are, and what their attitudes are toward other people'.[38] In this view, the coming of democracy is like 'a change of climate': it results from 'the spread of new ideas, new ways of thinking about relations between the people and the government, and the general acceptance of a new point of view, because *democracy is first a state of mind*'.[39] Thus, the envisaged order of events for democratising the Union would be: the collective body of its citizens develops a common public awareness; formulates large-scale democratic assumptions; and then directs its democratic claims to, and via, the central institutions. This, combined with the necessary institutional reforms, summarises the road to greater and better democracy in the transnational unit.

This line of thought contends that the role of the member publics will be decisive in determining the democratic quality of the polity of which they want to be and act as integral parts. It follows that the extent to which they develop a sense of fellow-citizenship resting upon what Tassin calls 'a politically-constituted public space'[40] will be critical for the nature of public involvement in EU affairs. To put it bluntly, the democratic awakening of the currently fragmented European *demos* will provide the popular base upon which a certain philosophy of collective governance be reflected in the internal workings of the Union: a transnational democracy, setting the standards for the quality of performance to be exhibited by the central institutions.

The point of this contention is that the scholar ought to shift the emphasis from purely institutional considerations to grass-roots political developments, examine the chasm between democratic theory and practice, and formulate comprehensive arguments on what democracy should be about in the Union. This, of course, requires both a definitional approach to democracy and a clarification of what democracy is not. It also relates to the examination of what the role of the European public should be in a regional system of mutual governance which, at this particular stage of its development, can be classified best as an 'unfulfilled democracy': a transnational democracy in the making which, although possessing some democratic qualities, should open up its political processes and institutions to its fledging *demos*.

All in all, the EU paradigm, as a polycentric arrangement among democracies where political authority tends to be diffused as much as possible to their executive branches, reflects a striking paradox: it is a politically uncrystallised collective entity in which democracy is losing its normative characteristics, whilst showing a notable potential for democratic self-development. Whereas on the one hand it appears as a living manifestation of a 'part-formed' body politic whose nascent *demos* still lacks the vantage point from which to see the larger system as a coherent political whole, on the other it displays a psychological need to cultivate its civic consciousness and create a new democratic environment by transcending pre-existing territorial and ideological boundaries. It is our contention that the struggle for transnational democracy will be won when the emerging European *demos* consolidates its civic personality and sees the purpose of its own activities in the total structure. In other words, when an amorphous aggregation of apathetic voters, confused about the role they share in EU politics, transforms itself into a politically conscious citizen body.

This said, the remedy to the democratic deficit appears to be as simple to state as it is difficult to achieve: political support for, democratic control over, and citizen identification with the decisions produced by the central institutions. Yet, as long as the European public acts only as a passive receiver and not as a potential transmitter of political initiatives, it will be this distinctive pattern of 'consensus elite government' which will continue unchallenged to steer the Union, control the fate of its citizens and command the major hierarchies of power within its structures by enforcing what Michels called 'the iron law of oligarchy'.[41] This time, however, it will be not in the form of dominant party structures, but of a 'regional regime' led by a management coalition of co-operative elites.[42] This uniquely observed pattern of 'managerial elitism' should be recognised as a poor substitute for democratic shared rule, leaving little, if any, space at all for citizens to share in a complex system of joint decision-making.

But this is not to suggest that one should turn to radical democratic theory to 'revive a sense of civic spirit throughout society'.[43] Rather, the object is to find appropriate ways to stop the Union from falling short of public accountability and policy responsiveness by means of reforming its institutional base and changing popular attitudes so that democratic participation be effectively guaranteed. Indeed, democratic reform is not the cause but the consequence of popular determination to be governed in a more democratic way: it follows rather than precedes public pleas for democracy. And although it may be crucial for correcting existing democratic deficiencies, it is certainly not an end in itself. For democratisation presupposes a self-conscious unit within which it actually takes place. This much-needed civic consciousness, if it is ever to be found in the Union, would have to spring from the European public itself and not from a 'good-will' declaration of intent among a cluster of national governmental elites. Otherwise, transnational democracy will remain largely ineffective, inconclusive and, hence, essentially unfulfilled.

And since no single democratic doctrine can claim to have the last word on what democracy is and how it actually works, it may be better to understand first what popular democratic assumptions are all about, and then establish a distinction between democratic and non-democratic systems of government. To borrow again from Schattschneider: 'Democratic government makes very little sense until we know why people should in any case at all have anything to say about how they are governed'.[44] He concludes: 'Unless we know why it is supremely important that people participate in their own government, the great effort required to make democratic government work will not seem worth the pains'.[45] In this way at least, one should not be disappointed in discovering how much EU practice deviates from academic definitions of democracy and good government. Or, as Dahl put it: 'Where, as in the European Community, there is a nascent *demos*, its representatives are weak... It is difficult to foresee when, if ever, the Community may adopt a government nearly as democratic as the polyarchies now existing within the member countries.'[46]

CONCLUSION

Let us close this introductory chapter with a touch of optimism, and argue that the Union provides a kaleidoscope of interdependent units whose multiple interaction derives its strength from the power of different constitutional traditions, diverse historical experiences, distinct political identities and cultural affinities; yet one in which the possibilities for increasing its democratic properties by means of transcending popular fragmentation and moving beyond 'executive elite dominance' are indeed limitless.

Notes on Chapter 1

1   Puchala, Donald J., 'Of Blind Men, Elephants and International Integration', *Journal of Common Market Studies*, March 1972, pp 267-84. Most of the discussion in this study will be concerned with the 'European Community' as the ascendant of the 'old' European Communities, and now the essential component of the three-pillar structure introduced by the Treaty on European Union. Unless otherwise specified, the terms 'European Community' and 'European Union' will be used interchangeably.

2   Scharpf, Fritz W., 'The Joint-Decision Trap: Lessons from German Federalism and European Integration', *Public Administration*, Autumn 1988, p 239. Cf Wallace, William, *Regional Integration: The West European Experience* (Washington DC, 1994, The Brookings Institution), p 46. Wallace notes: 'extensive collaboration interspersed with occasional confrontation characterize the policy style'.

3   Taylor, Paul, *The Limits of European Integration* (New York, 1983, Columbia University Press), p 56.

4   Webb, Carole, 'Theoretical Perspectives and Problems', in Wallace, Hellen *et al.* (eds), *Policy-Making in the European Community*, Second edn (Chichester, 1983, John Wiley & Sons), p 1.

5   Wallace, William, 'Europe as a Confederation: the Community and the Nation-State', *Journal of Common Market Studies*, September-December 1982, p 67.

6   Taylor, Paul, *The Limits of European Integration*, pp 60-92; Kaiser, Ronn D., 'Toward the Copernican Phase of Regional Integration Theory', *Journal of Common Market Studies*, March 1972, pp 207-32; Pinder, John, 'Positive Integration and Negative Integration', *The World Today*, March 1968,

pp 88-110; Langeheine, Bernd and Weinstock, Ulrich, 'Graduated Integration: A Modest Path Towards Progress', *Journal of Common Market Studies*, March 1985, pp 185-97; and Prize, Victoria C., 'Three Models of European Integration', in Dahrendorf, Ralf *et al.*, *Whose Europe? Competing Visions for 1992* (London, 1989, Institute of Economic Affairs) pp 23-37.

7   On these concepts see Paul Taylor, 'The Politics of the European Communities: The Confederal Phase', *World Politics*, April 1975, pp 342-3. Taylor states: 'scope refers to the horizontal extent of integration, the number of functional areas which are linked together in some way within the larger territory; level refers to the manner in which the areas are organised – in particular, the extent to which they are ruled from the new centres which can act independently of governments'.

8   Haas, Ernst B., *The Uniting of Europe: Political, Social and Economic Forces 1950-1957* (London, 1958, Stevens & Sons), p 5. He defines political community as a 'condition in which specific groups and individuals show more loyalty to their central political institutions than to any other political authority, in a specific period of time and in a definable geographic space'. Interestingly, 12 years later he asserted that 'the verbally defined single terminal conditions with which we worked in the past... are inadequate because they foreclose real-life possibilities'. See his 'The Study of Regional Integration: Reflections on the Joy and Anguish of Pretheorizing', *International Organization*, Autumn 1970, p 631.

9   See Wallace, William (ed.), *The Dynamics of European Integration*, (London and New York, 1990, Pinter), pp ix-x.

10   Tassin, Etienne, 'Europe: A Political Community?', in Mouffe, Chantal (ed.), *Dimensions of Radical Democracy* (London and New York, 1992, Verso) p 171. 'Whatever the difficulties posed in defining a European *identity*,' Tassin notes, 'it is clear that the idea of Europe has denoted, and continues to denote, a common tradition of thought and culture rooted in that constant interchange over two millennia which have given this part of the world a certain unity of the mind'.

11   Laffan, Brigid, *Integration and Co-operation in Europe* (London and New York, 1992, Routledge) p 3.

12   *Ibid.*

13   Deutsch, Karl W., *The Analysis of International Relations* (Englewood Cliffs NJ, 1971, Prentice-Hall) p 158. Quoted in *ibid*, p 3. Deutsch has also defined integration as 'the attainment, within a territory, of "a sense of community" and of institutions and practices strong enough and widespread enough to assure, for a "long" time, dependable expectations of "peaceful" change among its population'; and Haas as 'the process whereby political actors in several distinct national settings are persuaded to shift their loyalties, expectations and political activities toward a new centre whose institutions possess or demand jurisdiction over the pre-existing national ones'. See, respectively: Deutsch, Karl W. *et al.*, *Political Community and the North Atlantic Area*, (Princeton NJ, 1957, Princeton University Press), p 2; and Haas, Ernst B., *The Uniting of Europe*, p 12. Cf. Lindberg, Leon N., *The Political Dynamics of European Economic Integration*, (Stanford MA, 1963, Stanford University Press), pp 4-8.

14 Kolinski, Martin, 'The Nation-State in Western Europe: Erosion from "Above" and "Below"?', in Leonard Tivey (ed.), *The Nation-State: the Formation of Modern Politics* (Oxford, 1981, Martin Robertson), p 84. Cf. Hoffmann, Stanley, 'Reflections on the Nation-State in Western Europe Today', *Journal of Common Market Studies*, September-December 1982, pp 21-37. For a recent account of the subject see Selder, David, 'The Nation-State in Europe, East and West', in Wyn Rees, G. (ed.), *International Politics in Europe* (London and New York:, 1993, Routledge), pp 57-68.

15 Hallstein, Walter, *Europe in the Making*, (London, 1972, Allen & Unwin), p 18.

16 Kolinski, Martin, 'The Nation-State in Western Europe', pp 82-3.

17 Taylor, Paul, *International Organization in the Modern World: The Regional and the Global Process* (London and New York, 1993, Pinter), p 94.

18 Kirchner, Emil J., *Decision Making in the European Community: The Council Presidency and European Integration* (Manchester and New York, 1992, Manchester University Press), p 6. He states: 'Clearly, there is a strong element of national control in the process of integration which allows the pooling of sovereignties in certain fields but ensures that there is not a zero-sum transfer of competences from the national to the Community context'.

19 Taylor, Paul, *International Organization in the Modern World*, p 104. In the preface he makes the point that 'sovereignty survives as the fundamental principle but its implications are the result of changing conventions and culture'.

20 Wallace, William, 'Europe as a Confederation', p 66.

21 See Lindberg, Leon N. and Scheingold, Stuart A., *Europe's Would-Be Polity: Patterns of Change in the European Community* (Englewood Cliffs NJ, 1970, Prentice-Hall), esp. pp 38-63.

22 Laffan, Brigid, *Integration and Co-operation in Europe*, p 122.

23 Wallace defines 'formal' integration as 'deliberate actions by authoritative policy-makers to create and adjust rules, to establish common institutions and to work with and through those institutions'; and 'informal' integration as 'those intense patterns of interaction which develop without the intervention of deliberate governmental decisions, following the dynamics of markets, technology, communications networks and social exchange, or the influence of religious, social or political movements'. See Wallace, William, *The Transformation of Western Europe*, (London, 1990, Royal Institute of International Affairs), p 54.

24 See Brugmans, Henry, *L'idée Européenne: 1918-1965* (Bruges, 1965, De Tempel).

25 Hallstein, Walter, *Europe in the Making*, p 30; quoted in Slater, Martin, 'Political Elites, Popular Indifference and Community Building', *Journal of Common Market Studies*, September-December 1982, p 69.

26 Averyt, William F., 'Eurogroups, Clientela and the European Community', *International Organization*, Autumn 1977, pp 949-72.

27 For an account of the notion of 'symbiosis' and European integration see Taylor, Paul, 'The European Community and the State: Theories, Assumptions and Propositions', *Review of International Studies*, April 1991, pp 109-25. Cf. Hoffmann, Stanley, 'Obstinate or Obsolete? The Fate of the

Nation State in Western Europe', *Daedalus*, Summer 1966, pp 862-915; Wallace, William, 'Europe as a Confederation', p 66; and Lindberg, Leon N. and Scheingold, Stuart A., *Europe's Would-Be Polity*, pp 94-5.

28 Quoted in Wallace, William, 'Europe as a Confederation', p 65. See 'European Union', Report by Leo Tindemans to the European Council, *Bulletin of the European Communities*, Supplement 1-1976.

29 On the concept of 'executive-centred elites' see Mezey, Michael L., *Comparative Legislatures* (Durham NC, Duke University Press, 1979), pp 53-4.

30 Williams, Shirley, 'Sovereignty and Accountability in the European Community', *Political Quarterly*, July 1990, p 306.

31 A similar definition of legitimacy appears in Kaiser, Karl, 'Transnational Relations as a Threat to the Democratic Process', in Keohane, Robert O. and Nye, Joseph S. (eds), *Transnational Relations and World Politics* (Cambridge MA, 1981, Harvard University Press), p 357.

32 Lodge, Juliet, 'EC Policymaking: Institutional Dynamics', in Lodge, Juliet (ed.), *The European Community and the Challenge of the Future*, Second edn (London, 1993, Pinter), p 22.

33 See Chryssochoou, Dimitris N., 'Democracy and Symbiosis in the European Union: Towards a Confederal Consociation?', *West European Politics*, October 1994, pp 1-14.

34 Bowler, Shaun and Farrell, David M., 'Legislator Shrinking and Voter Monitoring: Impacts of European Parliament Electoral Systems upon Legislator-Voter Relationships', *Journal of Common Market Studies*, March 1993, p 46.

35 Neunreither, Karlheinz, 'The Democratic Deficit of the European Union: Towards Closer Co-operation between the European Parliament and the National Parliaments', *Government and Opposition*, Summer 1994, p 299.

36 For a brief account of the first two transformations see Dahl, Robert A., *Democracy and its Critics* (New Haven and London, 1989, Yale University Press), pp 1-9.

37 Forsyth, Murray, *Unions of States: The Theory and Practice of Confederation* (Leicester, 1981, Leicester University Press), p 15.

38 Schattschneider, Elmer E., *Two Hundred Million Americans in Search of a Government*, (New York, 1989, Holt, Rinehart and Winston), p 42.

39 *Ibid.*

40 Tassin, Etienne, 'Europe', p 188.

41 See Michels, Robert, *Political Parties* (Glencoe, 1915, Free Press).

42 On this concept see Taylor, Paul, *International Organization in the Modern World*, pp 2-3.

43 Parry, Geraint, *Political Elites* (London, 1969, Allen & Unwin) pp 152-6.

44 Schattschneider, Elmer E., *Two Hundred Million Americans in Search of a Government*, p 43.

45 *Ibid.*

46 Dahl, Robert A., *Dilemmas of Pluralist Democracy: Autonomy vs Control* (New Haven and London, 1982, Yale University Press) p 15 (emphasis added).

CHAPTER 2

Democratisation in a System of Democracies

THE EUROPEAN RESURGENCE OF DEMOCRACY

Before reflecting upon the various definitions given on the 'democratic deficit' of the Union, a general discussion is in order, to act as a prelude to the current debate on the inadequacy of existing institutional arrangements to exercise effective democratic control over European legislation. Such a discussion is also expected to reveal that irrespective of how one defines the concepts of democracy and legitimacy, without these two indispensable ingredients for the building of any viable polity, the forces that move the Union towards further integration would find it all the more difficult to motivate the member publics to shift their democratic expectations to, and identify with, the central institutions. These democratic concerns were arguably given greater currency after the collapse of communism in Central and Eastern Europe.

Whereas by the turn of the 1980s the states in this region started to reassert their right to self-determination, EU members showed a firm determination to expand the common arrangements, strengthen the bonds among their peoples and, in brief, 'deepen' the integrative process in almost all areas of public activity. As Ascherson put it, for the East Europeans 'birth meant rebirth' in the sense that '1989 transformed sham nation-state independence within the Soviet empire into something more "real": approximating to popular memory of what independence has meant in the post-Versailles period'.[1] By contrast, the end of the same year found the Heads of State and Government of the Community agreeing at the Strasbourg European Council on the establishment of an Inter-Governmental Conference (IGC) on Economic and Monetary Union (EMU) by the end of 1990, which was soon to be running in parallel with its political counterpart on European Political Union (EPU).

In Eastern Europe, the demise of communist rule was accompanied either by a proliferation of a large number of nation-states, courtesy of the disintegration of the Soviet Union or, in the case of its former satellites, by a 'return to normality' in terms of political pluralism, parliamentary democracy and the rule of law.[2] Western Europe on the other hand has witnessed a *relance* of integration, culminating in the signing of the Treaty on European Union (TEU) in February 1992. As its name implies, and Art. A explicitly states, the new treaty was intended to mark a new stage in the creation of 'an ever closer union among the peoples of Europe,' although a large part of the original treaties, as amended by the Single European Act (SEA) in February 1986, still stands in its own right (see chapter 8).

In attempting to link these parallel processes – integration in the West, disintegration (or regeneration) in the East – it is no exaggeration to suggest that the cataclysmic consequences of the '1989 events' paved the way towards a rapid reappraisal of what democracy should mean in a Community embarked on the achievement of a genuine 'European Union' by the end of the millennium. The new post-cold war order in Europe, along with the polity's internal momentum for far-reaching institutional reforms, forced the Community to re-examine the quality of its own democracy. Such an internal enquiry soon acquired the status of a virtual necessity, not least because advocates for further adjustment to the new conjuncture drew attention to the 'demonstration effect' the Community had on its Eastern neighbours. As Lodge observed with a touch of irony, at a time when the EC is 'enjoining others to follow liberal democratic practices, it must itself practice democratic decision-making'.[3] Or, as Martin sarcastically put it: 'If the EC was a state and applied to join the Community it would be turned down on the grounds that it was not a democracy'.[4]

Soon after the realisation of the need to democratise the Community, voices were raised severely criticising the current state of its legislative processes. The rationale underlying these criticisms was that as long as the principle of responsible government was to be constantly undermined in EC law-making, any subsequent parliamentary deficiency at both levels of government would clearly highlight a distinctive pattern of institutional development whereby 'Executives decide and Parliaments abide'. 'To be sure,' Hoffmann and Keohane attest, 'national parliaments have seen their role diminish in all parliamentary democracies, either because the bills they vote are usually initiated by cabinet, or because... the legislature is less important than the directorates of the parties in power'.[5] Although integration reinforces these trends by depriving parliaments of their traditional powers, it does not challenge their prominent position as the hallmark of national governmental legitimacy, 'both because they are elected by the people, and because the executive emanates from them'.[6]

Whilst these 'peaceful revolts' were taking place, a change of priorities became evident, shifting the emphasis from market-oriented issues to those concerning the establishment of transparent structures of public accountability at the larger level. It was believed that only through the injection of a massive dose of democracy would the Community be able to transform itself from a 'Business Europe' into a 'People's Europe', and break away from the ill-effects of unfettered executive dominance. For one thing, the regional system seemed to be heading towards a distinct form of joint ministerial rule, with the decisions taken by the Council being far removed from the real needs and concerns of the citizen. As Bogdanor and Woodcock asserted, 'the shortcomings of the Community lie in the feelings of remoteness and lack of influence and involvement on the part of many of its citizens'.[7]

More specifically, European citizens are asked to vote every five years for what Martin calls 'a democratic "fig leaf" on an undemocratic system'.[8] Ranged against these comments, democracy, as 'a form of government in which ultimate control rests in the hands of the people,'[9] far from being achieved at the larger level, is something which still must be striven for. Holden's less abstract definition of democracy as 'a political system in which the whole people, positively or negatively, make, and are entitled to make, the basic determining decisions on important matters of public policy'[10] exemplifies the problem of the democratic deficit in the sense that these 'basic determining decisions' fall within the sphere of responsibility of decision-making structures that transcend national boundaries. Extending the argument that national polities with some elements of democracy are not necessarily democracies, to include also systems composed of democracies, we may conclude that the existence of some democratic arrangements in the Union do not render it really democratic.

Hence, the question of the democratic deficit comes to the fore of any discussion about the political future of the transnational system, pointing to the need to affirm the position of European citizens in the determination of 'the basic decisions', making them, in Parry and Moran's terms, 'choice-making agents'.[11] To achieve this, however, careful qualification is required, for it may be accompanied by a significant increase in political competition among the different institutional settings involved in the management of integration. For the process of democratising the Union touches upon the sensitive issue of power-sharing among the central institutions, and among them and their national counterparts. Thus, it is not merely by chance that a strong relationship has been established between the democratisation of the larger polity and the granting of new legislative powers to the popularly-based European Parliament; a development that for many Eurosceptics takes the form of a 'concealed conspiracy' towards a European federal state, imposing an immediate threat to national sovereignty.

On the other hand, if existing democratic shortcomings continue to be seen as the price ordinary voters must pay for the efficient management of integration, then large-scale democracy-building will eventually become the sole victim of an intensive and highly destructive power struggle between national and European structures of government. Most importantly, whatever the outcome of this dynamic conflict is, it will certainly constitute a hindrance to a more democratic process of union in that the gap between the power of central executive branches and their political responsibility to the European citizen body will dangerously widen. Hence, the flourishing of democracy at the larger level inevitably depends upon certain intangibles, the most pervasive and gripping of all being what Cohen called 'the spirit of union': 'the feeling of the members that their common membership is somehow deeper and more important than any issue over which disputes may arise among them'.[12] Applied to the Union, the survival and further endurance of this 'presupposition of democracy' rest upon the institutional capacity of its citizens to make possible the amicable resolution of any situation of conflict which may arise as integration proceeds.

Indeed, if we subscribe to Cohen's dictum that 'the more perfect realisation of democracy requires a community that is inclusive, self-conscious, and above all united,'[13] then, not only does the political viability of the Union depend vitally upon democracy, but democracy itself depends upon its communal foundation. The American federal experience on the protection of the 1787 Constitution – perceived not as 'a temporary partnership of states' but as 'an ordinance of the people'[14] – offers a useful analogy in emphasising the importance of preserving the 'Union' at all costs.[15] This somewhat altruistic pattern of political behaviour toward the sustaining of the bonds of unity among EU partners is not an alternative description of utopia. For it adds up to the need for 'strength through mutual support', or what is often termed the principle of 'Community solidarity': the willingness of the segments to overcome internal conflicts of any kind by reference to their common membership.

TOWARDS A MORE DEMOCRATIC PROCESS OF UNION

But what do we mean by 'a more democratic process of union'? What does it imply for the conduct of transnational politics? And also, what are the necessary steps to be taken toward its achievement? To provide an answer, it is appropriate to distinguish between the 'directional principles' of EU democracy-building and its 'operational dynamics', through which these principles can be put into practice. The former relate to the achievement of a higher degree of citizen participation in transnational affairs via the involvement of national and European parliamentary institutions, as well as to the issues of openness and transparency in the decisional context of the Council. For instance, national parliaments can mark their impact on the life of the Union via their European scrutiny committees, and via joint committees with the European Parliament (see chapter 5).

The incorporation of these directional principles in the workings of the Union is deemed urgent, not least because of its unique ability to produce binding legislation upon states and citizens alike which, once adopted, cannot be amended or revoked unless a member state decides to do so through its relevant constitutional procedures. This, however, the British case notwithstanding (since a decision by parliament to negate Community law can be taken as having constitutional status), constitutionally feasible as it may be, would result in serious implications for the system's legal and political cohesion.[16] Overall, the strengthening of the polity's parliamentary element implies a more representative mode of interaction between governors and governed, whilst embodying the fundamental values of Western European political thought in all fields of EU responsibility. And yet, however crucial these principles may be, if the democratic transformation of the Union is to materialise, equal consideration must be given to the operational dynamics of the process, its very limitations included.

Clearly, on the basis of the preceding comments, EU democratisation does not necessarily imply or even justify the transfer of a particular pattern of national democratic organisation to European structures. For, to transplant a model of nation-state democracy to the Union would be as if one were to equate the larger political system with those of its long-established subsystems. The crucial question would be, then, which of the member states provides the most suitable democratic system to the larger association? But this line of argument is misleading, for it fails to incorporate in its logic the *ceteris paribus* clause: when we change the scale of democracy – ie, from a smaller to a larger political unit – we also change the 'qualifiers' (structural, procedural or other) which determine its actual

26

operation. It also leads us to a problem concerning the optimal unit of democracy (see chapter 3). Here, suffice it to stress that if a misleading question can only lead to a misleading answer, it is analytically more profitable, although no less bewildering, to base our methodology on Cohen's premise: 'Rational discourse about any particular democracy presupposes some understanding of the community in which that democracy is (or could be) realised'.[17]

That being the case, and keeping in mind Edwards's suggestion that 'different accounts of democratisation may appear to yield different answers chiefly because they add different qualifiers,'[18] a new argument is in order: the introduction of new democratic arrangements in the Union, as well as the strengthening and extension of older ones, must be compatible with the very peculiarities of the regional process which, at least so far, has managed to combine and accommodate various national and transnational norms and identities in a symbiotic, rather than competitive manner. Accordingly, equal attention should be paid to the organisational aspects of EU democratisation so that any alteration of the polity's 'constitutional' position should not disrupt the delicate balance achieved so far between the collectivity and the segments. This 'qualifier', although rarely stated by contemporary scholarship, constitutes the basis of our theoretical commitment and empirical engagement.

At a theoretical level, although an authoritative statement concerning relations between 'democracy' and 'efficiency' is next to impossible, there is no escaping the fact that democratic claims will have to be set and balanced against other ends such as the 'decisiveness' and 'effectiveness' of governmental action.[19] This assertion, far from implying that the awkward choice between equally important ends can always be avoided, suggests that it is possible to resolve the tension between concepts which, *prima facie*, appear to be irreconcilable. Also, it enables us to take into account the more significant aspect of the discussion: although the various approaches to EU democratisation are more usually than not presented as if they were totally isolated from each other, focusing on different criteria of relevance, they all face the same problem: how to transform a 'sham' democracy into a 'real' one.

From a rational democratic theory perspective, notwithstanding Lucas's contention that 'there is no one single argument for democracy, any more than there is a single form of government that should be reckoned a democracy,'[20] democracy arises very neatly from a definite basis epitomised in the phrase that the *demos kratein* (or that the people should govern themselves). In this sense, Sartori asserts, 'democracy is intended very much less as a device for controlling power than as a system in which the people ought actively to govern... [and] not be *mis*governed'.[21]

27

In defence of these rationalist claims comes the term 'governing democracy', suggesting that the *demos* in modern polities is less governed and more governing, and emphasising the merits of a literal approach to the Greek term *demokratia* as 'rule by the people'.[22] Yet again, the problem is not between 'etymological democracy' and a more compromised version to that of popular self-rule but, given the absence of a 'miracle-producing recipe', of how to incorporate the *demos* in the process of generating political decisions, instead of being passively submitted to them.[23] This discussion highlights one of the greatest dilemmas of modern democracies: whether to pursue a strategy for a maximisation of 'democracy in input' through direct citizen involvement in public affairs or one favourable to the maximisation of 'democracy in output' through a 'deciding *demos*' resting on periodically elected representatives.[24]

Moving the debate onto the regional level, the search for new and flexible interinstitutional arrangements assumes particular importance, especially if the focal point of such an endeavour is centred around the emergence of a balance between the institutional capacity of citizens to democratically sanction EU decision-makers and the achievement of high levels of 'policy responsiveness'. The latter term is defined as the ability of a given political system to provide adequate responses to citizens' problems, whilst articulating through its policy channels their needs and demands. This definition draws largely on Dahl's understanding of democracy as a political system in which the responsiveness of government to the preferences of its citizens is effectively ensured by giving the latter the opportunity to formulate and signify them to 'their fellow citizens and the government by individual and collective action,' and have them 'weighted equally in the conduct of government'.[25]

In general, the concept of democratisation refers to the process of introducing and maintaining in the internal structures of a polity conditions conducive to the rise of democratic government (see chapter 3). It is thus a process which has as much to do with the philosophy of 'democratic transition' from authoritarian rule (or non-democracy) to a system of democratic rule (or full democracy), as it has with that of 'democratic consolidation' in terms of promoting sustainable democratic processes. Both dimensions may well involve lengthy phases and complex instruments, as well as a plurality of procedural means towards democratisation. But they both aim at the same destination: a democratic process in relation to a *demos* that meets the following criteria, indicated by Dahl: effective participation, voting equality at the decisive stage, enlightened understanding, final control over the agenda, and inclusion.[26]

In the context of the Union, a new democratic *modus operandi* needs to be established between the European Parliament and the Commission as a means of achieving a balance between technocratic responsibility and administrative efficacy, as well as to accommodate the notion of executive accountability with that of technical expertise. Equally, the device of new procedural arrangements for consistent co-operation among national legislatures in the area of scrutinising European legislation, combined with a corresponding strengthening of their bonds with the European Parliament, is an appropriate start for redressing some of the structural aspects of the democratic deficit. Such was the rationale behind the setting up of The Assizes in November 1990 in Rome, a forum assigned the task of bringing together national and European parliamentarians (173 and 85 respectively) for an open exchange of views over institutional issues. Or, as Lodge put it: 'It wanted to create the basis for a symbiotic relationship between the national and supranational arms of a functioning parliamentary system'.[27] It is noteworthy that this meeting resulted in the adoption of a Final Declaration which was submitted to the IGCs that begun their deliberations later that year.[28]

Based on the premise that citizens must have a say in the affairs of their polity, one may venture to suggest that the success of EU democratisation rests on the ability of the European citizenry as a whole to claim democratic control over the making and taking of large-scale decisions. To that end, it is absolutely essential that its members should develop an active awareness with regard to the way in which the affairs of the Union should be handled, and be determined to engage themselves as real participants in regional political life. Although the process of 'transnational *demos*-formation' will be explored in greater detail at a later stage of this study (see Chapter 4), the following need to be set out: first, democratic participation in common affairs presupposes the existence of a 'political community' whose members, far from being a numerical accumulation of individuals with no common public concerns, represent a *demos* conscious of its political identity; and second, in order to fulfil the real meaning of citizenship, not only as a legal status but also as 'a form of identification, a type of political identity,'[29] the voter must be offered the institutional mechanisms through which he or she can influence the actual process of government.

More specifically, for all the validity and respect that the doctrine of popular sovereignty enjoys within each member-state, no visible evidence can persuade the European citizen that transnational decisions are, in Shonfield's words, 'part of the rough and tumble of politics,'[30] instead of being taken behind his or her back. Put differently, we have not yet witnessed the establishment of concrete institutional avenues for the expression of the 'sovereign power' of European citizens in relation to the larger unit. Such a power presupposes the existence of an 'inclusive' citizen body in the form of a European *demos*. But this conflicts with the current EU reality which is characterised by a fragmented citizenry in the sense of a 'polycracy': 'a separable multiplicity made up of the unit "each one"'.[31]

Indeed, when we shift our focus from the national to the Union level, each 'sovereign people' of the member states are reduced to the status of being merely a 'semi-sovereign people'.[32] Furthermore, if the contention that the people are sovereign only to the extent that they participate in the making of public decisions is valid, then the mere recognition of the people as sovereign will not suffice when there is no way of enforcing their 'sovereign will' in the actual process of government. And as long as this continues to be the case in the Union, no one should be surprised to discover that it is a far cry from being a polity based on the foundations of democratic citizenship.

Whereas in the sphere of the traditional nation-state the difficulty lies in balancing the relation between state and society – mainly through the politics of representation – in the sphere of the Union it lies in motivating large-scale civic activity, generating citizen identification with, and ensuring public accountability over, the central institutions. And it is exactly because of the unique nature of the Union that what is most required is not a new theory of representation, but the striking of a new balance between the constituent publics and those who are entitled to decide on their behalf. In short, the dynamic enmeshing of different spheres of authority in EU decision-making dictates the search for new political arrangements that will equally respect the principal values, operational attitudes and behavioural characteristics of all actors involved in its multi-layered context.

Further, if transnational democracy is to be achieved not only in theory but also in practice, political responsibility to the governed and parliamentary supervision over executive decisions should be primarily reflected in the organisation of the central institutions. This is fully in accord with J.S. Mill's idea that the people should 'exercise through deputies periodically elected by themselves the ultimate controlling power,'[33] as well as with Montesquieu's dictum that 'power should be a check to power'.[34] It also corresponds to the belief that the institution of parliament is a vital component of 'large-scale democracy',[35] necessary for the maintenance of a democratic culture: 'a system of values and beliefs that defines the context and meaning of political action,'[36] according to the formal (or constitutional) and informal (or ethical) limits of acceptable political behaviour.

The preceding reflections on the operational dynamics of EU democratisation point to the following set of propositions. First, the democratic transformation of the Union should not disrupt the symbiotic relationship established between national and European institutions, but rather enhance its mutually reinforcing character. Second, stronger representational devices must be introduced linking the wishes of the European electorate with EU policies and decisions, and restoring public confidence in the central legislative process. Third, the procedural arrangements for public accountability over the executive branches of the Union should respect, but not be compromised to, the principles of decisional efficiency and administrative efficacy. And fourth, EU democratisation will have to ensure that makers of law and policy at the larger level are ultimately responsible to the European citizenry as a whole. These suggestions are fully compatible with the member states' constitutional traditions, and their explicit emphasis on institutional 'checks and balances' over political authority.

On the other hand, it should be equally remembered that the demo-cratisation of the Union is not an end in itself, but rather a multifaceted, ongoing experiment in multinational shared rule. And since the regional unit is composed of democracies which have explicitly reiterated their commitment to responsible government, the importance of filling the disjunction between democratic theory and practice in the EU '*should* display even *more* concern with respecting democratic principles in its application of professed/declared principles'.[37] But let us now turn to the no less demanding task of defining what has become known as the 'democratic deficit'.

DEFINING THE DEMOCRATIC DEFICIT

According to what we may call the 'orthodox view', the democratic deficit of the Union stems from the fact that the transfer of national par-liamentary responsibilities to the governmentally appointed Commission (in drafting legislative proposals) and the intergovernmental Council (in transforming these proposals into binding legislation) has not been matched by a commensurate increase in the competences of the European Parliament as the only directly elected European institution. This view, by perceiving the European Parliament as the principal repository of democratic legitimacy in the Union, claims that both facets of the malaise could be corrected by increasing its legislative and controlling powers.[38] Other perspectives have found such an approach to be, at least, disputable. Indeed, a variety of opinions have been reported on the 'real' nature of such a deficit, implying that it springs essentially either from the absence of mechanisms of direct democracy in the Union or from the marginal, if not non-existent, role of national parliaments in influencing European decision-making. These views need to be given equal consideration if we are to fully appreciate the dynamic nature of the problem.

Before doing so, however, it must be noted that whatever the methodology employed toward its understanding, the acknowledged deficit reveals a 'parliamentary vacuum' in the way that the Union has organised its legislative function.[39] This gap extends equally to both levels of government. Partial as it may be, since it does not account for the socio-psychological dimension of the polity's democratic pathology, this definition implies that the role of parliamentary institutions, irrespective of their geographical origins, remain particularly weak in EU processes. From this interpretation, which in a way bridges the gap between the 'orthodox view' and what we may term 'other approaches', the democratic deficit can be explained best as an institutional deficit in general, and an accountability deficit in particular: an apparent chasm between the powers of the Union and their political responsibility to the directly elected representatives of its citizens. The crucial question is whether this general identification is alone capable of capturing the dynamic within the relationship between representative democracy, as a system of 'indirect *demos* control', and European integration, as a process of uniting previously separate nation-states into a new regional unit. In attempting to answer this question, the following limited − but reflective of the current debate − definitions need to be discussed.

To begin with the 'orthodox view', Williams defines the democratic deficit as 'the gap between the powers transferred to the Community level and the control of the elected Parliament over them, a gap filled by national civil servants... and to some extent by organised lobbies, mainly representing business'.[40] Moreover, she argues that whilst 'these civil servants are acquiring a detailed knowledge of the Community which complements their knowledge of their own countries' administration... most national politicians, leading members of the opposition and backbenchers alike, have no role in the Community'.[41] In brief, since this loss of influence experienced by national parliaments 'has not been Strasbourg's gain,'[42] a democratic deficit exists.

Lodge, by severely criticising the state of secrecy in the Council's legislative functions, has added yet another constraint on the ability of national parliaments to scrutinise European legislation. But national governments, she claims, find this state of affairs highly convenient, since their Council representatives can escape parliamentary influence and control which 'are believed to be the hallmarks of open, liberal democracies'.[43] Thus, neither the European Parliament, as the 'conscience' of the Union, nor national parliaments, as the embodiment *par excellence* of national sovereignty, can apply sanctions against the Council. Instead, 'what we really have, is decision-making by executives'.[44] Herein lies her central argument: 'The democratic deficit refers to weaknesses... in inter-institutional relations and specifically to the idea of inadequate parliamentary influence over the Commission and the Council'.[45]

In line with the preceding definitions, Martin, author of the European Parliament's reports on EPU,[46] has observed that 'the democratic deficit results from the fact that powers transferred by national parliaments to the European Community are not being exercised by the democratically-elected representatives of the people in the Community'.[47] In other words, although a great many decisions affecting the lives of European citizens are no longer made in their representative assemblies, the fact remains that these decisions 'do not evolve from what we would understand as a *democratic process* at the European level,'[48] constituting 'a severe violation of the elementary principles of democracy'.[49] Also, he criticises the Community for having a sclerotic decision-making process in which laws are made in the secretive Council, aiding undemocratic government within national structures as well. He concludes: 'The process of moving towards European Union presupposes and implies a deepening of the democratic basis on which the EC is founded... This means that the European Parliament must be made into a real legislative and monitoring body'.[50]

A report drawn up on behalf of the European Parliament's Committee on Institutional Affairs in 1988 defined as a 'democratic deficit' the combination of the following phenomena: the transfer of powers from the member states to the Community and the exercise of those powers by institutions other than the European Parliament, 'even though before the transfer, the national parliaments held powers to pass laws in the area concerned'.[51] In particular, the European Parliament recognises that the acknowledged deficit not only flows from its 'over-restricted legislative powers', but also has its counterpart within the states themselves: 'member parliaments too have been considerably weakened *vis-à-vis* their respective governments, whilst these have become legislatures'.[52] From this perspective, the democratic deficit points to the 'de-parliamentarisation' of national systems explained best by the increasing fear that 'parliaments would not be able to cope effectively with the challenges of decision-making in modern political systems' (see chapter 5).[53]

Departing from the 'orthodox view', and moving on to the 'other approaches', Bogdanor argues his case for the introduction of instruments of direct democracy in the Community, such as the direct election of a proper Executive and the use of the referendum to decide certain common issues.[54] The rationale behind his thinking is that 'if it is not possible to articulate the will of the electorate at European level through direct elections' – since they can legitimise decisions that have already been made – 'why should one not consider the use of other democratic instruments that could give the electorate a genuine choice free from the constraints imposed by the party systems of the member states?'[55] The point he makes is that since the Community cannot be forced into the mould of a parliamentary system, 'the natural alternative would be direct election of the Commission... by the universal suffrage of electors in the member states'.[56] This 'electoral enterprise' is expected to allow the voter to allocate political responsibility within the Community by choosing a genuine European Government. But it will also provide a further incentive to generate popular excitement in European affairs, recognise the principle of popular sovereignty and broaden the political liberties of the European peoples to include 'the self-government of the citizen'.[57] Defining the democratic deficit as 'the gap between elite proposals and popular perceptions,'[58] he argues that its correction lies on the transformation of the Community into a presidential system in which the Council 'would be faced with more powerful counterweights than the appointed Commission and the nearly powerless Parliament'.[59]

Teasdale and Huxham, in a 1991 Bow Group memorandum, counsel against investing too much political capital in the European Parliament to redress the deficit in question. Rather, they urge an immediate increase in the levels of public accountability over the central institutions, thus 'making them more open, more responsive and less technocratic in character,' by bringing national parliaments closer to the locus of European decision-making.[60] To that end, they propose the creation of a 'Council of National Parliamentarians' to which the Council would be held accountable, and the establishment of a series of joint delegations between national parliaments and the EP for the discussion of issues of mutual concern. These reforms would mesh with the Council's philosophy that its members are individually accountable to the national parliaments, making responsibility 'more visible, substantive, and communautaire'.[61] In addition, they would create the basis for an increased 'partnership' between national and regional authorities 'of benefit to the European citizenry as a whole'.[62] In brief, they maintain that no attempt to democratise the Community will be credible unless it recognises the 'institutional logic' of asserting the role of national parliaments in European legislative processes, without transferring additional law-making powers to Brussels.

In a comparatively moderate approach, Welsh argues that the democratisation of the Community requires that national parliaments and the EP should join forces 'in maintaining democracy and consent as the European Union takes shape'.[63] And since 'the principle source of the democratic deficit lies in the way the Council operates through a network of Committees and Working Groups made up of national civil servants who... are subject to no scrutiny whatever,' 'no room for institutional complacency and self-satisfaction must be offered, if the rights of electors are to be protected'.[64] What he actually has in mind is the evolution of the Council into a 'Chamber of States' whose members would be individually accountable to their national parliaments, and the setting up of a 'Standing Conference of National Parliaments' with a mandate to produce regular reports on European policy. He also argues that 'a decision by the Council to fix Brussels as the single Seat of the European Parliament' would reveal whether 'those who have been in the forefront of calls for greater accountability will be prepared to stand up and be counted'.[65] In brief, he maintains that in order to provide 'good government' which responds to the public needs, it is essential to recognise that both parliamentary domains should work together to assert the democratic rights of citizens.

As must already be clear, a large number of interrelated interpretations of the deficit concerned can be presented without, however, altering in any substantive way what the above reflections have so far revealed about its nature.[66] Instead, let us summarise the various approaches discussed by offering the following general definition: the 'democratic deficit' of the Union refers to the growing dissonance between the way in which representative democracy operates in the member nation-states and the actual conditions upon which the political management of integration effectively rests.

DOES DEMOCRACY MATTER?

A central question to address is whether the process of integrating democratic nation-states inherently presupposes a diminution of democratic processes in the newly-integrated polity, as compared to the pre-existing smaller political units.[67] To rephrase the question, whether a larger union composed of national democracies should not itself be democratic. That being the case, the issue of identifying, understanding and rectifying transnational democratic deficiencies should not concern us, at least with the same intensity and vigour as it presently does. For if it is axiomatically true that the controlling powers of citizens via elected representatives over the compound polity is weaker than in the older independent, and now 'component' parts, then questions of a democratic nature are somewhat irrelevant to the political organisation of the 'inclusive' community. This could even explain, although not justify, why so little attention has been paid by some theories of regional integration, especially those stressing the 'functional imperative', to the transformation of intergovernmental relations based on the 'relative power' of states into relations among citizens based on the essentials of the democratic process (see chapter 6).

However tempting and convenient the adoption of this analytical logic, the position taken in this study is that these arguments hardly correspond to reality, let alone substantiate the reasoning they advocate. And that, because in a period when the very art of government is increasingly determined by the forces of interdependence, no single state that aspires to democracy can convincingly assert that the formation of a union composed of smaller entities should neglect the importance of democratically monitoring the decisions taken within its structures. All the more so if these decisions enjoy the status of having direct public effect. This is particularly true now that both leaders and led unequivocally accept the indispensability of democracy, which has so masterly survived even the most stormy winds of change.

But for all the respect the democratic ideal seems to enjoy today, it would be false to assume that democracy has indeed reached its full potential in producing a system of government capable of effectively articulating an ever increasing array of public demands. The previous approaches to the democratic deficit clearly made the point that the apparent 'loss of democracy' at the national level, as a result of EU membership, has not meant a corresponding gain in democratic participation within the larger unit. Moreover, the consolidation of a largely undemocratic regime at the Union level contradicts the constitutional traditions of the component polities. And so too, the assertion that the 'democratic principle', as the ability of the *demos* to exert political influence over the taking of publicly binding decisions, should be strictly confined within national boundaries. Should this be allowed to happen, however, it would amount to the fallacious assumption that democracy is not a prerequisite for any form of political organisation beyond the level of national states. In brief, these points suggest that one of the primary objectives of the Union should be to transform the potential of the constituent *demoi* from being the recipients of decisions taken at forums far removed from the public gaze into an integral part of integration processes.

It is no coincidence that the European Court of Justice (ECJ) has made the following ruling with regard to the European Parliament's participation in the life of the EU: 'Although limited, it reflects... the fundamental democratic principle that the peoples should take part in the exercise of power through the intermediary of a representative assembly'.[68] Likewise, the Commission has stated: 'if the Community is to develop,

Parliament must be given a bigger role to play. Indeed, any strengthening of Parliament's position widens the Community's democratic basis.'[69] Finally, in their Declaration on Democracy, adopted at the European Council in Copenhagen in April 1978, European leaders solemnly declared 'to safeguard the principles of representative democracy, of the rule of law, of social justice and of respect for human rights'; confirming that 'the application of these principles implies a political system of *pluralist democracy* which guarantees both the expression of opinions within the constitutional organisation of powers and the procedures necessary for the protection of human rights'.[70]

Notwithstanding this celebration of political rhetoric or 'leaflet democracy' (democracy in words rather than in deeds) the Union is still far from being democratic. Instead, it is characterised by an increasing gap between the powers of its citizens and those entitled to decide on their behalf. This democratic discrepancy points to a clear violation of the democratic process and renders the nascent European *demos* as the sole victim of a loss of national democratic autonomy (see chapter 5) and of an illusion of transnational democracy (see chapter 3). Hence, the task of detecting the democratic shortfalls of Union governance is no less imperative than that of any national polity. For democracy *does* matter whether its principles and procedures are to apply within a purely national context or within a 'system of "open states"' determined to jointly bear the fruits of their partnership.[71] Especially if they share an active commitment to openly debate, challenge and defend public policies in a parliamentary arena (where the voice of the opposition can be also heard), rather than in a 'closed' ministerial council in conjunction with an unelected bureaucracy, both supported by extensive structures of 'comitology' which 'largely determine the manner in which powers under primary legislative instruments are exercised in practice'.[72]

From the perspective of the constituent governments, the explanation for the poverty of democratic arrangements in the Union is partly to do with their reluctance to extend democracy across national frontiers on the basis that such a move would question their domestic constitutional orders, weaken popular attachment to territorial communities, loosen the bonds of unity within their substructures and erode national identity. A less convincing but rather convenient argument might be that if the parts that are to be joined together by mutual agreement to form a new 'body politic' were committed to the democratic functions of government, so would the compound entity, as the sum total of the participating democracies. As a result, the invention of broader participatory structures that transcend, but not necessarily replace, those of the nation-state would not qualify as a democratic condition for the governance of the Union.

Moreover, whatever democratic legitimacy would be needed to keep the Union functioning would derive from the democratic properties of its constituent units. From this view, 'democracy across borders' can only follow from 'democracy within borders'.[73] Yet, the application of these ideas to 'the creation of a democratic community which both involves and cuts across democratic states' can only have a negative effect on transnational democracy-building.[74] For the latter requires much more than merely bringing together a number of democracies in a larger unit. Be that as it may, the current EU system sharpens this point for, although it is compounded of democracies, it is certainly not nearly as democratic as any of its constituent polities.

To the extent, therefore, that the institutional development of the Union has not followed the traditional lines of national democratic organisation, especially those concerning the functions of the member legislatures, there is justifiable criticism for having a weak parliamentary input in its processes. Not that the national experience is a panacea to our understanding of democratic achievement within a regional setting, or for guiding the future strategy of the European Parliament to assert its role in a complex system of joint decision-making (since it is not part of a political order identical to a nation-state).[75] Yet, it does bring to the surface a number of inconsistencies with regard to the application of the democratic process within transnational political structures.

A CONCLUDING NOTE

After considering these points, it cannot be denied that the process of union must respond and correspond to the wishes of the member publics, whose lives are directly affected by the shared exercise of power. And if we subscribe to an old saying that 'the best is the enemy of the good', then the real enemy of democracy (the resurgence of tyrannical or authoritarian rule aside) is none other than the achievement of greater and better democracy, and with it of an ever-more responsible political authority. Having outlined the definitional and operational map of EU democratisation, and the two general schools of thought on the democratic deficit, we can now turn to the historical roots, theoretical origins and conceptual foundations from which such a deficit derives its acclaimed significance. This will give us the opportunity to elaborate further on the concepts and theories of democracy, national and transnational.

Notes on Chapter 2

1 Ascherson, Neil, '1989 in Eastern Europe', in Dunn, John (ed.), *Democracy: The Unfinished Journey, 508 BC to 1993* (Oxford, 1993, Oxford University Press), p 222.

2 Ascherson writes: 'there was an almost universal feeling that the revolutions meant a "return" to "European standards"... and therefore to broad democratic values to which every single one of these nations or nationalities had aspired... On the other hand, democratic systems (as opposed to aspirations) were certainly not "normality" in the region before the Communist period'. *Ibid*, p 222.

3 Lodge, Juliet, 'The Democratic Deficit and the European Parliament', Fabian Society, Discussion Paper no 4, January 1991, p 7.

4 Martin, David, 'European Union and the Democratic Deficit', John Wheatley Centre, June 1990, p 22 and p 19. He also adds that 'at a time that Eastern Europe is rapidly democratising, the building where the Council of Ministers meets in Brussels is referred to as "Kremlin West"'.

5 Keohane, Robert O., and Hoffmann, Stanley, 'Conclusions: Community Politics and Institutional Change' in Wallace, William (ed.), *The Dynamics of European Integration* (London and New York, 1990, Pinter), p 294.

6 *Ibid.*

7 Bogdanor, Vernon and Woodcock, Geoffey, 'The European Community and Sovereignty', *Parliamentary Affairs*, October 1991, p 492.

8 Martin, David, 'European Union and the Democratic Deficit', p 19.

9 Miller, David, 'Democracy and Social Justice', in Birnbaum, Pierre *et al.* (eds), *Democracy, Consent and Social Contract* (London, 1978, Sage), p 76.

10 Holden, Barry, *Understanding Liberal Democracy* Second edn (London, 1993, Harvester Wheatsheat), p 8.

11 Parry, Geraint and Moran, Michael, 'Democracy and Democratization', in Parry, Geraint and Moran, Michael (eds), *Democracy and Democratization* (London and New York, 1994, Routledge), p 274.

12 Cohen, Carl, *Democracy* (University of Georgia Press, Athens GA 1971), p 47. In a rather sceptical fashion, he states: 'The commitment to union largely explains why compromise can prevail among widely divergent views within a democracy, but often does not prevail between democracies'.

13 *Ibid.*, p 49. This self-encompassing character of the political community, however, should not imply that this community will become isolated from the outside word – ie, a 'fortress Europe' – but rather that a sufficient degree of social and political coherence will emerge within its context.

14 See Beer, Samuel H., *To Make a Nation: The Rediscovery of American Federalism*, (Cambridge MA, 1993, Harvard University Press), pp 308-40. In this study Beer contrasts the 'compact theory' of American federalism with what he calls the 'national theory'.

15 Cohen, Carl, *Democracy*, pp 47-8. He explains: 'Our Civil War, beyond its economic and moral causes, was above all a struggle to protect that without

which there could be no continental democracy – the unity within which differences, however bitter, might be discussed and in time resolved'.

16 For more on this debate see Parlement Européen, 'Symposium sur les Relations entre le Droit International Public, le Droit Communautaire et le Droit Constitutionnel des Etas Membres', Document no 8 du Service Juridique du Parlement Européen, Bruxelles, 21-22 Juin 1995, PE 213. 411/8.

17 Cohen, Carl, *Democracy*, p 41.

18 Edwards, Alistair, 'Democratisation and qualified explanation', in Parry, Geraint and Moran, Michael (eds), *Democracy and Democratization*, p 102.

19 Although the moral dilemma between democracy and efficiency has always been a crucial issue to resolve, it has embellished the nature of the conflict between these principles. As Aberbach *et al.* put it: 'Excessively bureaucratic policy-making may lead to a crisis of legitimacy, but excessively political policy-making threatens a crisis of effectiveness'. See Aberbach, Joel D. *et al.*, *Bureaucrats and Politicians in Western Democracies* (Cambridge MA, Harvard University Press, 1981), p 255.

20 Lucas, John R., *Democracy and Participation* (Harmondsworth, 1976, Penguin) p 11.

21 Sartori, Giovanni, 'Electoral Studies and Democratic Theory: A Continental View', *Political Studies*, February 1958, p 12. Yet, he defines democracy in a negative way, as 'a system in which no-one can choose himself, no-one can invest himself with the power to rule and, therefore, no-one can arrogate to himself unconditional and unlimited power'. See Sartori, Giovanni, *The Theory of Democracy Revisited* (Chatham NJ, 1987, Chatham House), p 206.

22 On this point see Sartori, Giovanni, *The Theory of Democracy Revisited*, p 121.

23 For an account of 'etymological democracy' see *ibid.*, pp 21-38.

24 For instance, Plamenatz writes: 'A political system is democratic if it operates in such a way as to ensure that makers of law and policy are responsible to the people'. See Plamentanz, John, *Democracy and Illusion* (London, 1978, Longman), pp 69-70.

25 Sørensen, Georg, *Democracy and Democratization* (Boulder CO, 1992, Westview Press,), p 12. For the original argument see Dahl, Robert A., *Polyarchy: Participation and Opposition* (New Haven, Yale University Press, 1971), p 3.

26 Dahl, Robert A., *Democracy and its Critics* (New Haven and London, 1989, Yale University Press), pp 108-14. The last criterion, which practically means that the *demos* ought to include all adults subject to its laws, except transients, is cited in his *Dilemmas of Pluralist Democracy: Autonomy vs Control* (New Haven and London, 1982, Yale University Press) p 6. Since no country perfectly meets these criteria, however, Dahl prefers the term 'polyarchy' for contemporary political systems, reserving the term 'democracy' for the ideal type.

27 Lodge, Juliet, 'EC Policymaking: Institutional Dynamics', in Lodge, Juliet (ed.), *The European Community and the Challenge of the Future*, Second edn (London, 1993, Pinter), p 22. The rationale behind this statement is that both parliamentary settings will have to increase the quality of democratic accountability in EC structures at the expense of highly unanswerable governments rather than at the cost of each other's vital interests.

28 See Martin, David, *Europe: An Ever Closer Union* (Nottingham, Spokesman, 1991), pp 94-101.

29 Mouffe, Chantal, *The Return of the Political* (London and New York, 1993, Verso), pp 65-6. Mouffe puts forward a meaning of citizenship according to which to be a citizen is to be associated in terms of the recognition of a set of political principles specific to the liberal democratic tradition such as freedom and equality. Thus, citizenship is 'something to be constructed, not empirically given'.

30 Shonfield, Andrew, *Europe: Journey to an Unknown Destination* (London, 1973, Allen Lane), p 82.

31 Sartori, Giovanni, *The Theory of Democracy Revisited*, p 22.

32 Schattschneider, Elmer E., *The Semisovereign People: a Realist's View of Democracy in America* (New York, 1960, Rinehart and Winston). Although Schattschneider's characterisation refers to the *substance* of American democracy rather than its *form*, in the case of the EU it covers both dimensions.

33 Mill, J.S., 'Considerations on Representative Government', in Acton, H.B. (ed), *Utilitarianism, Liberty, and Representative Government* (London, 1972, Dent & Sons), p 228. Quoted in Held, David, *Models of Democracy* (Cambridge, 1992, Polity Press), p 93.

34 Baron de Montesquieu, 'Of the Laws which Establish Political Liberty with regard to the Constitution', in Norton, Philip (ed.), *Legislatures* (Oxford, 1990, Oxford University Press), p 24.

35 On the distinction between the terms 'small-scale democracy' and 'large-scale democracy' see Dahl, Robert A., *Dilemmas of Pluralist Democracy*, pp 12-6.

36 Sørensen, Georg, *Democracy and Democratization*, p 26.

37 Stavridis, Sterlios, 'Foreign Policy and Democratic Principles: The Case of European Political Cooperation', unpublished PhD. dissertation, University of London, London School of Economics and Political Science, 1991, p 324.

38 European Parliament, Directorate General for Research, 'Symposium on the European Parliament in the Community System', National Parliaments Series no 5, Summary Report and Plenary Debates, November 1988, p 20.

39 Herman, Valentine, 'The European Parliament and National Parliaments: Some Conclusions', in Herman, Valentine and van Schendelen, Rinus (ed.), *The European Parliament and the National Parliaments* (Westmead, 1979, Saxon), 1979, pp 270-1.

40 Williams, Shirley, 'Sovereignty and Accountability in the European Community', *Political Quarterly*, July 1990, p 306.

41 *Ibid.*

42 *Ibid.*, p 303. According to Williams, even more worrying is the fact that national parliaments 'have been suspicious of attempts by the European Parliament to demand greater powers, and have been unwilling to work closely with it in establishing a joint structure of Parliamentary accountability'.

43 Lodge, Juliet, 'The Democratic Deficit and the European Parliament', p 10.

44 *Ibid.* Cf Lodge, Juliet, 'European Union and the "Democratic Deficit"', *Social Studies Review*, March 1991, pp 149-53. In this article, Lodge argues that because parliamentary control over the Council is imperfect, its representatives

'can pass off unpopular decisions as the "fault" of the Commission or of the other member states... [and] act as though they were "forced" into accepting a decision in the making of which they had no part'. See p 150.

45 Lodge, Juliet, 'EC Policymaking', p 22.

46 See European Pariament, '1993: The New Treaties', Luxembourg: Office for Official Publications of the European Communities, 1991.

47 Martin, David, *Europe*, p 60.

48 *Ibid.*, p 59 (emphasis added).

49 *Ibid.*, p 64.

50 *Ibid.* For a similar point of view see Klepsch, Egon A., 'The Democratic Dimension of European Integration', *Government and Opposition*, Autumn 1992, pp 407-13; Dunn, Bill N., 'Why the Public Should be Worried by the EEC's Democratic Deficit', European Democratic Group, Discussion Paper, EPPE, 1988; and Plumb, Lord, 'Building a Democratic Community: The Role of the European Parliament', *The World Today*, July 1989, pp 112-7.

51 European Parliament, 'Report on the Democratic Deficit in the European Community', Committee on Institutional Affairs, Session Documents, Series A, Doc. A-2-0276/87, February 1988, pp 10-11.

52 *Ibid*, p 11.

53 *Ibid.*

54 Bogdanor, Vernon, 'Democratising the Community', London, Federal Trust for Education and Research, June 1990, p 11.

55 *Ibid.* Cf his 'Direct Elections, Representative Democracy and European Integration', *Electoral Studies*, December 1989, pp 205-16; and 'The June 1989 European Elections and the Institutions of the Community', *Government and Opposition*, Spring 1989, pp 199-214. In these articles Bogdanor explains the reasons why direct elections to the European Parliament are unable to provide the legitimacy which advocates of European integration so desperately seek. On this point see also Stavridis, Stelios, 'The Forgotten Question of the European Parliament's Current Lack of Legitimacy', *The Oxford International Review*, Spring 1992, pp 27-9.

56 *Ibid.*

57 *Ibid.*, p 15. 'Democratic institutions', Bogdanor notes, 'are not merely a mechanism designed to ensure government by the people's choice. Government is also to be evaluated by its concequences for the citizens, by what J.S. Mill called in *Representative Government* "the degree in which it tends to increase the sum of good qualities in the governed, collectively and individually"'.

58 *Ibid.*

59 Bogdanor, Vernon, 'The Future of the European Community: Two Models of Democracy', *Government and Opposition*, Spring 1986, pp 174-5.

60 Teasdale, Anthony and Huxham, Quentin, 'National Parliaments and the European Parliament: How to Improve Democratic Accountability in the European Community', London, A Bow Group Memorandum, April 1991, p 5.

61 *Ibid.*, p 6. 'The merit of such ideas', they note, 'is that they could replicate the benefits of the pre-1979, *indirectly* elected European Parliament without

prejudicing the benefits that have flowed from the *direct* election of the Parliament in 1979'.

62 *Ibid.*, p 10.

63 Welsh, Michael, 'Accountability and the European Institutions: The Complementary Roles of Westminster and Strasbourg', London, Tory Reform Group, 1990, p 5.

64 *Ibid.*, pp 5-6.

65 *Ibid.*, p 10. He states: 'The present "provisional" arrangement, which has lasted since 1962, requires the Parliament to hold its plenary sessions in Strasbourg; most other activities take place in Brussels, while the official home of its Secretariat remains in Luxembourg'. He concludes that this situation 'has made the Parliament a part-time institution, unable to influence events because it can never be sure of being in the right place at the right time'.

66 See Kirchner, Emil J., *Decision Making in the European Community: The Council Presidency and European Integration* (Manchester and New York, 1992, Manchester University Press), p 14; Nugent, Neil, *The Government and Politics of the European Community*, second edn (London, Macmillan, 1991), p 309; Vogel, David, 'The Making of EC Environmental Policy', in Andersen, Svein S. and Eliassen, Kjell A. (eds), *Making Policy in Europe* (London, 1993, Sage), p 117; Nicol, William and Salmon, Trevor, *Understanding the New European Community* (New York, 1994, Harvester, Weatsheaf), p 280; Dinan, Desmond, *An Ever Closer Union? An Introduction to the European Community* (London, 1994, Macmillan), p 288; Shaw, Josephine, *European Community Law*, (London, 1993, Macmillan), p 67; Close, Paul, *Citizenship, Europe and Change*, (London, 1995, Macmillan), p 242; and Holland, Martin, *European Integration: From Community to Union* (London, 1994, Pinter), p 86.

67 For a similar discussion see Weiler, Joseph H.H., 'After Maastricht: Community Legitimacy in Post-1992 Europe', in Adams, William J. (ed.), *Singular Europe: Economy and Polity of the European Community After 1992* (Ann Arbor MI, 1992, The University of Michigan Press), pp 20-7.

68 See the ECJ's ruling on 30 October 1980 in Cases no 138 and 139/79 (Isoglucose), European Court Reports (ECR) 1980, p 3333, para. 33. In this case, the ECJ maintained that the principle of democracy is applicable to the EC, while the EP gained a *de facto* delaying power before giving its opinion to the Council. For details see Jacobs, Francis *et al.*, *The European Parliament*, Second edn (Harlow, 1992, Longman Current Affairs), pp 180-2; and Kirchner, Emil J. and Williams, Karen, 'The Legal, Political and Institutional Implications of the Isoglucose Judgements', *Journal of Common Market Studies*, December 1983, pp 173-90.

69 Introduction to the Andriessen Report of 7 October 1981, *Bulletin of the European Communities*, Supplement 3-1982.

70 Quoted in European Parliament, 'Concepts of Democracy in the European Community', Political Affairs Committee, Directorate General for Research and Documentation, 6 November 1980, p 3 (emphasis added). For a brief account of the pluralist democracy model see Holden, Barry, *Understanding*

Liberal Democracy, pp 109-11, and the bibliography therein. On the problems of pluralist democracy see Dahl, Robert A., *Dilemmas of Pluralist Democracy*, pp 31-54; Sartori, Giovanni, *The Theory of Democracy Revisited*, pp 152-156; Held, David, *Models of Democracy* (Cambridge, 1992, Polity Press), pp 192-5 and the table in p 204; and Birch, Anthony H., *The Concepts and Theories of Modern Democracy* (London and New York, 1993, Routledge), pp 160-8.

71 Wessels, Wolfgang, 'The EC Council: The Community's Decision-Making Centre' in Keohane, Robert O., and Hoffmann, Stanley (eds), *The New European Community: Decisionmaking and Institutional Change* (Boulder CO, Westview Press, 1991), p 151.

72 Shaw, Josephine, *European Community Law*, p 85. According to the author, 'the term "comitology" refers to the practice within the Council of delegating implementing powers by primary legislation to the Commission, to be exercised in conjunction with committees of national civil servants which wield varying degrees of influence over the executive process'.

73 This partly explains why 'democratic theory has examined and debated the challenges to democracy that emerge from within the boundaries of the nation-state,' without seriously questioning 'whether the nation state itself can remain at the centre of democratic thought'. See Archibugi, Daniele and Held, David, 'Editors' Introduction', in Archibugi, Daniele and Held, David (eds), *Cosmopolitan Democracy: An Agenda for a New World Order* (Cambridge, 1995, Polity Press), p 7.

74 For this quotation see *ibid.*, p 13. This discription derives from a cosmopolitan conception of democracy, 'founded on a new account of international relations and of the possibility of accountability among nations'. See p 8.

75 European Parliament, 'Symposium on the European Parliament in the Community System', p 15. Hence, the Summary Report has asserted that in order to understand how the European Parliament relates to the wider issues of European integration and to traditional ideas of parliamentarism, it is essential to understand the 'constitutional' system of the Community itself.

PART II

Conceptual Foundations

CHAPTER 3

On Democracy, National and Transnational

'THINKING BEHIND' EXISTING DEFINITIONS

The crucial question to be addressed in this chapter is whether it is merely by chance that, for all their marginal differences, most definitions presented so far perceive the democratic deficit as the growing chasm between the powers transferred to the executive branches of the Union and the inadequacy of parliamentary control over them. In other words, what actually lies behind these highly interrelated, if not tautological, definitional approaches? And also, what is the theoretical justification for the recognition of this essentially 'political' phenomenon? It is to these issues that we now turn in an attempt to 'think behind' the existing definitional formulas.

A first point to make is that the theoretical origins and conceptual foundations of the deficit in question derive from the essentials of responsible government, in that decisions affecting the lives of individuals must be subject to public accountability. This suggests that if the Union is ever to meet even the minimum requirements of a large-scale democratic polity, it needs to adjust its present arrangements to ensure the closeness, representativeness and accountability of the governors to the governed. Hence, a corresponding concern for the student of integration is to assess the 'generic properties' of democratic government, and then connect the findings of such an enquiry to the limits and possibilities of developing democracy among democracies.

DILEMMAS OF DEMOCRATIC THEORY

The notion of democracy as a value concept directly invokes the age-old debate about how to organise, promote and articulate in the best possible way the primary needs, interests and concerns of the citizen within the body politic. In its broadest sense, the democratic ideal implies a some-what utopian form of civic association whereby a variety of actors pursuing different and often competing goals find themselves harmo-niously co-existing under the umbrella of a concrete, generally acceptable and (preferably) constitutionally entrenched set of governing rules and procedures.

In practice, however, this type of political interaction is supervised by rule-enforcing instruments, and it is the institutionalisation of the demo-cratic ideal which becomes the crucial factor in converting public demands into policy outputs. Needless to say that the success of this conversion process should not always be taken for granted, but rather it should be seen and assessed in the light of both the intrinsic and contextual chal-lenges confronting the democratic functioning of a given political system.[1] Thus, for all its innately idealistic nature, democracy primarily refers to an 'organising method' of structures, processes and procedures through which democratic purpose can be transformed into actual political achievement. From this perspective also, democracy can be seen as a distinctive form of government comprising its own internal structures, behavioural characteristics and operational dynamics.

In the context of the Western liberal-democratic tradition, the conception of democracy as an institutional arrangement points to the existence of a distinct democratic form for organising political life, its ultimate task being to successfully channel and reflect the wishes of the majority in both policy-formation and policy-execution stages. Accordingly, the genius of democracy lies in its capacity to articulate the interests of 'the many' (the majority), as opposed to those expressed by 'the few' (the minority), by allowing the *demos* to participate, directly or indirectly, in the political process. Echoing an observation made by Arblaster, the democratic principle implies that 'the people should, as far as possible, make or participate in making the decisions that affect them most closely and importantly'.[2]

There is nothing new in arguing that a large number of problems arise when one tries to present a definitive view of democracy, let alone examines its qualities in the actual process of government. For it is a dynamic conceptual scheme, invented and re-invented in the course of time. In the interests of our present discussion it is sufficient to present the following ways of approaching its meaning. The first is to perceive democracy as a 'political method' which, according to Schumpeter, refers to 'that institutional arrangement for arriving at political decisions in which individuals acquire the power to decide by means of a competitive struggle for the people's vote'.[3] Thus sketched, democracy is 'incapable of being an end in itself, irrespective of what decisions it will produce under given historical conditions'.[4] This 'neoclassical' interpretation – baptised by Schumpeter himself as 'another theory of democracy' and by others as the 'competitive model of democracy'[5] – is qualitatively distinct from the 'classical doctrine of democracy' which views the 'democratic method' as a means of 'realising the common good by making the people itself decide issues through the election of individuals who are to assemble in order to carry out its will'.[6] More recently, Zolo has attempted to reconstruct democratic theory through the conceptual lenses of a 'post-classical doctrine of democracy', involving the constitutionalisation of political parties, a new division of powers between legislative, executive and administrative agents, and the promotion of 'communicative democracy'.[7]

And yet, whatever the definitional approach may be, the fact remains that in some way or other democracy is linked to both safeguarding the continuation of a pluralistic form of society (usually resulting in only partial accommodation among the various interests involved in the political process) and upgrading the civic virtues of the *demos* through its active engagement in the political process. Notwithstanding Pickles's contention that one of the greatest difficulties in defining democracy is that 'political systems are in a continual state of evolution',[8] an element common to all definitions of the term is that political authority ultimately rests with the *demos* whose members enjoy the full rights (and duties) of citizenship. As Arblaster put it: 'Any claim that a certain state of government, regime or society is "really" or "in the final analysis" democratic, however implausible it may seem, must involve the implication that in some way or other... the "real" will of the people is expressed through it'.[9]

Taken together, the preceding reflections conceive of democracy as a mixture of both an ideal, moral or theoretical system and an institutional arrangement having to do more with procedures than structures: a nexus of patterns that guarantees the fullest possible participation of the *demos* in the actual process of government. This definition, by perceiving democracy as an ensemble of principles and processes for broadening public participation in the exercise of common affairs, sets the bases for a continuous interactive relationship between political authority and those subject to it.

Overall, the meaning of democracy appears to be two-fold: first, it involves the existence and acceptance of a number of specific principles and values held by the *demos* of a political community; and second, it provides the machinery for the embodiment of these ideals in the daily process of government. Thus, the concept of *demos* and the quality of its involvement in the shaping of its political environment reveal the core meaning of such a highly contestable and even 'critical' concept: contestable, since for some 2,500 years democracy has lost nothing of its inherently debatable nature; and critical since it continues to be associated with a variety of norms and ideals 'by which reality is tested and found wanting'.[10]

The democratic quality of a political system or regime is vitally determined by the extent to which a creative synthesis can be achieved between the recognition of the principal values inherent in the concept of democracy and the way in which its normative characteristics are put into practice. Put differently, there is a strong and intimate connection between the operational and the ethical dimensions of democracy, the former being a complex web of procedural arrangements and the latter providing for their moral justification. From this view, democracy can be both a universal ideal and a method of arriving at binding decisions: a political condition taking the form of a fixed democratic order and a political process towards the achievement of its ideals. In short, it is a political *virtue* which nonetheless ought to be practically attained.

Admittedly, due to the very dynamism inherent in the contemporary process of government, students of politics have been compelled to acknowledge that these two highly interrelated concepts of democracy indicate that a viable democratic order, far from implying a static system of axiomatic principles and values, is more closely related to a flexible set of institutional arrangements constructed according to the particular characteristics of the political community in which they apply. Indeed, contemporary scholarship perceives democracy as an on-going process of interaction between state and society, with the former representing the established governmental apparatus and the latter the community of citizens; that is, as a dynamic process in which the *demos* should be given the opportunity to participate to the maximum possible degree in public decision-making at every level.[11] But for democracy to exist as a process of interaction between the 'dominant' and the 'subordinates',[12] as well as a process of decision-making, some further requirements must be met. The most crucial of these is the maintenance of adequate levels of popular control over the public authorities. As Arblaster put it: 'It is important to democracy that government should be not merely ready, but also obliged, to listen to what the people... has to say'.[13]

As far as the need for democratic accountability (or indirect *demos* control) is concerned, it has been suggested that its significance rests upon a higher moral principle: 'political authority should flow from the people, in distinction to flowing from another political source'.[14] Equally, the need for political responsibility to the governed or 'upward control',[15] stems from the axiom that a responsible government not only has to give an account of itself to its citizens, but also needs to be prepared to listen to, and answer questions in, the legislature – the place where the representatives of the *demos* assemble – about its actions and inactions.[16] Otherwise, what we might have is not democracy, but rather 'a parody of democracy or a pseudodemocracy'.[17]

So far, our discussion on the essential conditions of modern democracy has been deliberately conducted under the prism of an institutional, rather than a philosophical approach. For the latter, Pickles comments, 'can easily become escapist or even utopian since it is not possible to discover how far principles and ideas are realistic until attempts are made to put them into practice'.[18] As Birch has argued, the justification of 'institutional democracy' as 'the best practicable system of government' rests upon Mayo's following premises: the peaceful settlement of disputes; the peaceful change and orderly succession of rulers; the protection of diversity in society; the minimisation of injustice; and the promotion of human freedom.[19]

As against this, idealist theorists have asserted that democracy is not merely an institutional method for arriving at governmental decisions, but rather an end in itself, including claims about 'human equality, human self-development, civic virtue, or the maximisation of the public interest, all of which may be regarded as possible candidates for inclusion in a book of democratic values'.[20] Such an approach has been taken by Lively, who explicitly states that democracy cannot be defined 'in terms of particular institutions or methods, but only in terms of the ends which are to be maximised'.[21] This, however, runs the danger of equating democracy with a static design of civic rule or even with a 'good-will' declaration of intent. For these reasons, the institutional approach seems to be a more pragmatic method of conceiving democracy.[22] It is thus hardly surprising that democratic theory has been extended to new fields of enquiry, exhibiting distinctive emphasis on answering the question of which set of procedures can best transform democratic norms into policy structures.

In general, the building of stable democratic polities which, in Dahl's words, constitutes 'the most difficult of all the arts of politics',[23] requires that essentially, and not just potentially, democratic characteristics are embodied in the workings of political institutions, the fulfilment of which entails the device of procedural methods for supervising the activities of governmental agents, keeping them in close contact with public preferences. Hence, looking at democracy in terms of institutions does not exclude the possibility of having in mind their essential purposes.[24] In brief, the more the *demos* is involved in the process of arriving at binding decisions, and the more these decisions become subject to its control, the more operationally meaningful democracy is. At least, this is the premise on which this study is founded.

REPRESENTATIVE DEMOCRACY IN THEORY AND PRACTICE

Reflecting upon its modern dimension, the term 'democracy' came into use during the later stages of the eighteenth century to describe a system of government in which the representatives of the *demos*, chosen through competitive periodic elections, were invested with the means to take publicly binding decisions. With regard to the 'democratisation' of the franchise, it was not until the end of World War II that universal suffrage applied in most Western European countries. Thus, representative democracy is a very recent development in the history of politics, although a rapidly spreading one to all geographical directions. In 1951, a UNESCO report drawn up by McKeon concluded: 'For the first time in the history of the world... [the] acceptance of democracy as the highest form of political and social organisation is a sign of a basic agreement in the ultimate aims of modern social and political institutions... that the participation of the people and the interests of the people are essential elements in government and in the social relations which make good government possible'.[25]

Elaborating on the 'newness' of representative democracy, Hunson indicates that for more than two millennia politicians and philosophers regarded it as an inferior form of government, agreeing, explicitly or not, with Plato's view of democracy as 'a state in which the poor, gaining the upper hand, kill some and banish others, and then divide the offices among the remaining citizens, usually by lot.'[26] Plato's *Politeia* of course referred to the Athenian model of direct democracy where 'a fear of class rule underlay his opinion'.[27] By contrast, when McKeon reported his views on the state of democracy in the early 1950s, what he actually had in mind was its contemporary dimension, where citizens elect deputies who in turn make decisions on their behalf. But any discussion on representative democracy presupposes some understanding of the concept of representation – described by McLean as 'one of the slippery core concepts of political theory'[28] – and its changing nature over time. Notwithstanding the fact that in order to capture all possible shades of its meaning would inevitably require an exhaustive enquiry of the very foundations of modern European political thought, the following should nevertheless be set out.

Deriving from the Latin 'repraesentare', the term 'representation' had nothing to do originally with people representing other people in the process of government. Rather, it was confined to images and inanimate objects which 'stand in the place of or correspond to' something or someone.[29] Although the real expansion of the term occurs in the early fourteenth century, when the Pope is often said to represent the person of Christ, not until the end of the sixteenth century is there an example of representing as 'acting for someone as his authorised agent or deputy'.[30] In fact, the term moved into the realms of political activity when the summoning of knights and burgesses in Parliament began to involve the presentation of grievances to the King, making the redress of those grievances conditional upon consenting to taxes.[31]

The next steps in its evolution appeared when the 'members' of parliament were given 'specific instructions' by their communities, and were required 'to give an account of' their actions in parliament.[32] As this process of consultation advanced, the members of parliament gradually developed an awareness as a single body.[33] These developments were linked with the belief that 'all men are present in parliament, and the idea that the ruler embodies the whole realm'.[34] In this context, Hobbes defined representation in terms of authorisation: 'a representative is someone given authority to act by someone else, who is then bound by the representative's action as if it had been his own'.[35] Thereafter, its elaboration continued against the background of the French Revolution and, more recently, of the various struggles over the relationship between legislative and executive functions.[36]

Since the French Constitution of 1791, and its explicit recognition of Burke's famous 'conscience clause',[37] sovereignty was to reside with the nation as a whole, whilst Parliament was to embody 'the will of the nation'. Political representatives were no longer to be thought of as delegates sent to the assembly with *pouvoir restrictifs* – ie, as agents representing 'constituent interests' – but were to act as independent makers of laws, as well as 'the voice of the nation'.[38] Interestingly, the vast majority of Western European countries have either copied or closely followed the French constitutional provisions.[39] Even in Britain, where no written constitution formally exists, a similar attitude is embodied in the doctrine that sovereignty belongs to Parliament, there being no mention of the people.[40]

As the meaning of political representation changed, so did the meaning of popular sovereignty and the status of representative assemblies. Seen by James Mill as 'the grand discovery of modern times' in which 'the solution of all difficulties, both speculative and practical, will perhaps be found,'[41] the representative system became the foundation of modern democracy; a 'discovery' which, for Loewenstein, 'was as decisive for the political evolution of the West... as the mechanical inventions... have been for man's technological evolution'.[42] Yet, as Dahl has asserted: 'the change in democracy resulting from its union with representation created its own problems'.[43]

More explicitly, an associated dissatisfaction attached to the practice of representation becomes inevitable due to the difficulties involved in achieving a correspondence between representatives and represented.[44] Following Wright's analysis, 'there is an inherent tension between a pluralistic approach to representation and the straightjacket of sovereignty,' each pointing towards different kinds of politics: 'the former towards a negotiated politics of social partnership, the latter towards a politics of *dominium*'.[45] He concludes: 'representative government with electoral democracy does not exhaust the range of representative possibilities available to, and required by, the democratic governance of modern states'.[46]

These normative comments imply that representative government cannot always guarantee the plurality of forces that seek meaningful representation in the context of modern electoral democracies. A brief look at the many possibilities of electoral devices substantiates Wright's argument that a parliamentary majority may claim to represent 'the people' on the basis of an 'electoral mandate', although the people concerned may be a minority of those voting or entitled to vote.[47] It also brings to the fore the 'potency' and 'elusiveness' of representation: 'Potent, because here is the axial legitimating principle of modern democratic politics, the foundation of the claim to rule; and elusive, because its meanings are effortlessly blurred, merged and exchanged before they can be pinned down and put into service'.[48]

But there is something more to add to this sceptical syllogism: representation has been largely perceived from the outset as an inherently problematic historical achievement of modern democratic polities: as 'the thin veneer of snatched moments and single channels' or even 'a fading badge of legitimacy', rather than 'a matter [or better a combination] of rich textures,' and hence 'the active democratic constituent of big government'.[49] Wright's advice is to take representation rather more seriously than it has been taken in the past and transform its potential from being merely a 'flag of governmental legitimacy' into 'an active agency of control'.[50] In accordance with this comes Schwartz's assertion that whatever the definitional requisites ascribed to the concept in question, it remains 'an instrument of power' that links the *demos* to its government: 'an institutional technique by which power is structured in a political society,' providing 'a multilevel system capable of making public action possible'.[51]

Once direct public participation in the management of common affairs became impossible, the representational device emerged as a practicable means of providing democratic government: 'a way of making the participation of the membership of a community decisive so as to enable individual voices to be heard fairly, while increasing the likelihood that difficult decisions will be made wisely'.[52] Although representative government has often been advertised as a 'second-best' substitute for the meeting of the *demos* in person, it has proved to be equally 'democratic' to direct democracy. And despite the fact that representation has complicated the discussion about the meaning of democracy, its underlying value is that it offers a 'structured, civil and considered process of law-making'.[53] In Paine's words: 'By engrafting representation upon democracy, we arrive at a system capable of embracing and confederating all the various interests and every extent of territory and population'.[54]

Therefore, before one speaks about the 'superiority' of one form of democracy over the other, it is important to stress their respective virtues in relation to the polity in which they are to apply. For both direct and indirect systems of control have their own merits and demerits, rather than one being *ex definitio* more desirable to the other. The open dilemma is not between direct participation and indirect representation, but rather to strike a balance between the 'possible' and the 'unattainable' under the complexities of modern society. This requires that democratic thinkers and politicians be willing to discover new positive ways for upgrading the democratic quality of the governmental process.

These prescriptive considerations bring us to the central issue of how to put the theory of popular sovereignty into practice and transform its democratic dictates into political reality. In retrospect, the answer to this question is to be found in the device of competitive periodic elections for renewing the confidence of the *demos* to its government, as well as in a variety of procedural mechanisms for holding those in office accountable to its entrusted representatives. The evolution of representative government brought the locus of democracy closer to the institution of Parliament as the place where public policy was debated and decided upon. In this context, systems of indirect popular control were designed to give practical effect to the ever perplexed relationship between citizens and public policy-making. Accordingly, representative democracy can be defined as a system of indirect *demos* control of those who are entitled to exercise political authority on its behalf through the electoral process.

This definition shifts the emphasis from the transformation of individual relationships into what Eulau called 'the representation of the whole,'[55] to the question of how to ensure political responsibility of the governors to the governed. At this point, the issue of policy responsiveness comes to the fore of our discussion. For in an era where both 'mandate uncertainty' and the complexity of public policy-making tends to widen the gap between representatives and represented, the former are called to be sensitive to the wishes of the latter.[56] The premise underlying this point rests on the presence of continuous interactive ties between both arms of the representational relationship whereby elected representatives act as intermediary links between the *demos* and its government. In this sense, representative democracy is concerned with the idea of 'civic competence': the institutional capacity of citizens to hold their government to account for its actions or lack of action on a continuous basis.

It would be false to assume that representative democracy has been realised by simply giving every adult citizen the right to vote every four or five years. This fallacy has been called 'electoralism'.[57] Should this occur, what we may actually end up with is the 'electoralisation' of democracy, with enormous democratic gaps from one election to the next. Thus, continuous *demos* control over policy-makers emerges as the fundamental operating principle of democratic government. As Mayo asserted: 'Political systems can be classified as more or less democratic according to a number of criteria associated with popular control and designed to make it effective'.[58] And since it is far from self-evident that the exercise of power always operates in the interests of public accountability, the significance of devising the adequate machinery for citizens to control the actions of their representatives is of cardinal importance. In short, if we hold to the idea of democracy as 'popular power', such a power can only be embodied in the principle of public accountability. For the opposite inherently entails the danger for the prevalence of what might be described as a form of 'elective authoritarianism': a situation in which the absence of internal checks over public policy may induce the representatives of the *demos* to act adversely to its interests.

In this context also, the idea of popular consent emerges as the hallmark of legitimate government, contrasting with other forms of arbitrary rule 'where the wishes of the people are ignored and their assent or support is not sought or considered necessary'.[59] In brief, the civic virtue of contemporary government relies on the premise that policies are decided by the representatives of the *demos*, for the interests of the *demos* and under the control of the *demos*. In Bealey's words: 'The inauguration of representative democracy does not abolish the exercise of power and the structures of hierarchy: it only results in greater precision in the definition of power and more supervision of the activities of the hierarchs'.[60] In summary, if democracy refers to a situation where sovereignty rests with the *demos* and nowhere else, representative democracy refers to that system of government where the abstract of popular sovereignty is transformed into effective *demos* control.

THE POLITICAL THEORY OF DEMOCRATIC ACCOUNTABILITY

Concern about the way in which the principle of accountability operates in practice gives rise to the following set of questions: How much accountability is needed to ensure a thriving democracy? From what sources does the accountability principle derive its meaning? And also, to what extent can active citizen participation contribute to the accountability process? To provide an answer, and before focusing on the institutional dimension of accountability, let us define the concept in question as a continuous process by which those who govern are publicly held to account for their actions and inactions by the elected representatives of the *demos*.

As Day and Klein have suggested, accountability has come to resemble a 'chameleon word' with an exasperating ability to slip between a whole range of meanings.[61] Notwithstanding the numerous difficulties involved in any attempt to distinguish between the many situations in which the principle can be made operative, what is absolutely essential is that 'continuously functioning big government should be accompanied by effective and continuous mechanisms for holding government to account'.[62] For as long as political authority is being concentrated in institutionally unaccountable hands, and the concerns of the *demos* cannot be articulated through the political process, no doctrine of responsible government can be actually marshalled, let alone practically realised. Instead, the gap between popular expectations and governmental performance as one of the most alerting of all political cleavages of our time will dangerously widen, and popular sovereignty will remain a distant ideal.

But there is also an additional concern related to the operational dimension of democratic accountability: in order to maintain the integrity of what J.S. Mill called 'the governing function', and hence advance the well-being of the *demos*, those empowered to take binding decisions across the institutionally defined limits of acceptable behaviour, should be dismissed whenever any mismanagement occurs. For representative government, although conventionally described as being merely 'a matter of ruling', is first and foremost 'a matter of checking and controlling' those entrusted with public power. According to J.S. Mill, all questionable governmental activities should be fully exposed and justified by their initiators, and if these activities conflict with 'the deliberative sense of the nation,' then those promoting them should be expelled from office and succeeded by others who hold the people's 'trust'.[63] Or, as Wright put it: 'being able to kick parties and governments out [through periodical elections] is indispensable, but so is being able to kick them while they are in'.[64]

Cutting through the conceptual maze, it is fair to describe account-ability as a dynamic, on-going process by which the doctrine of popular sovereignty is reflected in the process of government. In this sense, the accountability construct becomes the essence of liberal democratic theory and practice, compelling one to agree with Stavridis's remark that such a process 'cannot be stopped at a specific moment in time, or for that matter, being suspended even by a common consent'.[65] As Wright argues, although the holding of regular elections has been traditionally offered as 'the "democratic solution" to the problem of accountability,' thus implying that 'issues of accountability arise only in relation to those parts of govern-ment which are not elected,' in reality, 'this is patently not the case'.[66] On the contrary, 'the rhetoric of elections as synonymous with account-ability may, in fact, divert attention from the conditions that have to be met if accountability in the full sense is to be achieved'.[67]

This reflects the experience not only of national but also transnational systems of government, misinterpreting the real meaning of democratic control. In short, the comfortable belief that elections are a sufficient con-dition of public accountability — ie, 'he who says elections says account-ability' — diminishes the pursuit of the relevant principle on the part of the elected, 'with the additional irony that the absence of this belief on the part of the non-elected may even be a spur to accountability'.[68]

In conclusion, democratic accountability refers to a dynamic public process of interaction between government and the *demos*, in which the agents of the former are made politically responsible to the elected rep-resentatives of the latter on a constant basis rather than once every four or five years. Thus, for any system of government to fulfil this primary objective, it should complement the 'raw accountability' of elections, with 'a system of continuously functioning accountability'.[69] Otherwise, far from being characterised by strong devices of indirect *demos* control, it will be identified by their very absence. For only when the delegation of public authority to an elected government is accompanied by the insti-tutional capacity of the *demos* to control its actions is there evidence that sufficient levels of democratic accountability exist.

But let us now examine the institutional bases through which the principle of accountability can maximise its democratic potential. Since it has been generally acknowledged that of all the institutions of modern (representative) democracy, the most appropriate one to act as 'a centre for accountability' is none other than the institution of parliament, it is to this particular institution that we immediately turn.

PARLIAMENT AND THE DEMOCRATIC PROCESS

In a period when the claims of parliaments to monopolise the 'representative process' are practically unachievable,[70] the executive branches of government seem to have taken many of their traditional functions, often reducing their role to one of 'heckling the steamroller'.[71] Hence, there is a mounting concern over the widening distance between parliamentary practice in theory and in reality in Western European democracies, pointing towards the 'recentralisation' of national political power in favour of 'cabinet decision-making'.[72] This process is assisted by the transformation of the role of political parties, the appearance of advanced networks of technical expertise and the multiplication of interest group activities. Indeed, parliaments have found themselves trapped in a vicious circle of overgrown government and executive dominance, to the extent that one is compelled to agree with an oft-raised criticism that the history of government has passed from the sovereignty of the monarch to the sovereignty of parliament, and now to the sovereignty of the executive.

Although the course of parliamentary decline can be best visualised in rather erratic terms across a number of Western European countries, the optimum model of a parliamentary democracy according to which a parliament can effectively call a government to account is manifestly not the case in contemporary Europe. For indirect *demos* control over the executive has decreased to a situation where elected representatives can only exercise *ex post facto* scrutiny over the making of public policy and then with little, if any, chance of altering its original content. But even without taking this into account, the institution of parliament, as the place where the interests and concerns of the *demos* were met after extensive public debate, has been reduced to one where particular (or factional) interests effectively prevail. Although it is not in the interests of this section to engage in a lengthy discussion of how parliaments can find a way out of this impasse, it is important to shed some light on the decreasing status of their controlling powers so that the pathology of democratic accountability in the conduct of contemporary politics becomes readily apparent.

The inescapable diagnosis to make here is that the unprecedented expansion in the size and complexity of modern government along with the fact that the so-called 'nuclear' weapons in parliaments' procedural-controlling arsenal – ie, votes of confidence, motions of censure and impeachment – have been largely kept for threatening purposes only, has meant that they have been imperfectly matched by an expansion of the instruments of parliamentary control.[73] As Chapman has remarked: 'In one way or another, governments have escaped the rigours of direct parliamentary control and have themselves come to have a great deal of control over assemblies.'[74] Framing the same problem in different terms, Bobbio has spoken of 'a trend not towards the greatest possible control of those in power by the citizens, but towards the greatest control of the subjects by those in power'.[75]

Echoing the anxiety of an age where parliaments hardly correspond to the calls for a more efficient organisation of power, King asserts that what is really at issue is the policy-making capacity of representative democracy itself.[76] This criticism, valid as it may be now that other forms of 'functional representation' have acquired overwhelming attention by contemporary scholarship, does not say much about the way in which parliaments have found it all the more difficult to exercise control over executives, nor does it address the related question of how to accommodate the public will to the policy outcomes produced by the latter.

In attempting to elucidate one of democracy's greatest problems, namely the need to scrutinise governmental activities, the following set of arguments should be stressed: first, democratic decision-making implies that the *demos* should be able to shape the content of public policies before they are decided by governmental officials; second, institution-alised criticism does not suffice when elected representatives are excluded from the process of translating draft proposals into binding legislation; third, democratic procedures require repeated demonstrations of popular acceptance so that political decisions reflect at any given stage in time the real problems and concerns of the *demos*; fourth, legislative control by parliament presupposes that the latter possesses 'information powers' in the sense that its members are empowered to obtain information on executive activities; and fifth, if the previous requirement is to be achieved, parliament should also be granted extensive sanction and supervisory powers – ie, the power to modify a decision taken by the executive, the power of censure of government, the power to conduct investigations, etc.[77] On this basis, if the process of accountability is to meet the conditions of democratic government, then *all* of the above requirements should be available to parliament at the same time.

DEVELOPING DEMOCRACY AMONG DEMOCRACIES

These, then, are the essential requirements for making government democratic, with accountability taking the form of a one-way process towards the achievement of an optimal model of interaction between 'decision-makers' and 'decision-receivers'. And yet, we all know that procedural arrangements, as well as institutional tactics and political strategies, are in the final analysis related to 'the art of getting things done'. In other words, just as 'the decision to maintain civil rule… must be constantly renewed in the daily conduct of political relations,' so the process of accountability in any system of governance that wants to be called a 'democracy' should be equally confirmed and reinvented all the time.[78]

This observation applies equally whether the political system in question is confined to a purely national level, or to more advanced frameworks of transnational organisation such as the Union. In fact, the concept of accountability is all the more relevant in the latter case since the Union represents a constellation of democratic states embarked on an adventurous experiment of joint decision-making for the benefit of their respective *demoi*. Indeed, the regional process can be taken as an exercise in democratic creativity, allowing for the development of a transnational *demos ab intra*. This – combined with the need to restore the tradition of responsible government at the national level, and extend its qualities at a level beyond that – underlines the cause of reforming the Union to take it beyond executive dominance; something which, in turn, requires that the experience of national and transnational parliamentary deficiencies should be used as a guide of the shape of things to come.

Although the preceding reflections on the basic properties of a representative polity can be no more than a preface to yet another interminable intellectual debate in Western political thought, they do provide a logical justification of why the notion of a 'democratic deficit' in the Union has been almost exclusively confined to the absence of parliamentary controls. Thus, they set the theoretical scene enabling us to relate our previous discussion to the prospects for developing democracy across borders and defend a certain philosophy of democratic governance that goes beyond the sphere of 'normal interstate relations'.[79]

The primary aim here is to project a novel conception of transnational politics capable of forging democratic links among the member publics without challenging their respective democratic traditions. Drawing from the domain of democratic theory, as a coherent network of concepts and ideas concerning the art of good government, this body of thought aims at breaking away from the traditional dichotomy between the worlds of interstate and intrastate democracy, and transcend the divide between democracy within the member states and democracy in the Union. It is summed up in the concept of 'transnational democracy'.

TRANSNATIONAL RELATIONS AS A CHALLENGE
TO DEMOCRACY

In a period when the domestic as well as the international politics of states can be better understood against the background of transnational socio-economic and political dynamics, the theory and practice of democracy should be used in such a way as to indicate that democratic rule can equally be extended beyond the already familiar forms of national political organisation. This view, which arguably contradicts the Hobbesian 'realist' philosophy of international politics, in that relations among nations are not subject to moral principles,[80] corresponds to Gould's thesis that 'democratic theory, properly interpreted, can apply to the international domain as well as to the domestic domain'.[81]

But the transnational democracy theme goes even further, suggesting that democratic relations need to acquire a cross-frontier dimension, and for that reason it is to be found somewhere in the vast grey area which takes shape between the worlds of interstate and intrastate democracy. Far from denying or rejecting either the moral or legal significance of existing territorial boundaries, it essentially opposes those who argue in exclusive terms in favour of their totality or even indispensability. Thus it challenges the view that democratic legitimacy and representation is exhausted by national representative institutions, whilst emphasising a new paradox of democracy: that democratic 'extension' and 'deepening' in and between countries becomes an essential condition for democracy to retain its relevance in the next millennium, where political relations are expected to be neither 'symmetrical' nor 'congruent'.[82] It follows that for domestic democracy to be sustained and cope with this new challenge it needs to keep pace with the development of larger polities such as the Union.

The rationale behind this line of reasoning is that contemporary government is predominantly defined and conditioned by extensive networks of transnational interaction which can effectively 'diminish the range of decisions open to given national "majorities"'.[83] Indeed, the chronic intensification of levels of intrastate and interstate interdependence seem to substantiate Held's argument that 'the chains of political, social and economic activity are becoming world-wide in scope,' placing questions on the political agenda that 'go to the core of the categories of modern democratic thought'.[84] These developments, product of the changing conditions of governance, by creating new political uncertainties, 'become,' in Held's words, 'open to question as soon as the issue of national, regional and global interconnectedness is considered and the nature of a so-called "relevant community" is contested'.[85]

Especially in the case of the Union, where its citizens primarily belong to different national and subnational communities, an increasingly timely and acute problem has emerged: that of holding transnational decision-makers accountable to a nascent *demos*, in terms of publicly discussing and openly defending their large-scale activities. Against these evolving problems for the conduct of responsible government in the composite 'body politic', transnational democracy emerges as a promising alternative to the logic of secretive, technocratic and unaccountable governance.

The proposed 'model', as an ensemble of concepts so arranged as to reveal the properties of large-scale governance, emphasises the importance of commonly shared democratic procedures within a collectivity of democracies such as the Union. The aim is to provide democratic guidance over its processes by building across the frontiers of the constituent units instruments of democratic decision-making, whose outcomes correspond with the wishes of a fledgling European *demos*. By perceiving democracy both as a concrete political system (form of governance) and a definable 'code of practice' accompanying this system (act of governance), we propose that no principles of democracy which are compatible in its domestic context should be seen as incompatible above that level. And since there are very few studies dealing with the question of how different spheres of political authority, linked both horizontally and vertically, interact within a larger polity, the task of reinventing democracy beyond a purely national scale still remains a fundamental challenge to democratic thinking.

According to Held, transnational interconnections are in a position to contest traditional resolutions of central democratic questions, with profound implications for all the key ideas of democratic thought: 'the nature of a constituency; the meaning of accountability; the proper form and scope of political participation; and the relevance of the nation-state...'[86] Especially now that the very process of government seems to be effectively escaping some of the categories of a nation-state 'faced with unsettling patterns of national and international relations and processes as the guarantor of the rights and duties of subjects'.[87] This leads to the question posed by Dahl of 'how this new change of scale transforms the limits or possibilities of democracy?'[88]

Although the process of European integration has changed a number of established perceptions about the exercise of sovereignty, large-scale democratic deficiencies should not be seen as the price citizens must pay for their governments' European activities. Instead, their proliferation is in itself a legitimate enough reason for reinforcing the institutional capacity of citizens to become the decisive subjects of EU politics. Finally, if we accept that over the next years the quest for democratising the Union will grow stronger, then the questions that further formal integration generates for the theory and practice of democracy are far from easy to resolve.

ON THE UNSETTLED TALE OF DEMOCRACY

Notwithstanding Fukuyama's celebrated proclamation of the triumph of Western liberal democracy, its transnational aspects raise some serious questions confronting contemporary political discourse. As Hirst argues, the vision offered by Fukuyama, far from being one of hope, creativity and inventiveness, implies that the future would be 'the endless repetition of more of the same, with no ideological *sturm und drang*, but rather a politics centred on bureaucratic problem-solving, limited social engineering and liberal compromise'.[89] Yet, if this is all there is to it, it can hardly be said that the tale of democracy had a 'happy ending' after all. For, according to 'the end of history' thesis, its future will be a highly monotonous exercise, offering 'a vision of a world purged of ideology,'[90] leading towards the total atrophy of the imagination.

The search for a new democratic 'path' points towards 'the third democratic transformation' as a means of redressing the institutional limitations of what is known as 'the dominant idiom' of liberal representative democracy.[91] In analytical terms, this implies an essential departure from state-centric approaches to democracy so that the extension of its ideals across borders be adjusted to the changed conjuncture, whilst responding to the problems that contemporary pluralism generates for multinational governance. Applied to the Union, the aim is to mobilise the democratic energies of its incipient *demos* toward the recognition of 'the other' as 'a legitimate present',[92] and the eventual framing of a politically viable system of mutually reinforcing structures (symbiosis), co-operative conflict resolution (accommodation), constructive public interaction (communication) and political responsibility to the *demos* (accountability).

But perhaps the model's greatest merit lies in the fact that it does not aim to construct a larger political entity *de integro* by means of subsuming the democratic traditions of the component parts into a 'superior' form of polity. Instead, it represents a polycentric arrangement which is flexible enough to take account of the very complexities and peculiarities of the EU system, and specific enough to develop a symbiotic relationship between national and transnational authorities. In this sense, transnational democracy requires neither a 'constitutional revolution', in terms of a radical break with existing central arrangements, nor the construction of a new authoritative centre and, hence, a single locus of decision-making. Rather, this new democratic design aims to build strong democratic ties among the member publics and guarantee that democratic 'checks and balances' will form the basis on which the constituent governments are prepared to jointly manage their individual sovereignties. Moreover, by embedding the democratic qualities of the 'component' communities in an 'inclusive' community based on mutually legitimising structures of government, it aims to restore the confidence of citizens in the exercise of public affairs without threatening their 'individuality' by the force of institutional centralisation. This is an appropriate basis for a plurality of identities to group themselves together under a mutually accommodating environment of multiple loyalties, cross-frontier group affiliations and political allegiances and, eventually, transnational citizenship.

THE JUSTIFICATION OF TRANSNATIONAL DEMOCRACY

The arguments mounted in support of transnational democracy can be found, *inter alia*, in the complexity of modern government; the prevalence of executive-elite dominance inside as well as outside national boundaries; the dependence of governmental elites upon 'quasi-public bureaucratic agencies' for advice, information and technical expertise;[93] the decreasing levels of public accountability over national and European legislation; the limited popular support which transnational political groups enjoy in European elections; the intensification of corporatist and 'neocorporatist' networks of interest intermediation for the settlement of conflicting social interests by means of by-passing parliamentary institutions; the ill-founded but still dominant paradigm of democratic legitimation based on citizen election or majority decision;[94] and finally, the concentration of much political and economic power in hierarchically structured technocracies and business corporations.[95]

The preceding list, exhaustive as it may seem, is far from complete, not to say a relatively limited sample of an ever increasing catalogue of democratic deficiencies. Yet, the point is clearly made that if the ideals of democracy are to be adequately entrenched, public participation will need to acquire its proper status at the larger level. Equally, if the political interaction between agents of transnational authority and the fledging European *demos* are to develop in accordance with the dictates of the democratic process, a new approach to EU politics emerges as a prerequisite for large-scale governance to achieve its democratic potential. All in all, transnational democracy aims to strike a new balance between the principles of democratic autonomy of the parts and 'ever closer union' of the whole.

Doubtless, if the Union is to be understood as a pioneering experiment in transnational democracy-building, then the complex variants of such a novel construction, as well as the inescapable intermeshing involved between them, need to be thoroughly explored. According to our interpretation, this type of democracy refers to a multifocal form of governance applied within and across national boundaries whereby the *demos* of the 'inclusive' political community can exercise significant control over the making and taking of publicly binding decisions. This definition suggests that power to produce joint decisions should be distributed according to the following four principles of democratic organisation: political pluralism, institutional decentralisation, decisional closeness to the *demos* and policy responsiveness.

In conclusion, transnational democracy, both as a new integrative dynamic (since it strengthens the democratic bonds between the member states) and a new form of democratically supervising transgovernmental activities (since it presupposes adherence to the principle of public accountability), far from leading to a considerable diffusion of national democratic autonomy (see chapter 5), is ideally suited to the development of a more civic and participatory process of union. But how are we to appreciate the relevance and importance of transnational democracy with the reality of EU politics? It is on this question that we now focus.

DEMOCRATIC GOVERNMENT AND UNION GOVERNANCE

The proper establishment, successful operation and further endurance of transnational democracy vitally depends upon the incorporation of the fundamental principles of democratic government in the relations between the Union and its state/citizen parts. Among those principles that will determine the democratic physiognomy of the collectivity, emphasis should be given to the following: meaningful legislative representation of both states and citizens in central decision-making; openness and transparency in the making of European legislation; collective and individual executive responsibility – ministerial and administrative – to the European Parliament and national parliaments, respectively; and continuous and effective *demos* control over the setting of the integrative agenda through a functional distribution of responsibilities between these bodies.

In a democratic regime, the task of controlling the executive is assigned to parliament, implying political responsibility to the *demos*. The justifying principle here can be found in one of Lively's democratic requirements that 'rulers should be accountable to the representatives of the ruled'.[96] Does this essential requirement of responsible government, however, apply to the Union? As most definitions of the democratic deficit illustrate, the existing system of 'checks and balances' among the major central institutions applies to the detriment of popular control over the executive branches of the Union. This situation owes much to the role that the representation of territorial interests play in the larger system (see chapter 7). Thus, a new institutional balance has to be struck between the two forms of popular representation that currently take place: the direct one between the European public and the European Parliament, and the indirect one between the former and the Council, representing the interests of the component states.

More specifically, the Union should be based on a 'double democratic legitimacy': of the European *demos*, as a self-conscious body of citizens; and of the constituent governments, as instruments for the articulation of territorial interests. Yet, one should be very cautious in transferring the debate on representative politics from the national to the Union level. For in the latter case, the difficulty is not about striking a reciprocal arrangement between state and society, but rather how to secure a transnational representative regime capable of meeting the democratic requirements of both territorial and electoral representation.

This is not to imply that since the Union is not a state as conventionally understood, any attempt to relate the transnational dimension of representation with familiar notions of democracy is inherently problematic. What it does imply is that instead of placing undue emphasis on the representation of the *demos*, as traditional political discourse does, a more balanced approach is required so as to recognise the representation of territorial government as an institution equally decisive for the 'democrativeness' of the Union; especially so if one perceives the latter as a co-operative system striving to achieve a reasonably balanced resolution between territorial and non-territorial claims. As these issues will be examined in greater detail in chapter 7, it is to the more traditional aspects of the relationship between democracy and representation in the larger system to which we now turn.

True as it may be that many prominent writers on democracy – from Burke, Hamilton and Madison to present day theorists – have taken representation as a means of limiting popular participation and control,[97] given the current asymmetries in the division of legislative powers among the core EU institutions, rectifying part of the democratic deficit points in the opposite direction; all the more so if one subscribes to the view that there is a necessary link between representative democracy and the actual implementation of the popular mandate. For democratic representation and indirect *demos* control should be seen as the two sides of the same coin, that is as the operational principles of modern democratic rule, national and transnational.

As democratic experience suggests, the mere existence of a parliamentary body is not proof that representative democracy has actually been achieved in a given political system. Nor is it alone a sufficient condition for determining the depth and range of popular control over the actions of government. Thus, to say that democracy has been achieved in the Union simply by enabling its citizens to determine the composition of the European Parliament is something that should be dismissed from the outset. Admittedly, voting alone cannot ensure the reality of representative democracy if it is not accompanied by other equally essential democratic requirements. In this sense, EU politics does not neatly correspond to the original notions of representative and responsible government. Put simply, how is the European citizen body to make effective use of its voting entitlement if the representatives that have been vested with the popular mandate are not entrusted with the necessary powers to achieve their aims? This accords with Cohen's point that there is indeed 'an enormous difference between a system in which the citizen does little more than vote, and one in which the many other channels of participation are ever-more widely and more fully used'.[98]

In this context, one may even consider that phenomena like political apathy, public estrangement and, eventually, voting abstention can in many cases – the Union being only one striking instance of them – constitute a reflection of citizen rationality. Echoing Morris's colourful remark, what do they have to gain by voting anyway, if they are perfectly well aware of the fact that the parliament they are going to elect will be a toothless and thus a subordinate organ to the wishes of the executive?[99] This assertion substantiates the point that when democracy operates through elected representatives, its depth will ultimately depend upon the quality of their participation in the governmental process, that is, on the opportunities they are given to influence, always according to the popular will, the decisions produced by government.[100]

This said, a further argument is in order: for the public to enjoy a greater sense of participation in the regional process, it is essential that the current state of secrecy under which the Council exercises its legislative powers be eliminated. Writing about the British House of Commons some 30 years ago, Beer has noted that 'it is not plausible to expect people to identify with the output of the governmental process when only the product and not the process itself is revealed to public gaze'.[101] Doubtless, as long as joint decision-making is to be conducted in a way that member states' differences in approaching draft European legislation are kept from the public, it is natural to expect that this unacceptable state of affairs will continue to exacerbate public discontent and abate the channels of communication between the people and the governing elites. As Crick put it: 'if anything useful and significant is to be done in a free society, it must be done publicly and in such a way as to consult, involve and carry with it those affected'.[102] For when a popular view prevails that 'something is going on out there and they are making decisions we will not like in ways we cannot hope to understand,'[103] then the conditions of democracy are obviously lacking.

Paradoxically, Bobbio notes, the relationship between democracy and 'invisible power' has been neglected by students of democratic politics. Perhaps this has to do with the fact that democracy itself was seen as a form of government whereby major decisions would be reached '*au grand jour*', rather than *in camera*, bringing about 'the transparency of power' or 'power without masks'.[104] The failure to do so, however, has been described as one of democracy's 'broken promises' at the national level, and an almost unknown property of decision-making beyond that level. For the idea of visible government in the Union has not evolved into a major political issue until very recently, when the need for greater transparency was recognised.[105]

Without wishing to exhaust a subject which goes to the heart of the debate on democratic political conduct, the following points are set out. First, the doctrine of *arcana imperii* defined as 'the secret and hidden deliberations or resolutions of those who hold power in the state,'[106] contradicts the idea of democracy as 'the rule of public power in public'[107] on at least two fronts: the right of the people to have access to governmental acts, and their equally deserved entitlement to use such information to expose possible incidents of public misconduct or maladministration. Second, 'closed government', as opposed to 'open government', deprives citizens of the possibility to acknowledge the grounds on which those in power decide issues of public interest. Third, it questions the foundations of popular legitimacy, in that citizens cannot exhibit their confidence in the procedures that bring about binding decisions if these procedures remain hidden from public scrutiny. Fourth, it challenges the idea of constructive public dialogue since the *demos* is no longer in a position to follow the debate on secretively produced legislation. Finally, it discredits the common defining property of all democratic political systems: that the *demos* is empowered to participate as fully as possible in the actual process of government.

THE RELEVANCE OF DEMOCRATIC THEORY TO
EU PRACTICE

The problems of democratic organisation faced by the Union are not entirely different from those found within the traditional structures of its constituent units. In fact, in both cases there is a mounting concern over the future role of parliamentary institutions. In this respect, EU democratisation may set in train analogous processes within national polities, by which the *demos* will assert the authority it ought to have within the democratic process. Although it would be wrong to assume that these ideas are without their own problems, it would be equally wrong to miss the point that, for all the uncertainties that surround the process of EU democracy-building, they are nothing compared to the anguish imposed by the ferocious alternatives to representative and responsible government.

As must already be clear, our analysis has been conducted in close relation to the conceptual foundations of Western democracy. The question is whether such an approach is relevant to the discussion of the Union's democratic deficit. Although a proper response would inevitably require a rather exhaustive analysis of descriptive and normative arguments, for the interests of clarity and the purposes of this chapter, we will confine our answer to merely stating that if one subscribes to Dahl's dictum that democratic theory 'is concerned with processes by which ordinary citizens exert a relatively high degree of control over leaders,'[108] then the theory's relevance with the deficit in question becomes immediately established.

For what the democratic deficit ultimately reveals is an ever widening chasm between the 'part-formed' *demos* of the equally partial European political community and its unaccountable centres of decision-making. Consequently, any sort of controlling powers acquired by the European citizen body can be seen not only as a step closer to the elimination of the democratic deficit, but also as a clear justification of the relevance of democratic theory to EU practice in that the dissonance between the essentials of responsible government and the actual conditions upon which the governance of the Union is largely based would eventually wane.

INSTEAD OF A CONCLUSION

The problems that will confront the Union of the next millennium will be problems of a democratic nature, whose resolution will require a new integration strategy to break through the politics of secrecy, indecision and unaccountability, whilst releasing the 'untapped energies' of its inchoate but nascent *demos*. This rather optimistic scenario, however, presupposes the embodiment of the value of democratic participation in the transnational process, as well as the consolidation on the part of European citizens of a lively sense of community; something which leads us on to the next chapter.

Notes on Chapter 3

1   The former set of challenges stem from the actual workings of democratic government, whilst the latter grow autonomously out of the external environments in which democracies operate. See Crozier, Michael *et al.*, *The Crisis of Democracy* (New York, 1975, New York University Press), pp 3-9.

2   Arblaster, Anthony, *Democracy* (Milton Keynes, 1987, Open University Press), p 105.

3   Schumpeter, Joseph A., *Capitalism, Socialism and Democracy* (London, 1994, Routledge), p 269. Influenced by Schumpeter's view of democracy as competitive leadership, Lipset defines democracy as 'a political system which supplies regular constitutional opportunites for changing the governing officials, and a social mechanism which permits the largest possible part of the population to influence major decisions by choosing among contenders for political office'; Schattschneider as 'a competitive political system in which competing leaders and organisations define the alternatives of public policy in such a way that the public can participate in the decision-making process'; Vanhanen as 'a political system in which ideologically and socially different groups are legally entitled to compete for political power and in which institutional power holders are elected by the people and are responsible to the people'; and Dahl as the 'system of decision-making in which leaders are more or less responsible to the preferences of non-leaders'. See respectively, Lipset, Seymour M., *Political Man: The Social Bases of Politics* (London, 1983, Heinemann), p 27; Schattschneider, Elmer E., *The Semisovereign People: A Realist's View of Democracy in America* (New York, 1960, Rinehart and Winston), p 138; Vanhanen, Tatu, *The Process of Democratization: A Comparative Study of 147 States, 1980-88* (London, 1990, Crane Russak), p 11; and Dahl, Robert A., 'Hierarchy, Democracy and Bargaining in Politics and Economics' in Eulau, Heinz (ed.), *Political Behaviour* (Glencloe IL, 1956, The Free Press), p 7. The common defining properties of these definitions are free electoral competition between leaders and indirect citizen participation in political decision-making via elected representatives.

4   *Ibid.*, p 242. The problem with this definition, Holden argues, is that 'any kind of political system in which governmental power depends on winning competitive elections could be counted as a democracy'. See Holden, Barry,

Understanding Liberal Democracy Second edn (London, 1993, Harvester Wheatshaft), p 12.

5   See Miller, David, 'The Competitive Model of Democracy', in Graeme Duncan (ed.), *Democratic Theory and Practice* (Cambridge, 1985, Cambridge University Press), pp 133-55.

6   Schumpeter, Joseph A., *Capitalism, Socialism and Democracy*, p 250. This model consists of both representative and participatory theories of democracy. Yet, if we are to embrace Zolo's viewpoint that 'the "common good" and the will of the *demos* come to the same thing', then we may take the classical doctrine of democracy as a coherent body of thought in which 'the classical theory of political representation [becomes] a simple institutional variant of the theory of participation'. See Zolo, Danilo, *Democracy and Complexity: A Realist Approach*, translated by McKie, David (Cambridge, 1992, Polity Press), p 66.

7   Zolo, Danilo, *Democracy and Complexity*, note 1, p 184. As Dahl claims that what the systems known as democracies should be descibed best as 'poly-archies', Zolo asserts that these systems 'are more properly *differentiated and limited autocratic systems*, that is... liberal oligarchies'. See p 181.

8   Pickles, Dorothy, *Democracy* (London, 1970, Methnen & Co), p 11. In her view, democracy as 'a set of institutions' must fulfil the following two require-ments: it must be able to elicit the opinion of as many people as possible on how the country ought to be governed; and it must provide ways of ensuring that the actions of those chosen by the public correspond to the wishes of the latter. She concludes that democratic government is 'a dialogue between rulers and the ruled'. See pp 12-14.

9   Arblaster, Anthony, *Democracy*, p 9. Similarly, he states that the consent, acceptance and support of 'the people' has increasingly become the principle source of governmental legitimacy in contemporary polities.

10 *Ibid.*, p 6.

11 This description heavily draws from Arblaster's analysis of the relevance and importance of 'popular power' in assessing the real nature of democracy. See *ibid.*, pp 94-5.

12 Beetham, David, *The Legitimation of Power* (London, 1991, Macmillan), p 15.

13 Arblaster, Anthony, *Democracy*, p 97. Thus, it is essential to the proper func-tioning of democracy that extensive public debate takes place before the determination of governmental policy – the outcome of such deliberations being popular decisions since it is the people which is ultimately sovereign. See p 98.

14 Mayo, H.B., *An Introduction to Democratic Theory* (New York, 1960, Oxford University Press), p 94. Mayo distinguishes the following set of principles in a democratic system: popular control of policy-makers; political equality; and effectiveness of the popular control. Yet, he recognises that some criteria are more important than others, and all are a matter of degree. See pp 61-6 and p 69.

15 Bealey, Frank, *Democracy in the Contemporary State* (Oxford, 1988, Clarendon Press), p 5. To stress the importance of 'upward control' in the democratic

process, he uses the example of the German Empire from 1870-1918, arguing that although it provided for periodic elections with manhood suffrage, as well as for organised political parties and considerable freedom of speech and of the press, responsible government did not exist because the Chancellor was responsible to the Kaiser alone and neither to the Reichstag nor to the electorate as a whole.

16 *Ibid.*, p 46. This may well imply, in Bealey's words, a disposition to answer questions and explain and justify policy; but it may result in the reversion, or even withdrawal, of policy. In any case, government will be disposed to be more responsive to the electorate.

17 Arblaster, Anthony, *Democracy*, p 95. Cf Bealey, Frank, *Democracy in the Contemporary State*, p 5. The term 'pseudodemocracy' is defined by Green as 'representative government, ultimately accountable to "the people" but not really under their control'. See Green, Philip, *Retrieving Democracy: In Search of Civic Equality* (London, 1985, Methuen), p 3.

18 Pickles, Dorothy, *Democracy*, p 18. For instance, to try and define democracy as 'a way of life in a society in which each individual is believed to be entitled to an equality of concern as regards the chances of participating freely in the values of that society', gives no guidance to government as to how society can be organised to provide justice, equality, liberty, fraternity and the like.

19 Birch, Anthony H., *The Concepts and Theories of Modern Democracy* (London and New York, 1993, Routledge), pp 243-4.

20 *Ibid.*, p 244.

21 Lively, Jack, *Democracy* (Oxford, 1975, Basil Blackwell), p 49. Arguing that 'it is perhaps impossible to define democracy in any very concrete institutional terms,' he concludes that democracy 'has to do with political equality, equality of influence over political decisions'. See p 49 and p 35.

22 Pickles, Dorothy, *Democracy*, p 18.

23 Dahl, Robert A., *A Preface to Democratic Theory* (Chicago and London, 1956, The University of Chicago Press), p 151.

24 Pickles, Dorothy, *Democracy*, p 19. The question that logically follows is how to put democratic principles into practice and provide more effective contacts between citizens and their government. See pp 27-8.

25 McKeon, Richard (ed.), *Democracy in a World of Tensions* (Paris, 1951, UNESCO), pp 522-3. Quoted in Hanson, Russell L., 'Democracy', in Ball, Terence *et al.* (eds), *Political Innovation and Conceptual Change* (Cambridge, 1989, Cambridge University Press), p 68.

26 Hanson, Russell L., 'Democracy', in Ball, Terence *et al.* (eds), *Political Innovation and Conceptual Change*, p 70. In *The Laws*, Plato coins the term 'theatrocracy' to describe the behaviour of the *demos* in the *ekklesia* (the Greek term for popular assembly), where political discourse and public decisions actually took place. Although today, as Hanson writes, the odious connotations of democracy have totally receded, one should not forget that 'it was not until the latter part of the eighteenth century that "democracy" and its

cognates, "democrat" and "democratic", became important in western European political rhetoric'. See p 72.

27　*Ibid.* On the politics of Athenian democracy see the first three chapters in Dunn, John (ed.), *Democracy: The Unfinished Journey, 508 BC to 1993* (Oxford, 1993, Oxford University Press).

28　McLean, Iain, 'Forms of Representation and Systems of Voting', in Held, David (ed.), *Political Theory Today* (Cambridge, 1991, Polity Press), p 172.

29　Pitkin, Hanna F., 'Representation', in Ball, Terence *et al.* (eds), *Political Innovation and Conceptual Change*, p 133 and p 135.

30　*Ibid.*, pp 133-4.

31　*Ibid.*, p 136.

32　*Ibid.*

33　*Ibid.*, pp 137-8.

34　*Ibid.*, p138.

35　*Ibid.*, p 141. In fact, Pitkin notes that Hobbes was the first to examine the idea of representation from a political theory perspective. More importantly, perhaps, he stressed the implications of representation for the sovereignty of the King. 'By calling the sovereign a representative,' Pitkin explains, 'Hobbes constantly implies that the sovereign will do what representatives are expected to do, not just whatever he pleases'. For further details see Hobbes, Thomas, *Leviathan* (Penguin, 1968, Harmondsworth).

36　*Ibid.*, p 142.

37　See Hampsher-Monk, Iain (ed.), *The Political Thought of Edmund Burke* (London, 1997, Longman), pp 109-10. Burke, in his eminent *Speech to the Electors of Bristol* in 1774, stated: 'Your representative owes you, not his industry only, but his judgement; and he betrays, instead of serving you, if he sacrifices it to your opinion... Parliament is not a *congress* of ambassadors from different and hostile interests... but parliament is a *deliberative* assembly of *one* nation, with *one* interest, that of the whole... You chose a member indeed; but when you have chosen him, he is not the member for Bristol, but he is the member of *parliament.*' Similarly, the 1791 French Constitution states that 'the representatives elected in the departments will not be representatives of a particular department but of the whole nation, and they may not be given any mandate'. Quoted in Birch, Anthony H., *The Concepts and Theories of Modern Democracy*, p 58.

38　Birch, Anthony H., *The Concepts and Theories of Modern Democracy*, p 58. 'Before this,' he asserts, 'the political representative had been viewed on the continent as a delegate, so that there were three parties in the representative process: the principle, the representative, and the authority to whom representations were to be made'.

39　*Ibid.*, p 59.

40　*Ibid.* As Allum put it, 'the people's active political participation has been discouraged in the English conception of democracy, and so it is no accident that the Schumpetarian model was theorized on the basis of British praxis'. See Allum, Percy, *State and Society in Western Europe* (Cambridge, 1995, Polity Press), p 99. A different point of view is expressed by Finer, suggesting that eighteenth and mid-nineteenth century legislatures were not sovereign since 'they had to act in conjuction with an executive power which even in Britain still retained a certain autonomy,' whilst 'they were conceived as a check and balance, an authorising or corrective instrument for the actions of the executive'. See Finer, S.E., 'The Contemporary Context of Representation', in Bogdanor, Vernon (ed.), *Representatives of the People? Parliamentarians and Constituents in Western Europe* (Gower, 1995, Policy Studies Institute), p 289.

41 Mill, James, *An Essay on Government* (New York, 1937, Cambridge University Press), p vi. Quoted in Dahl, Robert A., *Democracy and its Critics* (New Haven and London, 1989, Yale University Press), p 29.

42 Loewenstein, Karl, *Political Power and the Governmental Process* (Chicago, 1957, The University of Chicago Press), p 40. Quoted in Eulau, Heinz, 'Changing Views of Representation', in Eulau, Heinz and Whalke, John C. (eds), *The Politics of Representation* (London and Beverly Hills, 1978, Sage), p 53.

43 Dahl, Robert A., *Democracy and its Critics*, p 30.

44 Wright, Tony, *Citizens and Subjects: An Essay on British Politics* (London and New York, 1994, Routledge), p 93. 'It is relatively easy,' he argues, 'especially for those with a predilection for treating the study of politics as a branch of mathematics or economics, to demonstrate the inability of electoral systems to produce genuinely representative outcomes.'

45 *Ibid.*, p 96. It is not surprising, he notes, that this political tradition 'encounters particular difficulties in finding an agreed and durable basis for the achievement of social and economic objectives'.

46 *Ibid.*, pp 93-4. Not that he dismisses the importance of elections in the context of representative democracy. Rather, he argues that if elections become too blunt (ie, in the relationship between votes and outcomes) then there may well be an associated loss of legitimacy. Cf Hirst, Paul, 'Representative Democracy and its Limits', *Political Quarterly*, April-June 1988, pp 190-205; Nohlem, Dieter, 'Two Incompatible Principles of Representation' and Rose, Richard, 'Electoral Systems: A Question of Degree or Principle?', in Lijphart, Arend, and Grofman, Bernard (eds), *Choosing an Electoral System: Issues and Alternatives* (New York, 1984, Praeger), pp 83-9 and pp 73-81 respectively.

47 *Ibid.*, pp 92-3. He explains: 'A legislative assembly claims to be "representative" even though whole sections of the represented (in age, class, gender and ethnic terms) are hardly represented at all'.

48 *Ibid.*, p 93.

49 *Ibid.*, p 94 and p 96.

50 *Ibid.*

51 Schwartz, Nancy L., *The Blue Guitar: Political Representation and Community*, (Chicago and London, 1988, The University of Chicago Press). See respectively p 23 and pp 12-13.

52 Cohen, Carl, *Democracy* (The University of Georgia Press, Athens, 1971), p 77. 'If democracy,' he notes, 'is to be judged as government through participation, representation helps to make that participation effective'.

53 Bealey, Frank, *Democracy in the Contemporary State*, p 3.

54 Paine, Thomas, *Rights of Man* (Harmonsworth, 1984, Penguin), p 180.

55 On this point see Eulau, Heinz (ed.), *Political Behaviour*, pp 48-9.

56 *Ibid.*, p 49. See also Eulau, Heinz and Karps, Paul D., 'The Puzzle of Representation: Specifying Components of Responsiveness' in *ibid.*, pp 62-7; and Schwartz, Nancy L., *The Blue Guitar*, p 25.

57 On this point see Schmitter, Philippe C. and Karl, Terry L., 'What Democracy Is... And Is Not', *Journal of Democracy*, Summer 1991, p 78.

58 Mayo, H.B., *An Introduction to Democratic Theory*, p 60. Cf Bealey, Frank, *Democracy in the Contemporary State*, p 36.

59 Arblaster, Anthony, *Democracy*, p 90.

60 Bealey, Frank, *Democracy in the Contemporary State*, p 26. The author defines democracy as 'a decision-making process which can only exist when public contestation, inclusiveness, and responsible government are present'. See p 28.

61 Day, Patricia and Klein, Rudolf, *Accountabilities: Five Public Services* (London, 1987, Tavistock). Quoted in Wright, Tony, *Citizens and Subjects*, p 99.

62 Wright, Tony, *Citizens and Subjects*, p 100.

63 Quoted in *ibid.* For the original argument see Mill, J.S., 'Considerations on Representative Government' in Acton, H.B. (ed.), *Utilitarianism, Liberty, and Representative Government* (London, 1972, Dent & Sons), p 239.

64 *Ibid.*, p 98.

65 Stavridis, Stelios, 'Democratic Principles and Foreign Policy: The Case of European Political Cooperation', unpublished PhD dissertation, University of London, London School of Economics and Political Science, 1991, p 324.

66 Wright, Tony, *Citizens and Subjects*, p 101.

67 Day, Patricia and Klein, Rudolf, *Accountabilities*, pp 228-9. Quoted in Wright, Tony, *Citizens and Subjects*. Wright states: 'It is not just that the traditional doctrines about accountability are inadequate, but that they positively get in the way of new approaches'. See pp 100-1.

68 Wright, Tony, *Citizens and Subjects*, p 101.

69 *Ibid.*, p 104.

70 On this point see Williams, Raymond, 'Democracy and Parliament', A Socialist Society Pamphlet, London, 1982.

71 For the original argument see Mitchell, Austin, *Government by Party* (London, 1966, Whitecombe and Tombs). Quoted in Wright, Tony, *Citizens and Subjects*, p 100.

72 On the concept of 'cabinet decision-making' see Andeweg, Rudi, 'A Model of the Cabinet System: the Dimensions of Cabinet Decision-Making Processes', in Blondel, Jean and Müller-Rommel, Ferdinand (eds), *Governing Together: The Extent and Limits of Joint Decision-Making in Western European Cabinets* (London, 1993, St. Martin's Press), pp 23-42.

73 Herman, Valentine and Lodge, Juliet, *The European Parliament and the European Community*, (London, 1978, Macmillan), p 19.

74 Chapman, Donald, 'Parliament and European Union', in European Parliament, 'Symposium on European Integration and the Future of

Parliaments in Europe', DG for Research and Documentation, October 1975, p 181.

75 Bobbio, Norberto, *The Future of Democracy: A Defence of the Rules of the Game* (Cambridge, 1987, Polity Press), p 35.

76 King, Jeffrey H., 'Publicity, Commodification and Democratic Representation', in Köchler, Hans (ed.), *The Crisis of Representative Democracy* (Frankfurt, 1987, Verlag Peter Lang), p 79.

77 Stavridis, Stelios, 'Democratic Principles and Foreign Policy', pp 324-5. For instance, he argues that 'information without the power to change some action or decision is only an illusory power'. See p 326.

78 This argument draws from Stavridis's analysis of democracy as a dynamic state of affairs rather than an end in itself. See Stavridis, Sterlios, 'Democracy in Europe: East and West', in Conference Proceedings, 'People's Rights and European Structures', Manresa, Centre Unesco de Catalunya, September 1993, p 130. The quotation belongs to Jones, Roy E., *Principles of Foreign Policy: The Civil State and its World Setting* (Oxford, 1979, Martin Robertson), p 104.

79 On this term see Forsyth, Murray, *Unions of States: The Theory and Practice of Confederation* (Leicester, 1981, Leicester University Press), pp 10-16.

80 See Hobbes, Thomas, *Leviathan*, pp 187-8. Cf Held, David, 'Democracy: From City-States to a Cosmopolitan Order?', in Held, David (ed.), *Prospects for Democracy*, (Cambridge, 1993, Polity Press), 1993, p 28.

81 Gould, Carol C., *Rethinking Democracy* (Cambridge, 1993, Cambridge University Press), p 308.

82 Held, David, 'Democracy: From City-States to a Cosmopolitan Order?', in Held, David (ed.), *Prospects for Democracy*, p 14 and p 26.

83 Held, David, *Democracy and the New International Order* (London, 1993, Institute for Public Policy Research), p 5.

84 *Ibid.*, p 7.

85 *Ibid.*, p 7.

86 Held, David, 'Democracy, the Nation-State and the Global System', in Held, David (ed.), *Political Theory Today*, p 204.

87 *Ibid.*

88 Dahl, Robert A., *Democracy and its Critics*, p 319. He explains: 'the answer requires one to judge whether the trend towards transnationalism is reversible – reversible, that is, without costs that too many people will be unwilling to accept'. In general terms, Dahl's analysis provides a further justification for the imperative need to extend the democratic idea beyond national frontiers.

89 Hirst, Paul, *Associative Democracy: New Forms of Economic and Social Governance*, (Cambridge, 1993, Polity Press), p 12. Cf Fukuyama, Francis, 'The End of History', *National Interest*, Summer 1989, pp 3-18.

90 *Ibid.*

91 Hirst, Paul, 'Representative Democracy and its Limits', p 190. He notes: 'Representative democracy is such a powerful tool of legitimation of the

actions of government that no serious politician, even if they have just lost an election, will question it'.

92 Held, David, *Democracy and the New International Order*, p 24.

93 Hirst, Paul, *Associative Democracy*, p 22. Against the background of these democratic deficiencies, Hirst proposes the model of 'associational democracy' as the only practicable means of striking a delicate balance between democratic accountability and effective and efficient government.

94 *Ibid.*, p 20. Hirst characteristically states that 'democratic governance does not consist just in the powers of citizen election or majority decision, but in the continuous flow of information between governors and governed, whereby the former seek the consent and cooperation of the latter'.

95 *Ibid.*, p 22.

96 Lively, Jack, *Democracy*, p 30.

97 Arblaster, Anthony, *Democracy*, p 62.

98 Cohen, Carl, *Democracy*, p 21.

99 See Morris Jones, W.H., 'In Defence of Apathy', *Political Studies*, February 1954, pp 25-37.

100 The need for active citizen participation in the political process has been regarded by many contemporary scholars as an 'ideal' rather than a 'necessary' condition of democracy; at best inadequate and at worst overoptimistic. Dahl, for instance, once wrote: 'what we call democracy – that is a system of decision-making in which the leaders are more or less responsive to the preferences of non-leaders – does seem to operate with a relatively low level of citizen participation'. He concluded: 'it is innacurate to say that one of the necessary conditions for "democracy" is extensive citizen participation'. This view conflicts with J.S. Mill's political thought that the quality of a democracy should be judged by the extent of citizen participation in common affairs. In his exact words, 'nothing less can be ultimately desirable than the admission of all to share in the sovereign power of the state'. Quoted in Pickles, Dorothy, *Democracy*, pp 14-16. For a valuable selection of ideas on political participation see, *inter alia*, Pateman, Carole, *Participation and Democratic Theory* (Cambridge, 1970, Cambridge University Press); and Lucas, John R., *Democracy and Participation* (Harmondsworth, Penguin, 1976).

101 Beer, Samuel H., 'The British Legislature and the Problem of Mobilising Consent' in Norton, Philip (ed.), *Legislatures* (Oxford, 1990, Oxford University Press), p 78.

102 Crick, Bernard, *The Reform of Parliament* (London, 1964, Weidenfeld and Nicolson), p 177.

103 Bealey, Frank, *Democracy in the Contemporary State*, pp 265-6.

104 Bobbio, Norberto *The Future of Democracy*, p 33. For an excellent discussion on the subject see pp 79-97.

105 For a detailed account of this among other related issues see Lodge, Juliet, 'Transparency and Democratic Legitimacy', *Journal of Common Market Studies*, September 1994, pp 343-68.

106   For details on this definition see Bobbio, Norberto *The Future of Democracy*, p 33. For an excellent discussion on the subject see pp 86-7, and note 21, p 168.

107 *Ibid.*, p 79.

108 Dahl, Robert A., *A Preface to Democratic Theory*, p 3.

CHAPTER 4

The Process of Transnational *Demos*-Formation

PRELIMINARY REMARKS

Little doubt exists that the more democracy becomes a major concern for the student of European integration, the greater the chances for developing a better understanding of its transnational dimension. However, as no existing body of theory is capable of providing 'the final statement' on the subject, so our thesis professes no absolute truths in this respect. Rather, it is to be viewed not as a definitive conclusion, but as part of a continuing process of civic deliberation. After all, where democratic knowledge is most developed, it has been acquired not by the recognition of faultless statements, but by the less startling, yet all the same demanding, refinement of an archetypal set of democratic assumptions and ideas. Whilst we do not claim to possess the one and only prescription for curing the democratic pathology of the larger polity once and for all, we do venture to focus more on the treatment of the disease, rather than merely on its symptoms: that the Union suffers from a severe case of deficient civic 'we-ness'. But let us now pose the central question of this chapter: what is it that small- or large-scale democracy 'requires always and everywhere, and would be inconceivable without'?[1]

THE PREREQUISITE OF DEMOCRACY

From a democratic theory perspective, the answer to this question is of primary importance, for if democracy presupposes the meeting of certain conditions 'without which it cannot exist', thus not being merely based on 'the logic of circumstances', we have good reasons not to equate it with occasionally occurring political phenomena. On the other hand, the mere presence of what democracy presupposes does not necessarily guarantee its successful operation. As Cohen writes: 'its successful practice requires that a number of further conditions be met'.[2] Since the operational conditions of democracy have been extensively discussed in chapter 3, what needs to be presented here is the 'prerequisite' of democracy: the existence of a 'political community' within which democratic principles can be put into practice.[3]

Of equal importance is to identify those characteristics which actually make a group of people a political community, as well as the elements which can hold such a community together and even strengthen it. An answer to these interrelated questions was offered by de Grazia: 'Holding it together are systems of beliefs, flexible bands weaving through and around each member of the community, compacting it, allowing some strength at times, coiling like a steel spring at others... Without them... no political community can be said to exist.'[4] Here, the term 'belief-system' refers to the existence of a coherent and identifiable body of truly common (maximalist view) or at least compatible (minimalist view) political and democratic values which the members of a political community share about their relationships to one another and to those possessing decision-making powers.[5] Conversely, when no such body of values exists amongst them, they form a collection of individuals grouped together by something less than political or democratic bonds. That being the case, no 'real' political community, as opposed to an 'invented' or 'imagined' one, can exist.

Another premise of fundamental importance to the relationship between democracy and community is that the underlying structure of relations which develop within the latter should be closer to a *Gemeinschaft* (community), rather than to a *Gesellschaft* (society), in Tönnies's sense of the terms.[6] For it is in this type of association that one may perceive the embryo of a 'constitutive' community, as opposed to an 'instrumental' one: 'a community that would constitute the very identity of the individuals'.[7] Further, *Gemeinschaft* is more suitable for the prospering of democratic relations, since the individuals forming it have developed a 'sense of community', also known as 'community spirit' or 'community of attachment', strong enough to overcome and even transcend most of democracy's potentially disturbing effects such as unequivocal compliance to majority rule. Equally, where the community spirit is less intense and profound, democracy is less secure when it encounters internal issues with which it cannot cope effectively: when the members of a political community lack the necessary bonds of unity in and through which their differences might be openly discussed and, in time, amicably resolved. Here, the '*Gemeinschaft* factor' appears one of democracy's indispensable 'common spheres'.

To give an example: the application of majority rule in a democratic polity presupposes the existence of certain levels of social unity among its component parts. Following Cohen's line of reasoning, 'there can be no larger part unless the larger part and the smaller parts are indeed parts of one whole'.[8] Indeed, the successful operation of majority rule implies an *a priori* recognition that the 'opponents' who constitute the larger number are also an integral part of a self-conscious whole within which 'minorities can be distinguished and the majority may legitimately claim to rule'.[9] As Weiler put it: 'People accept the majoritarian principle of democracy within a polity to which they see themselves as belonging'.[10] Thus, both democracy and *Gemeinschaft* refer to the same desirable state of affairs: they are ultimately expressions of an overarching relation between the members of a political community and between them and their rulers. Whereas democracy constitutes an expression of these relations as viewed 'from within', *Gemeinschaft* is an expression of them as seen 'from outside'. Yet, what they both have in common is that in order to retain their generic properties, they have to be formed 'from below' instead of being imposed 'from above'.

Before elaborating on the various interrelated aspects of these concepts, and bearing in mind that our focus is centred on the interwoven worlds of transnational democracy and political community (comprising the basic properties of a politically organised *Gemeinschaft*), the following points need to be made. Although the different theoretical approaches and empirical methods employed to 'master' the disorderly universe of democracy have always been open to challenge, this should not impose too great an obstacle to associating the democratic process with a set of transnational arrangements.[11] Moreover, despite the fact that the political nature of the Union will probably remain unsettled among its students, the presuppositions of this unique exercise in large-scale democracy-building, should nevertheless be set out.

The aim is to complement our previous theoretical account of what EU democracy is or should be about, of what fundamental principles lie beneath its often puzzling meaning, and of how it may be operative within the realm of a distinctive political unit, capable of regulating both interstate and intrastate relations. Having presented the theoretical justification of transnational democracy, this part of the study focuses on the socio-psychological dimension of the Union's democratic deficit. It should be stressed from the outset that – as in any other exploration of small- or large-scale democracy-building, so in this undertaking – there is no place for dogmatic thinking. For any such enquiry combines a variety of democratic traditions, making it 'the exclusive property of none of them'.[12] Echoing Cohen's eloquent phrase: 'There may be dogmatic democrats; there can be no democratic dogma'.[13]

THE CONCEPTS OF *GEMEINSCHAFT* AND *GESELLSCHAFT*

According to Kamenka, no actual society or institution will ever conform completely to Tönnies's theoretical selections.[14] For they are conceptual entities representing two ideal types of social organisation, rather than an accurate description of existing kinds of societies; instead, they can be better understood as 'mental constructs', suggesting hypotheses and lines of investigation in dealing with social issues.[15] As Sorokin notes, both before and after Tönnies, the *Gemeinschaft-Gesellschaft* typology has been widely used within various academic disciplines.[16] But it is Tönnies's theoretical system that assumes utmost significance for contemporary theorists: a conceptual scheme that outlives its founder; a living paradigm of intellectual excellence.

In fact, it continues to reaffirm its multidimensional significance even when taken to apply in such a novel experiment in large-scale community-formation as the EU, based on prototypical political institutions. For the *Gemeinschaft-Gesellschaft* construct is one constantly shaped and re-shaped, invented and reinvented and, finally, debated and challenged in the context of both domestic affairs and transnational relations. From Plato to the great medieval thinkers, and from them to present-day analysis, these different types of association constitute the two opposite sides of the same interminable search for a 'viable polity'.[17] But let us now reflect upon Tönnies's sociological thinking which, in our view, wields so much influence even on this relatively 'new' subject of inquiry, as the process of democratising the Union is.

To begin with the concept of *Gemeinschaft*, it describes 'a sense among the individuals forming it of belonging together, of having common loyalties and values, of kinship', so that the tasks performed within its structures stem from 'a feeling of contributing something worthwhile to the good of the whole'.[18] Thus it is something qualitatively distinct and presumably higher than the numerical sum of the private well-being and prosperity of its members. In this type of society, people associate themselves together because they think of their relationships as valuable in the dual sense of being important both as an end in and of itself. Thus it is perceived as an internal, living and organic 'collective entity' – organic in terms of being considered and conceived in relation to its parts[19] – whose 'norms of order' are based upon 'concord', as opposed to *Gesellschaft*-like relationships which rest on a contractual arrangement or 'convention'. For such a contract to be successful, the wills of the individuals need to reflect what the law of contract calls 'a meeting of minds'.[20]

Gemeinschaft on the other hand, Tönnies argues, is conditioned by an existing social or 'integral' will of a higher type: a 'natural' will which springs or unfolds naturally *ab intra*, like a growing embryo, as opposed to an 'orthological' will – itself the conditioning and originating element of *Gesellschaft*.[21] Based on relationships of mutual affirmation of a 'federative' kind, representing 'unity in plurality and plurality in unity', the members of a *Gemeinschaft* gradually come to develop strong feelings of 'togetherness', 'we-ness' or even 'oneness', to the eventual framing of a collective consciousness: they are bound together in mutually reinforcing relationships, thinking of their collective existence as dominating their respective individualism and perceiving their close association as a means of improving their domestic conditions of living.

An entity which is formed through this positive type of relationship is called a *Gemeinschaft*, pointing to 'a lasting and genuine form of living together,' as opposed to its counterpart form of 'human *Gesellschaft*' which is considered as a mere co-existence of people independent of each other.[22] Whereas, then, the common sphere of a *Gesellschaft* rests on the concept of contract, with its 'secret' lying in 'a rational coming together of ends that remain individual,'[23] that of a *Gemeinschaft* rests on the concept of 'one people' – and in political terms of one *demos* – with its 'secret' lying in an 'internally-oriented relationship' developed among its members, rather than in a mechanical or artificial fusion of separate, private wills. Accordingly, the distinctive characteristic of a *Gemeinschaft* is that the collectivity is not considered a mere aggregation of its parts, but rather as an organically structured social body which is made up of smaller collectivities that depend upon the larger collectivity.

By contrast, the members of a *Gesellschaft* are often reduced to the status of being merely a collection of individual consumers – a mass of utilitarian oriented wills – behaving in a manner similar to that acted upon 'the fictional unattached men in the theories of classical economics'.[24] Tönnies's term 'exchange *Gesellschaft*' (or market) captures the meaning of that 'convention': a body of individuals grouping together for the conduct of profit-making transactions. In practice, *Gesellschaft*-like relationships are characterised by high levels of competitiveness, and the 'exchanges' resulting from them reflect a materialistic *quid pro quo* situation: 'only for the sake of receiving something that seems better to him will he be moved to give away a good'.[25]

In brief, a *Gesellschaft* type of society points to a system of conventional rules whereby 'the relations with visible, material matters have preference'.[26] In such an 'artificial being' of contractual arrangements, no common values can exist as 'objective qualities': whereas in a *Gemeinschaft* the individuals remain united 'in spite of all separating factors,' in a *Gesellschaft* they are essentially separated 'in spite of all uniting factors'.[27] Hence, the latter can be best seen as a multitude of competing individual wills that are devoid of affirmative relationships and affective/identitive ties. The result is the emergence of a 'web' of market-oriented ties which, for all their intensity, fall short of forming the nucleus of a political community as the highest type of a 'complete' *Gemeinschaft*: a *communio totius*, embracing all the rest.

On the other hand, the organic nature of *Gemeinschaft* rests on the assumption of perfect unity of human association as a natural condition which is preserved even 'in spite of separation'.[28] Accordingly, in *Gemeinschaft*-like relationships the ensemble of individual wills mutually direct each other towards an 'equilibrium of forces' somewhat close to Kuper's 'equilibrium model of society', as opposed to the 'conflict model' which may well be the case in a *Gesellschaft* (see chapter 7).[29] Moreover, in a *Gemeinschaft*, authority is not viewed as an all-powerful centre which produces binding decisions without the prior consent of the affected *demos*, but rather as a dialectical process of structuring civic relations.[30] In conclusion, *Gemeinschaft* implies an *a priori* social unity: a 'community of people' whose members constantly manifest their 'united will' and 'community spirit' towards the attainment of common goals, through their co-ordinated action.[31] As will be shown later, in political terms, this type of collective entity refers to a polity guided by a self-conscious *demos* whose collective will marks its impact on the shaping of the public affairs.

THE '*GEMEINSCHAFT* FACTOR' IN THE DEMOCRATISATION OF THE UNION

Moving the debate onto the Union level, there seems to be a strong link between the concept of *Gemeinschaft* and the democratic dimension of European integration. The point to make here is that the process of democratising the Union is inextricably linked to grass-roots politics in general, and the development of 'a sense of community' in particular, in that the positive feelings of the sub-units must be somewhat stronger and deeper than any decisive issues that may arise as integration proceeds. As a result, the stronger the 'sense of community', and with it the bonds of unity at the popular level, the more durable transnational democracy is likely to be, and the greater the propensity of the Union to withstand even the most bitter internal conflicts.[32]

Indeed, it is imperative that there be some common concerns which bind the European peoples into what Cohen calls a 'self-conscious unit'.[33] From this view, the proper functioning of democracy in the Union presupposes the existence of at least a nascent *Gemeinschaft* (see chapter 8). In brief, the relationship between transnational democracy and political community is a symbiotic one, suggesting that the more the viability of the larger political entity relies on the quality of democracy exhibited by the central institutions, the more such a quality remains dependent upon the extent to which elements of *Gemeinschaft* have been developed among the constituent *demoi*.

The difficult question arising here concerns the necessary steps to be taken towards the qualitative transformation of the current *Gesellschaft*-like EU system (see chapter 7) into one where the European citizen body will be the principal actor in the transnational process. Put in another way, what are the prospects for transforming the European peoples from a fragmented *demos* – a politically amorphous aggregate of separate publics which amount to no more than a dispersed citizen body – into a cohesive *demos* in the symbiotic meaning of the term? That is, 'a mode of coexistence reaching... a very strong sense of "we"'.[34] To answer these questions, which in our view lie at the very heart of democratic deficit, we present the following arguments.

A first point to make is that EU democracy is intimately linked with both its sociological and communitarian base; namely, with the appearance of new forms of citizen identification based on the power of a common democratic belief-system as a necessary, albeit not always sufficient, condition for sustaining them. The existence of common values among the subcultures of the larger political unit contributes substantially to its 'social legitimacy'. Weiler explains: 'Legitimacy is achieved when the government process displays a commitment to, and actively guarantees values that are part of, the general political culture'.[35] Just as the quality of progress towards further integration vitally depends upon popular support, so transnational democracy-building is inseparably linked with 'the construction of a "we" in a context of diversity' that reflects the core values of the 'uniting' parts.[36]

Both processes – democracy-building and community-strengthening – are concerned with the creation of a common belief-system so that a plurality of actors could democratically co-exist by allowing a new transnational political culture to blossom and bear fruit. For this to materialise, however, it would have to rely on a new paradigm of multiculturalism focused around community-building devices, and on a new philosophy of 'symbiotic pluralism'. The first part of the term stresses the necessity for mutual toleration among the component publics; the second refers to 'the rich fabric of various groupings, subcultures, and viewpoints'.[37] Such a conception does not require either assimilative or oppressive techniques of what is known among students of nationalism as 'enforced homogeneity'. Rather, it needs mechanisms capable of accommodating divergent claims without threatening the maintenance of democratic bonds among the subcultures. In brief, the formation of 'citizens' identities' patterned on a substantive corpus of democratic values is imperative for preventing the collectivity from what Garner calls 'smothering diversity'.[38]

But even without taking the rather abstract element of 'popular consensus' into account, as distinct from the concept of 'procedural consensus' that was related to the successful transfer of loyalties to supranational authorities,[39] what is imperative for the prospering of democracy in the Union is the existence of a 'transnational *demos*': a self-conscious and politically aware body of citizens capable of directing their democratic claims to, and via, the central institutions. The latter are seen as a necessary machinery for channelling, articulating and enforcing the 'public will'. Thus defined, transnational *demos* can be also understood as a new type of collective identity forged by the active will of a civic-minded European society – a 'community of civic communities' – whose members perceive themselves as parts of a composite *demos*.

The aim is to provide the larger configuration with the much-needed civic environment – a European public sphere – emphasising the possibilities, rather than the limits, for a politically organised community of peoples to be actively engaged in integration processes. The argument here is that it is somewhat irrelevant to speak of democracy in the conventional sense of the term – as government by the people – in a system composed of separate national *demoi*, unless their members are characterised by deep-rooted feelings of 'belonging to' an 'inclusive' community, in turn based on the common democratic properties of its 'component' communities. Here, the option of *demos*, nascent *demos* or '*demos*-to-be' overrides any territorial conceptions of political organisation, ethnocentric techniques of consciousness-raising, as well as assimilationist practices of community-formation. In this sense, it is more like a self-instituting process of civic identity-building that respects cultural pluriformity than a centrally planned strategy for constructing a *homo Europaeus* by means of learned doctrines, invented traditions, manufactured memories and artificial identifications. All of these constitute the very essence of homogenising nation-building strategies. Accordingly, the creation of a transnational *demos* is neither easily manageable nor a manipulative process of democratic self-transformation. Rather, its coming into being rests on the willingness and determination of the member publics themselves.

But for such a *demos* to exist, its constituent parts should be based on what Etzioni calls a 'core curriculum': a body of shared values which keep its members together as an identifiable entity;[40] one capable of escaping both the disuniting effects of 'unbounded pluralism' and the 'unnecessarily homogenising' forces of the 'melting-pot' type of society, whilst providing 'the frame of unity to contain the "plurals" from falling out'.[41] This model, defined by Etzioni as 'pluralism-within-unity', is based on the following premise: 'Constituent communities can follow their own subsets of values without endangering the body society', as long as they accept a set of shared core values.[42] Further, the more practical the means offered to the transnational *demos* to apply its 'civic commitment', the more powerful the linchpins that maintain the bonds of unity will grow to be, and the less probable the outbreak of potentially unchecked inter-segmental rivalries.

Although the assumption that small- or large-scale democracy presupposes the existence of both a political community and a *demos* is fundamental to this study, it is either not explicitly stated or totally missing from most contemporary reflections on the state of democracy in the Union. Whichever the case, it is our contention that, for a democratic Union to exist, its peoples must generate an active commitment to the democratic process in relation to its workings, analogous to that manifested in their own countries which, whether we formally acknowledge it or not, are still considered as their primary political units. For only a European *demos* conscious of its political identity and inspired by an underlying sense of community can create the bases of a self-directed (when it is the *demos* which steers the Union) and self-determining (when the *demos* has a say in the making of large-scale decisions) collectivity.

The above interpretation of the meaning and requirements of EU democracy places the emphasis on the process of *demos*-formation. Such a process, by emphasising the necessity for the creation of grass-roots European politics as stimuli for generating transnational civic activity, has a potential historical counterpart in the making of a federal *demos*. As Beer explains with reference to the USA, the united action of the American people gave birth to a democratic structure of government, enabling them 'to be brought to bear on the action of the general government', whilst leaving no doubt as to the ultimate source of political authority.[43]

All these, however, are not functions that European citizens 'can perform once and get done with'.[44] Rather, they require a continuing series of genuine concern and active participation in the public affairs of the 'inclusive' community, as well as citizen identification with its political institutions. These functions are absolutely essential for rendering the philosophy of government called 'democracy' in a polity composed of a plurality of constituent identities. In practical terms, their creative combination will decisively determine the effectiveness and responsiveness of the democratic process, the former relating to the ability of the *demos* to influence decisions made through systems of indirect control, the latter to the degree to which those in power remain responsive to public needs and demands.[45]

In conclusion, the application of these democratic conditions to the workings of a political community, whether national or transnational, will define what Cohen calls 'the sovereign range of democracy': the extent to which ultimate political authority lies in the affected public or in those deciding on its behalf.[46] The following definition of democracy offered by Cohen is of the utmost analytical importance in justifying the emphasis given to the relationship between democracy and community: 'Democracy is that system of community government in which, by and large, the members of the community participate, or may participate, directly or indirectly, in the making of decisions which affect them all'.[47] In support of this communitarian view comes Dewey's authoritative statement: 'Democracy is not an alternative to other principles of associational life but the idea of community life itself'.[48]

TRANSNATIONAL *DEMOS*-FORMATION VS NATION-BUILDING

Returning to the central theme of our inquiry, the formation of a European *demos* should not be confused with what has been described by Deutsch, among other political scientists, as 'the art of nation-building', and by many social scientists as 'the process of national development'.[49] Nor should it be confused with the possibility – rather entertaining for some, and feared by others – of creating a European 'super-nation' sustained by new forms of (supra)nationalism.[50] For should that be the case, it would be to confuse a potential loss of national identity with the development of a transnational democratic consciousness resting upon a profound popular base.[51] Likewise, it should not be confused with what has been described as 'a purely *political* European nationalism'.[52] Hence, a distinction needs to be made between the two: the process of (transnational) *demos*-formation and that of nation-building.[53]

The former process refers to a situation in which the members of a political community develop a common awareness about the way in which public affairs should be handled, and seek to join forces in demanding a more democratic way of government in relation to them. Thus a *demos* is a community of citizens linked to each other by strong democratic bonds and pressing to acquire a measure of effective control through formal or informal means over government. Although the actual *foci*, conditions and procedures around, by and through which this over-all result can be achieved are various, the end-purpose – democracy – is fairly easily recognisable. The making of a *demos* whose claims matter in the political process, as opposed to the building of a nation, does not suggest either a denying or a formal constitutional merging of pre-existing polities in a larger amalgamated unit governed by a single common government and, hence, by one supreme centre of decision-making.[54]

In other words, it does not imply a legally-based merger or fusion of two or more previously independent units into a 'classical' state, as a territorially-defined entity which possesses legal authority and maintains a general hierarchy of values, power and institutions upon which public life is organised. Nor does it imply a profound and disruptive effect of what Smith calls 'the European pattern of national identity'.[55] The sentiment of democratic consciousness among European citizens does not entail in any pragmatic sense either a loss of national identity, nor can it by itself make a separate 'nation' whose people is characterised by sentiments of patriotism, cultural homogeneity and ethnic solidarity. True, a group consciousness is needed, but one based on adherence to democratic values, rather than on a sense of common origins, a consciousness of sameness and commonality, religious or ethnonational ties and feelings of belonging to one state or of wishing to form one.[56]

Far from hinting at an amalgamative process in a Deutschian conception of the term, or at one whereby 'the inhabitants of a state's territory come to be the *loyal* citizens of that state,'[57] transnational *demos*-formation aims to improve potential democratic deficiencies: it does not imply the mutual assimilation of formerly independent entities into a single 'indivisible' body politic possessing the *de jure* or even the *de facto* status of a nation, let alone that of a 'super-state'.[58] As Weiler suggests: 'It would be more than ironic if a polity... set up to encounter the excesses of statism ended up by coming around full circle and transforming itself into a (super-) state, and it would be equally ironical if an ethos that rejected the nationalism of the member-states gave birth to a new European nation and nationalism'.[59]

Therefore, unlike formal political amalgamation, which tends to be seen as a 'nuclear process' whereby the populations of different territories legally come to form the core population of a larger territory by means of a higher constitutive act, transnational *demos*-formation is a process of bringing the democratic capabilities of the separate national *demoi* – of which the European peoples are composed – into the forefront of European integration. In this conception, the metaphor of the 'melting pot', in which the old identities are assimilated in a new supranational identity, should be dismissed from the outset. And so too the model of a 'mosaic society' in which 'primary' identities and identifications are not only preserved but also continue to be the central and irreplaceable focus of citizens' political life. Rather, the idea is for a *trans*national civic identity to be forged out of the kaleidoscope of pre-existing and mutually compatible belief systems.

In brief, transnational *demos*-formation is about a politics of 'civic inclusion' followed by a corresponding sharing of popular political sentiments and values so as to make the European peoples feel, look and act more as a *demos* than as several, fragmented and mutually alienated citizen bodies. It is only then that the Union, instead of being merely a 'union of states', can be seen as a 'union of peoples', guided in their relationships by a spirit of mutual affirmation, fortifying the bonds that unite them as one composite *demos* and perceiving the multicultural nature of their political being as a source of civic enrichment, rather than of divisiveness and fragmentation.

The logical outcome of this process is not a 'homogeneous polity' composed of 'one people, one government and one territory', but rather a new framework of unity out of diverse polities that preserves the integrities of their people whilst reflecting their common democratic aspirations without either destroying the subcultures that are joined together to form the larger *demos* or breaking the European society into a cluster of warring nationalities. This dynamic in the relationship between the member publics as individual units and as a composite but identifiable *demos*, and in Weiler's terms between 'the autonomous self' and 'the self as part of the larger community',[60] needs to be recognised as utterly important in the transformation of the Union from democracies to democracy. Such capabilities, supported by 'new modes of discourse and a new discipline of solidarity',[61] are about the ability of the larger *demos* to act as a coherent front pressing for greater political responsibility to its members.

In essence, transnational *demos*-formation can be best understood as the product of a general recognition by the citizens of the member nation-states of the imperative to be governed by more democratic processes than those currently operating within European structures. It also implies that the Union's governing process should be directed by the assertion of such a *demos* as the unchallenged unit of transnational authority, the ultimate focus of political purpose, the basic reason of active rational deliberation and, finally, the symbol and source of 'strong democracy'.[62] That is, as the political body which not only shares in civic entitlements, but also takes a prominent position in the governance of the larger unit.

Although both processes can facilitate political integration, the fundamental difference between them rests on the conception of an end-result: whilst nation-building perceives integration as a means of achieving a 'natural' community whereby the constituted unity lies in one nation and its respective conception of nationality, transnational *demos*-formation is assigned the task of creating a self-conscious citizen body without aiming either at a homogeneous citizenry or seeking to accomplish a 'cultural match' between states and peoples. On the contrary, cultural pluralism is seen not only as a feasible but also as an underlying feature of Western European civilisation itself. For these reasons, it is important to disentangle the 'state-factor' from the formation of a transnational *demos*. Bloom explains: 'Internally... nation-building has been successful when the nation-state has the ultimate or transcending claim on its people's loyalty... Internationally... when the state can rely upon the mass support of its citizenry in a situation of competition with external actors'.[63] Another fundamental difference is that whereas the viability of nation-building depends upon citizen identification with the nation as a whole, that of transnational *demos*-formation depends upon citizen identification with the political institutions of the larger entity.

This distinction is crucial, for it clears away any notion that the idea of forming a collective civic identity may itself evoke nationalism. Instead, it is concerned with the transformation of divided or conflicting loyalties to a balanced co-existence of multiple political loyalties – seen schematically as a dynamic network of concentric loyalties. No doubt, this is what Etzioni had in mind when he wrote that 'communities are best viewed as if they were Chinese nesting boxes, in which less encompassing communities (families, neighbourhoods) are nested within more encompassing ones (local villages and towns), which in turn are situated within still-more-encompassing communities, the national and the cross-national ones (such as the budding European Community)'.[64] As Reif put it: 'a stronger sense of belonging to the more immediate communities does not imply a rejection of a European political community'.[65]

Following Bloom's line of argument, nation-building 'only occurs when the mass of citizens, directly or indirectly, actually experience the actions of the state... These actions will evoke identification and, therefore, nation-building only if: (a) the state is perceived as being involved in a common endeavour in relation to an external threat; or if (b) the state acts beneficiently towards its citizens'.[66] Yet, García explains that the challenge now faced by the Union is 'to offer and be able to implement policies which justify to individual citizens the responsibilities involved in belonging to a European *political community*'.[67] This comment is suggestive of the need to create a congenial framework of citizen participation in integration processes, and to move away from any obstinately state-centric form of collective identification.

In this context, we can identify the following structural components or internal features of the transition from a plurality of *demoi* to a pluralistic *demos*: democratic self-consciousness of the collective body of citizens; emphasising of shared 'belief-systems'; public awareness of the political process; determination to direct democratic claims to, and via, the central institutions; and a sense of community, as necessary to support concerted political activities. Above all, however, at the socio-psychological level, a *demos* exists only if its members recognise their collective existence as such.

Equally, the degree to which a transnational political community is indeed established or not relates to the extent to which its composite *demos* is bound together by a web of shared understandings and develops positive feelings to the institutions of that community, rather than merely to those that reside in the component communities. In this sense, it has the political awareness of responsible citizens, and not the will of a higher central authority, to thank for its existence. Thus it is neither the creature of a body of law granting political rights to a community of people composed of different nationalities, nor is it a by-product of a process similar to that of national integration – 'consisting of government policies designed to change people's attitudes and loyalties'[68] – involving direct initiatives to create a sense of national identity and pride through national symbols, socialisation via the educational system, and measures to reduce the impact of segmental cleavages in society.[69]

Consequently, transnational *demos*-formation should not be seen as part of an irreversible 'melting process' of full assimilation where particular groups of people with strong territorial affinities have decided to leave their distinctive cultural milieu and become part of a new European nation. For if that were the case, it would be as if the peoples and leaders of the member states with long-established symbols, self-images and historical traditions would be willing to undergo a process of 'national deculturation' and confirm their allegiance to a larger 'us' of an incipient nation. This is a scenario which, even if we embrace Connor's view that Western Europe is far from being composed of 'fully integrated states',[70] should be dismissed outright. Otherwise, it would be as if we were to accept that the transnational political culture which sustains European integration, at least at the elite level, is a culture without a national form or, in Lenin's terms, 'an innational culture'.[71] This runs the danger of perceiving the Union as a polity detached from the distinctive characteristics of its sub-units.

Transnational *demos*-formation should be seen as an experiment constructed out of the elements of pre-existing identities; a desire to democratically shape the common fate of a plurality of highly interrelated peoples, without endangering the existence of that plurality: 'a many turned into one without ceasing to be many';[72] or, a willingness to maintain territorial boundaries and at the same time transcend them for the sake of democracy itself. As Connolly put it: 'The upshot will be to support a more cosmopolitan democratic imagination that desaggregates standard conceptions of democracy and distributes political identifications and democratic energies across disparate spaces'.[73] His conception of democracy as an 'egalitarian constitution of cultural life',[74] contrasts Schmitt's dictum: 'Democracy requires... first, homogeneity and second – if the need arises – elimination or eradication of heterogeneity'.[75]

However, Connolly's view exemplifies best the ethos of transnational *demos*-formation: 'to cultivate respect for a politics of democratic governance,' by pluralising 'democratic energies, alliances and spaces of action that exceed the closures of territorial democracy'.[76] Thus it reflects both upon a process of self-transformation, insofar as the pursuit of transnational democracy entails adherence to novel democratic engagements, and upon one of self-transcendence, insofar as national traditions get in the way of achieving better conditions of democratic shared rule.

Institutionally, these processes can be complemented with the following: by granting to the European Parliament full co-decisional powers with the Council and transforming the latter into a Second Chamber – a European Senate – along the lines of the German *Bundesrat* (see chapter 7); by reinforcing the democratic legitimacy of the Commission either directly through the popular mandate or indirectly through the selection (and not only approval) of its members by the European Parliament; by requesting stronger links between the European Parliament and the member state legislatures; by establishing genuine European political parties which are politically, administratively and financially unrestrained and independent from their national counterparts; by altering the current political status of the Committee of the Regions into a democratically elected body possessing more than consultative powers; by introducing pan-European referenda in case of regime creation or regime transition, these being the introduction of new formal Union competences or extension of the scope of pre-existing ones respectively; or even by adopting a comprehensive European constitution based on a double democratic legitimacy. In fact, the possibilities towards a more democratic and tightly-integrated Union seem limitless.

Interestingly, though, the current antipathy between intergovernmentalists and federalists generates two competing views on the sources of EU legitimacy: national governments (indirect legitimation) and the European public (direct legitimation). In Wallace's terms, their inability to reach a substantive consensus has left the Union 'uncertain about the application of liberal democracy within its *own* processes,' thus delaying 'the shift from policy to polity'; namely, from a 'policy-generating process' based on the practices of 'conference diplomacy' to 'an entity that might develop into a form of direct governance in its own right' founded on 'some shared values and... some form of collective identity'.[77] This is imperative not only for the process of citizen identification with the transnational polity as 'a deep sense of belonging to a significant, meaningful group,'[78] but also for the member publics to share in a commitment to render accountable those relations that contribute to their daily lives.

The central point stemming from the preceding analysis is that the concept of transnational *demos* is based upon certain democratic criteria, the quality of citizen involvement in political decision-making being the most prominent. This, in turn, depends on the existence, or not, of institutional avenues available to the *demos* to direct its claims to those who actually govern. But who is to determine, and how, what channels of communication are best suited for articulating public needs and demands? That no single democratic answer exists 'as such' to this question is obvious. A look at the different democratic experiences of the member states suffices to make this point. Yet this question raises a more fundamental one: can there be any sort of democratic polity without first there being a consolidated popular base on which its decisions are to apply? Whatever the answer to the first question may be, that to the second question should categorically be that it cannot. For no democracy, however approached, defined and analysed, has ever existed, exists or ever can exist without a *demos*, whether unitary or composite in kind. To borrow from Sartori, as '*demos* precedes *cracy*',[79] so democracy implies by definition the existence of a *demos*. Tautological as it may initially sound, we find this argument to be sufficient enough to support the case for a transnational *demos* as a *praesumptio juris et de jure*.

In summary, whereas nation-building suggests an 'architectural or mechanical model' which can take the form of a process of inventing or even imagining a nation where one does not exist,[80] *demos*-formation is motivated by a commonly shared public desire to replace an improper or unsatisfactory form of governance with one which meets the requirements of what Dahl calls '*a fully democratic process in relation to a demos*'.[81] In practice, however, its very success in the context of the Union seems to depend in considerable part upon the following two variables: the level of community feeling, concerning itself with the internal cohesiveness of the composite *demos*; and the level of capacity exhibited by the central institutions in responding to the demands made upon them by its members.[82]

This partly explains why one might consider the exploration of the relationship between *Gemeinschaft* and European integration as a means of gaining experience about the possibilities of transnational democracy. In brief, it raises a number of questions on whether this dynamic process of democratic self-transformation and self-transcendence will be driven by the aspirations of the member publics or, conversely, whether the demo-cratisation of the Union will be conditioned 'from above' guided by the short term self-interestedness of national governing elites. As García put it: 'Europe will exist as an unquestionable political community only when European identity permeates people's lives and daily exercise'.[83]

SOME FINAL RECOMMENDATIONS

Among the findings of this chapter, the most significant is that any diag-nosis or prescription which falls short of recognising the relevance of the '*Gemeinschaft* factor' to the process of democratising the Union, however illuminating, is bound to remain partial, omitting the socio-psychological dimension of the democratic deficit. And if one considers the recent democratic developments in the Treaty on European Union, such as the common citizenship provisions, as a practical means upon which new collective identities may arise, there is good ground for positive thinking; namely, that the Union is a strongly enough established collective entity to permit its citizens to determine questions of a democratic nature and, in time, allow for a transnational *demos* to be built *ab intra*.

However, to nominally hold citizen status does not automatically make a community of people(s) a fully-fledged *demos*. In other words, being a citizen, that is merely possessing legal and political rights, is one thing; acting as a citizen, in terms of belonging to a collectivity, developing an active concern about its future, and claiming active involvement in its political processes, is clearly another. Yet without citizenship, the latter requirements cannot fulfil their practical aims, not to mention being largely inconceivable. Moreover, the passing from one stage to the other will not be, to borrow an expression, an 'all-or-nothing' process analogous to the crossing of a narrow threshold, but rather a gradual exercise in collective civic identity-building. In Schlesinger's words: 'The production of an overarching collective identity [or of a "collective belief in the virtue of a civic order"] can only seriously be conceived as the outcome of long-standing social and political practice'.[84] In this sense, Union citizenship can be the practical pathway towards a transnational *demos*.

The rationale underlying this argument is that as there cannot be *demokratia* without the existence of a *demos*, the latter cannot exist without its members having a public role in determining their own destinies, as well as viewing their common citizenship status as important in its own right. That is, as a potential civic weapon for creating new and better politics in the best sense of the term: 'an activity consisting not merely in the use of power, but in open and rational inquiry into the common good'.[85] Arguably, in a Union of collateral nationalities and multiple co-existing loyalties and identities, common citizenship emanates as one of the most powerful instruments of transnational democracy, providing a means by which European citizens can take a direct and active part in integration processes.

As in any other polity which aspires to democratic governance, so in the Union, the quality of citizenship is an indispensable machinery available to the *demos* for measuring its future not only in terms of present-day realities, but also in terms of the democratic potential it entails by creating the opportunity for grass-roots civic activities. At the same time, it keeps alive the foundation upon which all forms of democracy, irrespective of their actual range, depth, intensity and extensiveness, heavily draw: the advancement of 'civic competence' through which ordinary people can mark their impact on the actual process of government. In brief, it fuels and links a sense of public participation, or what Dietz calls 'other types of citizen behaviour',[86] with the institutional reality of a transnational polity seeking to bridge the long-standing gap between the worlds of interstate and intrastate democracy. As Tinder remarks: 'Democracy has less justification as a system of rule than as a system of communication... [which] has a unique claim to respect: it is universal'.[87]

Overall, this chapter has tried to offer an answer to the intricate question of how the conception of a European *demos*, combining a plurality of national feelings and forms of intrastate fellowship, can maximise its democratic potential? The gist of the thesis is that this civic body is the *ultima ratio* of European political integration. This is not to underestimate the difficulty of the task, as summarised by Hedetoft: 'Solving the "democratic deficit" in Europe requires the squaring of a circle with politics, culture and identities'.[88] Rather, it implies that were the idea '*demos* before *ethnos*' to be crowned with success in the Union's multi-cultural context, there is an enormous field of history, theory and politics to be explored which effectively escapes the categories of conventional disciplines in the study of European integration. This is a reality too obvious to comment on, had it not been consistently ignored so far.

On the other hand, it suggests that the inchoateness of the current process of transnational *demos*-formation is but a transient stage, that is part of a historically-rooted, but by no means insurmountable, popular tendency for groups to stand by their own self-conceptualisations of national 'we-groups' *vis-à-vis* other national 'they-groups'. Also, it is an effort to prescribe a political *telos* for an integration process which passes through nation-state political structures without either totally enhancing or totally transcending them. Indeed, as democracy and integration themselves, the nation-state simultaneously undergoes a process of decline and renewal, decomposition and recomposition, degeneration and regeneration, whereby terms like 'crisis' and 'revival' are but two alternative ways of interpreting the same phenomenon: the interaction, on the one hand, between historical instance and political circumstance depending on the 'logic of the situation' and, on the other, between concerted institutional-engineering and emerging civic sensitivities over the exercise of public authority. In the final analysis, the belief in the forging of a transnational civic identity – common and yet differentiating in its respect for the constituents' actual diversities – out of the segments' traditions and cultures, to support a more *demos*-oriented process of union, is our testimony on the presuppositions of democracy in the larger political unit.

With these final recommendations on the concepts, politics and processes of democracy, community, identity, and integration, we can now concentrate on the structural factors which have also played a part in determining the origins and nature of the Union's democratic deficit. A Union, which neither basks in the sunlight of a complete *Gemeinschaft* – its citizens being 'members of the unit directly and not through membership of another political unit'[89] – nor shivers in the shadowland of an 'unmanaged' *Gesellschaft* on the road to disintegration. But neither does it wander somewhere in the dusk of an unspecified 'half-way-house' between the two. Rather, the Union approximates most closely to a new type of collective entity – itself a complicated mixture of familiar models of governance – summed up in the concept of 'Confederal Consociation': an ensemble of *Gesellschaft* and *Gemeinschaft* elements that results in a fairly co-ordinated system of democracies (see chapter 7).

Before moving on to Part III, a final remark is in order, reflecting the central thesis of this study: the democratic pathology of the Union can only be remedied through the combined impact of the processes of transnational *demos*-formation and further constitutional reform concerned, respectively, with the socio-psychological and the structural components of the democratic deficit.

Notes on Chapter 4

1   Cohen, Carl, *Democracy* (Athens, 1971, University of Georgia Press), p 41.
2   *Ibid.*
3   *Ibid.*
4   de Grazia, Sebastian, *The Political Community: a Study of Anomie* (Chicago and London, 1969, The University of Chicago Press), p ix.

5   As Barry suggests: 'Having a value is not just a *tendency* to do things of a certain kind. It means also believing that it is *right* to do these things'. See Barry, Brian, *Sociologists, Economists and Democracy* (Chicago, 1970, The University of Chicago Press), p 90.

6   See Tönnies, Ferdinand, *Community and Association*, translated and supplemented by Loomis, Charles P. (London, 1974, Routledge and Kegan Paul).

7   Mouffe, Chantal, *The Return of the Political* (London and New York, 1993, Verso), p 61.

8   Cohen, Carl, *Democracy*, p 46.

9   *Ibid.*, p 47.

10 Weiler, Joseph H.H., 'After Maastricht: Community Legitimacy in Post-1992 Europe' in Adams, William J. (ed.), *Singular Europe: Economy and Polity of the European Community after 1992* (Ann Arbor MI, 1992, The University of Michigan Press), p 22. Cf Shackleton, Michael, 'The Internal Legitimacy Crisis of the European Union', Occasional Paper 1, Europa Institute, The University of Edinburgh, 1994, p 13.

11 In light of the present discussion, it is worth recalling Raphael's point that 'democratic ideals' in the relations between states owe something to the analogy of democracy within the state itself. This explains why the international society of states includes certain democratic procedures, and why these procedures are accepted even by non-democratic countries. He concludes: 'Democracy is a matter of liberty as well as equality, and liberty includes the freedom to express one's opinions and one's criticisms of those who have the whip-hand'. See Raphael, D.D., *Problems of Political Philosophy*, revised edn (London, 1976, Macmillan), pp 156-7 and p 164.

12 Cohen, Carl, *Democracy*, p xiv.

13 *Ibid.*, p xv.

14 Kamenka, Eugene, *Bureaucracy* (Oxford, 1989, Basil Blackwell), p 81.

15 *Ibid.*

16 Tönnies, Ferdinand, *Community and Association*, Forward by Pitirim A. Sorokin, pp v-vii.

17 On this issue see Lehman, Edward W., *The Viable Polity* (Philadelphia, 1992, Temple University Press). Lehman makes the point that political viability must be seen along three interrelated dimensions: the capacity of a political system to pursue its goals effectively, its ability to elicit citizen participation efficiently, and the legitimacy of the prevailing (political) rules of the game.

18 Taylor, Paul, *The Limits of European Integration* (New York, 1983, Columbia University Press), p 3.

19 Tönnies, Ferdinand, *Community and Association*, p 160. Cf. MacIver, R.M., *Community: A Sociological Study* (London, 1936, Macmillan), pp 22-8. MacIver states: 'A community is a focus of social life; an association is an organisation of social life... but communiuty is something wider and freer than even the greatest associations'. See p 24.

20 Kamenka, Eugene, *Bureaucracy*, p 80.

21 On these concepts see Tönnies, Ferdinand, *Community and Association*, p 15 and p 119.

22 *Ibid.*, pp 38-9.

23 Kamenka, Eugene, *Bureaucracy*, p 79.

24 de Grazia, Sebastian, *The Political Community*, p ix. Plamenatz, in his attack on the utilitarian approach, writes that '[people] are not mere competitors, however benevolent, in a market for the supply of personal wants; they are members of a society, and their hopes and feelings, both for themselves and for others, would not be what they are apart from their group loyalties'. He concludes: 'They see themselves as having rights and duties, as moral beings, because they have some conception of social world with parts for themselves and others to play in it'. See Plamenatz, John, *The English Utilitarians*, Second edn (Oxford, 1958, Basil Blackwell), pp 173-5. Quoted in Barry, Brian, *Sociologists, Economists and Democracy*, p 176. Accordingly, a political community is not utilitarian insofar as it endows relations with a civic value of their own.

25 Tönnies, Ferdinand, *Community and Association*, p 87.

26 *Ibid.*, p 89.

27 *Ibid.*, pp 74-5 and p 78.

28 *Ibid.*, p 42.

29 On the distinction between these concepts see Kuper, Leo, 'Plural Societies: Perspectives and Problems', in Kuper, Leo and Smith, M.G. (eds), *Pluralism in Africa* (Berkeley, 1971, University California Press), pp 7-26. It is noteworthy that this work has been described as the most authoritative statement on the theory of the plural society.

30 On the relationship between *Gemeinschaft* and authority see Plant, Raymond, *Community and Ideology: An Essay in Applied Social Philosophy* (London and Boston, 1974, Routledge and Kegan Paul), pp 51-8.

31 Tönnies, Ferdinand, *Community and Association*, pp 69 and 74.

32 On this argument see Cohen, Carl, *Democracy*, pp 47 and 54.

33 *Ibid.*, p 49.

34 The phrase in quotation belongs to Sartori, Giovanni, *The Theory of Democracy Revisited* (Chatham N.J, 1987, Chatham House), p 36.

35 Weiler, Joseph H.H., 'After Maastricht', p 20.

36 Mouffe, Chantal, p 69.

37 Etzioni, Amitai, *The Spirit of Community: The Reinvention of American Society* (New York, 1993, Simon and Shuster) p 14. Etzioni argues that 'an important way to build community is to ensure that there are numerous occasions for active participation of the members in its governance'. See p 141.

38 Garner, John W., *Building Community* (Washington DC, 1991, Independent Sector), p 11.

39 On the distinction between these two types of consensus see Taylor, Paul, *The Limits of European Integration*, pp 6-7.

40 For details see Etzioni, Amitai, *The Spirit of Community*, pp 147-51.

41 For these quotations see *ibid.*, pp 155-7.

42 *Ibid.* Etzioni, Amitai, *The Spirit of Community*. He states: 'As I see it, there are two kinds of pluralism: the kind that is unbounded and unwholesome, and pluralism-within-unity. In the former, each group is out to gain all it can, with little concern of the shared needs of the community. In the latter,

groups vie with one another, yet voluntarily limit themselves when they impinge on common interests'. See p 217.

43 Beer, Samuel H., 'What is Wrong with European Federalism?', in Hill, Spephen (ed.), *Visions of Europe: Summing up the political choices* (London, 1993, Duckworth), pp 119-20.

44 Cohen, Carl, *Democracy*, p 6.

45 As Etzioni argues: 'A responsive society is one whose moral standards reflect the basic human needs of all its members'. He concludes: 'political institutions [cannot] effectively embody moral voices unless they are sustained and criticized by an active citizenry concerned about the moral direction of the community'. See Etzioni, Amitai, *The Spirit of Community*, pp 255-6.

46 Cohen, Carl, *Democracy*, pp 22-3. He goes on arguing that a representative system does not restrict the sovereign range of democracy when participation in the selection of the representatives is broad and deep, and if the representatives remain responsive to the needs of their constituents.

47 *Ibid.*, p 7.

48 Dewey, John, *The Public and its Problems* (New York, 1927, Holt), p 148. Quoted in Barber, Benjamin, *Strong Democracy: Participatory Politics for a New Age* (Berkeley 1984, University of California Press), p 119.

49 Deutsch, Karl W., 'Nation-Building and National Development: Some Issues for Political Research', in Deutsch, Karl W. and Foltz, William J. (eds), *Nation-Building* (New York, 1966, Atherton Press), p 3.

50 On the rejection of that possibility see Smith, Anthony D., *National Identity* (Harmondsworth, 1991, Penguin), p 152.

51 According to Bloom, 'national identity describes that condition in which a mass of people have made the same identification with national symbols... so that they may act as one psychological group when there is a threat, or a possibility of enhancement of, these symbols of national identity'. See Bloom, William, *Personal Identity, National Identity and International Relations*, Cambridge Studies in International Relations, no 9 (Cambridge, 1993, Cambridge University Press), p 52.

52 Smith, Anthony D., *National Identity*, p 197.

53 This distinction also appears in Chryssochoou, Dimitris N., 'Europe's Could-Be Demos: Recasting the Debate', *West European Politics*, October 1996, pp 787-801.

54 This approach to the process of amalgamation draws heavily upon Deutsch's point of view as presented in Deutsch, Karl W. *et al.*, *Political Community and the North Atlantic Area*, (Princeton, 1957, Princeton University Press), p 6.

55 Smith, Anthony D., *National Identity*, p 153.

56 For an excellent analysis of the term 'nation' see Connor, Walker, 'A Nation is a Nation, is a State, is an Ethnic Group, is a...', *Ethnic and Racial Studies*, October 1978, pp 379-88. For an interesting interdisciplinary collection of definitions see Snyder, Louis L., *The Meaning of Nationalism* (New Brunswick, 1954, Rudgers Univerity Press), pp 14-55. Cf Snyder, Louis L., *Encyclopedia of Nationalism* (New York, 1990, Paragon House), pp 230-4.

57 Bloom, William, *Personal Identity, National Identity and International Relations*, p 56. Bell and Freeman note: 'By "nation-building" we mean the formation and establishment of a new state itself as a political entity, and the process of creating viable degrees of unity, adaptation, achievement, and a sense of national identity among the people'. See Bell, Wendel and Freeman, Walter E., 'Introduction' in Bell, Wendel and Freeman, Walter E. (eds), *Ethnicity and Nation-Building: Comparative, International and Historical Perspectives* (London, 1974 Sage), p 11. Quoted in *ibid.*

58 'A "nation",' writes Giddens, 'can only exist when a state has a unified administrative reach over the territory over which its sovereignty is claimed'. See Giddens, Anthony, 'The Nation as Power-Container', in Hutchinson, John and Smith, Antony D. (eds), *Nationalism*, p 34.

59 Weiler, Joseph H.H., 'After Maastricht, p 39. He explains: 'Note, too, that the Preamble [of the Rome Treaty] speaks about the peoples of Europe, rejecting any notion of melting pot and nation building'. See note 54, p 38.

60 *Ibid.*, p 38.

61 *Ibid.* According to Weiler, in a transnational context, 'the idea of community seeks to dictate a different type of intercourse among the actors belonging to it, of self-limitation in their self-perception, of a redefined self-interest and, hence, redefined policy goals'.

62 The term 'strong democracy' has been used by Etzioni as the antithesis of 'faulty democracy' and, in particular, as a means for making government 'more representative, more participatory, and more responsive to all members of the community'. See Etzioni, Amitai, *The Spirit of Community*, p 155. Barber, on the other hand, by distinquishing it from 'thin democracy', defines 'strong democracy' as 'politics in the participatory mode where conflict is resolved in the absence of an independent ground through a participatory process of ongoing, proximate self-legislation and the creation of a political community capable of transforming dependent, private individuals into free citizens and partial and private interests into public goods'. See Barber, Benjamin, *Strong Democracy: Participatory Politics for a New Age* (Berkeley 1984, University of California Press), p 132.

63 Bloom, William, *Personal Identity, National Identity and International Relations*, p 58.

64 Etzioni, Amitai, *The Spirit of Community*, p 32.

65 Reif, Karlheinz, 'Cultural Convergence and Cultural Diversity as Factors in European Identity', in García, Soledad (ed.), *European Identity and the Search for Legitimacy* (London, 1993, Pinter), p 138. In fact, a survey conducted by the Eurobarometer in autumn 1992 has revealed that 62% of the respondents saw 'a sense of European identity as being compatible with a sense of national identity'. See Figure 8.2, p 141.

66 Bloom, William, *Personal Identity, National Identity and International Relations*, p 75.

67 García, Soledad, 'Europe's Fragmented Identities and the Frontier of European Citizenship', in García, Soledad (ed.), *European Identity and the Search for Legitimacy*, p 18 (emphasis added). According to Tassin, however, only 'the idea of a public space of fellow-citizenship' is capable of giving birth to such a community. See Tassin, Etienne, 'Europe: A Political Community?', in

Mouffe, Chantal (ed.), *Dimensions of Radical Democracy* (London and New York, 1992, Verso) p 189.

68 Birch, Antony H., *Nationalism and National Integration* (London, 1989, Unwin Hyman), p 37. He states: 'By developing national institutions and exploiting tactics of political socialisation, the attempt is made to replace local and sectional loyalties by an overriding sense of national loyalty. This process is known as nation-building'.

69 *Ibid.*, p 40.

70 Connor, Walker, 'Nation-Building or Nation-Destroying?', *World Politics*, April 1971, p 350. In this article, Connor tests the theory of 'nation-building' against the forces of ethnic diversity. Cf García, Soledad, 'Europe's Fragmented Identities and the Frontier of European Citzenship', p 10. García argues that national integration 'remains less difficult in those societies in which formal national institutions have acquired legitimacy and where the identity of the citizen, as a member of the political community, could develop within a democratic political culture'.

71 Lenin, Nikolai (Vladimir Ilich Ulyanov), 'Critical Remarks on the National Question' in Snyder, Louis L. (ed.), *The Dynamics of Nationalism: Readings in its Meaning and Development* (Princeton NJ, 1964, Van Nostrand Company), pp 11-12.

72 This phrase epitomises the pluralistic conception of the *demos*. On the organic conception of the *demos* see Sartori, Giovanni, *The Theory of Democracy Revisited*, pp 23-4.

73 Connolly, William E., 'Democracy and Territoriality' in Ringrose, Marjorie and Lehrner, Adams J. (eds), *Reimagining the Nation* (Buckingham, 1993, Open University Press), p 51.

74 *Ibid.*, p 65.

75 Schmitt, Carl, *The Crisis of Parliamentary Democracy* (Cambridge MA, 1998, MIT Press), p 9. Quoted in *ibid.*, note 31, pp 74-5.

76 For these quotations see Connolly, William E., 'Democracy and Territoriality' in Ringrose, Marjorie and Lehrner, Adams J. (eds), *Reimagining the Nation*, p 70, respectively. He states: 'Territorial democracy threatens to become a late-modern anachronism unless it is challenged and exceeded by a new pluralisation of democratic allegiances and spaces – and even that may not be enough'.

77 Wallace, Helen, 'Deepening and Widening: Problems of Legitimacy for the EC', in García, Soledad (ed.), *European Identity and the Search for Legitimacy*, pp 100-1. Likewise, Shackleton argues: 'From my perspective the [legitimacy] crisis is a product of the realisation that we do not yet have the means to move from a system essentially concerned with the *administration of things* to one concerned with the *governance of people*'. See Shackleton, Michael, 'The Internal Legitimacy Crisis of the European Union', p 5.

78 Poplin, Dennis E., *Communities: A Survey of Theories and Methods of Research* (London, 1979, Macmillan), Table 1-1, p 6.

79 Sartori, Giovanni, *The Theory of Democracy Revisited*, p 34.

80 Deutsch, Karl W., 'Nation-Building and National Development', p 3. He explains: 'As a house can be built from timber, bricks, and mortar, in different patterns, quicker or slowly, through different sequences of assembly, in partial independence from its setting, and according to the choice, will, and power of its builders, so a nation can be built according to different plans, from various materials rapidly or gradually, by different sequences of steps, and in partial independence from its environment'.

81 Dahl, Robert A., *Democracy and its Critics* (New Haven and London, 1989, Yale University Press), p 114.

82 For a similar discussion see Taylor, Paul, *The Limits of European Integration*, pp 12-13.

83 García, Soledad, 'Europe's Fragmented Identities and the Frontier of European Citizenship', p 15.

84 Schlesinger, Philip, 'Europeaness: A New Cultural Battlefield?', in Hutchinson and Smith (eds), *Nationalism*, p 321. He concludes, however, that this does not seem to be 'the most compelling mobilising cry for Europe in the 1990s'. Cf Smith, Anthony D., 'National Identity and the Idea of European Unity', *International Affairs*, January 1992, pp 55-76. Smith writes: 'A common European cultural identity, if such there be, does not yet have its counterpart on the political level; to date, each state of the European Community has placed its perceived national interests and self-images above a concerted European policy based on a single presumed European interest and self-image'. See p 56.

85 Tinder, Glenn, *Community: Reflections on a Tragic Ideal* (Baton Rouge and London, 1980, Louisiana State University Press), p 38.

86 Dietz, Mary G., 'In search of a Citizen Ethic', in Marcus, George E. and Hanson, Russell L. (eds), *Reconsidering the Democratic Public* (Pennsylvania, 1993 The Pennsylvania State University Press) p 177. Adopting a communitarian approach, Dietz focuses on which 'core' rights and duties an individual takes as appropriate to citizenship rather than whether these should be the central focus of citizenship.

87 Tinder, Glenn, *Community*, p 43. He states: 'Political community exists where power is reliably subordinate to common inquiry... where laws are passed only after parliamentary debate and where governmental acts are regularly subject to retrospective examination and criticism'. See p 38. This comment resembles Ross's description of the ideal type of (political) democracy as a 'form of government in which the political functions are exercised by the people with maximum intensity, effectiveness, and extensiveness in the parliamentary manner'. See Ross, Alf, *Why Democracy?* (Cambridge MA, 1952, Harvard University Press), p 90.

88 Hedetoft, Ulf, 'The State of Sovereignty in Europe: Political Concept or Cultural Self-Image', in Zetterholm, Staffan (ed.), *National Cultures and European Integration* (Oxford and Providence, 1994, BERG), p 35.

89 Zetterholm, Staffan, 'Why is Cultural Diversity a Political Problem? A Discussion of Cultural Barriers to Political Integration', in Zetterholm, Staffan (ed.), *National Cultures and European Integration*, p 73.

Interpretative Explorations

CHAPTER 5

Parliamentary Decline and National Democratic Autonomy

INTRODUCING THE PATTERNS OF INTERPRETATION

Part III of this study explores the origins and nature of the democratic deficit from the perspective of two different explanatory theses: the parliamentary decline thesis and the federal thesis. The first reflects upon the asymmetrical evolution of the powers of Western European executive and legislative institutions since the early days of the century. To properly assess, however, the questions that EU membership generates for a perceived loss of national democratic autonomy on the part of member state legislatures, this thesis will have to be complemented by a discussion on the transfer of responsibilities from national to transnational authorities. The second thesis (see chapter 6) represents one of the two competing visions of European unity: the federal vision for a democratic 'union of peoples', as opposed to a 'union of states' designed to tackle functionally-specific tasks. In particular, it links the origins of the Union's democratic deficit with the failure to reach a formal constitutional settlement at the larger level during the formative years of integration. Here, the crucial link is between federalism and democracy in that, although a democratic system need not necessarily be of a federal kind, federalism has come to symbolise an inherently democratic method of organising political life in the large-scale, pluralist societies of our time.

THE PARLIAMENTARY DECLINE THESIS

Students of politics have widely recognised that a feature common to the evolution of contemporary democracies is the (continuing) decline of parliaments, once regarded as the centre of enlightened public debate. Attributes like 'the crisis of parliamentary democracy', 'parliamentary decline', 'the pathology of legislatures' or 'the passing of parliament' have appeared with noticeable regularity in the relevant literature, revealing the main factors that contributed to the 'de-parliamentarisation' of twentieth-century democracy. Our analysis will try to take this discussion further by linking the implications of post-1945 parliamentary decline to the building of EU institutions. It will also test the strength of a common-place criticism that what actually exists at the Union level is to a large extent a mirror-image of national parliamentary deficiencies.

The question here is whether the democratic shortfalls of the Union can be seen mainly as a historical continuation of the wider phenomenon concerning the declining influence of the member state legislatures in the national governing process. The conclusion to be drawn on the validity of this thesis is that, although it does not provide a complete framework for interpretation of the genesis of the democratic deficit, it serves as a useful reminder of the structural factors leading to a distinctive pattern of Union governance which, when measured by liberal-democratic standards, can be classified as more or less undemocratic. Thus, the democratic deficit of the Union can be seen partly as an extension of national parliamentary deficiencies and partly as an institutional problem transferred from national to European structures of government.

Although the origins of modern parliamentary decline can be traced to the years following the end of the First World War, emphasis will be placed on the period following the collapse of totalitarian ideologies and regimes in Europe and the restoration of democratic rule in 1945. The special constitutional arrangements of each country aside, we will explore the principal reasons that made for the declining status of Western European representative assemblies, in terms of their legislative functions, policy-making responsibilities and, eventually, political prestige.

The analytical justification for this line of enquiry is that unless we outline their common weaknesses in the political process it will not be possible to determine whether a structural transformation of twentieth-century democracy or merely an ephemeral crisis of one of its traditional institutions has actually taken place. As Norton has observed, the study of legislatures has taken place within the inheritance of three interrelated axioms: first, that the fundamental tasks of legislatures is the making of laws; second, that legislatures since the nineteenth century have 'declined';

and third, that the explanation of such a decline lies in the growth of party politics.[1]

THE DECLINE OF LEGISLATURES AND ITS CRITICS

One of the most influential studies on parliamentary decline is Bryce's *Modern Democracies*, first published in 1921.[2] Considering the impact Bryce's normative and empirical findings had on the academic community, this study becomes an appropriate starting point. According to one of his oft-quoted criticisms on the British political system, the disappearance of a sense of 'social responsibility' among members of Parliament 'has made parliamentary deliberations seem more and more of a game, and less and less a consultation by the leaders of the nation on matters of public welfare'.[3] This remark has a wider political significance for the evolution of other Western democracies too. Convinced that something has been lost from the 'Olympian dignity' in the conduct of parliamentary politics, as compared to the standards of decorum that prevailed during the alleged 'golden age' of legislatures, Bryce asserted that 'the average standard of talent and character in their manners did not rise'.[4]

Much of his blame for the changing nature of parliamentarism was apportioned to the increasing importance of 'party machines' which made many parliamentarians feel themselves responsible to political parties, rather than to their constituencies. He perceived the effects of party discipline as detrimental to Burke's idea of the representatives' independence of mind. In addition to these problems came the complexity of modern public issues themselves, leading to a considerable extension of governmental responsibilities in almost all fields of national public life.

These developments accounted 'for the disappointment felt by whoever compares the position held by legislatures now, with the hopes once entertained of the services they were to render'.[5] With regard to Western Europe, although Bryce explicitly stated that 'it is rather the moral ascendancy than the legal power that has been affected', he also pointed out that it was due to the fact that 'when moral power drops legal power inevitably ceases to inspire affection and respect,'[6] that legislatures experienced a reduction in their once unchallenged authority in the realm of national politics. The gist of his thesis is two-fold: that the conception of legislatures as 'the driving-wheel of government' belongs to the past; and that whatever decline is visible in their influence, any country that wants to be called a 'representative democracy' must restore the institution of parliament as the vital centre of the governing function. But he did not specifically define how such a demanding task should be achieved.

Soon after their publication, Bryce's views were widely accepted by students of legislative behaviour, keeping their appeal even to this very day by symbolising the importance of parliamentarism for the attainment of responsible government. Indeed, although subsequent studies have gradually shifted their attention from moral issues to more practical questions such as executive-legislature relations, they have found it difficult to escape Bryce's dictum of parliamentary decline. Yet, however influential his study may have been, it was not without its critics. Notwithstanding Norton's view that Bryce's 'magisterial survey' produced a qualified perception of parliamentary 'decline',[7] '*Modern Democracies* provided a dogma for a new generation of old democrats who regard the influence of parties as precarious'.[8] Impressed by the educational level of parliamentarians in the nineteenth century, as well as by the eloquence of their debates, authors like Bryce established the myth of the 'golden age' of legislatures which was to become the rule for measuring their subsequent decline.[9]

Justifiably enough, Loewenberg embarked on a more cautious analysis of the changing circumstances that challenged the position of Western European legislatures. He sought to explain the shift in power from representative assemblies to executive organs by what he called 'the process of political modernisation' which 'brought about a multiplication of political structures, each more specialised than the multifunctional institutions of the old regime.'[10] In his view, political modernisation was a by-product of three successive developments: the democratisation of the franchise; the surge of political demands; and the emergence of new concepts of political legitimacy. The first resulted in the transformation of the composition of legislatures, creating the first modern crisis for political parties.[11] The second, product of the newly-industrialised societies, transformed the pattern of parliamentary activity in that, given the complexities of public policy-making, new measures should be taken to match the expertise available to ministers, the setting up of specialised committees being the most crucial.[12] As for the third, he asserted that the appearance of 'plebiscitary leadership' offered to executives a means of justifying their political authority by new concepts of representation and legitimacy, without the intermediary activity of parliamentarians.[13]

Loewenberg's final assessment, however, revealed that, despite the evident strains that political modernisation has placed upon legislatures, they have not ceased to perform important policy-making and communication functions. Indeed, the ability of parliaments to devise new procedural mechanisms and revise older ones has often in the past acted as an effective 'internal weapon', employed to defend their existing powers or extend their practical influence into new fields of political activity. What Loewenberg implies is that parliaments have only lost their monopoly in the performance of major political functions, which they now share with other, more specialised agencies. Hence he concludes not only that none of the Western European political systems have found the institution of parliament expendable, but also, by virtue of its multifunctional character, parliament has exhibited a remarkable flexibility in adapting to the changes imposed by the realities of political modernisation.[14]

Bracher, on the other hand, has argued that 'the transition from the old liberal parliamentarism... to egalitarian party-state parliamentarism led to a series of functional disturbances even in the tradition-bound older democracies of Europe'.[15] The assumption that 'rule by parliament' seemed to have reached its limits acquires further support when considering its inherent inefficiency to absorb the socio-political tensions of the 'age of the masses'.[16] In brief, basic problems of structural democratic change have been widely contrasted with the unprecedented prominence of European assemblies in the mid-nineteenth century. Smith writes: 'The absence of mass parties, party discipline, and even of meaningful party labels, gave the members of the assembly a unique freedom to control government... but the particular circumstances were not to last'.[17] With the dictates of 'party democracy' pressing towards the reorganisation of the popular vote in Europe, and the subsequent rise of national mass parties, a loss of power on the part of legislatures seemed inevitable.

But parliaments have not experienced a loss of their legitimising function, for they remain synonymous with popular sovereignty. Far from being equated with 'law-making factories',[18] parliaments have consolidated their image as strong symbols of representative and responsible government, providing 'a base from which a governing hierarchy emerges'.[19] Nevertheless, the dictates of a highly technocratic era after a period of 'legislative collectivism' increased the scale of governmental activities on matters which legislatures had previously shown little, if any, concern.[20] In brief, modern government suggests that the administrative agencies have become major policy-makers with an influential role in the legislative process.[21]

The new conditions of post-1945 Western Europe generated new pressures for democratic adjustment. The question widely posed was not only whether but also how could representative assemblies carry out what Bracher called 'the actual practise of national politics'? This role is still largely conceived in terms of control and decision-making.[22] The prevailing view was that parliaments could no longer be regarded as being of primary importance for the management of public affairs. Instead, they were often seen as a 'theatre of illusions' incapable of having the direct impact they once had on the legislative process. This accords with Smith's view that although traditional parliamentary functions continued unaltered in their form, the actual powers through which these functions could be achieved had to be seen in a different context to that hitherto.[23] The question was not about parliamentary performance *per se*, but rather about its very limitations in relation to government and bureaucratic administrations.

To appreciate this statement fully, it is essential to distinguish between the 'powers' and the 'functions' of a legislature. Whereas its powers can be better viewed as components of its functions, the opposite does not seem to apply.[24] And since parliaments are not functionally-specific bodies, although some of their functions can be commonly traced to different parliamentary settings, it is much more difficult to determine their functions than their powers. For, the former are wider in scope and more likely to vary from one constitutional system to another than are the latter, which almost universally can be found 'in the neatly numbered articles and clauses of a constitution, basic law, or similar documents'.[25] This also explains Smith's concern with those parliamentary powers that have been totally lost, altered in context, or gradually enfeebled, rather than with their respective functions as a measure for assessing their alleged 'decline'. Yet, wrong as it may be to equate the present role of legislatures with a nostalgic romanticism for a much-celebrated or even overvalued past, one should not ignore that the final product of national rule-making rarely looks very different from what the government had originally intended. In summary, the changing relationship between parliament and administration, combined with the need for 'expertocracy' in managing complex public affairs, the expanding role of central government, and the almost unhindered dominance of party politics, became the determining factors in challenging the viability of representative assemblies.

Any attempt to consider in greater detail the radical expansion of the role of the administration in national politics, and link it to the dynamics of parliamentary decline, should take into account the existence of three parallel developments: the changing nature of the law; the technical complexity of socio-economic legislation; and the emergence of organised parties in the European political scene.[26] Placing the emphasis on the first development, Grosser argued that while laws 'formerly served to make more explicit the rights and duties of citizens,' in the case of postwar Western Europe, it was the concerted action of administrative agencies that was destined to transform society, using the law as 'the privileged instrument for this transformation'.[27] He explains: 'It is not by chance that the constitutions framed since World War II no longer define the administration as an executive but as initiator of policy'.[28] In brief, Grosser reached the conclusion that, although parliamentarians 'continue, indeed, to call themselves collectively "the Legislative Power" in the law books... in most cases they merely participate in a procedure of registration'.[29]

On the other hand, modern bureaucracy was seen by many as 'part of a progress towards a more open society and even a step towards the democratisation of government'.[30] The justification here is two-fold: first, that bureaucracy offered 'a career open to the talents'; and second, that it 'appeared to provide constraints on the free use of governmental power' – the result being that 'governmental orders were issued in the form of general rules administered and applied in an impersonal and impartial manner'.[31] In Parry's words: 'Although government continued to be the possessor of absolute legislative authority, it committed itself to carrying out its laws according to known, formal procedures'.[32] He also points out that it 'enabled state power to be organised more efficiently than ever before,' allowing 'commands to flow smoothly from the top... to the bottom'.[33] But for all its organisational advantages, and irrespective of whether one views modern bureaucracy as a form of 'enlightened paternalism' or as the principle cause of 'red tape', it soon became 'the *de facto* policy-maker without being fully answerable to the public'.[34] For ultimately it is upon the *demos* itself that the impact of bureaucracy, positive or negative, assumes particular importance for the democratic functioning of any politically organised society.

EXECUTIVE-LEGISLATURE RELATIONS THEN AND NOW

This section addresses the following set of questions. Are we witnessing a dynamic, structural transformation of Western European democracy during the second half of the century? Or is it rather a transitory phase and, hence, a temporary or ephemeral 'crisis' flowing from the fact that assembly powers are measured in terms of an idealised past? And also, if we assume that parliamentary decline will continue into the future, what will its impact be in the governing process of democratic systems? To provide an answer, it is necessary to call attention to the way in which a gradual change in the perceptions of students of legislative behaviour has taken place on how legislatures perform their functions and exercise their powers in relation to executive agents.

From a classical democratic theory perspective, a legislature is taken to denote a rule-making body deriving its political legitimacy directly from the periodically expressed consent of the *demos*. As government by popular consent became the essence of modern democracy, it was believed that parliament should be concerned only with the most general rules. This idea, Blondel notes, 'appeared to be logical and tie liberal government... to the existence of healthy and lively legislatures'.[35] But the implementation of policies already adopted by parliament should be left in the hands of the administrators whose role was perceived as being largely apolitical at the time: they could neither propose legislation, nor alter its original context. In this sense also, they were considered neither as 'agents' of the *demos*, nor as an organic part of representative government. In retrospect, however, their role was never apolitical in absolute terms, not least because the so-called 'mere technicalities' involved in the implementation of public policies could variously alter the final product of policy-making. Further, how autonomous can policy implementation be when it depends on a wide range of institutions and public officials? To say, then, that public policy, even in nineteenth-century Europe, was entirely determined by assembly members would be too unrealistic an assertion, if not, in Hogan's words, 'a caricature of the facts'.[36]

On the other hand, there is no doubt that since the beginning of the second half of the century, the balance between legislatures and executives tilted in favour of the latter. The reasons for this change are as various as they are obvious, lying in the need for technical legislation and specialised agents, as well as for continually improved, rational organisation and planning in 'sensitive' societies which 'can no longer afford mere improvisation and dilettantism than can modern economies and industry'.[37]

Consequently, 'unpolitical' experts – ie, those who have 'the knowledge to make [effective] decisions' – along with the expansion of organised interest groups and 'superparty' planning, greatly disputed parliaments' claims to power of decision and control.[38] As Blondel has observed: 'in the postwar years, legislatures of Western European states often seemed to become increasingly streamlined and increasingly confined to obeying the fiats of strong executives backed by a disciplined party'.[39] He concluded: 'Whether or not legislatures had declined in quality in the nineteenth century, in the twentieth they were gradually reduced to minor or even negligible roles'.[40] All in all, although Western European polities remained both liberal and democratic, such was the influence of the executive that parliaments appeared on the verge of becoming mere decorative organs in the national governing process.[41]

A useful analysis on the conditions that strengthened the policy-making role of the Executive *vis-à-vis* the legislature was offered by Beer, who argued that the imperatives of modern policy – government intervention in the management of the economy and the development of the welfare state – made new calls upon executive action which resulted in the emergence of *ad hoc* 'managerial decisions'.[42] Moreover, he asserted that due to 'the increasing specificity of essential governmental decisions', government must rely less upon general laws and more upon this type of decision in its effort to manage and control the new socio-economic affairs.[43] Hence, the delegation of legislative power to the executive has grown immensely, with parliament contenting itself 'with a broad authorisation to the executive which then determines the more specific provisions'.[44] Although Beer focused his research on the British House of Commons, his normative assessments are equally valid when applied to other Western European legislatures. For their decline is also rooted in the same process of losing a substantial number of 'managerial' responsibilities over executive organs without gaining any corresponding powers to control their decisions.

This problem was compounded by the increasing influence of new organised groups in policy-making which, combined with the subsequent device of direct avenues of consultation between them and various governmental departments, gave rise to a system of 'functional representation', operating 'outside and alongside the established systems of parliamentary representation'.[45] In essence, the transformation of the consultation process into one of intensive bargaining and negotiation between interest groups and bureaucratic administration has further reduced the importance of legislatures as significant brokers for functional interests, a role widely recognised throughout the last century. In this context, Eulau's dictum 'If there is a crisis… it is a crisis in the theory of representation and not in the institution of representation,'[46] needs to be recognised as crucial in terms of shifting the emphasis from the practical considerations of parliamentary decline to the more theoretical debate concerning the meaning of representation itself. This step was taken by Hogan, who argued that in the modern process of government, executives can equally be considered agents of the people, 'with a positive function in the achievement of the common interest'.[47]

Defining representation as 'a specialisation of social function by which responsible agents are selected to perform political and governmental tasks,' Hogan pointed out that the ultimate task of a modern polity is to create a balanced network of representation with various devices as appropriate to different purposes.[48] He also suggested that the classic 'textbook model' of executive-legislature relations does not fit in contemporary societies since public policy is now largely determined by a complex web of administrative interactions and not by parliaments alone. Hogan reached the conclusion that in this new framework of policy-formation, representation becomes an essential device to make government operational and effective, the result being that parliament cannot be considered any more an autonomous controller of governmental activities.[49] But where do the preceding reflections leave us in terms of transnational political organisation? It is to this issue that we now turn.

PARLIAMENTS AND THE POST-1945 EUROPEAN ORDER

Soon after the end of World War II, it seemed as if the stability of Western European democracy was almost completely dependent upon the extent to which each nation's governmental apparatus was in a position to satisfy an ever expanding array of public demands. And although it can be argued that parliaments have lost nothing of their past legitimising primacy, they have entered into a new dynamic phase of political development, totally different from that which had previously elevated them as the focal point of political activity. More importantly, the once powerful weapons that enabled them in the past to hold the executive politically to account seemed under the new circumstances somewhat anachronistic. In essence, parliaments were faced with a complex and highly sophisticated network of party politics, domestic and external economic interdependencies, societal structural changes and technological advances that, along with the rise of new public demands, made the old parliamentary practice look both inflexible and unpromising in providing the new political direction.

As noted earlier in this study, at the *apogee* of this unfavourable situation for European parliamentarism, the states of Western Europe sought to strengthen their bonds and transform the traditional paths of diplomatic relations into novel patterns of interaction through the creation of common institutions. This phase reflected the search for new levels of decision-making amongst increasingly interdependent units. And yet, despite the negative developments which precipitated the decline of legislatures, new transnational parliamentary structures were set up, indicating that the institution of parliament was still attracting the hopes of the architects of 'New' Europe. Or, as Loewenberg put it, few polities, 'from neighbourhood associations to supranational organisations', could finally do without it.[50] Accordingly, what the parliamentary decline thesis leaves unsaid is that representative democracy has its own dynamics which make legislative institutions highly flexible and adaptable bodies, academic controversy over each stage of their adaptability notwithstanding.

But let us now attempt to capture the relationship between the thesis under scrutiny and the democratic deficit of the Union. At a general level, the emergence of structural democratic deficiencies in contemporary Western European polities can be seen as the result of a long, and not always easily traceable, series of socio-economic and political developments contributing to the changing relation between parliament and the executive. The latter, in its effort to move beyond traditional administrative tasks, became largely responsible for directing public policy. These changes in the relationship of different types of representation, be they 'functional', 'executive' or 'popular', have provided a further blow to the traditional image of parliaments as the decisive actors in proposing legislation and shaping its content before enactment.

The underlying assumption here is that the emergence and consolidation of structural parliamentary deficiencies has furthered the bases of an already acceptable pathology of modern political systems. Thus, attributes like 'democratic deficit', 'lack of democracy', 'parliamentary vacuum' or 'loss of national democratic autonomy' have their historical roots in the evolution of parliamentary democracy itself.[51] Whether this amounts to a structural transformation of Western European parliamentarism or to an ephemeral crisis of the institutions of representation, albeit a prolonged one, is really a matter of semantic argument. What is of vital importance, however, is that the parliamentary decline thesis has hardly been rested on systematic empirical evidence about the functions, powers and roles of legislatures in their alleged 'golden age'.

Moreover, this thesis has not adequately extended its focus beyond executive-legislature relations to include also those concerning the role of the *demos*. Not that its validity should be dismissed altogether. Rather, its contribution should be assessed within the realities not only of domestic, but also of transnational political processes. This assumes greater political weight when transferring the discussion from a purely national level to the realm of EU politics. To properly link the thesis in question with the origins and nature of the Union's democratic deficit, it is necessary to examine the shrinking role of member state legislatures in relation to the particular impact that membership of the Union had on their respective powers and functions.

MEMBER LEGISLATURES AND THE TRANSFER OF RESPONSIBILITIES

The transfer of certain 'responsibilities' from national parliaments to EU institutions – defined by the EP itself as 'the power to lay down legal and other rules, but also… the power to take decisions and shape policy'[52] – has run a parallel course with the diminishing influence of the former in a substantive part of national legislation. As Herman and Lodge have observed: 'the powers of the individual members' national parliaments have been reduced over various legislative and financial matters without a corresponding… increase in the powers of the European Parliament'.[53] Irrespective of how one perceives the actual impact of EU membership on national sovereignty, the fact remains that although the member governments have managed to exercise effective control over European legislation, either in the framework of their permanent representatives (COREPER) or in the workings of the Council, the same cannot be said of member legislatures.[54] Indeed, exactly the opposite is the case: their role has from the outset been marginalised in integration processes. Sbragia links this to the treaty-based character of the Union, arguing that 'the process of creating institutions by treaty maximises the power of the executive within all national governments concerned,' in the sense of making them, rather than the member legislatures, the major actors in controlling the timing and shape of such a process.[55]

In January 1984, the European Parliament published the results of the first systematic attempt to evaluate the extent to which responsibilities have been transferred to the Community and their implications for the erosion of parliamentary democracy in both spheres of government. The report confirmed that the transfer of responsibility in the fields of external relations, customs union, agricultural policy, competition policy, taxation, social policy and the right of establishment, had led to an erosion of democracy at the larger level, 'in that decision-making powers have been transferred from national parliaments to the Community but are exercised not by the European Parliament as the democratically elected representative body, but by the Council of Ministers'.[56] It went on to state that such a 'democratic deficit' was less clear in the case of commercial policy, transport policy and capital movement, and that only in respect of the Community's budget, where the European Parliament had already acquired substantial powers, was there an offset to the temporary decline in parliamentary democracy.

Although the European Parliament's report recognised that 'the extent of this democratic deficit differs within individual subject areas,' that 'in some Member States responsibility for certain areas... had already been transferred from Parliament to governments,' and that 'governments are still accountable to their respective parliaments,' it asserted that the transfer of responsibilities has gone hand in hand with the general decline in the influence of national parliaments in substantive decisions. It concluded: 'The contrast between the growing power of the executive and the declining capacity of parliaments to call that executive to account... raises the issue of the legitimacy of Community decision-making.[57] In brief, the point being made by the European Parliament is that 'a loss of democracy' has taken place between the responsibilities transferred to the executive branches of the Community and the exercise of indirect *demos* control over them.

This development has led to various criticisms which, for all their partial differences, commonly diagnose 'a reduction in the amount of legislative influence and parliamentary democracy in the Community'.[58]

In connecting our previous findings on the decline of legislatures with the setting up of transnational political authorities and structures of decision-making, one may be tempted to argue that the democratic deficit of the Union is but the European counterpart of pre-existing parliamentary shortcomings at the national level, in turn originating from the ever expanding role of central government in both executive and legislative spheres.

Following this line of argument, the appearance and evolution of the polity's democratic shortfalls reflect, by and large, a natural continuation of what has already been described as the 'de-parliamentarisation' of modern political systems. This development signals a predominantly 'legislative problem' that has been transferred, more or less intact, from one level of government to another. Thus the deficit in question becomes the mirror image of the intensity of various political and institutional constraints placed upon the member state legislatures. From this stems the assumption that, to redress the loss of national legislative influence, it is essential to affirm the role of national parliaments in scrutinising European legislation.

REGIONAL DYNAMICS AND NATIONAL DEMOCRATIC AUTONOMY

As previously noted, the member state governments sought to maintain and even enhance their individual capacities by reserving the final word on a considerable range of draft European legislation, largely at the expense of national parliamentary input. As a result, the member state *demoi* have experienced a considerable loss in their capacity to influence the affairs of the larger polity through the intermediary involvement of their representative assemblies. Accordingly, when the *demos* cannot employ its national parliaments to exercise control over the transnational political process a loss of national democratic autonomy can be said to exist.

The questions that such a loss generate for the democratic management of integration point to a weakening of national democratic accountability over the individual members of the Council, as the Union's major legislative branch.[59] The most radical meaning of this loss would be that since national parliaments, as the incarnation of popular sovereignty in systems of indirect *demos* control, have become impotent, the transnational political process does not comply even with the minimum requirements of modern democracy. A more limited use of the concept might be that the delegation of legislative powers to the Council and, hence, to national executives (which can always claim that they remain loyal and accountable to their parliaments), has disrupted whatever balance of power existed between executive and legislative bodies at the national level, thus further facilitating the recentralisation of national political authority in favour of the former and, inevitably, at the expense of the latter.

As Neunreither has pointed out: 'This balance differed... from one country to another, due to the political traditions and constitutional relationship between the two branches... in political systems where the executive is elected by a majority of the parliament, there is a different relationship than in systems where the executive is more independent of parliament'.[60] Whatever the differences involved, the deliberate exclusion of member legislatures from joint decision-making, combined with the fact that central legislation takes precedence over national law, has resulted in the creation of a 'parliamentary deficit', compounded by the fact that it is only the member governments that, courtesy of Article 235 EC, are empowered to revise the context of the regional arrangements – the Treaty of Rome and its subsequent (and already ratified) amendments as incorporated in the Single European Act and the Treaty on European Union – and extend the scope of their collective action.

Put differently, the process of integration has had a negative impact on the relationship between democracy in the member states and democracy within the Union. At least, the legislative process of the latter by-passes national parliaments, allowing them to exercise *ex post facto* scrutiny and control over its outcomes. At most, it offers them the possibility of rejecting treaty amendments through the ratification process and, hence, the delegation of new legislative powers to the central institutions. In both cases, however, it sets the limits of national democratic autonomy within a treaty-based system of multilateral rule-making which effectively rests on the joint management of separate sovereignties, leaving national parliaments to operate outside the realm of the Union's *locus decidendi*.

The crucial question is not so much which particular set of responsibilities has been transferred from national legislatures to the Union, but in which component of its institutional apparatus are these powers to be found. The answer is that such responsibilities have remained solidly confined to the executive branches of the larger management system since neither the Council nor the Commission can be regarded as parliamentary bodies either on the basis of their composition or their method of work.[61] This, combined with the difficulties involved in the process of reclaiming the lost responsibilities to national parliaments, leads us to conclude that democracy, as an effective balance between political authority and *demos* control, has been severely undermined in integration processes; especially in those fields of domestic legislation in which the member legislatures had a long-established role to play.

Notwithstanding Taylor's assertion that 'the failure of Assemblies to exercise their sovereign powers did not mean that this could not be done,'[62] and the fact that sovereignty is a quality attributed to the exercise of power, rather than a quantitative object of governmental authority, the truth is that the loss of national democratic autonomy persists, increasing the powers of national executives.[63] Although a possible line of opposition to this view is that the transfer of powers to the Union has been ratified by the member legislatures, it is only recently that the latter have come to 'think about specific internal structures which could help them to fulfil their role'.[64]

Indeed, all of the member legislatures have a body specialising in EU affairs. Drawing on an a document published by the European Parliament in March 1992,[65] we can distinguish between the following spheres of 'competence' that these bodies possess: to deliver opinions on European questions on their own initiative, or at the request of national or European parliamentarians, or of another standing parliamentary committee; to report to their parliament on the state of progress of the translation and application of European legislation in national legislation, and on bills which might be incompatible with the former; to exercise in the run-up to European Councils closer scrutiny of matters on the political agenda; to be informed by government of all EU legislative proposals relating to matters on which parliament has reserved the right to legislate; to formulate draft legislative proposals concerning the application of the treaties; to request to have hearings with ministers or members of the European Parliament; to request verbal or written evidence for government proposals relating to EU issues; to summon experts on crucial matters of transnational activity; to co-ordinate the relations between their parliament and the European Parliament and maintain contacts with other counterpart bodies; and to recommend the holding of plenary debates. In short, they were a 'valid representative' of their parliament on European issues, and keep a 'watching brief' on common policies.[66]

One of the problems associated with our discussion is that the efforts to exercise parliamentary control over the activities of an international organisation are almost exclusively confined to the workings of the Union. In particular, it has been suggested that under international law 'the democratic legitimisation of decisions of international organisations through parliamentary organs is not a necessary or constitutive element of any international organization'.[67] But this line of reasoning should not be seen as a justification for perpetuating the democratic deficiencies of a system whose institutions are capable of taking publicly binding decisions.

Although in economic terms, the Union has been classified as an economic confederation, representing 'the replacement of external economic relations between its members by economic relations similar to those that obtain within a single state,'[68] politically, it can be seen as a unique exercise in transforming a system of democratic governments into a democratic system of government. For the moment, however, the gradualness of this process leaves the Union *in limbo* between the two: a 'half-way house' between the interactive association of national *demoi* and the making of a new transnational one.

Whichever description may be closer to the evolving EU reality, one thing remains certain: the demands for higher levels of national democratic autonomy will continue to assume paramount importance for the proper functioning of the regional system. To borrow from Dahl: 'stronger democratic institutions [within countries] would provide whatever democratic control may be possible over authority delegated to transnational decisionmakers'.[69] He concludes: 'Democratic controls would help to prevent delegation from becoming alienation... In this way, while freedom and control might be lost on one front, they could yet be gained on others'.[70]

'DECLINE' AS A RELATIVE TERM

The growing power of the executive, along with the proliferation of transnational activities and the delegation of legislative powers to new centres of decision-making have considerably undermined the *de facto* ability of the *demos* to hold governments to account by means of 'classical' assembly controls. In this context, the parliamentary decline thesis, combined with the dialectics of national democratic autonomy, help us to develop a better understanding of the causes of the erosion of the democratic ethos at the Union level, and the consolidation of a distinctive pattern of transnational political management based on the properties of what Wright called 'dominocracy': 'a top-down, executive-dominated way of governing,' whose 'presiding spirit is not that of *demos* but of *dominus'*.[71] In the case of the Union, it may more accurately be termed as 'consensus elite government' (see chapter 7).

But this is not to exaggerate the overall validity of the thesis. For it is only a partial explanation, over-emphasising the pathology of the representative function by assuming the triumph of modern bureaucracy and of party organisations. In short, it points in the direction of what Bracher called 'the quasi-dictatorship' of the executive,[72] whilst underestimating or even ignoring the dynamics of parliamentary democracy itself. Thus

Wheare argues that instead of focusing on whether or not legislatures have declined in general, as Bryce does, it is more profitable to ask in what respect it is asserted that they have declined. He wonders: 'Is it a decline in power? Or is it a decline in efficiency?'[73] The point made by Wheare is that the two do not necessarily coincide: 'A legislature may be doing too much, it may be keeping control of too wide a range of functions and as a result may have not have the time or the capacity to perform them effectively'.[74] Overall, he concludes that in absolute terms the powers of legislatures have increased and that 'the increase of powers by the executive has not been the result of taking away from the legislature things which it did before'; for legislatures 'do more than they did, legislators work longer hours and interest themselves in a wider range of subjects'.[75]

A special issue of *West European Politics* on 'Parliaments in Western Europe' revealed that although the concept of 'decline' remains current in both comparative and country-specific literature, it is too relative a term to describe the course of contemporary parliamentarism.[76] Using Mezey's typology of legislatures as a framework for analysis, and particularly his three types on 'the policy-making axis',[77] the study concluded that all Western European parliaments fall into the category of 'modest' policy-influencing as opposed to policy-creating legislatures.[78] Despite the narrow empirical focus of the volume, its findings do offer some good ground for capturing the overall trend of Western European legislative politics. Three particular case studies examined therein are of crucial importance to our analytical purposes.

In the context of the Fifth French Republic, Frears describes the National Assembly as a 'loyal workhorse' but a 'poor watchdog', identifying its most serious shortcomings in 'its failure to be the arena for the nation's political debate... and its incapacity to act as a check on executive power'.[79] The reasons are to be found in 'a mixture of constitutional, procedural, historical and cultural events'.[80] Focusing on the first two, he argues that the features of the regime are 'complete executive supremacy in the legislative process, severely limited opportunities for general debates criticising the government, virtually no opportunities for scrutinising executive acts and making the executive give an account of them'.[81] But he also states that parliament does contribute to 'the health of the political system by its positive role in legislation, by the great value that public and local communities attach to the member of parliament, and by the habit of disciplined majority support for government that has developed... and sustained political stability'.[82] He concludes: 'Control of the legislature by government requires a disciplined majority and disciplined parliamentary majorities have contributed greatly to the political stability of the Fifth Republic'.[83] Thus, if one subscribes to Wheare's dictum that the most important role a parliament performs is to make government behave,[84] then the National Assembly cannot be accused of the contrary.

Regarding the British House of Commons, one would find it tempting to argue that it is on a 'continuing' decline in being asked to ratify what has already been determined by (prime) ministerial politics. Whilst there is little doubt that the lower house has witnessed a decrease in its 'decisional' or 'influence' functions, the same cannot be said for its overall legitimising effects on the British political system. Indeed, by producing and sustaining a strong government, it acts as 'agent of regime support', its equally important interest-articulation functions notwithstanding. In Norton's words: 'Though successive governments have tended to take Parliament for granted, the more government is forced to divulge information and to listen to parliamentarians, the greater the benefit to the system of which it is an intrinsic part'.[85] Whether Low's remark in *The Governance of England*, published in 1904 – 'The House of Commons no longer controls the Executive; on the contrary, the Executive controls the House of Commons'[86] – remains as justifiable a critique as it was at that time, is an open-ended question; one rooted in the constitutional tradition of collective political responsibility and the preferred line for its interpretation.

Looking finally at the German *Bundestag*, it has played a crucial role in avoiding government instability, albeit often at the expense of effective control over the federal government. This is partly due to the fact that 'chancellor democracy' limits direct parliamentary involvement in the formulation of public policy and the shaping of governmental guidelines.[87] As Saalfeld points out: 'Because of stable coalitions and cohesive party voting, important government proposals are hardly ever defeated'.[88] Also, 'environmental factors' have also contributed to a weakening of parliament's role as 'a check on the executive', intensifying neo-corporatist forms of decision-making.[89] This, together with the increased complexity of intergovernmental negotiations, has led to a proliferation of parliamentary committee work, increasing parliament's capacity to scrutinise legislation. The last point accords with Mezey's remark that 'Specialisation is a prerequisite to an effective oversight capacity'.[90] And since the committee stage proceeds the plenary session, the *Bundestag* is in a stronger position to influence legislation than other legislatures where the opposite is the case.

The aim of this cursory outline is only to illustrate that despite the cries regarding their impotence and inadequacy, legislatures have survived in the course of history by discovering new pathways for marking their impact on public life. An overall assessment might be that the long-term trend is not toward their 'decline', at least in Bryce's terms, but towards a gradual shift of the centre of gravity in scrutinising rather than directing executive decisions, influencing rather than dictating national policy-making, and legitimising the political system as a whole. In practical terms, this brief sketch highlights the difficulties involved in the process of reaching an authoritative statement on parliamentary decline. As Wheare put it: 'The fact is that the decline of legislatures may be an interesting question to discuss in general terms, but it is difficult, if not impossible to decide'.[91] For even where such a decline is more real than imagined, it still has to be visualised diagrammatically in rather erratic terms across a number of formal and informal parliamentary powers: what for some may constitute a loss of parliamentary capabilities for others may be interpreted as a potential gain in regime stability, governability and decisional efficiency.

The story, then, goes that the abstract and often normative arguments of Bryce's thesis are valid insofar as they can be supported by continuous empirical evidence in a comparative perspective and, to use a phrase, 'on the widest possible plane'.[92] It is comparative, however, in terms of being both intra-systemic (to compare the performance of the same legislature in different periods of time) and cross-systemic (to compare its performance with other legislatures at the same period of time). It is only along these lines that we can hope to reach a comprehensive assessment of the actual impact a legislature has on a given political system, whether federal or unitary.

A last point may be that legislatures should be analysed in the context of the political culture that surrounds them – how people see their parliament and what they expect from it – for such a culture 'affects the basic place of the legislature in the political life of the nation and the more mundane aspects of its existence'.[93] As Mezey notes: 'changes in legislative types... result from changes in expectations, which in turn result from the changes in the political culture of a nation'.[94] In this context, Lipset reveals that 'cultural factors' play a decisive part in determining the conditions for stable democracy in both parliamentary and presidential regimes.[95] Indeed, political culture becomes a crucial factor in evaluating the impact of legislatures on, and their contribution to, regime stability, especially in those cases where socio-political subcultures find it difficult to co-exist under a single government. It also helps us to assess the potential for integrating multinational societies characterised by a wide variety of cleavages. For instance, in the case of consociational democracies or in federal systems with acute problems of territorial diversity (see chapter 7).[96]

Norton is right to observe that legislatures, apart from their one core-defining function – 'they give assent, on behalf of a political community, that extends beyond the executive authority, to binding measures of public policy' – differ considerably.[97] And this is also true of their study, focusing on their policy-formulation functions and law-making powers to the legitimacy they enjoy from the *demos*, as well as that which they attribute to the polities in which they operate. Accordingly, different conclusions about their performance or its quality are often the product of the different ways of analysing legislative activity. Yet, traditional legislative theory has developed within a 'restrictive paradigm': 'the task of legislatures is of "law-making" or "law-giving"... [and]... their "best" form is one composed of men of independence... able to deliberate free of vested interests and the restrictive demands of an uninformed mass'.[98] It was mainly thanks to Blondel's resourceful analysis that a new direction was given to legislative research, both theoretically and empirically.

BLONDEL'S LEGACY AND BEYOND

Contemporary scholarship of legislative behaviour has shifted its attention from executive-legislature relations to the rise of administrative bodies of technical expertise, then to organised interests and the decision-making process and, eventually, to the realm of citizens themselves. Moreover, it has moved away from the 'old' dichotomy between the 'general' and the 'detailed' matters a legislature has to face, to what Blondel called 'the "real" question concerning the quantity of change over a whole variety of issues'.[99] This was made possible due to the emergence of a general academic consensus that the legislative process and the involvement of legislatures on a wide range of fronts had to take into account the dynamic nature of policy-making within the context of a changing society and/or one which actually resists change.

Such an analytical framework was proposed by Blondel, who was among the first to recognise the need for the theory of legislatures to replace the 'classical' model of legislative activity with one capable of embracing the role of individual legislators in 'the total decision process'.[100] He suggested: 'The overall influence of a legislature has to be assessed over time, the functions of a legislature being measured through its ability to adopt and pass on, on the one hand, and to initiate, on the other, a whole variety of reactions to existing situations and to previous policies'.[101] 'When examined in this way,' he explained, 'the functions of legislatures cover a much greater span than the classical theory was prepared to allow... This makes it possible to subsume in a single model the somewhat divided list of roles which are sometimes ascribed to legislatures in the contemporary literature'.[102] Similarly to Bagehot's ideas on the sociological functions of Parliaments – expression (or representation), teaching (or criticism) and informing (or publicity) – Blondel made clear that the function of the legislature, far from being one of 'really' passing the laws and statutes of the country, 'is to provide a means of ensuring that there are channels of communication between the people and the executive, as a result of which it is possible... for the executive decisions to be checked if they raise difficulties, problems and injustices'.[103]

Following this line of enquiry, one would have to embrace Blondel's central argument: 'We need to examine activities as well as influence, not hold as axiomatic that assemblies are reduced to very little role, but seeing whether and how across the world they vary in the scope of this role and how far it is possible to distinguish between those assemblies which clearly do not achieve much and those which do seem to make not too negligible a mark on the life of the polity'.[104] Irrespective of how one judges this suggestion, the overpessimistic reaction of holding legislatures as merely 'rubber stamps' bears little theoretical, and even less empirical, substance.

But where does Blondel's legacy leave us? A first point is that, as with any other political institution which claims to have some influence in modern government, legislatures are in the end conditioned by what the *demos* of a political community wants them to be. It follows that the future of legislatures is inextricably linked to the extent to which the *demos*, whether nascent, fragmented or well-established, believes in the democratic potential of parliament, and is determined to direct its democratic claims, channel its political demands and fulfil its civic expectations through the existing avenues of communication between its members and their elected representatives. Hence the political future of legislatures is conditioned by the extent to which the *demos* can convert its 'sovereign will' into actual political achievement by means of available assembly processes. And since the weight of the evidence is that legislatures do matter in the eyes of ordinary citizens, their future impact on the development of political societies is far from negligible. In fact, it is one of profound relevance for the democratic properties of both national and transnational systems of government.

CONCLUDING REMARKS

Despite the advances made so far toward a greater understanding of legislatures, no systematic effort has been attempted (as yet) to assess their relationship with the *demos* within and across countries. Once more, the Union offers an opportunity for scholarly research in this field. Indeed, if we accept the premise that for a system of government to remain viable over the long run, it must coincide with the expectations of its *demos*, then the significance of building strong parliamentary structures within the Union is almost self-evident. For wherever they are located, and whatever their formal powers, by signifying the place where public preferences are converted into political decisions, legislatures become a prerequisite for democratic participation.

This basic democratic ethic stems partly from the axiom that 'the legislature's proper function is to represent the views of citizens, influence the policy-makers, and reserve for itself the formal, final say on policy as the ultimate means of assuring policy responsiveness,' and partly from the contention that 'it is an elected body and therefore its actions can be advertised as decisions of the people'.[105] Especially in a period when direct forms of democracy are largely perceived as an impractical utopia, the institution of parliament becomes an active promoter of indirect *demos* control over the executive and, where and when needed, for restraining its actions and criticising its inactions in the name of popular sovereignty.

So far, and within the scope of existing analyses, the conclusion to be drawn is that stronger parliamentary institutions may indeed help to counter the democratic deficit of the Union. Yet, it is one thing to stress the importance of these bodies, and quite another to argue that *the* solution to this deficit rests solely upon them. In other words, although the transfer of legislative powers to the executive branches of the Union has exacerbated the institutional capacity of the constituent *demoi* to exercise effective control over transnational decision-making via their respective assemblies, such a deficit should not be entirely equated with the loss of national democratic autonomy. For structural democratic factors concerning EU constitutional reform are as crucial as are socio-psychological factors (see chapter 4).

In other words, to merely concentrate on the former would be to miss the point that equally important questions extend beyond institutional competences; namely, in the limits and possibilities for the development of a transnational *demos ab intra*. In conclusion, however valid the parliamentary decline thesis may be in throwing some light on the conditions which make up the pathology of modern legislatures, it remains far from complete when taken as a sole explanation for the democratic pathology of the Union. From this stems the need to shift our focus to the second explanatory thesis, which classifies the democratic deficit as being one of a federal or a constitutional kind. It is to this federal thesis that we now turn.

Notes on Chapter 5

1   Norton, Philip, 'General Introduction' in Norton, Philip (ed.), *Legislatures* (Oxford, 1990, Oxford University Press), pp 4-5.
2   Bryce, James, *Modern Democracies* (New York, 1921, Macmillan).
3   Bryce, James, 'The Decline of Legislatures' in Norton, Philip (ed.), *Legislatures*, p 51. This chapter is extracted from Bryce, James, *Modern Democracies*.
4   *Ibid.*, p 53.
5   *Ibid.*
6   *Ibid.*, p 55.
7   Norton, Philip, 'General Introduction', p 11.
8   Loewenberg, Gerhard, 'The Role of Parliaments in Modern Political Systems' in Loewenberg, Gerhard (ed.), *Modern Parliaments: Change or Decline?* (Chicago, 1971, Aldine-Atherton), pp 6-7.
9   *Ibid.*, p 6.
10 *Ibid.*, p 13.
11 *Ibid.*, p 5.
12 *Ibid.*, p 10
13 *Ibid.*, p 14.
14 *Ibid.*, p 15.
15 Bracher, Karl D., 'Problems of Parliamentary Democracy in Europe', *Daedalus*, Winter 1964, p 179.
16 *Ibid.*
17 Smith, Gordon, *Politics in Western Europe* Fifth edn (Aldershot, 1990, Dartmouth), p 190.
18 Quoted in Wahle, John C., 'Policy Demand and System Support: The Role of the Represented' in Norton, Philip (ed.), *Legislatures*, p 157.
19 Smith, Gordon, *Politics in Western Europe*, p 198.
20 Parry, Geraint, *Political Elites* (London, 1969, Allen & Unwin) p 15. For instance, these include the limitation of work, the regulation of working conditions and issues relating to the functions of the welfare state itself.
21 Whitherson, Joseph P., 'The Bureaucracy as Representatives', in Pennock, Ronald and Chapman, John W. (eds), *Representation*, Nomos X, (New York, 1968, Atherton Press), p 235.
22 Bracher, Karl D., 'Problems of Parliamentary Democracy in Europe', p 181.
23 Smith, Gordon, *Politics in Western Europe*, p 190.
24 Herman, Valentine and Lodge, Juliet, *The European Parliament and the European Community* (London, 1978, Macmillan), pp 16-17.

25 *Ibid.*, p 17
26 Grosser, Alfred, 'The Evolution of European Parliaments', *Daedalus*, Winter 1964, pp 162-3.
27 *Ibid.*, p 162.
28 *Ibid.*
29 *Ibid.*
30 Parry, Geraint, *Political Elites*, p 15.
31 *Ibid.*, p 16.
32 *Ibid.*
33 *Ibid.*
34 *Ibid.*, p 17.
35 Blondel, Jean, *Comparative Legislatures* (Englewood Cliffs NJ, 1973, Prentice-Hall), p 4.
36 Hogan, Willard N., *Representative Government and European Integration* (Lincoln, 1967, The University of Nebraska Press), p 77.
37 Bracher, Karl D., 'Problems of Parliamentary Democracy in Europe', pp 184-5.
38 *Ibid.* and p 190.
39 Blondel, Jean, *Comparative Legislatures*, p 6.
40 *Ibid.*, p 7.
41 *Ibid.*
42 Beer, Samuel H., 'The British Legislature and the Problem of Mobilising Consent' in Norton, Philip (ed.), *Legislatures*, pp 65-6.
43 *Ibid.*, p 66.
44 *Ibid.*
45 *Ibid.*, p 67.
46 Eulau, Heinz, 'Changing Views of Representation', in Eulau, Heinz and Whalke, John C. (eds), *The Politics of Representation* (London and Beverly Hills, 1978, Sage), p 32.
47 Hogan, Willard N., *Representative Government and European Integration*, p 77.
48 *Ibid.*, p 91 and pp 120-121.
49 *Ibid.*, p 87.
50 Loewenberg, Gerhard, 'The Role of Parliaments in Modern Political Systems', p 19.
51 For more on this point see Hayward, Jack (ed.), 'Special Issue on The Crisis of Representation in Europe', *West European Politics*, July 1995.
52 European Parliament, 'Transfer of Responsibilities and the Democratic Deficit', Research and Documentation Papers, Political Series no 4, January 1984, p 3.
53 Herman, Valentine and Lodge, Juliet, *The European Parliament and the European Community*, p 20. Cf Williams, Shirley, 'Sovereignty and Accountability in the European Community', *Political Quarterly*, July 1990, p 302.
54 *Ibid.*
55 Sbragia, Alberta M., 'Thinking about the European Future: The Uses of Comparison', in Sbragia, Alberta M. (ed.), *Euro-Politics: Institutions and Policymaking in the 'New' European Community* (Washington DC, 1992, The

Brookings Institution), pp 273.

56　European Parliament, 'Transfer of Responsibilities and the Democratic Deficit', p 38.

57　*Ibid.*, p 39.

58　Herman, Valentine and Lodge, Juliet, *The European Parliament and the European Community*, p 20.

59　For a detailed comparative account of these issues see Norton, Philip (ed.), 'Special Issue on National Parliaments and the European Union', *The Journal of Legislative Studies*, vol. 1, no 3, 1995.

60　Neunreither, Karlheinz, 'The Democratic Deficit of the European Union: Towards Closer Cooperation between the European Parliament and the National Parliaments', *Government and Opposition*, Summer 1994, pp 299-300.

61　European Parliament, 'Transfer of Responsibilities and the Democratic Deficit', p 3.

62　Taylor, Paul, *International Organization in the Modern World: The Regional and the Global Process* (London and New York, 1993 Pinter), p 96.

63　On this point see Neunreither, Karlheinz, 'The Democratic Deficit of the European Union', p 300.

64　For details see *ibid.*, p 303. Cf Weiler, Joseph H.H., 'After Maastricht: Community Legitimacy in Post-1992 Europe', in Adams, William J. (ed.), *Singular Europe: Economy and Polity of the European Community after 1992* (Ann Arbor MI, 1992, The University of Michigan Press), p 19. Weiler notes: 'Thus, in the formal sense, the existing structure and process could be said to rest on a formal approval by the democratically elected parliaments of the member states; and yet, undeniably, the Community process suffers... from a clear democratic deficit'.

65　European Parliament, 'Bodies within National Parliaments Specialising in European Community Affairs', DG for Research, 'National Parliaments' Series and ECPRD, March 1992.

66　*Ibid.*, p 47. It is worth noting that the Danish Common Market Committee (*Markedsudvalget*), acting by a majority of its members, can oblige the government not to give its final acceptance on draft European legislation of which it disapproves. Further, in the *Bundesrat*, following the set up of a Chamber for the Scrutiny of Documents of the European Communities in June 1988, the *Länder* may send representatives to EU negotiations when questions concern exclusively legislative matters or their vital interests. Finally, the Spanish 'autonomous regions' have established in their regional assemblies bodies specialising in EU affairs with a strong subnational interest in EU developments.

67　On this discussion see Ress, Georg, 'Democratic Decision-Making in the European Union and the Role of the European Parliament' in Curtin, Deirdre and Heukels, Tom (eds), *Institutional Dynamics of European Integration: Essays in Honour of Henry G. Schermers* vol. II (Dordrecht, 1994, Martinus Nijhoff), p 154. Cf Forsyth, Murray, *Unions of States: The Theory and Practice of Confederation* (Leicester, 1981, Leicester University Press), pp 186-7.

68 Forsyth, Murray, *Unions of States*, p 184.

69 Dahl, Robert A., *Democracy and its Critics* (New Haven and London, 1989, Yale University Press), pp 320-1.

70 *Ibid.*, p 321.

71 Wright, Tony, *Citizens and Subjects: An Essay on British Politics* (London and New York, 1994, Routledge), pp 23-4.

72 Bracher, Karl D., 'The Decline of Modern Parliament', in Macridis, Roy C. and Brown, Bernard E. (eds), *Comparative Politics: Notes and Readings*, Third edn (Homewood, 1968, Dorsey Press), p 424.

73 Wheare, Kenneth C., *Legislatures*, Second edn (New York and Toronto, 1968, Oxford University Press), p 147.

74 *Ibid.*, pp 147-8.

75 *Ibid.*, pp 148-9.

76 Norton, Philip, 'Conclusion: Legislatures in Perspective', in Norton, Philip (ed.), 'Special Issue on Parliaments in Western Europe', *West European Politics*, July 1990.

77 Mezey, Michael L., *Comparative Legislatures* (Durham NC, Duke University Press, 1979), pp 47-59.

78 Norton, Philip, 'Conclusion'.

79 Frears, John, 'The French Parliament: Loyal Workhorse, Poor Watchdog', in *ibid.*, p 33.

80 *Ibid.*, p 32.

81 *Ibid.*, p 33.

82 *Ibid.*, p 31.

83 *Ibid.*, p 51.

84 On this point see Wheare, Kenneth C., *Legislatures*, pp 77-96.

85 Norton, Philip, 'Parliament in the United Kingdom: Balancing Effectiveness and Consent?', in Norton, Philip (ed.), 'Special Issue on Parliaments in Western Europe', p 30.

86 Low, Sidney, 'The House of Commons and the Executive', in Geoffrey Marshall (ed.), *Ministerial Responsibility* (Oxford, 1989, Oxford University Press), p 20. Cf Lord Hailsham's 'elective dictatorship' thesis in his *The Dilemma of Democracy* (London, 1978, Collins).

87 Saalfeld, Thomas, 'The West German Bundestag after 40 Years: The Role of Parliament in a "Party Democracy"', in Norton, Philip (ed.), 'Special Issue on Parliaments in Western Europe', p 68.

88 *Ibid.*

89 *Ibid.*

90 Mezey, Michael L., *Comparative Legislatures*, p 54.

91 Wheare, Kenneth C., *Legislatures*, p 156.

92 Blondel, Jean, *Comparative Legislatures*, p xii.

93 Norton, Philip, 'Conclusion', p 147.

94 Mezey, Michael L., *Comparative Legislatures*, p 284.

95 Lipset, Seymour M., 'The Centrality of Political Culture', *Journal of Democracy*, Fall 1990, pp 80-3.

96 On the integrative role of legislatures see Mezey, Michael L., *Comparative Legislatures*, pp 255-74.

97 Norton, Philip, 'Parliaments: A Framework for Analysis', in Norton, Philip (ed.), 'Special Issue on Parliaments in Western Europe', p 1.

98 *Ibid.*, p 2.

99 Blondel, Jean, *Comparative Legislatures*, p 14.

100 *Ibid.*, p 15.

101 *Ibid.*, p 16.

102 *Ibid.*, p 17.

103 *Ibid.*, p 135. For a discussion of Bagehot's views on the subject see Allum, Percy, *State and Society in Western Europe* (Cambridge, 1995, Polity Press), pp 310-1.

104 *Ibid.*

105 Mezey, Michael L., *Comparative Legislatures*, pp 283-24 and p 270.

CHAPTER 6

European Federalism and Democratic Principles

INTRODUCTORY NOTES

In visible contrast to the parliamentary decline thesis which traces the origins of the democratic deficit to the predominance of executive institutions in national and EU processes, the federal thesis calls attention to the concerted efforts of those committed to the creation of a European federation. It focuses on a series of federalist-inspired arguments for replacing the anachronistic European system of nation-states with a new framework of political interaction capable of guaranteeing public participation in the affairs of the envisaged polity, whilst offering a new flowering of democratic diversity among its sub-units. The gist of the thesis is that the democratic deficit of the Union is essentially a 'federal deficit', stemming from the absence of a European constitution that could guarantee the fundamental rights of the constituent *demoi*, ensuring that meaningful legislative representation of, and political responsibility to, the governed will apply in a 'bottom-up' process. And yet an alternative method for achieving unification prevailed, known as the 'gradualist' approach to integration. Resting upon an incrementalist philosophy for integrating markets and peoples, whilst drawing partly on Mitrany's functionalism and partly on Haas's revised version of it,[1] the application of this method proved to have little to do with the federalist projects of radical political change against and even beyond the nation-state.

The triumph of this hybrid functionalist method, best described as a case of 'functional federalism',[2] had far-reaching implications for the democratic nature of EU institution-building. Following this line of interpretation, the incrementalist scope of what has generally been termed Monnet's 'strategy of small steps' – as opposed to Spinelli's 'head-on approach' towards federation – constituted *the* crucial factor in the emergence of an elite-dominated system of shared management with a technocracy at its centre. This partly explains why the gradualist process fell short of establishing new patterns of interaction between citizens and central institutions, focusing instead on the development of utilitarian bonds between them. In general, the comparative study of these two 'integrationist fronts' for unification, and in Burgess's terms these 'two faces of federalism',[3] helps to develop a better understanding of the underlying conditions which determined the political nature of European integration.

More important, perhaps, is to assess the consequences of the repeated failures of the early federalist strategies to mobilise public support for a supranational authority. These shortcomings were apparent in the modest outcome of the 1948 Hague Congress, namely the Council of Europe, as well as to those associated with the creation of the European Defence Community (EDC) and the collapse of the European Political Community (EPC). The inglorious end of the last two interconnected designs represented the conclusion of the federal phase of early continental attempts at unification, furnishing to successive integrative initiatives a modest democratic potential. On the other hand, the inner logic of the federal thesis rests heavily upon a variety of negative-premise arguments, in that the lack of democratic arrangements at the larger level owes much to the fact that the ideals of federal democracy have not been fulfilled in integration processes. To properly evaluate the validity of the thesis in question, one should take into account the deeper aspects of the relationship between federalism and democracy in both historical and contemporary terms. This will enable us to descend from the 'general' to the 'particular' and determine the extent to which the prevalence of one operational method of integration over the other contributed to the democratic pathology of the Union. It will also help us to assess the way in which federalists envisaged the qualitative transformation of Western Europe from a loose association of sovereign states into a democratically structured 'union of peoples'.

FEDERALISM AND THE IDEA OF DEMOCRACY

It is fair to suggest that no single body of theory has so far been able to provide an in-depth and complete evaluation of the relationship between federalism and democracy. One reason for this is that both concepts, by virtue of their dynamic nature, are liable to different interpretations at different moments in time. For instance, it is no accident that Conlan has identified 267 different, yet overlapping, definitions of federalism.[4] Likewise,

Dahl's observation speaks for itself: 'Today the term *democracy* is like an ancient kitchen midden packed with assorted leftovers from twenty-five hundred years of nearly continuous usage'.[5] Notwithstanding these analytical constraints, there is a striking resemblance in the way in which students of politics have tried to approach these concepts, using them either as ends in themselves, that is as terminal states of political development, or as dynamic processes towards the achievement of concrete political objectives. In addition, they have been vested with the status of distinguished forms of government intended to solve particular problems. As regards the first equation, federalism and democracy have been largely viewed as constantly searching for an accommodation of the varying interests of different collectivities within a viable political framework based on the explicit consent of the *demos*, the amicable settlement of societal disputes, and the rule of law as an indispensable instrument for the protection of essential liberties.

Alternatively, conceived as models of government embracing their own theories and ideologies, their advocates have tried to defend their principal moral values, using every available means to put them into practice. In general terms, the relationship between federalism and democracy can be seen as a by-product of the dialectical interchange of operational, structural and conceptual variables. Since, however, they both tend to operate more often than not through processes than structures, the conception of these political phenomena as a static design regulated by fixed rules should be dismissed from the outset. Instead, one should speak of an evolving pattern of changing relationships, capable of taking endless forms of organisational expression. But let us now place their dynamic relationship in its historical and contemporary context.

In its historical dimension, the discussion of linking federalism and democracy goes back to the political philosophies of Rousseau and Kant.[6] The former, also known as the philosopher of the 'general will', recognised in *The Social Contract* that democracy can only flourish in small communities that could effectively guarantee public involvement in the management of common affairs. Acknowledging, however, that due to their limited size these communities run the danger of being overwhelmed by others of a larger territory, he asserted that democratic stability can be maintained through their incorporation into a larger union based on the principle of popular self-rule. As Levi has observed, it was Rousseau who first suggested the remedy of the *confederation* as 'the instrument for joining the external power of a great people with the simple rule and the good order of a small state'.[7]

Kant, on the other hand, in his seventh thesis on the *Idea for a Universal History with a Cosmopolitan Perspective*, carried these ideas further by urging mankind 'to step from the lawless condition of savages into a union of peoples'.[8] The rationale behind Kant's thinking was that his proposed *foedus amphictyonum* would provide even to the smallest states an additional platform for exerting some influence to secure peace and justice 'not from their own power... but from the united power of the union, acting according to the decisions reached under the laws of their united will'.[9] But he also recognised that the mere existence of such a union was not a sufficient condition for achieving peaceful co-existence among the sub-units. To that end, he asserted that it should be democratically structured in the dual sense that the 'federal covenant' must be 'a free pact among free peoples', and that the larger union must rest upon a government based on 'the free choice and consent of the governed'.[10] Thus Kant was also among the first to enunciate that democratic institutions are 'the only political basis for a federal community', stating in his *Perpetual Peace* that 'the civil constitution of every nation should be republican'.[11] In summary, both philosophers chose a more or less federal path to develop democratic ideas on a scale larger than the state, aiming to establish a novel civic order among citizens belonging to different communities based on the 'united will' of a wider political unit.

No comment, however, on their historical dimension can be complete without prior reference to the 'great American experience'. For it was not until the drafting of the 1787 American Constitution that large-scale democratic questions were addressed. Indeed, the application of the 'federal principle' contributed to the enlargement of the size of democratic government in the United States of America, 'reconciling,' in Hamilton's words, 'the advantages of monarchy with those of republicanism'.[12] Thus federalism in general, and the federal principle in particular, were viewed as new instruments of government capable of developing democracy beyond a purely national level, where 'the international clash of national wills is scarcely regularised through the promotion of rational and democratic procedures'.[13]

In its contemporary dimension, the same discussion witnesses a change in the centre of gravity from an effort to prevent a world political power from becoming 'a universal tyranny',[14] to the no less demanding task of balancing democratic diversity with overall 'federal cohesion', defined as the ability of a federal system to overcome the internal rivalries arising among the constituent units. In particular, students of democracy hold the view that federalism, by denoting a diffusion of political power, contributes to a moderation of political conflicts, whilst offering greater opportunity for 'political schooling', itself an essential condition for furthering the socialisation of minority groups into 'a democratic political culture'.[15] From this also stems the importance of devising adequate

institutional arrangements for the meaningful representation of each associate collectivity within the federal polity without either disturbing the
central effectiveness of the system, or challenging the authority and/
or popular legitimacy of the central institutions. Modern federalism, by
transcending the traditional tension between peaceful co-existence and
intersegmental fragmentation, is concerned with the establishment of a
co-operative democratic ethos in the relations between the federal government and the component governments.

In practice, it aims to reconcile the demands for wider political integration and segmental diversity, or in Watts's terms for 'unity without
uniformity and diversity without anarchy'.[16] From this view, the appro-
priateness of federal organisation 'would appear to lie in those instances
where the existence and vigour of the forces that press both for wider
unity and for autonomous regional diversity are relatively balanced'.[17]
Accordingly, the striking of an effective balance between the parallel
demands for 'unity in diversity' emerges as the strongest catalyst for the
attainment of sufficient levels of overall federal cohesion: a precondition
for federal polities to survive the test of time. Here, the question of democratic representation in federal systems becomes a crucial balancing factor
for the political viability and successful operation of the federation.

DEMOCRATIC REPRESENTATION IN FEDERAL SYSTEMS

As Preston King argues, the representation of the sovereign people, either
as a whole (when taken as a single entity) or as parts (when taken as a
plurality of entities) becomes the prior object of the federation.[18] 'What is
distinctive about federations,' he explains, 'is not that "the people" are
viewed as sovereign, but that the expression of this sovereignty is tied to
the existence and entrenchment of regional, territorial entities'.[19]
Consequently, in a given federal system there are two possible, but not
antithetical ways of perceiving 'the people': as united and as diverse; a
duality which, in his words, 'for the life of the federation, is implicitly
inexpungible'.[20] But in both cases, it is the federal *demos* which is to be
served by the central arrangements.

Although federations encompass a considerable range of purposes,
identities, cultural traditions, organisational structures, possibilities for
power-sharing among the constituent units, as well as different means of
protection for the constitution,[21] democratic representation of the participating communities is an essential feature common to all federal entities.
The issue here is not so much about creating direct links among different 'levels of government',[22] but rather about establishing concrete and

accessible avenues of interaction between the *demos* and the central institutions. And since in federal systems the latter are free to exercise considerable power over the former without being dependent upon prior agreement between state governments or local authorities, these direct links become central to the democratic legitimacy of the federal polity. It follows that federalism requires effective built-in democratic arrangements for the constituent populations to operate under conditions of 'good government' in the sense that the central institutions should be responsible and responsive to the federal *demos*. Put differently, federalism suggests the presence of democratic mechanisms to ensure citizen participation in political decision-making both within the 'component' communities, through their own means of representation, and in the 'inclusive' community, by directly electing a 'house of peoples' as one component of a bicameral legislature, the other being a 'house of states' representing territorial units.

Furthermore, in a federal system, unlike a unitary state model, the degree of democratic participation is linked to the extent to which legislative autonomy in the form of 'reserved powers' (powers not delegated to the general government) has been conferred to each participating collectivity by the constitution. Thus, the question of public participation is intrinsically woven into the particular degree of autonomous action granted to each distinct level of government in which the *demos* exercises its sovereign rights. But the extent to which democratic diversity, and in Harrison's terms 'a co-ordinated expression of it',[23] can be maintained without endangering the political cohesion of the federation is conditioned by the ability of the central arrangements to produce viable constitutional equilibria. Seen from a different angle, the intersection of federalism and democracy passes through the capacity of the compound polity to generate a common commitment to federal unity, whilst preserving the integrities of the constituent entities. This corresponds to Burgess's view that the idea of federation emerges as a living, pluralist and organic political order which 'builds itself from the grounds upwards,' constructing its tiers of authority so as to create an environment in which 'the public authorities of each political community... can carry out their tasks, fulfil their duties and exercise their rights with greater security'.[24] It also accords with the view that 'federalism promotes, or is promoted by, "democracy"'.[25]

According to Friedrich, however, 'those who would... identify democracy with the absolute and unrestrained will of the majority of a given community are confronted with an unresolvable dilemma by federalism' since the 'sovereign will' of a constituent people might have 'to adjust to what other people want or reject'.[26] Further, because classical constitutional federalism, due to its dualistic nature, may allow decisions to be taken against the wishes of even the majority of the *demos*, it is less 'democratic' as a method of organising political life than 'co-operative federalism' where each governmental level 'can influence, bargain with, and persuade the other'.[27] Although co-operative federalism, by stressing the indispensability of policy co-ordination and the need for extending concurrent competences, represents a means of enhancing the autonomy of constituent entities, 'this new form of organisation of the federal state has not modified the nature of federal institutions'.[28] In any case, this paradigm relates to 'joint decision systems' and can be summed up in the concept of 'co-determination' among participants in national policy-making (see chapter 7).

Leaving aside the alleged advantages of jurisdictional co-existence *vis-à-vis* a dualistic conception of federalism based on the model of exclusive jurisdiction, the fact remains that the above 'undemocratic' features of federalism should be set against the benefits of mutual control exercised by the 'checks and balances' in a system based on a separation of powers seeking to combine 'a maximum of freedom with the necessary authority'.[29] In addition, if we subscribe to Friedrich's view that in any federal system a given group of individual citizens 'belong' not only to their concurrent settings but also to the 'inclusive' community,[30] then, far from clashing with democracy, federalism implies the existence of an organic, albeit composite, whole within which all the segments are entitled to participate in the workings of the federation. Hence the latter can be seen as a 'corporate union', including states and citizens, aiming to articulate a whole variety of views, 'conveyed,' in Gagnon's words, 'by the image of checks and balances towards a state of equilibrium'.[31] This system can be described best as dynamic 'equilibrium pluralism' (see chapter 7).

In conclusion, the relationship between federalism and democracy, at least in its broader sense, is the same that exists between liberalism and individual freedom, socialism and social justice, corporatism and interest intermediation, as well as pluralism and interest differentiation, to mention but a few examples. It is thus predominantly an 'osmotic' relationship, since both concepts are indissolubly linked, and find themselves in constant interpenetration with each other. In this sense, federalism may be seen as a particular type of democracy: a federal democracy based on a constitutional system of delegated, reserved and/or shared powers between relatively autonomous, yet interrelated, structures of government whose multiple interactions aim to serve the sovereign will of the federal *demos*.

THE FEDERAL IMPULSE TO POSTWAR EUROPEAN UNITY

With the postwar circumstances in Western Europe corresponding 'to those which often in the past have led nations to undertake the initial steps towards federation,'[32] federalism emerged as an inspiring remedy for Europe's organisational problems. At the same time, the interposition of a central authority beyond pre-existing boundaries acquired, mainly thanks to Italian federalist thinking, the status of a desirable political ideology. In this sense, the process of federating Western Europe consti-tuted a unique experiment, making it particularly difficult for students of politics to classify it under a single pattern of federalisation, normative or empirical. Rather, it is better assessed on its own merits and limitations, requiring the careful examination of the prevailing ideology which stood behind the launching of the federal alternative. But let us reveal some of the many literary responses elaborated by federalists during this era of hope, and capture the way in which their writings reflected the con-sciousness of the time.

Although the ideal of a united Europe predated the specific postwar attempts, what actually distinguished these efforts is that 'the unity concept moved into the foreground of popular thinking with both an emotional and practical appeal'.[33] For much of the original impetus stemmed out of a recognition that Europe, once the 'hub of the universe', had run its course as a world power, and was hence in desperate need of devising 'a new ordering of its corporate life' capable of ensuring peace and stability in the region.[34] Deeply shocked with the suicidal effects of nationalism in general, and the inelastic ideology of 'dogmatic nationess' in particular, the federal impulse to postwar European unity arose as an attractive alternative to a challenge which, according to Bowie, 'went to the very foundations of social existence'.[35]

The devastating experience of two highly destructive European 'civil wars' provided a golden opportunity for neighbouring states and publics to put forward a new set of political arrangements for the transformation of long-established interstate relations into some sort of federal union. At least that was the aim of early federalist aspirations, which stressed the projection of other comparable developments of federal government, the American federal experience being the most prominent. Although the idea of a 'United States of Europe' has found no equivalent paradigm, all that was needed at the time was 'a solid institutional structure to allow this common elaboration to develop and determine itself'.[36] This phrase clearly states the problem: any other path toward unification was instantly perceived as yet another sophisticated form of escapism from the real problems that confronted European civilisation. To fully appreciate this current of federalist thinking, it is important to outline the way in which federalists perceived the concept of national sovereignty and the nation-state.

Far from conceiving the nation-state as an *a priori* fact of existence, but rather as 'a historic accident', European federalists proposed its supercession by a process of 'rational federal development'.[37] In all their different guises, be they 'radical', 'integral' or 'incremental' federalists, the champions of the federal cause were most sceptical about the long-term capacity of states to co-operate harmoniously with each other. This premise is clearly reflected in Jameson's point that Realpolitik, as the hallmark of interwar politics, was 'a disbelief in the value and dignity of the individual' and that 'the root-cause of the decay of civilisation in the twentieth century was nothing more and nothing less than atrophy of the imagination'.[38] Convinced that the immediate cause of war lies behind the divisive effects of nationalism, federalists argued their case for a 'union of peoples' to end the existing anarchy among states. Doubtless, common opposition to Hitler's *Neue Ordnung* had greatly facilitated the consolidation of the federal idea among continental democratic forces. A draft declaration issued by the European Resistance Movement in July 1944 put it thus: 'Federal Union alone can ensure the principles of liberty and democracy in the continent of Europe'.[39]

Following this somewhat teleological line of argument, any federal surrender of sovereignty seemed better than allowing the European states system, described by Curry as 'an antiquated and destructive nuisance,'[40] to consolidate itself once more, especially after its 'great moral and material bankruptcy'.[41] Reflecting upon the 1944 Ventotene Manifesto, Burgess has observed: 'The real cause of international anarchy was seen as "the absolute sovereignty of national States", which is the source of power-politics in the international sphere and of totalitarianism in the national one'.[42] Similarly, Spinelli has argued that the nation-state had become for those who sought guidance 'a compass which has ceased to give any bearings'.[43] To complete the picture, Brailsford wrote: 'If we abandon the concept of the sovereign state, it will not be because we have changed our views about a legal theory. It will be because we have reached an idea of human fraternity that embraces our neighbours who in other languages think the same civilised thoughts.'[44] These statements provided the moral justification of the postwar federalist design, demanding the immediate replacement of Europe's historic fragmentation into sovereign states by 'better' forms of political organisation.[45] The choice of European nations was one between federalism and anarchy, rather than between the former and some measure of interstate co-operation.

Overall, federalists built their case by exploiting to the highest possible degree the inadequacy of nation-states to cope with the new set of problems that could no longer be tackled by their individual capacities alone. According to Smith, the utter purposes of this uncompromised 'anti-statist' campaign can be summarised as follows: to denounce the ability of the nation-state to present a cohesive and self-sufficient front to the outside world; to doubt its role both as the sole guardian of national territorial integrity and as a guarantor of economic autonomy; and to challenge its actual performance in delivering welfare and prosperity to its citizens.[46] Above all, by stressing the inability of states to provide new means of democratic participation, federalists have argued that an unprecedented 'legitimacy crisis' had shaken their once powerful structures: a deep-rooted structural crisis which prompted them to look above the nation-state itself as a means of resolving its acute legitimation problems.

Underlying the various federalist diagnoses is a higher political purposeness, amounting to the belief that 'new loyalties will arise in direct conflict with the nation-state,'[47] opening up much wider horizons than those afforded by the latter. This is exactly what European federalists had in mind: the multiple pressures on the nation-state would lead to the recognition that new democratic arrangements would have to be devised so as to meet the challenges of the postwar era. Spinelli, for instance, had strongly opposed the idea proposed by national governments of a 'partial' European union without first creating a democratic infrastructure upon which common institutions would be based. In this sense, federalism provided the means not only to overcome the structural crisis of the nation-state itself, or even 'to transform the very essence of national statehood into a larger loyalty going beyond its territorial affinities,'[48] but also a powerful stimulus to the extension of the democratic process. As Levi has observed, federalism took the form not only of an operational method for achieving unification, but also that of a political ideology 'which brings to light the sense of a new phase in history of the affirmation of new institutions and values'.[49]

Inspired by two interrelated ideas, that of democracy against totalitarianism and federalism against nationalism, federalism was taken as being totally antithetical to the *ancien régime* of nation-states, where the identification of the state with the nation had brought 'centralisation and authority within the state and imperialist wars outside'.[50] In fact, their fusion was viewed as the basis upon which 'governments demanded exclusive loyalty from the citizens' whilst destroying 'all the links of communities which were smaller or larger than the state'.[51] Having thus dismissed the traditional ideologies which, in Levi's words, 'insofar as they pursue the illusion of national renewal... ultimately remain prisoners of this political formula, suffering its decadence and thus remaining in the field of conservation,'[52] the federalists called for the creation of central institutions and 'federalised economic and administrative structures'.[53] This was seen as the only way for Europe to defend a certain spiritual value of its civilisation: the democratic conquests of its peoples. As Bosco put it: 'If it is true that the ideals of the French Revolution found in the nation-state a political form which was indispensable for their realisation, it is also true that they found in the nation-state the limit to their success at the international level'.[54] Hence the belief that integration was part of the historical evolution of European democracy itself.

DEMOCRATIC PRINCIPLES AND THE POLITICS OF EUROPEAN FEDERALISM

Whatever the title ascribed to the envisaged polity, it was widely recognised that the federal system would have to strike a delicate balance between such extreme concepts as stability and change, interdependence and autonomy, democracy and efficiency and, above all, unity and diversity. In order, however, to convince the European peoples of the merits of federalism as a means of safeguarding their cultural traditions and civic autonomy, the federalists stressed the representative character of the central institutions. In particular, it was maintained that the latter should be left free to exercise the political authority conferred upon them by a written constitution in direct relation to the European public without having to depend upon the convergence of short-term national interests for the formulation of common policies and decisions.

Moreover, federalists were constantly reminding that 'both the United States and Switzerland abandoned confederal forms of political organisation because of their inability to deal adequately with common problems'.[55] A further reason for dismissing confederalism was that it was seen as intergovernmental co-operation in disguise, resting on the inelastic practices of 'conventional' international diplomacy such as 'horse-trading', 'side-payments' and 'log-rolling', to mention but a few. As Harrison put it: 'The federalist position... leads... to a profound distrust of mere confederal solutions, international functional co-operation and economic incrementalism as instruments of integration'.[56] Herein lies its greatest contribution to the cause of European unification: that in the larger political community, power and responsibility should be seen as being mutually supportive, rather than as a competitive tussle for political authority between the collectivity and the segments.

In addition, it was proposed that the central institutions should derive their legitimacy directly from the European peoples, so that the exercise of power would be consistent with the requirements of the democratic process. Indeed one of the motives behind the federal unification of Europe was the furthering of large-scale democracy without undermining the democratic qualities of the parts that were to be federated. Writing on the strategic aims of the Federalist Movement, Levi refers to 'the objective of changing the character of exclusive communities which nation-states have and unify them in a federal community thus transforming them into member states of the European Federation, in such a way that they can coexist peacefully though maintaining their autonomy'.[57] In support of this view comes Friedrich's remark that 'not only does [federalism] unite without destroying the shelves that are uniting, but also it tends to strengthen them'.[58] More specifically, it was believed that federalism could encourage democratic diversity by establishing a system of co-ordinate but independent spheres of authority based on a division of powers among state and federal agents. According to this design, the member legislatures would hold their executives accountable to their respective publics, whilst a European legislature would act as a potential barrier against the danger of central executive dominance.

Convinced that the viability of any federation rests firmly on these democratic conditions, the federalists perceived the creation of direct channels of communication between governors and governed as a prerequisite for polities based on representative democracy to transfer a substantial part of their sovereignty to a central authority. Hence the quest for democracy was not just another decorative rhetoric but rather a *conditio sine qua non* for the successful realisation of the federal project. Pinder explains: 'There was to be a [bicameral] legislature comprising a house of states and a house of the people; containing the citizens' directly elected representatives; and a federal government that was to be responsible either to those representatives or to the voters direct'.[59] 'The rule of law, based on fundamental rights,' he continues, 'was to be the responsibility of a federal supreme court'.[60] These ideas were the creative marriage of the Proudhonian and the Hamiltonian tradition of federation, the former advocating 'a community of free persons, organised in a variety of groups which together comprise the federation,' the latter 'entrusting a part of sovereignty to a European federal authority based on representative democracy and the rule of law'.[61]

Resting on a 'firm constitutional structure', the main powers of the federation were to lie in the sphere of defence, foreign affairs, commerce across state lines, international exchange, communication and, in Pinder's words, 'enough tax to sustain the necessary expenditure'.[62] The envisaged pattern of federal-state relations was closer to the dualistic model of federalism, requiring a constitutional separation of policy responsibilities between state governments and the general government, rather than to a system of shared rule based on concurrent competences, conceived at the time as a potential source of internal disputes. Interestingly, the current debate on the principle of subsidiarity and the mounting scholarly comparisons between the Union and the properties of the German system of 'interlocking responsibilities' is reflective of the evolutionary nature of European federalist thought and the search for an appropriate (federal) model of transnational governance (see chapter 7).

SPINELLI'S 'CONSTITUENT METHOD' AND THE AMERICAN FEDERAL EXPERIENCE

It soon became evident, however, that if the federal project was to be crowned with success it would have to overcome national governmental resistance to an immediate relinquishing of state sovereignty to a federal polity. For all nations – irrespective of their size, economic and military potential – far from willing their own demise, become highly sensitive over their capacity to exercise their sovereign rights, in which, as Beyen notes, they see 'the incarnation of their national self-respect'.[63] Doubtless, Western Europe was no salutary exception to this rule. The answer to this difficult question came from Spinelli, who proposed a strategy based on a campaign of public persuasion for the drafting of a federal constitution. This task was to be carried out by a directly elected European Constituent Assembly (ECA).[64]

Drawing on the experience of the League of Nations, which has ended up with merely advisory powers, Spinelli rejected the partial character of intergovernmental solutions. The federalist criticism of all systems of states or leagues of governments was that, by being 'necessarily concerned with making the world safe for national sovereignty and not for either democracy or the people,' they lose sight of the fact that 'the essential unit in a true democracy is not the government but the citizens'.[65] Spinelli's constitutional approach to unification was an attempt to fill this vacuum. To borrow a phrase, it was 'a question of uniting nations by uniting people'.[66] As regards the moral justification of Spinelli's 'constituent method', it lay in the belief that the ECA was the only acceptable body to give federal democracy its due and transform the possibility of popular participation in the affairs of the federation into reality.

The premium placed on the institution of parliament stemmed from the fact that binding decisions should be taken openly, as opposed to the secretive methods of consensus-building where the defence of each separate interest often outweighed acceptance of the common interest. The proposed constitution was to be based on a declaration of fundamental rights, democratic institutions, and the separation of powers. As for the third criterion, it was believed that a balanced structure of national and federal competences based on the principle of dual federalism could preserve national identity and diversity in a way compatible with the federal democratic ethos. Thus it was agreed that the federation should exercise limited but real powers, with the remaining spheres of competence resting upon state jurisdiction.

The resemblance of these early federalists aspirations to the American federal experience is obvious, especially if one recalls the classical arguments expressed in the *Federalist Papers* for devising a system of effective restraints upon excessive central power. Based on the belief that the basic function of a federal constitution is 'to combine a maximum of freedom with the necessary authority,'[67] the federalists tried to promote a constitutional pattern for balancing the authority of the federal government with the powers reserved to the states. This led Pistone to assert that Spinelli's 'constituent method' was inspired by 'the way the first federal Constitution in history was drawn up... worked out by the Philadelphia Convention in 1787.[68] In a word, Spinelli sought to transplant to Europe 'the great American experience'.[69] The latter was seen as a promising analogy since it was the first democratic form of government ever applied to a vast territory composed of many peoples with a strong sense of cultural diversity, but which had showed their determination, only ten years after the 1774 Continental Congress, to form a united nation.

In conclusion, the gist of the federalist thesis was that 'federalism is the only international democratic bond which can create a reign of law among nations,' as well as the only possible means for enlarging 'the sphere of democratic government from the ambit of the state to that of a group of states'.[70] The object was a European federation characterised by democratic performance and strong organic bonds among the component parts: a constitutional system in which Lincoln's eminent resolve for 'government of the people, by the people, and for the people,' would find its proper meaning. As most federalists have acknowledged, however, the difficulty of the task lay not so much in convincing the European peoples of the need for a federation, but in convincing them that they, rather than their national governments, must create it. This brings us to the very limitations of European constitution-making itself.

FROM THE COUNCIL OF EUROPE TO MONNET'S 'FUNCTIONAL FEDERALISM'

The first real test for the federalist design came with the convention of the 1948 Hague Congress. But the end-product of the process inaugurated at The Hague in the form of the Council of Europe did not live up to federalist expectations. Instead, it represented 'a triumph of the unionists', a group not particularly inclined to federalists ideas.[71] In particular, the Council of Europe was endowed with a consultative Assembly formed by members appointed by national parliaments, whose role was confined merely to the sphere of issuing recommendations to a Committee of Ministers. But even the latter was given the modest power of issuing recommendations to national governments, thus being incapable of enforcing its own unanimous decisions. Its influence rested on the seriousness with which national governments considered its recommendations.[72]

Moreover, it remained ultimately unaccountable either to the Assembly or to national parliaments, a reality which forced Beyen to observe that the Committee 'is not really in any sense a responsible body: it is not an organ at all'.[73] Described by Pentland as 'an almost invisible functionalist workshop promoting intergovernmental co-operation by means of consensus and specialised standing conferences,'[74] the Council of Europe failed to replace the classical dogma of state sovereignty with what the federalists had in mind: a federal entity capable of influencing the political culture of its sub-units.

At the time, however, that the federal movement was losing its original momentum and whatever popular appeal it initially displayed, an alternative method of institutional development started to consolidate its strength: Monnet's 'functional federalism'. Being functionalist in conception but federalist in prospect, this approach represented a new, albeit modest, integration philosophy which would finally shape the future of Western Europe. The term 'functional federalism' has been employed as an analytical tool to explain the composite character of Monnet's gradualist approach: an eclectic synthesis of elements of functionalism and neo-functionalism, without being fully in accord with either of them. For instance, Monnet's pragmatism did not share Mitrany's concern for the development of a 'socio-psychological community' at the popular level as a precondition for any viable transfer of sovereignty and of citizens' loyalties from the nation-state to international institutions.[75] Rather, his method seemed more in line with Haas's dictum that 'functional integration requires pluralism' in the sense of involving processes like the joint lobbying of organised interests, the *engrenage* of national and international bureaucracies and the active participation of governments in complex negotiations.[76]

Monnet's 'functional strategy of elite bargaining' does not essentially depart from the neofunctionalist-inspired process of 'elite socialisation'.[77] But it does deviate from Mitrany's understanding of 'the integrative dynamic' which, Taylor notes, 'is the learning process of citizens who are gradually drawn into the co-operative ethos created by functionally specific international institutions devoted to the satisfaction of real welfare needs'.[78] In Mutimer's words: 'neofunctionalism… provides relative rigorous formulation of the means of political integration developed *ad hoc* by Jean Monnet and his colleagues in the 1950s'.[79] Or, as Milward and Sørensen put it: 'the theory's technocratic elitism appealed strongly to European Community officials who naturally saw the extensive theorising about the workings of the Community as a confirmation of their historical role as guardians of European integration processes'.[80]

Although Monnet has explicitly stated in his *Memoirs* that Europe was above all a 'moral idea',[81] his emphasis on 'concrete achievements' and 'continuing change', rather than on 'grand designs', made him look more of a 'functionalist' and less of an 'incremental federalist'.[82] But his original and ultimate goal was, like Spinelli's, a European federation. Their main difference, however, was that for Monnet this goal was never an *idée fixe* but rather part of his 'controlled idealism': the ability to combine the 'desirable' with the 'feasible' in a single integrative blueprint. As he stated in his autobiography, he was 'a man of beginnings' who firmly believed that 'anticipating the result blocks the spirit of invention'.[83] To borrow from Burgess: 'Monnet seems to have been an advocate of federalism without ever having been a federalist'.[84] But let us now offer some further insights into the two basic components of the gradualist approach to integration: functionalism and neofunctionalism.[85]

Convinced that the unification of Europe was not so much interested in end-products as in evolutionary steps and processes, the functionalists criticised the federal alternative for being totally impractical and idealistic, 'offering,' in Harrison's words, 'merely the prospect of the unattainable'.[86] Instead, by recognising that integration – seen as a *process* and not as a *condition* – had nothing to do with formal constitution-making, they stressed the point that Europe cannot be unified 'by a stroke of the constitutional lawyer's pen'.[87] In general, they criticised the federalists as advocates of an immediate objective which was largely overtaken by a naive sentimentalism, deceiving themselves with the illusion of radical political change. Likewise, Spinelli's proposed pathway to unification was viewed as over-ambitious and legalistic, resting on the fallacious assumption that the termination of the war had also signalled the 'withering away of the nation state,' to use Mitrany's terms.[88]

Most important of all, the federalist project was believed to be consciously undermining the necessary gradualness of the integration process in order to achieve a rigid constitutional settlement, thus losing sight of the dynamics of 'functional incrementalism' as one of its dominant characteristics. Moreover, the functionalist conception of 'Union' was part of an evolutionary process of achieving functionally-specific objectives, and not of a deterministic situation leading, either immediately or necessarily, towards a federal state (or state-like entity). Although it would be wrong to assume that the functionalists saw federalism as an uncontrolled homogenising force eroding national diversity, they maintained that it was in the interests of integration itself to proceed in a piecemeal fashion for fear that a federal surrender of sovereignty would be too big a sacrifice for national governments on the altar of their unification.

The key concept of the functional method can be identified in the perception of a common interest among the various actors involved in the integration process. This was vitally important for Europe to develop the necessary machinery to produce common policies and decisions. Thus the pursuit of common tasks was linked from the outset with the creation of common institutions possessing a responsibility of their own, albeit limited in scope. As Kitzinger has pointed out, the main difference between functionalists and federalists was that whereas the former were preoccupied with defining the 'general interest' first, and then finding common answers to common problems, the latter sought joint action as a means for obtaining more effective central institutions.[89] Being confined to technical and economic areas, functional integration does not postulate the creation of a new sovereign power at a higher level. Instead, by trying to eschew politics, in terms of depoliticising communal issues rather than being inherently apolitical itself, it presents no immediate challenge to the sovereignty of states.[90] In short, the 'functional imperative', as the law governing the evolution of integration, rejected the inevitability of constitutional requirements, focusing on problems which, although they cannot be ignored, cannot be solved separately by each government acting alone. This has been termed the 'unitary trap'.[91]

The functionalist approach to integration, which soon became the prototype on which most European activities were to be based, was practically illustrated in the 1950 Schuman Plan, proposing the establishment of 'supranational' institutions for regulating the European coal and steel industries, and resolving, in a mutually acceptable way, the long-standing Franco-German rivalry. According to Bowie, far from trying to create at once a fully-fledged federation, the plan was to set up institutions patterned on the federal model, but with authority limited to a specific function.[92] In general terms, if the process inaugurated by the Schuman Plan is seen in the light of the desperate realities of the day, then its final product, namely the European Coal and Steel Community (ECSC), represented too moderate an alternative to early federalist proposals for the establishment of a European Government based on popular consent.

It was only in the eyes of the most optimistic functionalists, later to be called neofunctionalists, that an inner compulsion towards integration was evident from the outset, in that the creation of common institutions would set in motion a process for the accumulation of wider functions, leading towards the creation of a 'political community'.[93] The underlying assumption here was that the very incompleteness of the project would create the need for new central arrangements and, in time, for a directly elected European Parliament to ensure democratic control over the larger, and by then federated, European polity. For the moment, however, direct democratic legitimacy was not viewed as a prerequisite for the political management of the larger entity.

Moreover, the neofunctionalists, by abandoning the central integrative role of attitudinal change, whilst exhibiting a strong normative commitment to elite-driven integration, placed the emphasis on a 'procedural consensus' about the institutional rules of the game: they stressed 'the psychology of elites in an integration process ideally culminating in the emergence of a new political system...'[94] Further, they conceptualised integration as resulting from what Haas called an 'institutionalised pattern' of interest politics.[95] Such concentration on institutional developments had important implications on their conception of sovereignty. Taylor writes: '[neofunctionalists] implicitly accepted the view that sovereignty is strengthened by an expanding legal competence'.[96] Like the older functionalism, neofunctionalism allows for an open-ended single terminal condition of integration. Attributes like 'political community', 'supranational authority', 'federal union' and so on, add little to the precise institutional form the end-product is expected to take. Perhaps the only relatively discernible outcome of integration in neofunctionalist terms is the creation of what Harrison called a 'self-regulating pluralist society'.[97]

In conclusion, Monnet's incremental method was far too limited in scope, and heavily reliant on 'a combination of benevolent technocrats and interest-propelled economic groups to build transnational coalitions in support of European policies'.[98] Hence, the ECSC was an instrument for reaching decisions above the state level without, however, disposing of (national) political power in areas 'which normally demand a real government'.[99] What is also important is the institutional implications of

Monnet's method, and the way in which the concepts of democracy and technocracy fit in its context. To properly address this issue, we need to give an account of ECSC institutions and then link our analytical findings with the second *relance*, and subsequent failure, of federalist projects in the mid-1950s, and up to the signing of the Rome Treaties in March 1957. But let us first summarise the basic properties of the different theoretical approaches discussed so far, in the following table.

Table 6.1 Basic properties of European integration theories

	Federalism	**Functionalism**	**Neofunctionalism**
Basic premises	'Unity in diversity' (Montesquieu)	'Form follows function' (Mitrany)	'Functional integration requires pluralism' (Haas)
Key actors	Bicameral legislature (Double democratic legitimacy)	International civil service (management committee government)	Enlightened technocracy (rational problem-solving, internationalisation of power)
Process dynamic	Popular constituent assembly (constituent process)	Technical self-determination (internationalisation of domestic issues)	Spill-over effect (Expansive logic of integration)
Operational Framework	Co-ordinate but independent spheres of government (fixed division of competences)	Enmeshment process (technical administration and decision-making)	'Community method' (Commission initiative, Council-Commission dialogue and joint lobbying of organised interests)
Integrative conditions	Formal constitution-making (politicisation of issues)	Popular consensus (depoliticisation of issues, functional interdependence)	Procedural concensus (Institutionalised pattern/ elite socialisation
Constitutional implications	Creation of sovereignty (higher legal order)	Retention of sovereignty (identifiability of states)	Pooling of sovereignty (system of shared management)
Form of democracy	Federal democracy (constitutionalism)	Working democracy (associationalism)	Pluralist democracy (elitism)
Envisaged polity	Federation or federal state	Network of international functional agencies	Self-regulating pluralist society

FUNCTIONALISM AND DEMOCRACY RECONSIDERED

The institutional blueprint of the ECSC included a curious mixture of supranational or federal-like institutions, its greatest innovation being the High Authority (HA). Such a body was to act as the central executive of the ECSC and its decisions were to apply directly to the member states. Its members were chosen as individuals, and were given the explicit mandate not to receive instructions from national governments; their task was to upgrade the 'Community interest' independently of the demands expressed by national governments. With regard to the Council of Ministers, its primary task was to approve or reject policy measures proposed by the High Authority either by majority voting or unanimity according to the issue in question. The third institutional component of the ECSC was the Common Assembly, a body composed of national parliamentarians mainly entrusted with advisory powers. Although it had no real impact on the central legislative process, it could dismiss the High Authority as a body through the passing of a motion of censure, requiring a two-thirds majority. Finally, a Court of Justice was established to ensure adherence by the other ECSC institutions to the provisions of the Treaty.

Monnet's quasi-federal edifice had to a certain extent departed from the traditional type of international organisation. It can be better classified as a partial economic confederation: partial, since it did not cover all the economic relations among the member states; and confederal, since the states did not cease to be states by joining the wider association. After a careful qualification of its 'embryonic' federal structure, one could argue that, far from implying any straightforward threat to the sovereignty of the member states, the ECSC represented a system of pooled responsibilities and resources in functionally-specific areas for the fulfilment of joint tasks. Monnet was perfectly aware of the fact that national governments would never have agreed to relinquish their individual sovereignties to a powerful European Government, and least of all immediately. In his view, the 'second-best' way to move towards unification was by small incremental steps in areas where sovereignty was not seriously challenged, that is mainly in technical and economic co-operation.

It was also believed that as more and more activities came under the control of supranational agencies, national barriers of all types would eventually be eroded, creating new pressures for widening the Community's democratic bases. At that time, however, its daily operation relied on a numerically small technocratic elite of policy-makers. Thus it was not political responsibility but 'technocratic unaccountability' that was the hallmark of its institutional infrastructure. In addition to that, Pinder observes, no one appeared to have foreseen how much the

Council would come to dominate ECSC politics 'as the political structures of member states came to assert themselves against the realisation of the federal idea'.[100] This institution gained in importance over time, ensuring that the European construction remains predominately intergovernmental in the sense that it was the member governments alone, rather than a central political authority beyond their boundaries, that effectively defined the 'rules of the game'.

Whereas for the European federalists the device of constitutionally entrenched democratic arrangements was the premise rather than the consequence, for the adherents of Monnet's method, the complete fulfilment of the purposes of integration depended on the successful operation of functional institutions, with democracy having to follow rather than precede any move towards an 'ever closer union'. To underline the federalist point, while integration could not survive without democracy, since the former cannot solely depend on the convergence of short-term interests among national governments, Monnet's functionalism implied that integration was an 'elite-pull' rather than a 'mass-push' phenomenon, guided by 'interest politics' and not by popular political sentiments.[101] These differences between Monnet and Spinelli's orthodoxy became manifest when the next step towards federal integration was proposed: the creation of the European Defence Community, counterbalanced in democratic terms by the European Political Community.

In the autumn of 1950, Monnet persuaded French Prime Minister Pleven to endorse the idea of a common European army made up of national units but operating as one force under a joint command. A few months later, the idea was approved by the French National Assembly, 348 to 224. The partisans of the Pleven Plan, as the project was named, or *cédistres*, immediately sought to grasp the opportunity for extending its scope through the foundation of a supranational political authority. The rationale behind the formation of the EPC was that the EDC's implied limitations on national sovereignty could never enjoy the consent of national parliaments unless accompanied by a democratic political centre to control the new military force.[102] In this way, both national parliaments and their electors would know how such an authority would be organised, administer its own powers and be held publicly accountable.[103] Art. 38 of the EDC Draft Treaty mandated the envisaged Assembly to propose plans for putting the EDC 'on a democratic basis', and for integrating its political framework with that of ECSC within a 'federal or confederal structure'.

Soon after the EDC Treaty was signed in May 1952 by the 'Original Six', there was an increased belief that Art. 38 could be carried ahead of schedule. To this end, a Constitutional Committee, chaired by Spaak, urged the Six to entrust the Common Assembly of the ECSC with the task of undertaking the role of a constituent body, called the 'Ad Hoc Assembly'. On 10 September 1952, the inaugural meeting of the ECSC Council opened the way for the Assembly to prepare the constitutional draft. The EPC Statute envisaged the establishment of a parliamentary form of federal union based on a bicameral legislature, an Executive Council and a High Court.

The legislature comprised a Peoples' Chamber that was to be directly elected by universal suffrage, and a Senate composed of delegates selected by national parliaments;[104] the executive was to be headed by a President chosen by the Senate, its other members being subject to the approval of the lower house. This was an important reinforcement of those who preferred a confederal structure. Through that body, the states, by retaining their right of veto, could maintain their sovereignty. However, it was to be held politically responsible to both houses, which also retained the right to censure it. Finally, the High Court was to be chosen 'with the participation of the Senate, upon nomination of the several states on an equal basis'.[105]

Overall, the proposed draft was a balanced mixture of federal and confederal structures, exercising supranational functions as defined by the treaties. Since the EPC project was based on a bicameral legislature and the principle of the separation of powers, it is hardly surprising that federalists attached to it so much importance. Also, the EPC had the additional power, as compared to the ECSC and EDC, to levy taxes directly on citizens as well as to progressively build a common market. In the end, however, these hopes collapsed when the French Parliament failed to ratify its Statute in August 1954, putting an end to the EPC project as well, and with it to the prospects for a more democratic relationship between peoples and central institutions.

Once more, the limits of integration played an adverse role in redressing Europe's 'federal deficit'. And, if we subscribe to Bosco's view that 'the ECSC succeeded because it did not involve the creation of a federal state,'[106] we can perhaps understand the deeper reasons for the collapse of both projects. Not surprisingly, the next step to integration was based again on Monnet's approach, this time concentrating its efforts on the economic aspects of unification, namely the creation of a Common Market. The European Economic Community (EEC), product of the Messina *relance* in 1955, by remaining 'remarkably similar to that designed between May and July 1950,'[107] fell short of enhancing the democratic ethos of integration. Instead, it approximated more closely a standing diplomatic conference in which the member states retained the right to block any decision of which they strongly disapproved.

In conclusion, Spinelli's famous dictum 'federate or perish' was overwhelmed by what Burgess has referred to as 'a vision of a Europe united by a bureaucracy,'[108] involving a partial sharing of national sovereignty. By the late 1950s, the 'maximalist' conception of Europe, resting on a directly elected European Parliament possessing substantive controlling and legislative powers, an executive council collectively responsible to the European peoples, and a Constitutional Court on the lines of the American judiciary, was in retreat. As Monnet has summarised the debate: 'I have never believed that one fine day Europe would be created by some great political mutation, and I thought it wrong to consult the peoples of Europe about the structure of a community of which they had no practical experience'.[109] Partly in response to this confession, Spinelli has commented that 'Monnet has the great merit of having created Europe and the great responsibility to have built it badly'.[110]

EUROPEAN FEDERALISM AND ITS CRITICS

The early school of European federalist thought, by relying on the American federal experience, seemed to have undermined the *sui generis* character of postwar European integration. In their unrestrained passion for a united Europe, Beloff asserts, federalists were misguided in looking to the US pattern for a promising analogy.[111] For this 'self-created people', united under the new federal compact, 'was the constituent power which created and shaped the new republican state… reduced the powers of the states and aided those of the general government… in such a way that their application could be extended as new needs arose'.[112] At the same time, each component state 'was considered to have an "individuality" which made it the primary political community of its particular people'.[113] In Albertini's words: 'as a new form of the modern state, federalism is an American product. But the United States of America had not to overcome historically-constituted nations to constitute itself'.[114]

By contrast, the federal conception of Europe was not only based on the fallacious premise that the traditional nation-state had nothing else to offer its citizens, but it has also profoundly overestimated the popular impulse to integrative schemes. As a result, they failed to recognise that their vision was not the primary goal for a sufficient number of Europeans, and also that the principles of federal democracy did not acquire sufficient persuasive power to win the confidence of national governments. But most significant of all was the fact that both 'unionists' and 'centralists', unlike their American counterparts whose 'frequent division into "conservatives" and "radicals" actually helped them arrive at a balanced and practical consensus,'[115] failed to understand each other, leaving their original confrontation at the Hague Congress to mark the whole post-1945 history of the federal movement.

On the other hand, it would be unjust not to reiterate the commitment of European federalists towards a democratic process of integration, and their opposition to an essentially utilitarian basis of (economic) interest-convergence as a precondition for any public loyalty transfers. For they have unequivocally maintained, time and again, that parliamentary democracy was too closely related to the political traditions of Western European states to be denied at a level beyond them. Finally, it was they who first stressed the importance of linking the idea of a European constitution with the legitimation of the larger political edifice based on an open parliamentary system so that any transfer of sovereignty from national to common institutions be immediately counteracted by transparent structures of indirect *demos* control.

From these reflections, one may conclude that the emergent democratic deficiencies in the institutional structures of both the ECSC and EEC are strongly linked to the fact that their governing processes did not arise out of a genuine federal blueprint based on the active and understanding consent of citizens, but rather from two international treaties negotiated under the conditions of 'summit diplomacy' by states: the Treaty of Paris, named as the 'Treaty of Laws' after its detailed legalistic nature, and the Treaty of Rome, often described as a 'framework treaty' because of its open-ended character. Indeed, both blueprints fell short of providing the necessary popular authority and democratic guarantees for the proper functioning of the regional system, thus confirming Featherstone's assertion that 'technocrats had to build Europe first before the politicians and the people could get their hands on it'.[116]

Summing up the political lessons to be learned from the early federalist attempts to create a 'union of individuals in a body politic', as opposed to a 'union of states in a body politic,'[117] the prevalence of Monnet's 'functional federalism' produced no such grass-roots politics as those envisaged by Spinelli. In defence of Monnet, Holland asserts that 'before effective democratisation could be introduced the Community had to prove itself worthy of supranational authority'.[118] What is actually missing from this view is the recognition that 'democracy across borders' is not about giving formal power over a 'supranational' centre, but rather it is about the mobilisation of popular consent which can effectively sustain joint decisions.

To underline the point, transnational democracy is about the generation of a genuine commitment by the *demoi* of the 'component' parts to the prospects of creating an 'inclusive' whole founded upon the democratic functions of government. In a word, only a European *demos* can create a truly democratic Union.[119] Assessing the democratic properties of these two competing approaches, Bosco has remarked: 'the disadvantage of Monnet's strategy is that it cannot be carried out in a democratic manner because it requires European decisions which are no longer controlled by national parliaments and not yet controlled by the European Parliament... The advantages of Spinelli's strategy are derived from the fact that with federal power as the starting point it would be up to European democracy to determine the ways and means, structures and deadlines for European unification'.[120]

POLITICS AS THE ART OF CREATING THE POSSIBLE

Spinelli's method recognised that those individuals who are to come under the federal compact must be moved by such strong 'we-feelings' as to propel them not only to use this 'instrument of government' but also to support its outcomes. 'That means,' Beer notes, 'having opinions, expressing them in political organisations, taking part in public debate, voting in elections and accepting the disappointments of defeat as well as seeking the joys of victory'.[121] In this sense, the gains of those committed to a federal Europe have not matched their far-reaching democratic claims. Although such a distinctive account of the genesis and exegesis of the democratic deficit seems to be only a partial illustration of its composite character, it does suggest, albeit with a touch of concealed idealism, that for some people politics is something more than merely 'the art of the possible': it is the art of *creating* the possible.

Notes on Chapter 6

1   See Mitrany, David (1943), *A Working Peace System* (Chicago, 1966 Quadrangle Books); Haas, Ernst B., *The Uniting of Europe: Political Social and Economic Forces 1950-1957* (London, 1958, Stevens & Sons).

2   The term has been initially employed by Chiti-Batelli to describe a 'middle-way' approach to international integration, based on such premises as 'federation through functional arrangements' or 'utilising functionalism for the federal cause'. This moderate path to unification has found practical appeal in the mixed nature of integration in the early 1950s, in that it was functionalist in strategy and federalist in prospect. For details see Chiti-Batelli, Andrea, 'Functional Federalism', *Common Cause*, April 1950, pp 472-7;

and Mitrany, David, 'Functional Federalism', *Common Cause*, November 1950, pp 196-99. Cf Harrison, Reginald J., 'Neo-functionalism', in Groom, A.J.R. and Taylor, Paul (eds), *Frameworks for International Co-operation* (London, 1990, Pinter), p 139; and Burgess, Michael, *Federalism and European Union: Political Ideas, Influences and Strategies in the European Community, 1972-1987* (London and New York, 1989 Routledge), p 56.

3   Burgess, Michael, *Federalism and European Union*, p 43.

4   Conlan, Timothy, *New Federalism* (Washington DC, 1988, The Brookings Institution), p xxiv. Quoted in Bolick, Clint, 'European Federalism: Lessons from America', Occasional Paper No 93, (London, 1994 The Institute of Economic Affairs), p 9.

5   Dahl, Robert A., *Dilemmas of Pluralist Democracy: Autonomy vs Control* (New Haven and London, 1982, Yale University Press) p 5.

6   Friedrich, Carl J., 'Federal Constitutional Theory and Emergent Proposals' in Macmahon, Arthur W. (ed.), *Federalism: Mature and Emergent* (New York, 1955, Garden City), p 513. Some of their most important statements on the subject are Jean-Jacques Rousseau, *The Social Contract* (Harmondsworth, 1968, Penguin); and Immanuel Kant, 'Perpetual Peace' and 'Idea for a History with a Cosmopolitan Perspective', in Reiss, Hans (ed.), *Kant's Political Writings* (Cambridge, 1970, Cambridge University Press), pp 93-130 and pp 41-53 respectively.

7   Levi, Lucio, 'European Elections and International Democracy' in Bosco, Andrea (ed.), *The Federal Idea: The History of Federalism Since 1945* vol. II (London and New York, 1992, Lothian Foundation Press), p 289.

8   Quoted in *ibid.*

9   Quoted in *ibid.*, pp 287-8.

10   *Ibid.*, pp 288-9.

11   Quoted in *ibid*, pp 287-8.

12   According to Wheare's classic definition, the federal principle refers to a 'method of dividing powers so that general and regional governments are each, within a sphere, co-ordinated and independent'. See Wheare, Kenneth C., *Federal Government*, Third edn (London, 1953, Oxford University Press), p 11. For Hamilton's quotation see Levi, Lucio, 'European Elections and International Democracy', p 289; and Beloff, Max (ed.), *The Federalist, or the New Constitution*, No 9, Second edn (Oxford, 1987, Basil Blackwell), p 38.

13   Levi, Lucio, 'European Elections and International Democracy', p 288 and p 290.

14   Friedrich, Carl J., 'Federal Constitutional Theory and Emergent Proposals', p 513.

15   On these points see Hadenius, Alex, 'The Duration of Democracy: Institutional vs Socio-economic Factors', in Beetham, David (ed.), *Defining and Measuring Democracy* (London, 1994, Sage), p 73.

16 Watts, Ronald L., 'Federalism, Regionalism, and Political Integration', in Cameron, David M. (ed.), *Regionalism and Supranationalism: Challenges and Alternatives to the Nation-State in Canada and Europe* (London, 1981, The Institute for Research on Public Policy), p 10.

17 *Ibid.*, p 13.

18 King, Preston, 'Federation and Representation', in Burgess, Michael and Gagnon, Alain-G. (eds), *Comparative Federalism and Federation* (New York, 1993, Harvester Weatsheaf), pp 95-6. Cf his *Federalism and Federation* (London and Canberra, 1982, Croom Helm), pp 88-95.

19 *Ibid.*, p 96. According to Elazar, 'one of the characteristics of federalism that flows from its popular base is the reduction of the question of political sovereignty to an incidental one'. He concludes: 'the federal principle represents an alternative to (and a radical attack upon) the modern idea of sovereignty'. See Elazar, Daniel J., *Exploring Federalism* (Tuscaloosa, 1987, The University of Alabama Press), pp 108-9.

20 *Ibid.* King writes: 'It is precisely because of this (minimal) dual principle of representation that federations have often been supposed to be unstable or evanescent. Duality of representation, however, has nothing to do with fragility and impermanence...the inclination to see federations in particular as abstractly less permanent than other forms, as structurally prone to either dissolution or seamless integration, has no basis in it.'

21 Watts, Ronald L., 'Federalism, Regionalism, and Political Integration', pp 13-14.

22 In speaking of such 'levels' one might assume that they are sharply separated from each other, 'like boxes piled on top of one another', to use Friedrich's visual metaphor. In reality, however, as the author makes explicit, these different levels of government are never thus sharply divided. See Friedrich, Carl J., *Trends of Federalism in Theory and Practice* (London, 1968, Pall Mall Press), p 3.

23 Harrison, Reginald J., *Europe in Question: Theories of Regional International Integration* (London, 1974, Allen & Unwin), p 43.

24 Burgess, Michael, 'The European Tradition of Federalism: Christian Democracy and Federalism', in Burgess, Michael and Gagnon, Alain-G. (eds), *Comparative Federalism and Federation*, p 149. The second quotation is taken from Fremantle, Anne (ed.), *The Papal Encyclicals in their Historical Context* (London, 1963, Mentor-Omega), p 420.

25 Quoted in Burgess, Michael, 'Federalism as Political Ideology: Interests, Benefits and Beneficiaries in Federalism and Federation', in Burgess, Michael and Gagnon, Alain-G. (eds), *Comparative Federalism and Federation*, p 109.

26 Friedrich, Carl J., 'Federal Constitutional Theory and Emergent Proposals', p 518.

27 Vile, M.J.C., *The Structure of American Federalism* (London and New York, 1962, Oxford University Press), p 199.

28 Levi, Lucio, 'Recent Developments in Federalist Theory', in Levi, Lucio (ed.), *Altiero Spinelli and Federalism in Europe and in the World* (Milano, 1990, Franco Angeli), p 37.

29 Friedrich, Carl J., 'Federal Constitutional Theory and Emergent Proposals', p 517. He defines federalism as 'the *process of federalising a political community*, as the process by which a number of separate political organizations, be they states or any other kind of associations, enter into arrangements for making joint decisions on joint problems, or reversely the process by which a hitherto unitary political organisation becomes decentralised to the point where separate and distinct political communities arise and become politically organised and capable of making separate decisions on distinct problems'. See p 514. For an illuminating account of the doctrine of the separation of powers see Vile, M.J.C., *Constitutionalism and the Separation of Powers*, (Oxford, 1967, Clarendon Press), pp 1-20.

30 *Ibid.*, p 519.

31 Gagnon, Alain-G., 'The Political Uses of Federalism', in Burgess, Michael and Gagnon, Alain-G. (eds), *Comparative Federalism and Federation*, p 27.

32 Bowie, Robert R., 'The Process of Federating Europe', in Macmahon, Arthur W. (ed.), *Federalism: Mature and Emergent*, p 497.

33 *Ibid.*, p 496. For an account of past attempts to unite the continent see Bailey, Sydney D., *United Europe: A Short History of the Idea* (London, 1948, National News-Letter).

34 *Ibid.* Nevertheless, the success of the federal project would ultimately depend upon the foundation of a balance of interests and power between need and resistance.

35 *Ibid.*, p 497. In fact, Bowie writes: 'As important as its economic and political decline was the spiritual malaise that affected much of its population'. See p 495.

36 Burgess, Michael, *Federalism and European Union*, p 30. On the concepts of federalism and federation see his *Federalism and Federation in Western Europe* (London, 1986, Croom Helm), pp 15-33.

37 Harrison, Reginald J., *Europe in Question*, p 45.

38 Jameson, Storm, 'Federalism and a New Europe', in Channing-Pearce, Melville (ed.), *Federal Union: A Symposium* (London, 1991, Lothian Foundation Press), p 253 and p 249.

39 Draft Declaration by the European Resistance Movement, July 1944. Quoted in Kitzinger, Uwe, *The European Common Market and Community* (London, 1967, Routledge), pp 29-33.

40 Curry, W.B., 'Federalism and Democracy', in Channing-Pearce, Melville (ed.), *Federal Union: A Symposium*, p 133.

41   Kitzinger, Uwe, 'Time-Lags in Political Psychology', in Barber, James and Reeds, Bruce (eds), *European Community: Vision and Reality* (London, 1973, Croom Helm), p 8.

42   Bosco, Andrea, 'The Federalist Project and Resistance in Continental Europe', in Bosco, Andrea (ed.), *The Federal Idea: The History of Federalism Since 1945* vol. II, p 52. See Spinelli, Altiero and Rossi, Ernesto, *Il Manifesto di Ventotene* (Pavia, 1944), pp 19-20. Cf Albertini, Mario, 'The Ventotene Manifesto: The Only Road to Follow', in Levi, Lucio (ed.), *Altiero Spinelli and Federalism in Europe and in the World*, pp 127-40.

43   Spinelli, Altiero, 'European Union and the Resistance', *Government and Opposition*, April-July 1967, pp 321-9. Quoted in Ionescu, Ghita (ed.), *The New Politics of European Integration* (London, 1972, Macmillan), p 2.

44   Brailsford, H.N., *The Federal Idea* (London, 1939, Federal Union), pp 15-16.

45   For a similar discussion see Jameson, Storm, 'Federalism and a New Europe', p 255; and Bowie, Robert R., 'The Process of Federating Europe', p 496. The underlying assumption here is that 'unless we destroy the nation-state, the nation-state will destroy us'. As Robbins put it, the 'remedy' is plain: 'independent sovereignty must be limited'. See Robbins, Lionel, *The Economic Causes of War* (London, 1939, Jonathan Cape), pp 104-5. For Mitrany, however, 'the real issue is not between federalism and some other loose political form, but between social performance through national action or through international planning and action'. See Mitrany, David, 'Functional Federalism', p 199.

46   Smith, Gordon, 'The Crisis of the West European State', in Cameron, David M. (ed.), *Regionalism and Supranationalism*, p 22.

47   *Ibid.*, p 25.

48   Levi, Lucio, 'Altiero Spinelli, Mario Albertini and the Italian Federalist School: Federalism as Ideology', in Bosco, Andrea (ed.), *The Federal Idea: The History of Federalism Since 1945* vol. II, p 214.

49   *Ibid.*, p 217.

50   Bosco, 'The Federalist Project and Resistance in Continental Europe', p 51.

51   Levi, Lucio, 'Recent Developments in Federalist Theory', p 66.

52   *Ibid.*, p 55.

53   Pentland, Charles, *International Theory and European Integration* (London, 1973, Faber and Faber), p 170.

54   Bosco, Andrea, 'What is Federalism? Towards a General Theory of Federalism', paper presented at the Second World-ECSA Conference on 'Federalism, Subsidiarity and Democracy in the European Union', Brussels, May 1994, p 4.

55   Watts, Ronald L., 'Federalism, Regionalism, and Political Integration', p 12.

56   Harrison, Reginald J., *Europe in Question*, p 44. Cf Greilsammer, Ilan, 'Some Observations on European Federalism', in Elazar, Daniel J. (ed.), *Federalism*

and Political Integration (Ramat Gan, 1979, Turtledove), pp 107-31; and McWhinney, Edward, *Federal Constitution-Making for a Multinational World*, (Leyden, 1966, A. W. Sijthoff), pp 112-22.

57   Levi, Lucio, 'Recent Developments in Federalist Theory', p 62. Cf Watts, Ronald L., 'Federalism, Regionalism, and Political Integration', p 4.

58   Friedrich, Carl J., *Trends of Federalism in Theory and Practice*, p 176. As Pentland asserts, 'federalism thus accepts the possibility of multiple levels of political orientation: men can participate in and feel loyalty to several sets of political institutions at the same time and in the same space without experiencing inner conflict'. See Pentland, Charles, *International Theory and European Integration*, p 174.

59   Pinder, John, 'The New European Federalism: The Idea and the Achievements', in Burgess, Michael and Gagnon, Alain-G. (eds), *Comparative Federalism and Federation*, p 45.

60   *Ibid.*

61   Mayne, Richard *et al.*, *Federal Union: The Pioneers* (London, 1990, Macmillan), p 91.

62   Pinder, John, 'The New European Federalism: The Idea and the Achievements', p 45.

63   Quoted in Lindsay, Kenneth, *European Assemblies: The Experimental Period 1949-1959* (London, 1960, Stevens & Sons) p xiv.

64   Pistone, Sergio, 'Altiero Spinelli and a Strategy for the United States of Europe', in Bosco, Andrea (ed.), *The Federal Idea: The History of Federalism from the Enlightenment to 1945*, vol. I (London and New York, 1991, Lothian Foundation Press), pp 351-7. For a more recent account of the federal legacy of Altiero Spinelli see Burgess, Michael, 'Federal Ideas in the European Community: Altiero Spinelli and European Union', *Government and Opposition*, Summer 1984, pp 339-47.

65   Bosco, Andrea, 'What is Federalism?', p 9.

66   *Ibid.*, p 2.

67   Friedrich, Carl J., 'Federal Constitutional Theory and Emergent Proposals', p 517.

68   Pistone, Sergio, 'Altiero Spinelli and a Strategy for the United States of Europe', p 354. Levi, Lucio, 'The Federalist Papers and the Choices Before the American People', in Bosco, Andrea (ed.), *The Federal Idea*, vol. I, pp 29-38.

69   An excellent comparative study of the politics of European integration and the American federal experience is provided by Elazar, Daniel J. and Greilsammer, Ilan, 'Federal Democracy: The USA and Europe Compared: A Political Science Perspective', in Cappelletti, Mario *et al.* (eds), *Integration Through Law*, vol. 1, book 1 (Berlin and New York, 1986, Walter de Gruyter), pp 71-167.

70　Bosco, Andrea, 'What is Federalism?', p 2.

71　De Rougemont, Denis, 'The Campaign of European Congresses', in Ionescu, Ghita (ed.), *The New Politics of European Integration*, p 25.

72　Lindsay, Kenneth, *European Assemblies: The Experimental Period 1949-1959*, p 75.

73　This point was made by Beyen in his opening address to the 1951 Hague Conference on European Assemblies. Quoted in *ibid.*, p 18.

74　Pentland, Charles, 'Political Theories of European Integration: Between Science and Ideology', in Lasok, Dominik and Soldatos, Panayotis (eds), *The European Communities in Action* (Brussels, 1981, Brylond), p 553.

75　This type of community, Taylor notes, stresses superordinate 'co-operative' goals without, however, posing any apparent threat 'to the existing cultural attachments of groups and individuals'. See Taylor, Paul, 'Introduction', in Mitrany, David, *The Functional Theory of Politics* (London, 1976, Martin Robertson), p x.

76　For this quotation see Haas, Ernst B., *Beyond the Nation State: Functionalism and International Organization* (Stanford, 1964, Stanford University Press), p 447. Yet Haas states that 'pluralism must be redefined to allow for its "industrializing" and "post-industrial" variants' and that 'pluralism at the national level must be differentiated from its international manifestations'.

77　This process exists when 'the immediate participants in the policy-making process, from interest groups to bureaucrats and statesmen, begin to develop new perspectives, loyalties and identifications as a result of their mutual interactions'. See Lindberg, Leon N. and Scheingold, Stuart A., *Europe's Would-Be Polity: Patterns of Change in the European Community* (Englewood Cliffs NJ, 1970, Prentice-Hall), p 119. Quoted in Harrison, Reginald J., 'Neofunctionalism', p 144.

78　Taylor, Paul, 'The Concept of Community and the European Integration Process', *Journal of Common Market Studies*, December 1968, p 86. Further, from a certain body of democratic theory, that of 'functional democracy', Mitrany's functionalism should not be dismissed as undemocratic due to the distrust it places on traditional Parliaments to exercise control over complex processes of public policy-making. Guided by the quest to watch closely for the 'relation of things', Mitrany argued his case for replacing old-style, non-specialist assemblies by new forms of representation and ways of obtaining public control such as 'functional' assemblies composed of experts whose technical knowledge would guarantee greater and better efficiency in supervising governmental actions. In *The Functional Theory of Politics*, he noted that 'no-one would share in power who did not share in responsibility' and that 'the functional structure could be made a union of peoples... directly concerned in any specific function, by giving them functional representation'. See p 119. Mitrany's rationale was that 'in acquiring formal representative status, [pressure groups] also assume a corresponding democratic responsibility'. See p 261. No doubt, however, that this form of democracy, labelled by Mitrany himself as 'working democracy', as opposed to 'voting democracy', is seen by many democratic theorists as a hindrance to established notions of representative and responsible government. Others, like Hirst, are partly in favour of these views, that is, insofar as 'different forms of representation are not seen as a substitute for representative democracy, but rather as a supplement to it'. See Hirst, Paul, *Associative Democracy: New Forms of Economic and Social Governance*, (Cambridge, 1993, Polity Press), pp 16-17.

79 Mutimer, David, 'Theories of Political Integration', in Michelmann, Hans J. and Soldatos, Panayotis (eds), *European Integration: Theories and Approaches*, (Lanham, 1994, University Press of America), p 33.

80 Milward, Alan S. and Sørensen, Viebeke, 'Interdependence or Integration? A National Choice', in Milward, Alan S. *et al.*, *The Frontier of National Sovereignty: History and Theory 1945-1992* (London and New York, 1993, Routledge), p 3.

81 Monnet, Jean, *Memoirs* (New York, 1978, Doubleday and Co.), p 329.

82 See Burgess, Michael, *Federalism and European Union*, p 44. For the latter characterisation see Pinder, John, 'European Community and nation-state: a case for a neo-federalism?', *International Affairs*, January 1986, p 42.

83 Quoted in Fontaine, Francois, 'Forward with Monnet', in Douglas Brinkley and Hackett, Clifford (eds), *Jean Monnet: The Path to European Unity* (London, 1991, Macmillan), p 55.

84 Burgess, Michael, *Federalism and European Union*, p 51.

85 For differences between the two theories see Taylor, Paul, *The Limits of European Integration* (New York, 1983, Columbia University Press), pp 1-25.

86 Harrison, Reginald J., *Europe in Question*, p 48.

87 *Ibid.*

88 Mitrany, David, *The Functional Theory of Politics*, p 239.

89 See Kitzinger, Uwe, 'Time-Lags in Political Psychology', p 13. As a result, Kitzinger asserts, the functionalists sought 'to set up only that minimum of political institutions that was indispensable in order to direct the common action that was most urgently required'.

90 This point is analysed further in Taylor, Paul, 'Functionalism: The Approach of David Mitrany', in Groom, A.J.R. and Taylor, Paul (eds), *Frameworks for International Co-operation*, p 132. Taylor states: 'the functionalist approach, indeed, allows the view that there is no point at which the state would *necessarily* lose its sovereignty, in the sense that power would now need to be finally transferred, or that the state would lose its legal right to act, if it so wished, against the wishes of the functional agency'.

91 Quoted in Bosco, Andrea, 'What is Federalism?', p 15.

92 Bowie, Robert R., 'The Process of Federating Europe', pp 501-2.

93 The term 'political community' is used here in accordance with Haas's definition, that is, as 'a condition in which specific groups and individuals

show more loyalty to their central political institutions than to any other political authority'. See Haas, Ernst B., *The Uniting of Europe*, p 5.

94 Taylor, Paul, *The Limits of European Integration*, p 7.

95 Haas, Ernst B., *Beyond the Nation State*, p 35. Quoted in Taylor, 'The Concept of Community and the European Integration Process', p 87.

96 Taylor, Paul, 'The Concept of Community and the European Integration Process', p 87.

97 Harrison, Reginald J., 'Neo-functionalism', p 145.

98 Wallace, Helen, 'European Governance in Turbulent Times', *Journal of Common Market Studies*, September 1993, p 300. Quoted in Featherstone, Kevin, 'Jean Monnet and the "Democratic Deficit" in the European Union', *Journal of Common Market Studies*, June 1994, p 155.

99 Bosco, Andrea, 'What is Federalism?', p 18.

100 Pinder, John, *European Community: The Building of a Union* (Oxford, 1991, Oxford University Press), p 6.

101 Shepherd, Robert J., *Public Opinion and European Integration* (Farnborough, 1975, Saxon House), p 227.

102 Bodenheimer, Susanne J., *Political Union: A Microcosm of European Politics* (Leyden, 1967, A. W. Sijthoff), p 53.

103 Preda, Daniela, 'From a Defence Community to a Political Community: The Role of De Gasperi and Spinelli', in Bosco, Andrea (ed.), *The Federal Idea*, vol. II, p 192. For further details on the EPC plan see Cardozo, Rita, 'The Project for a Political Community (1952-54)', in Pryce, Roy (ed.), *The Dynamics of European Union* (London, 1987, Croom Helm), pp 49-77.

104 Friedrich, Carl J., 'Federal Constitutional Theory and Emergent Proposals', pp 505-6. For an excellent collection of information on the development of the EDC Draft Treaty and the EPC Statute see Bowie, Robert R. and Friedrich, Carl J. (eds), *Studies in Federalism* (Boston and Toronto, 1954, Little, Brown and Company).

105 *Ibid.*, p 523.

106 Bosco, Andrea, 'What is Federalism?', p 18.

107 Pinder, John, 'European Community and nation-state', p 43.

108 Burgess, Michael, *Federalism and European Union*, p 59. Quoted in Featherstone, Kevin, 'Jean Monnet and the "Democratic Deficit" in the European Union', p 150.

109 Quoted in *ibid.*, p 54. On Monnet's role during these formative years see Richard Mayne, 'The Role of Jean Monnet', *Government and Opposition*, April-July 1967, pp 349-71.

110 George Ball, 'Introduction', in Monnet, p 11. Quoted in Burgess, *Federalism and European Union*, pp 55-6.

111 Beloff, writing in *The Times*, asserted that 'what one is struck with is not the parallel... but the immensity of the difference'. He concludes: 'those who

believe in furthering European unity must seek elsewhere than in American federalism.' See Beloff, Max, 'False Analogies from Federal Example of United States', *The Times*, 4 May 1950. Quoted in Elazar, Daniel J. and Greilsammer, Ilan, 'Federal Democracy', p 71. Cf MacFarquhar, Roderick, 'The Community, the Nation-State and the Regions', in Burrows, Bernard *et al.* (eds), *Federal Solutions to European Issues* (London, 1978, Macmillan), pp 17-24.

112 Beer, Samuel H., 'What is Wrong with European Federalism?', in Hill, Stephen (ed.), *Visions of Europe*, p 119.

113 *Ibid.*, p 120. For an excellent account of the politics of American consti- tutionalism, see Bruce Ackerman, *We the People: Foundations* (Cambridge MA, 1991, Harvard University Press).

114 Quoted in Bosco, Andrea, 'What is Federalism?', p 13.

115 Beer, Samuel H., 'What is Wrong with European Federalism?', p 119.

116 Featherstone, Kevin, 'Jean Monnet and the "Democratic Deficit" in the European Union', p 160.

117 Burgess, Michael, *Federalism and European Union*, p 13.

118 Holland, Martin, *European Integration: From Community to Union* (London, 1994, Pinter), p 144.

119 From a federalist perspective, Beer has concluded: 'Only a European people can create a United States of Europe'. See Beer, Samuel H., 'What is Wrong with European Federalism?', p 121.

120 Bosco, Andrea, 'What is Federalism?', p 14.

121 See Beer, Samuel H., 'What is Wrong with European Federalism?', p 121.

PART IV

Contemporary
Reflections

CHAPTER 7

Confederal Consociation in Theory and Practice

THE CHALLENGE TO CONCEPTUAL INNOVATION

The theses presented so far as alternative interpretations of the genesis and exegesis of the democratic deficit, for all their analytical insights, fail to provide an overall explanatory framework. Even when taken as complementary, rather than mutually exclusive, to each other, they fall equally short of capturing the dominant character of the relationship between democracy and integration, as the latter has unfolded against the background of the two major revisions of the original treaties in the mid-1980s and early 1990s respectively. To that end, we introduce the concept of 'Confederal Consociation' in the already long list of relevant theories and models that comprise the fields of exploration. As in any other similar undertaking, so in the proposed typology, it is the creative tension between the 'familiar' and the 'unique' that lies behind the intellectual challenge of defining the political physiognomy of the Union.

Various pieces of evidence suggest that the consociational dimension of Union governance effectively weakens the infrastructure of transnational democracy by making 'executive-centred elites' the decisive subject of EU politics. In particular, the democratic pathology of the Union springs, by and large, from the fact that the management of integration rests firmly in the hands of national governmental elites which compromise the interests of responsible government in the name of decisional efficiency. The latter term is defined as the ability of the segment elites to reach amicable agreements through accommodationist patterns of joint decision-making.[1]

These problems are compounded by the fact that, on the basis of existing typologies, the Union still remains, almost axiologically, an unsolved puzzle: a 'half-way house' between the worlds of 'federal state'

and 'federal union of states'.[2] Although it is often taken to imply something more than the mere aggregate of its constituent units, political
authority has not yet moved towards a larger sovereign entity. It is thus
neither a 'conventional' international organisation, nor is it becoming an
ordinary state, as generally understood. Equally puzzling is the nature
of its legal structure, for some based on international treaty rules, whilst
others prefer to speak of an incipient constitutional system driven by aspirations similar to those involved in traditional state-building processes. In
terms of regional integration theory, although the Union is more than a
Deutschian 'pluralistic security-community', it has failed to meet either the
socio-psychological conditions of the older functionalists or those related
to the formation of a neofunctionalist-inspired 'political community'.

Profoundly uncrystallised in its political superstructure, the Union
remains an integrative venture whose final destination is yet to become
discernible. Attributes like 'partial polity' and 'part-formed political
system' clearly demonstrate the lack of confident scholarly assertion,[3]
rendering the whole enterprise 'a challenge to the continuing separation
of international relations from political science'.[4] But even without taking
into account the series of neologisms invented over time to describe its
distinctive political properties and functions, the vigorous intermeshing of
federal and confederal processes, and of centralised and decentralised
tendencies, render its institutional structure far from comprehensive in
the eyes of its citizens.

To simply argue, however, that the Union is nothing but yet another
sui generis political phenomenon, and should thus be examined either in
terms of new conceptual paradigms, or *ad hoc* theoretical interpretations,
or even a combination of both, runs the danger of complying with undis-
ciplined and often ill-founded formulations that perpetuate its present
stance in the vast grey area of 'normal interstate' and 'normal intrastate
relations'.[5] Embarking on this interminable search for a clear model, or
indeed for a less nebulous one, we claim that the construct of 'Confederal
Consociation' is the closest possible approximation to this particular stage
of EU development, as well as a promising analogy in filling the existing
gap between traditional state-centric and federalist-driven approaches to
European integration.[6]

CONCEPTUALISING THE UNION

As previously noted, the Union is largely unclassified as a system of governance. To give a brief account of the complexity surrounding the
subject: Wallace argues that what has now been created by member

governments is 'a constitutional system which has some state attributes, but which most – or all – of its constituent governments do not wish to develop into a state, even while expecting it to deliver outcomes which are hard to envisage outside the framework of an entity which we would recognise as a (federal) state'.[7] He concludes: 'The retreat from a federal objective for the European Community, while retaining a constitutional agenda which implied the need for a federal state-framework, has left a shadowy area at the centre of EC construction which substitute concepts such as "democratic deficit" and "subsidiarity"... have failed to illuminate'.[8] Hence, Sbragia asserts that it is perhaps more useful to think of the Union as 'an ongoing experiment in fashioning a new structure of governance, one that accepts a great deal of cultural diversity as well as incorporating politics based on the state-society model *and* politics based on relations between governments'.[9] Behind this statement lies the concept of *symbiosis* between national and transnational structures of government, adding credence to Kirchner, Bulmer and Wessels's insistence on using the German system of co-operative federalism as a model for explaining current integrative arrangements, as well as to Taylor's understanding of the constitutional implications of the symbiotic process for the sovereignty of states.[10]

McKay, for his part, has put it thus: 'What we have witnessed in Europe... is a movement towards federation which has indigenous rather than external roots, over which there is near-unanimity among elites and which has already produced real results in terms of the delineation of power between national and supra-national (or federal) authorities'.[11] Moravcsik, by developing a 'liberal intergovernmentalist' approach, describes the Community as a regime that makes interstate bargaining more efficient, whilst enhancing the autonomy of national leaders;[12] a definition close to Puchala's 'Concordance Systems' approach.[13] But whilst Wallace accepts that the Community is 'more than an inter-national regime but less than a fully-developed political system,' questioning whether it can be seen as 'a political "community" in the widest sense,'[14] Webb takes it to be 'a partially-integrated policy-making system at the regional level,'[15] making Cameron's 'institutionalised intergovernmentalism' sound like a relatively specific analogy.[16]

Writing on the inappropriateness of classical statist, purely intergovernmental, and traditional federal forms of organisation, Keohane and Hoffmann have visualised the evolving EU reality as 'an elaborate set of networks, closely linked in some ways, partially decomposed in others, whose results depend on the political style in the ascendant at the moment'.[17] But perhaps one of the most insightful analyses offered so far is Scharpf's 'joint-decision system' in which the pathology of public policy-making is conditioned by a 'systemic tendency towards sub-optimal substantive solutions'.[18] Embracing Wallace's dictum that the Union is 'stuck between sovereignty and integration', but recognising that the effectiveness of common policies are greatly influenced by what Taylor called the 'interdependence trap', Scharpf argues that the European polity 'seems to have become just that "middle ground between cooperation among nations and the breaking of a new one" which Stanley Hoffmann thought impossible'.[19] Although this statement contradicts our earlier view that progress towards the formation of a transnational *demos* should not be seen as a prelude to a European 'political nation', it certainly adds something to the current debate. If anything, the above scholarly review suggests that the questions of what exactly the Union is, or towards what it is developing, have yet to be sorted out.

Given the numerous conceptual and analytical difficulties in reaching an authoritative statement on its defining properties, we suggest that instead of placing undue emphasis on the peculiarities of the EU system, it is more profitable to examine those aspects of its internal organisation which can be paralleled, with a greater or lesser degree of accuracy, with already familiar models of governance. This is not to imply that new conceptual tools should not be employed, or that a new theoretical thesis should not be attempted to elucidate further the conditions and dynamics that constantly form and reform the transnational process. What it does suggest is that such a thesis will not only have to take into account pre-existing classifications, but also to use them constructively so as to substantiate its findings both theoretically and empirically. In Groom's words: 'There must be acknowledgement of the old Europe, but also a realisation that in building a new one, there are many original aspects that do not fit easily into the customary conceptual frameworks of integration theory'.[20]

In overall terms, the fusion of confederal and consociational elements in a new structure of collective governance aims to provide an alternative interpretation of EU political life to 'the thesis of federalism and the antithesis of intergovernmentalism' which stress either the influence of the central institutions or that of constituent governments, respectively.[21] And since the construct of Confederal Consociation derives its theoretical substance from Lijphart's general model of 'consociational democracy' and Forsyth's dynamic conception of confederation, eventually it takes the form of a creative synthesis of the two. Such a composite analysis of theories, concepts and knowledge drawn from the study of other discernible models of governance will help us to reconceptualise the rules of the integrative game, and explain why the Union still lacks a substantive relationship with its nascent, yet fragmented, *demos*. Having done this, it will be easier to evaluate the contribution of the TEU to the democratic properties of the transnational system (see chapter 8). As for now, it is to a closer examination of the model's conceptual ingredients that we wish to turn our attention.

THE CONCEPTS OF CONFEDERATION AND CONSOCIATION

To begin with the concept of confederation, just as a federal state differs essentially from a unitary one, so does a confederation from a federation. Whereas the latter is based on a constitutive act which gives birth to a higher, superordinate legal order, a confederation is based on a *foedus* or treaty among sovereign states, thus representing a 'contractual union of states' in which the participants voluntarily decide to band together by way of 'mutual agreement' in order to transform their existing patterns of relations into something akin, yet not identical, to the internal relations of one state.[22]

Sharma and Choudhry epitomised the distinction between these models thus: first, 'a confederation is a loose union over confederating independent states, whereas a federation is a union deriving its authority from the citizens of the union'; second, 'a confederation is the outcome of an agreement or treaty made generally for a specific period... whereas a federation is the result of a true constitution supreme over all other instruments from which both [levels of] government[s]... derive their respective powers'; third, 'in a confederation, the powers of the common body or authority are narrow and extremely limited, whereas in a federation the powers of the general government are wider, largely exclusive, and capable of being exercised through its own agencies'; fourth, 'in a confederation, the units are free to dissociate themselves from the union, whereas in a federation the units are united with the general government on a co-operative basis'; fifth, 'in a confederation the units retain their sovereignty, whereas in a federation the authority of government is shared by them with the general government'; and sixth, 'in a confederation the general government is subordinate to the regional governments, whereas in a federation the general government co-exists with the regional governments and is independent from them'.[23]

Seen from a different perspective, in the case of the confederation, a plurality of previously independent states gives way to a 'treaty-constituted political body',[24] in which 'the condition of "the last say"', to use Dahl's terms,[25] rests with the partners to it and not with an independent authoritative entity having a monopoly of legislative and coercive powers. Hence, Forsyth views confederation as being 'far more directly a contractual creature than the normal state', manifesting itself not as 'the constituted unity of one *people* or *nation*, but a unity constituted by *states*'.[26] He explains: 'the constitution of a confederation is not, by definition, the unilateral act of *one* people... considered as a homogeneous entity... a confederation is formed precisely because a nation or people in this sense is not deemed to exist, because the sense of identity and thus of trust between the citizens of each member state does not run to that depth'.[27]

In practice, confederation takes the form of a 'half-way house' between 'normal interstate' and 'normal intrastate relations', with the constituent units reserving the right of self-determination: 'a union that falls short of a complete fusion or incorporation in which one or all the members lose their identity as states'.[28] Or, as defined by Elazar: 'Several pre-existing polities joined together to form a common government for strictly limited purposes... that remains dependent upon its constituent polities in critical ways and must work through them'.[29] This type of union, similarly to a 'mutual pact' among self-determining body politics, signifies a 'joint agreement to be independent'.[30] Forsyth explains: 'The contract which lies at its base is not a contract to abide by the will of the majority regarding the government to which all shall be subordinate, but simply a contract between equals to act henceforth as one'.[31]

This is not to imply that a confederation possesses merely a 'legal' personality of the type of 'conventional' international organisations; rather, it is capable of developing a 'real' personality of its own: 'an original capacity to act akin to that possessed by the states themselves'.[32] At a more specific level, its underlying characteristic as 'a system of governments' is that, by focusing on intergovernmental relations between a number of legally and politically equal centres of authority, rather than between these centres and a single federal government, it provides the component parts with a variety of opportunities to achieve mutually advantageous co-operation without resigning their individual sovereignty to a single government.

According to the German political theorist von Treitschke: 'A Confederation of States... is recognised by international law as an association of sovereign States, who have bound themselves together, without resigning their independence, to further certain common goals... Consequently the members of a Confederation exercise their natural *liberum veto*'.[33] In other words, although confederations may have a considerable freedom in determining their internal organisational structures, the rule is that 'they cannot as organisations make general rules or measures which are directly binding upon the states that create them'.[34] Forsyth's remark on the subject sharpens this point: 'Thus the individual states must give their express assent, or at the very least withhold their express dissent during a fixed period, before a convention, treaty, or any kind of general resolution made within or by an interstate organisation becomes binding upon them'.[35] All in all, confederations do not fundamentally challenge, at least in constitutional terms, the legal capacity of the constituent units to determine the fate of their own polities. In this context, the idea of a 'condominium of powers' in which the management of certain policy areas are voluntarily put into a limited but joint pool of sovereignty does not conflict with the above description.[36]

Forsyth argues that 'the permanence accorded to a confederation is more than merely the standing "disposability" of the institutions of the typical international organisation.[37] Instead, 'it is a profound locking together of states themselves as regards the joint exercise of fundamental powers,' driven by a common determination to prevent hegemony and, hence, a monopoly of power.[38] Accordingly, confederation can be also seen as a process by which a group of separate states commit themselves by a treaty of union to mutually beneficial interaction which may well extend beyond the traditional patterns of international co-operation. And since it aims to reconcile the concurrent demands for preserving the sovereignty of the parts and high levels of co-ordination amongst them, this model is indeed capable of embracing a wide range of institutional possibilities. Thus it can be seen, in line with Friedrich's dynamic model, as a 'federation-to-be',[39] or even taken to denote, according to Forsyth's theory, a 'genuine federal body', albeit of a looser kind, insofar as the constituent units become parts of a new whole.[40] In conclusion, irrespective of whether the analytical dichotomy between the two forms of polity springs, as Friedrich believes, from 'the quintessence of the static and formalistic approach,'[41] what seems to be certain is that the concept of confederation 'remains a useful part of the federal vocabulary'.[42]

Changing the focus of our discussion to the concept of consociation, it may be useful to preface our inquiry by presenting a brief etymological account of the term. 'Consociation', a much rarer term than 'confederation', derives from the Latin 'consociare' which means 'the action or fact of associating together', 'union in fellowship', or 'combination'.[43] It appears as early as 1603 in Althusius's *Politica Methodice Digesta*, partly as an attempt to analyse the process of building up a new polity in the early seventeenth-century Low Countries, 'without either a strong governmental apparatus or an articulate national identity,'[44] and partly as a response to Bodin's *Les six livres de la Republique* and his novel conception of sovereignty. According to its founding father, Vasovic notes, consociation refers to some kind of *contractus societatis* in which 'the constitutive parts of the state... retain not only the right to resist the ruler who broke the contract... but also the right to secede from one state and to make a contract with another'.[45] So far, no clear-cut distinction can be drawn between confederation and consociation: they both appear to be collective entities which do not possess genuine sovereignty of their own, and where the central authority is evenly divided among the sub-units in order to avoid the subordination of any one segment to the other(s). Consequently, equal partnership, as opposed to segmental dominance, emanates as their common defining property.

The first modern exponent of consociationalism was Apter who, in the early 1960s, defined it as a 'Joining together of constituent units which do not lose their identity when merging in some form of union'.[46] Yet it was Lijphart who first ascribed to the term a comparative politics dimension, stressing its stabilising effects in plural societies characterised by 'cumulative, reinforcing, and, specifically, "isolative" cleavages'.[47] Thereafter, the consociational model, comparable types of which are Lembruch's *Proporzdemokratie* (proportional democracy) and *Konkordanzdemokratie* (concordant democracy), and Bluhm's 'contractarianism' (contractarian democracy),[48] has tried to explain how democracy is able to survive in polities where no commonly-shared values exist. As Stevenson has pointed out, the explanation the theory offers is that 'in such countries the population is segmented in subgroups, each represented by political elites who are trusted to bargain with other elites on behalf of the group's interests'.[49] In particular, it aims to strike a balance between 'positive-sum' and 'zero-sum' decision-making by means of replacing majority rule by 'joint consensual rule'.[50]

Reflecting upon the 'paradoxical' nature of the Dutch political system – in terms of combining democratic stability, religious differences, social fragmentation and legislative fractionalisation – Lijphart offered, in Boulle's words, 'a refinement of pluralist theory'.[51] The gist of his thesis was that there could be stable democracy in 'plural', 'vertically segmented' or 'communally divided' societies if there was overarching co-operation among the segment elites, based on a set of unwritten 'rules of the game'.[52] In *Democracy in Plural Societies*, Lijphart developed a general model of consociational democracy which was an essential departure from classical pluralist theory insofar as the latter required 'criss-crossing conflicts and multiple loyalties to produce stability'.[53] Lijphart's model comprised the following defining characteristics: grand coalition, mutual veto, proportionality and segmental autonomy.[54] As Boulle suggests, these characteristics 'give rise to a system of power-sharing at the national level of government, and group autonomy at the subnational level'.[55]

'Grand coalition' is a blanket term referring to a 'summit diplomacy forum', a 'coalescent style of leadership', a 'coalition cabinet' and a 'grand council', where bargains are struck by what Dahrendorf called 'a cartel of elites'.[56] Although the grand coalition can take various institutional forms, what is imperative is that all segments in society are proportionally represented in its context. But its very efficiency depends upon the availability of a second structural requirement in the form of a mutual veto or 'negative minority rule', a practice synonymous with Calhoun's model of 'concurrent majorities'.[57] Lijphart has established the need for a mutual veto on the following grounds: 'Although the grand coalition rule gives each segment a share of power at the central political level, this does not constitute a guarantee that it will not be outvoted by a majority when its vital interests are at stake'.[58] At the other extreme, Powell warns, it is possible that mutual vetoes can be used by recalcitrant groups to block decisions, 'to the great advantage of the supporters of the status quo and the disadvantage of the have-nots'.[59] As regards 'proportionality', its basic function is 'to ensure that all groups influence decisions in proportion to their numerical strength,' in contrast to the 'winnertakes-all' outcomes in systems of 'majority rule democracy'.[60] Finally, 'segmental autonomy' completes the picture by allowing 'autonomous rule-making and rule application by each of them without interference from the others, or the joint authorities'.[61] It may well reinforce segmental cleavages in society through a form of 'personal jurisdiction' over specific issues: 'each (minority) segment is enabled to take decisions on matters of exclusive concern to it'.[62]

These, then, are the defining characteristics of consociation, whose successful operation, Lijphart notes, 'presupposes not only a willingness on the parts of elites to cooperate but also a capacity to solve the political problems of their countries'.[63] This means that apart from the 'cooperative efforts' of rival segment elites exhibited in the bargaining process, what is also required is the deployment of such accommodative techniques, which can maintain the stability and integrity of the system, and 'counteract the centrifugal tendencies of cultural fragmentation'.[64] This is practically ensured by 'continuing procedural guarantees' for reaching substantive intersegmental accommodation. In short, consociationalism, both as a process of consensual decision-making and a pattern of elite behaviour, can be better understood as a strategy of 'co-operative conflict resolution' whereby the segment elites attempt to transcend inter-group fragmentation by enforcing the terms of institutionalised compromise through the politics of accommodation. In fact, politics itself becomes, to borrow a phrase, 'the institutionalised art of compromise'.[65] But where do these observations leave us in terms of democracy? Should the striking of a politically weighted compromise be seen as a welcome development, even when reached outside the realm of democratic politics? In other words, do political ends sometimes justify less democratic or even non-democratic means of decision-taking?

The crucial point to make here is that consociational polities require neither a 'sense of community' at the popular level nor a popular affirmation of commonly-shared values, nor the existence of a single and undifferentiated *demos* united by the overarching power of a higher civic 'we-ness'. In fact, they are defined exactly by their very absence: in a consociation there are two or more distinct politically organised people, and a positive aggregation of segmental interests hardly ever exists as such. Holden explains: 'Due to the fundamental nature of the sectional divisions and conflicts, demands cannot be simply aggregated or synthesised'.[66] This is why consociationalism often 'ceases to be a theory about the nature of democratic decision making and becomes instead a theory about how much decision making remains possible in the face of grave difficulties'.[67]

Moreover, conflict-regulating practices are employed as 'closed', highlighting the elitist character of the regime, whilst rendering the relationship between 'decision-makers' and 'decision-receivers' highly problematic. As a result, overall *demos* control over elite activities is the exception rather than the rule of the game, in contrast to Almond's 'Anglo-American' democracies where, in principle, the existence of 'cross-cutting cleavages' make systems of collective public accountability easier to apply.[68] Instead, each section of the fragmented citizen body exercises controlling functions over the segment elites through its own procedures. For instance, one cannot exclude the possibility that, by hiding behind the ever convenient excuse that the mobilisation of public opinion around sensitive or controversial issues will be detrimental to democratic stability, the members of the elite cartel may succeed in excluding themselves from extensive public scrutiny and control. In this case, 'the faith of democracy' seems to lie more in a 'belief in the principle of compromise itself,'[69] than in the principles of decisional transparency, indirect *demos* control and open public debate.

At times, however, a compromise based on reciprocal concessions among the elites can become an almost self-sufficient condition for the articulation of divergent interests without resort to exclusion: where majority rule is unacceptable to 'cleavage minorities', consociational practices provide a balanced structure for keeping all sections of the population under a common political roof or, as Kellas has pointed out, 'several nations in one state'.[70] Notwithstanding Sartori's observation that 'in all democracies most decisions are not majoritarian,'[71] the successful operation of a consociational democracy rests on the ability of consensual practices to provide unanimous decisions. Having described the conceptual ingredients of Confederal Consociation, the tantalising question which remains to be addressed is where does the present EU system fit in the complex worlds of confederation and consociation, and what the proposed model implies for the polity's democratic organisation.

THE CONFEDERAL CONSOCIATION THESIS

Applied to the Union of the 1990s, the first part of this complex term – confederal – refers to the structural properties of the system, suggesting that not only has the role of the state remained effective, but also that the constituent governments have found ways of strengthening their position domestically, regionally and internationally. Although the right of a member state to invoke the Luxembourg Accords of January 1966 in order to 'block' central decision-making cannot be said to correspond directly to the actual conditions under which the constituent units of the chief historical examples of confederations exercised their 'natural' *liberum veto*, a certain degree of resemblance becomes apparent in the way in which EU partners wish to protect their vital national interests through consensus-building mechanisms, and achieve a certain goal of unity.

The confederal character of the Union has been pointed out by a number of scholars over the years, recently summarised by Keohane and Hoffmann thus: 'If any traditional model were to be applied, it would be that of a confederation... since the central institutions are (a) largely intergovernmental, (b) more concerned with establishing a common framework than with networks of detailed regulations, and (c) apparently willing to tolerate a vast amount of national diversity'.[72] Similar descriptions are to be found, *inter alia*, in the subtitle of an article written by Brewin, 'A Union of States without unity of government'; in the term 'Confederence' used by Church; and in Elazar's view of the Union as a 'new-style confederation of old states'.[73] The second part of the term – consociation – refers to the process of arriving at collective decisions. Their consociational aspects were first pointed out by Taylor.[74] All four major characteristics of a consociation can be found in the Union: a fair separation of its segments; its domination by a management coalition of co-operative elites; a proportional representation of the states to the central institutions; and the existence of a qualified right of a mutual veto for the protection of minority interests. The consociational model suggests that the Union maximises the influence of states in areas of common concern, whilst allowing them to enjoy what Lijphart earlier defined as 'a high degree of secure autonomy in organising their own affairs'.[75]

This is not to imply that the Union is the 'jewel' in the consociational 'crown'. For what distinguishes it from being a 'normal' consociation is that its sub-units take the form of nation-states whose populations have a strong national identity. In other words, the 'pillars' of the transnational society are composed of national electorates, each represented by a sovereign government; they are not parts of a single pluralist state. Put simply, it is the governance of the Union that rests on the principles of (territorial) segmental autonomy and grand coalition, since 'decision-making authority is delegated to the separate segments as much as possible',[76] and since 'on all issues of common interest, the decisions are made jointly by the segments' leaders, but on all other issues, decision-making is left to the segments'.[77]

Moreover, in matters of common concern, there is a continuous search by the segments for the lowest common denominator. This, supported by an accommodative mutual veto, replaces the logic of 'mutual antagonism' or 'mutual exclusion' with that of 'mutual reconciliation', which practically means 'reversible dissensus'. The latter property of the system's *modus decidendi* has been termed by Taylor 'confined dissent', implying that the higher the level of integration, and the higher the stakes involved in central decision-making, the higher the propensity of the states to produce consensus outcomes for the accommodation of major political claims.[78] Finally, proportionality serves the Union as the basic standard for the allocation of votes when majority rule is formally required, and as the working method for central administrative appointments (especially for the staffing of the Commission). Taylor explains: 'Whereas integration theory predicts an increasing preparedness to accept appointments in the central bureaucracy on the basis of ability... consociationalism suggests an increasing determination to insist upon proportionality in the central institutions...'[79] Overall, member governments get a fair share of their representative quota in the key decision-making bodies of the Union.[80]

Consociationalism lends support to the view that 'the strengthening of the regional functional systems may help to sharpen rather than soften the cleavages in the existing society of nations.[81] It also suggests that integration provides the means by which the power of the dominant elites that represent the collective interests of each segment at the larger level can be significantly enhanced, enabling them 'to present themselves as leaders and agents of a distinct clearly-defined community'.[82] Also, they may well resist 'any tendency towards the strengthening of the horizontal links between the segments, since that would also weaken their constituencies,' and promote *vertical* integration which allows leaders to strike deals with other bloc leaders while retaining authority within their own subculture'.[83] In brief, it provides the members of the elite cartel with an additional platform from which they can move on to consolidate their domestic power base,[84] influence the articulation of territorial interests and obtain a greater level of independence in the world community.

This approach to the workings of the Union suggests an increasing determination by the segment elites to exercise managerial control over integration, even if 'progressive' initiatives reflecting the wider 'Community interest' will have to be compromised out of a generally-held awareness that a less ambitious settlement is better than one which might overlook the vital interests of a member state. The operational code adopted by the members of the Council of Ministers and the European Council for taking positive decisions despite the reality of mutual vetoes, provide a perfect test for this hypothesis: both institutions become sites for inter-elite accommodation, performing functions similar to those of a grand coalition in a consociational system. In other words, collective shared-rule turns into a 'summit diplomacy forum' in which consensus-building, the process of co-opting divergent expectations, is not sought at the grass-roots level, but rather at the leadership level. This is fully in accord with consociationalism as a theory of political stability and its explicit distinction between 'elite political culture' and 'mass political culture'.[85]

Here, one could add the decisive impact of the Presidency arrangements as the institution *par excellence* for sustaining the symbiotic process in reconciling interstate differences at both pre-legislative and decision-making stages. In fact, the Presidency has gradually taken over the Commission's role as an autonomous 'package-broker' in multilateral negotiations, as well as a policy-initiator, offering various possibilities for accommodating state and Union interests through its active involvement in joint decision-making. Of such dynamic accommodation, Almond's classical dictum that 'politics is not a game', provides not only the theoretical justification of inter-elite compromise but also the main operational tool toward its achievement. In brief, the evolving role of the Presidency has gone hand in hand with a more creative type of inter-governmentalism in the management of EU affairs since the mid-1970s, acting as a crucial link between national and European dynamics: a point where two different incentives of transnational politics are brought together.[86]

A further insight from consociationalism points to viewing the Union as an ensemble of 'territorial communities',[87] as opposed to a single civic entity, aiming at the amicable settlement of divisive issues against the danger of fragmentation. Here, the model highlights an important function of the system: 'the maintenance of stability in a situation of actual or potential mutual tension'.[88] Thus, Confederal Consociation takes the form of a polycentric structure of mutual governance whose ultimate aim is the attainment of a creative synthesis or symbiosis among the separate segments and identities involved in its dynamic, multi-layered context. This means that the states achieve mutually auspicious interaction without fear of having their vital national interests overwhelmed by the force of 'general' interests in a neofunctionalist fashion.

Moreover, by emphasising the internal conditions under which nations decide to do certain things in common in favour of consensually-predetermined objectives, Confederal Consociation sets the bases of creative co-existence and acceptable behaviour through multiple networks of formal and informal arrangements. In this sense, it performs a crucial dual function: it defines the limits of integration whilst increasing the possibilities for national and transnational 'games' to go along side-by-side, supporting rather than excluding each other. Finally, by offering a spectrum of possibilities for national authorities to pursue their own agendas in relation to the interests of the Union (when exercising their Presidency duties) it provides the states with a 'sense of security' to further the pace of collective action, without forcing them to 'commit state or national suicide'.[89] All-in-all, the model refers to a compound polity whose distinct culturally defined and politically organised units are brought together in a consensually pre-arranged form of Union to further certain common ends, without either losing their sense of forming collective national identities, or resigning their individual sovereignty to a higher central authority.

THE PRINCIPLES OF TERRITORIALITY AND INVERSE FEDERALISM

Thus sketched, Confederal Consociation – both as a distinct form of political interstate organisation and a new integrative dynamic between polities which effectively retain their freedom in organising a substantial range of their internal affairs autonomously – does not pose any fundamental threat to the sovereignty of states. 'Indeed,' Taylor writes, 'as with consociationalism and the various segments within states the common system in some ways helps to consolidate the sub-units,' and even 'develop their sense of forming distinctive identities'.[90] Thus the Union has an interesting analogue with a system of horizontal *Kooperative Staaten*, in that the formulation of common policies rests upon the existence or not of prior agreement between state and federal actors, whilst their implementation relies on the administrative systems of states. This term, which essentially describes the basic properties of the German system of 'interlocking federalism' or *Politikverflechtung*[91] captures the co-operative nature of European integration.

In both systems, the power of the constituent governments is well protected, whilst political authority originating in different orders of government is commonly managed after intensive intergovernmental bargains. The same cannot be said of the US federal system, where state governors do not share in national policy-making. Whereas Washington represents a 'centre' composed of institutions capable of regulating the interactions stemming from the activities of the state governments, Bonn is best described as the 'meeting point' of state and federal agents that jointly decide upon the formulation of national policies.[92] Hence, Sbragia notes that it is not the American but the German type of federalism which 'allows one to conceptualise a Community in which a "centre" is created that is not completely independent from its constituent units'.[93] But in both models federal institutions are ultimately responsible to the (federal) *demos* rather than to the state governments. It is the absence of one sovereign *demos* that brings the Union closer to being a Confederal Consociation.

It follows that only if electoral representation is linked to the development of the Union independent of its sub-units, and a political centre is established that is intended 'to represent the European interest,'[94] can we speak of a truly federated Union; one in which the European Parliament will be given the chance to evolve into a legislative authority analogous to other lower federal chambers and, hence, to a real 'co-player' in central decision-making. As the Union now stands, such legislative functions are a far cry from those presently exercised by the European Parliament. Yet the implied analogy should be seen in relative terms, even in relation to German federalism where a strong system of territorial representation co-exists with a federal government with considerable legislative and fiscal powers. As Scharpf put it: 'the German federal government can draw on its parliamentary and electoral legitimation to exert political pressure on the states, and in negotiations it can bring to bear the weight of its larger budget. In contrast, the European Commission is completely dependent on the governments of the member state governments in both political and fiscal terms'.[95]

But what is instructive in the German system as a source of inspiration for EU institution-building is that its democratic properties stem from the recognition of two distinct representational bases: state executives and federal *demos*. Whereas the former are represented in the *Bundesrat* as an 'assembly of *Land* ambassadors',[96] the latter represents the 'constituent power' which confers sovereignty on the federation as a whole. As Sbragia put it: 'The German model... represents an important institutional innovation in federalism and helps us to grasp how the constituent units of a system may, as institutions, participate in central decision-making... [it] treats state governments as institutions seriously'.[97] This largely *sui generis* type of federalism based on the practice of co-determination between federal and state agents can be represented schematically as follows.

Figure 7.1 The co-operative federalism pyramid

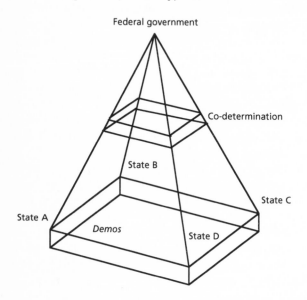

On the other hand, the 'interlocking' functions of German federalism make it extremely difficult for the individual citizen 'to identify responsibilities for specific policy decisions in an increasingly intransparent decision-making process in which every level of government is partly involved and thus only partly accountable'.[98] Also, the predominance of negotiations between *Länder* and federal agents 'generally lessens the effectiveness of parliamentary controls on both levels; state parliaments, in particular, usually find themselves called upon to merely rectify outcomes which they are not expected to influence'.[99] Or, as Wessels put it: 'In such a process the decision-making is shifted to common institutions and bodies which cannot be controlled according to traditional democratic standards'.[100] Hence Kirchner's warning that 'without adequate provisions to the contrary, the prevailing "democratic deficit" in EC decision-making would probably continue under the system of co-operative federalism'.[101] The transformation of state representation into state participation in national policy-making thus moves the German polity away from the traditional type of federal democracy where the emphasis is on the representation of the *demos* in a conventional 'centre'. This alternative democratic design to the old 'center-periphery model' institutionalises state participation in the exercise of the federal power.[102]

But irrespective of whether the member state legislatures will one day become the functional equivalents of the German *Länder*, setting the bases for a bicameral legislature composed of a *Bundesrat*-like chamber for the participation of member state executives and a European Parliament representing the transnational *demos*, as the *Bundestag* claims to represent the German *demos*, co-operative federalism raises the possibility for 'a federal-type organisation to operate without a centre traditionally conceptualised... constructed by member governments without its being detached from the collectivity of constituent units, in this case national governments'.[103]

This polycentric and multilogical pattern of federalism co-existing with a more favourable version of intergovernmentalism as a method of promoting integration, and based on the premise that the defence of each separate interest coincides with the need to strike a deal in the context of an intersegmental 'positive-sum' game, may be best defined as a case of 'inverse federalism': a situation in which political power tends to be decentralised as much as possible to the constituent governments rather than to the central institutions, and where the allocation of competences among the different levels of decision-making is controlled by the former – schematically seen as an 'inverse pyramid'.[104] Although this unique type of federalism addresses the issue of the territorial dimension of EU politics, it takes the form of a joint-decision system based on formal and informal veto-unit arrangements.

The growth of this mode of interaction, as the nub of the idea of Confederal Consociation, its emphasis on balancing territorial and non-territorial claims, as well as its 'special' relationship with the principle of segmental autonomy, corresponds best to the *ad hoc* evolutionary character of the Union. For the latter has so far managed to give meaningful institutional expression to the principle of territoriality through its intergovernmental components, and permit the channelling and articulation of non-territorial claims via its 'supranational' institutions.

Despite the alleged advantages of inverse federalism in accommodating the interests of the collectivity with those of the segments, it falls short of meeting the requirements of those who proclaim the demise of the (Western) European nation-state, envisage the immediate creation of a common European identity, support the formation of a fully-blown European *demos*, and expect a transfer of loyalties to take place on a 'zero-sum' basis. It is our contention that the appearance or lack of a creative balance between such neighbouring concepts as inverse federalism, territoriality and segmental autonomy will in the end define 'the possibility of movement toward a closer political bond as federalism',[105] and with it the actual shape of Europe's could-be *demos*.

From the perspective, therefore, of 'the national "game" being played in Europe',[106] as the lower component of the two-level game metaphor, one should not underestimate the principle of territoriality in the evolution of the integrative system. On the contrary, there are good reasons for thinking that over the last few years territorial politics has played an ever-more influential role in EU political life. Thus any attempt to understand and explain the polity's operations from a classical federalist perspective becomes too nebulous a framework for analysis. Instead, it is more preferable to link the role of territorial interests and institutions with a pattern of federal organisation that recognises both the felt need of the member states to protect their vital interests and the claims made by non-territorial institutions such as the EP to be involved in substantive terms in central decision-making. The result of this combination takes the form of a structure of mutual governance in which the condition of territoriality co-exists with that of non-territoriality in a symbiotic, rather than competitive, manner, and where the dynamics of inter-elite accommodation shape the forms that transnational federalism is allowed or indeed prohibited from taking.

In summary, EU politics can be thought of as based on an inverse type of federalism, rather than on a federalism founded upon notions of institutional centralisation and hierarchical, vertically-linked authority structures. This form of institutional development should be recognised as a discernible overall integrative stage in which territorial politics is becoming stronger as the scope of integration is being extended. For the more optimistic, however, it can be also seen as part of an evolution in which today's quasi-federal and quasi-democratic central arrangements may be replaced one day by a formal constitutional framework whereby *in camera* decision-making, unaccountable bureaucratic management and executive elite dominance become the exception rather than the rule of EU practice. In this sense, a self-determining 'political community' might emerge, and be governed by democratic standards, adding substantively to the dynamics of transnational *demos*-formation. This move towards the final European vocation, by representing the culmination of a process of conscious large-scale community-strengthening, points towards the qualitative transformation of the Union from democracies to democracy.

REFLECTIONS ON THE PLURALIST CHARACTER OF THE SYSTEM

The significance attributed to the concept of Confederal Consociation is that it aims to provide a consensual form of mutual governance out of, by and for sovereign entities. At least, it can be seen as one possible form of applying consociational processes in a confederation of states which might gradually evolve into a more congruent federal body.[107] At most, it can be used as a new pattern of political interaction in which the 'inclusive' and the 'component' polities engage themselves in a process of union which often transcends the territorial dimension of politics, and with it the ill-effects of subcultural fragmentation, through the application of co-operative arrangements. In both cases, it opens a wide range of possibilities for reconciling the parallel demands for segmental autonomy and overall systemic stability within a common framework of power characterised by strong pluralistic tendencies.

Essentially, this co-operative interplay between national and EU political life, by involving the simultaneous building up, down and across of a multiplicity of interactive ties,[108] addresses the more general issue of the transformation of the classical concept of 'self-determination' – and its implications of 'what a nation does or can do'[109] – into one of 'co-determination', involving the common management of national sovereignties. As Groom has remarked: 'Since governments feel themselves ultimately to be in control, they are willing to contemplate a far-reaching pooling of sovereignty which they jointly manage'.[110] This gradual transformation has been largely sustained by the emergence of a transnational political culture among the dominant governing elites, pointing towards the consolidation of a moderate version of nationalism co-existing with a conscious effort to avoid systemic polarisation. This 'decentralised, though co-ordinated, system in which participating actors... have a high level of interdependence with each other, but, nevertheless, preserve and even augment their autonomy', has been defined by Taylor as 'managed *Gesellschaft*'.[111]

In such a diverse network of interactions facilitated by a highly flexible treaty framework, there are no permanent coalitions of power nor any fixed 'code of practice' regarding the role that each actor has, or is expected, to perform. In procedural terms, the system is loose enough to allow consensual and majoritarian patterns of decision-taking to co-exist and determine the outcome of specific policies. Its generic properties are cultural distinctiveness and civic autonomy of the parts; its legal nature rests upon the individual constitutional orders of states, as opposed to a superordinate, federal legal order; whilst political power tends to be diffused as much as possible to the executive branches of the constituent units.

Also, the dynamic enmeshing of personal, functional and territorial loyalties, together with the gradual development of cross-national allegiances and multiple group affiliations, by enhancing the pluralist character of the system, prevent the emergence of exclusive loyalties which may exacerbate conflict among the sub-units. And since it is possible for a plurality of loyalties and identities to co-exist in such a 'corporate union' – including states'/Union's, states'/citizens' and Union's/citizens' interests[112] – there is no reason for national authorities to stop contemplating higher levels of co-determination within the larger management system.

Put simply, there is no need for zero-sum competition between the interests of the collectivity and the ascending plurality of claims stemming from the subcultures. Equally, the process of 'macro-level loyalty-building' should not be associated with the integration of the masses into a common political form that overrides citizens' 'fixed primary loyalties'.[113] Nor should attempts to manage or even extend the scope of the central arrangements be equated with a direct loss of capabilities at the national level. Indeed, by perceiving the system as inclusive of various forms of fellowship, Confederal Consociation mitigates the fears that integration in the 1990s is about the subordination of states to some form of a higher central authority, let alone about the collection of exclusive citizen loyalties.

Rather, by dismissing an 'either/or' conception of EU politics, it sharpens the point that a division of jurisdictional competences between states and international organisation is compatible not only with the very idea of statehood itself, but also with further national state-building processes, subnational community-strengthening and multiple identity holding. In brief, the model contains a suggestion of the flexibility of the system, of the non-conflictual character of power-sharing, and of the means through which the separateness of the segments is compatible with notions like systemic stability, inter-elite accommodation and institutionalised compromise.

This is perhaps why the initial concentration of law-making and law-enforcing power in the state gives way to a continual structuring and restructuring of power within the shared undertaking without the former losing its individual sovereignty. In other words, the system employs a looser notion of pluralism to the British and American political traditions, which tend to emphasise the importance of individual liberty *vis-à-vis* state activity and the sharing of power between relatively autonomous groups and government agencies, respectively.[114] In essence, EU pluralism is based on the realisation that 'economic and political interests are best advanced by staying together in a sensibly arranged political union'.[115] For one thing, the Union retains the basic properties of a voluntary association of states and, hence, the possibility of secession by the segments which are united for specific ends. Although such a system is flexible enough to exhibit varying degrees of pluralism according to the separate interests involved in the transnational process, the outcome of the various claims is controlled by the relevant political elites. Hence pluralism is an important variable of the integrative game, seen best as a 'matter of degree' rather than an 'all-or-nothing' phenomenon between dominant and subordinate elites; the latter being usually the case in the 'conflict' model of plural, highly segmented or deeply divided societies.

The persistence of this form of *controlled pluralism* – lying in the midst of a continuum whose two poles are represented by dynamic 'equilibrium pluralism' (congruent federations) and 'conflict pluralism' (consociational systems) – is conditional upon the extent to which a delicate balance of power and interests can be struck within the elite cartel.[116] Evidently, then, the 'winner-takes-all' ethos which persists in the majoritarian Westminster model and its 'government-versus-opposition' logic do not suit the present Union, for they imply that the wishes of some constituent *demoi* will be enacted in central legislation at the expense of others. Indeed, the model's essential constitutional properties, such as 'parliamentary supremacy, unitarianism, single-party executive, adversarial two-party system, and plurality elections,'[117] conflict with the currently fragmented nature of the European *demos*.

Moreover, the inclination of the EU system is such that it induces the segment elites to adopt the working principles of 'joint consensual rule'. This is not required in the Westminster model where 'an elected majority enjoys extensive power for the duration of its majority status'.[118] In brief, the consociational management of pooled sovereignties reinforces the symbiotic nature of European integration, providing a barrier to the prevalence of adversarial politics. Yet, this system of consensus elite government is not without serious implications for the quality of transnational democracy.

CONSENSUS ELITE GOVERNMENT VS *DEMOS* CONTROL

The preceding comments on the elite-controlled character of EU pluralism should not be seen merely as an anti-elitist attack on a mode of political interaction which has been firmly established over the years in European structures. Although government in the self-interest of elites conflicts with the dictates of democratic participation and popular legitimacy, our

intentions reflect the need to assess the limits and possibilities of democracy in a polycentric union whose current democratic properties remain
weak in comparison to the average Western European state. The central
proposition to make here is that although a minimum democratic condition is that the *demos* should be entitled to participate as fully as possible
in the actual process of government, the sustenance of democracy
inevitably rests on the solders of the few who are entitled to decide for
all. This has been termed by Zeigler 'the irony of democracy' in that
'elites must govern wisely if "government by the people" is to survive'.[119]

Students of democratic elitism perceive political power as resting
firmly in the hands of a relatively small body of individuals, and they thus
distance themselves from classical democratic theory and its insistence on
'rule by the many'. They also view the divide between elites and non-
elites as a feature common to modern societies. For even under the best
possible democratic conditions, 'a few exercise a relatively great weight
of power, and the many exercise comparatively little'.[120] Yet, should we
accept that the key political decisions will always be made by 'tiny
minorities', then the crucial issue is not how many exercise public power
but how wisely and closely to the interests of the *demos* they exercise it.
The question that all these interrogations generate for our discussion is
whether it is possible to organise a transnational polity along conventional democratic lines, given that the foundations of its governance
are concerned with the building of a joint decision-making system that
sustains 'demo-distributions' controlled by national executives, and not
with the creation of political institutions whose workings reflect some
form of what Sartori calls 'demo-power'.[121]

It is definitely not our intention to elevate the discussion to the level
of an abstract philosophical framework, for all the obvious interest such
a normative undertaking might entail. Nor do we intend to explore 'the
nuts and bolts' of elite theory from Mosca and Pareto to Michels and
Dahl: this has already been done by Parry.[122] Instead, our aim is to find
appropriate analogies in order to explain why the present EU system
operates in the way it does, and how it would be possible to rectify its
most acute democratic deficiencies without endangering its greatest
achievement so far: the building of a new transnational political culture
favouring the resolution of common problems by common procedures.

This 'silent revolution' in the perceptions and attitudes of the dominant Western European political elites is sustained by the development of
an active awareness at the leadership level that the idea of joint sovereignty, even when it does not always adequately articulate all interests
pursued in intergovernmental bargains, is better than foregoing the
privileges offered by common membership. On the other hand, this is

not a self-sufficient condition for reinforcing the process of developing a transnational 'socio-psychological community' at the grass-roots. All it does is to provide the infrastructure upon which the dynamics of integration may create pressures for further democratic reforms, even at the expense of territorially defined interests.

The negotiations leading to the signing of the Single European Act (SEA), which extended majority rule in new policy areas and introduced a co-operative legislative procedure, is a perfect illustration of the fact that democratisation can proceed against a particular elite's self-interests when non-compliance with the wishes of the majority may threaten its future participation in the system.[123] A similar point can be made for the signing of the TEU, although in this case a more careful examination of the final product is needed, especially if we are to capture the problematic relationship, and in Stavridis's terms the 'democratic disjunction', between the wishes and interests of Europe's political elites and popular political sentiments (see chapter 8).

But let us return to the central questions posed in this section: what are the political implications that Confederal Consociation generate for the advancement or obstruction of a more democratic process of union in which the concept of indirect *demos* control would be compatible with that of decisional efficiency? More generally, what are the limits and possibilities of transnational democracy in such a complex framework of consensus elite government? And also, is it possible to imagine a terminal democratic state of union, given Taylor's view that 'there may be cases indeed that regional integration helps to reinforce the anti-democratic tendencies of elites'?[124] To offer an answer, the following should be set out.

As in any other consociational system, so in the Union, 'political process and democracy is mainly limited to the sphere of interelite communications,'[125] not least because its nascent *demos* does not have the means either to set the agenda of the integration process, or to influence, in any substantive terms, the shaping of central legislation. Instead, both processes are controlled by national governmental elites which, acting in the interests of unfettered executive dominance, remain highly unaccountable to the European citizen body as a whole, either directly (through referenda) or indirectly (through elected representatives).

Because consociations are collective entities governed by 'a cartel of elites', 'the individual loses the status of being the active and decisive subject in politics'.[126] As Bachrach might have added, politics becomes a form of 'democratic elitism', where multiple elites determine public policy through bargaining and compromise.[127] It is no accident, therefore, that elites employ the theory of democratic elitism as an apology for elite rule to defend their often shortsighted behaviour and governmental inaction.

It can be also used as a means of legitimising a situation in which 'the rules of the game are only for insiders', entertaining the criticisms of the apparent 'lack of appropriate "transmission" channels between EC decisions and the citizen'.[128]

The point being made here is that as long as the norms, principles and values of transnational democracy are consciously undermined in integration processes, any consequent democratic deficiency at the Union level will merely be a reflection of a certain philosophy of governance whereby the member publics abide by the decisions taken within the elite cartel. In this sense, the subversion of the democratic process, and the preservation of a 'democratic deficit', spring from a conscious effort to maintain political stability by avoiding intersegmental confrontation and the ill-effects of institutional immobilism. As Moravcsik put it: 'Ironically, the EC's "democratic deficit" may be a fundamental source of its success'.[129] In short, the price of stable governance practically takes the form of various democratic shortfalls which in a different context – ie, in a non-segmented society – would simply be unacceptable.

Seen as a pluralistic community of 'territorial communities' in search of a lasting symbiosis among its various segments and identities, the Union is primarily concerned with the elimination of conflictual situations which may arise through the use of majority rule in areas which can be seen as antithetical to the prerogatives of national sovereignty. Put differently, the proper functioning of the central arrangements are conditional upon the extent to which broad agreement can be achieved without resort to what Riker calls the 'minimum winning coalition' principle,[130] even when majority rule is formally required by the treaties. For the 'embarrassment' of being outvoted in a vital decision is such that the rule of the game prescribes that the greater the importance of the outcome for a particular member state or group of states, the greater the consensus required to achieve a 'balanced' resolution. Whilst this might not be positively unanimous, it does 'reflect a "negative unanimity" or general consensus'.[131]

Evidently, the device of a mutual veto minimises the risks of 'winner-takes-all' outcomes, enabling each member of the elite cartel to function without the anxiety of having its vital interests 'subsumed' either by the force of other territorial interests, or by the combined strength of non-territorial ones. What, therefore, *prima facie* appears to be the violation of the principle of majority rule, is a distinctive accommodationist pattern of joint decision-making which helps to promote vertical integration among the member publics and horizontal co-operation among the elites. As previously noted, when the stakes are not too high, majority voting, far from endangering the peace and unity of the system, becomes the rule for the normal transaction of EU business. This explains why democracy in the common system acquires the status of a sufficiently flexible organisational device for seeking widely acceptable solutions, rather than being conceived as an end in itself. As Barker put it: 'democracy is not a solution but a way of seeking solutions'.[132]

From this analytical prism, the embodiment of consociational procedures in EU decision-making can be seen as a by-product of a uniquely observed compromise between the traditional notions of responsible government and a deep-seated concern for achieving the conditions of stable democracy. It also explains why progress towards further integration depends upon the ability of coalescent-style institutions to strike a balance between the two apparently contradictory, but by no means mutually exclusive, principles: national autonomy and transnational unity. Thus although democracy survives as the fundamental principle of national political organisation, it does not exist *per se* in the workings of the larger entity. Instead, what we actually have there is a multiplicity of quasi-democratic arrangements concerned with the effects of joint decision-making, and dictated by the need for 'positive-sum' governing. In brief, by emphasising elite-driven, as opposed to *demos*-led, integration, Confederal Consociation addresses the implications that the dialectic co-existence of a plurality of forces pressing simultaneously towards a more centralised or decentralised, loose or coherent, technocratic or democratic, Union, generate for the political viability of the common system. Also, it suggests that the problems associated with the making of a transnational *demos* are far from ephemeral or easy to resolve.

The main differences between the basic properties of Confederal Consociation as a 'managed *Gesellschaft*', and as a democratic union in the form of a politically organised *Gemeinschaft*, each projecting two alternative modes of transnational political organisation, can be represented as two different pyramids composed of four interrelated parts equally important to the political viability of the whole edifice.[133]

Figure 7.2 Alternative modes of transnational political organisation

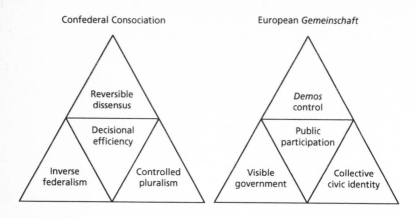

In conclusion, the Confederal Consociation thesis, by transcending the major political dilemma evident, explicitly or less so, in all classical approaches to federal integration, namely that of stressing the representation of the *demos*, as opposed to the representation of constituent governments, provides a comprehensive explanation of the inherent ambivalence in the process of EU democracy-building: despite the fact that over the last few years a number of significant steps have been taken towards the democratisation of the Union, no substantial progress has yet been made in bringing voters to the European polling-booths.[134] The explanation the model offers is that in a system where low-consensus politics among the elites prevail over democratic decision-making, citizen identification with the non-territorial institutions of the system can never be complete. In fact, political apathy may be interpreted as a consequence of popular wisdom: why should European citizens bother to vote if their directly elected representatives at the larger level are but a decorative feature in a predominantly arcane process of government? What, then, seems to be new about the relationship between democracy and European integration in the 1990s is that no terminal democratic state can be envisaged that is not essentially symbiotic, and not able to ease the tension between the territorial representation of governments and the incorporation of the nascent European *demos* in the politics of integration processes.

FROM *GESELLSCHAFT* TO *GEMEINSCHAFT*?

The present stage of EU development represents neither a movement back to the 'conventional' intergovernmentalism of the 1970s,[135] nor a qualitative leap towards a formally amalgamated federation similar to the USA, Canada or Australia. There, the processes of constitutional engineering were determined from the outset by a felt need to define the meaning of democracy within the federal architecture, whilst making it operative through the workings of 'general' institutions. For instance, what was produced at the Grand Convention of 1787 was a balanced resolution among the territorial, political and constitutional dimensions of federalism, whilst institution-building was partly a response to the problem of how to ensure government accountability via elected representatives without jeopardising the overall federal cohesion of the new American polity; or, conversely, without encouraging those subscribing to the dictum 'Let the States govern themselves'. In brief, in the well-consolidated federal systems of our time, a democratic culture could be developed *ab intra* and grass-roots politics established, leading to an 'inclusive' federal *demos*.

By contrast, the elasticity of EU institution-building, along with an overriding concern for securing the representation of what Scharpf calls the 'institutional self-interest of governments',[136] has itself set the limits of democratisation within the Union. Despite the polity's remarkable evolution from inception to the present day, the divide between territory and *demos* has effectively persisted, to the extent that Sbragia was compelled to confess that 'even if national governments as such did not participate in the Community's policy-making process, Community politics would certainly be shaped, and probably dominated, by territorial considerations'.[137] 'The option available to the Community,' she contends, 'is to implement the political dimension of federalism without its constitutional dimension'.[138]

In particular, Sbragia proposes a type of federal organisation which she calls 'segmented federalism' allowing for 'treaty-based federal arrangements in certain policy areas, without being founded on a formal, constitutionally based federation'.[139] Confederal Consociation sharpens this point since its operational code does not require the existence of a European Constitution to deal effectively with the pressing realities of the day. Indeed, one of the reasons why this type of organisation provides the best fit for the Union of the 1990s is that the various constitutional forms of the states, far from being formally amalgamated in a single constitutional arrangement, retain their status as distinctive legal orders. Further, by supporting the legality of the EU system, they seem to play a crucial part in the politics of European constitutional choice. Indeed, by providing transnational structures with the necessary authority to take publicly binding decisions in a wide range of functional policy areas, national constitutionalism remains a strong legitimising pillar for the viability of the larger edifice, leaving a range of possibilities open between the Union and the states.

For the time being, however, the Union exhibits more a dispersed system of national democracies rather than a transnational democratic system. One reason for this is that the interests of the 'territorial state' co-exist with those of the central institutions insofar as they are products of consensually-oriented inter-elite negotiations. And if one takes into account that the system continues to be regulated mainly by an international treaty, and that member governments withhold the right to withdraw from the larger association if and when they find it appropriate, it is easy to explain why the *locus decidendi* of the Union continues to rest on state agents rather than on non-territorial central institutions such as the European Parliament. This, in turn, frees the participants from 'the albatross of federalism' since the current balance of trends minimises the possibilities for the establishment of a European 'federal government', as a type of government concerned with the political organisation of a single state.[140] Yet, it is important to stress that EU institutions are not merely an instrument of national authorities, that is an extension of domestic politics at a higher level. Rather, state and international organisation perform complementary functions.

However, seen as a transitional arrangement, Confederal Consociation may give way, in time, to the emergence of a European *Gemeinschaft* through the application of the provisions of the TEU. For the greatest challenge posed to the presently dominant synthesis of confederal structures and consociational processes can be found in the elements of what Groom calls a transnational 'psycho-political community'.[141] But the extent to which the Maastricht process is alone capable of transcending the *Gesellschaft*-like qualities of Union governance, and bring a stronger *Gemeinschaft* element to its daily conduct, is yet to be seen. As for now, not only is the Union building up to larger units at a federal level, and across by governmental elites in a consociational manner, it is also building down to smaller entities at the subnational level.[142] Maybe the idea of a 'Europe of the Regions', as opposed to the traditional notion of a 'Europe of States' based on the principle of what Lijphart called 'government by elite cartel',[143] and Taylor 'government by alliance',[144] will create strong tendencies at the popular level to demand an immediate and substantive increase in the democratic properties of the transnational system.

But in the real world of territorial and non-territorial politics and interests, the achievement of an optimal model for balancing the 'public

sentiment' with the underlying objectives of governments and administrations is heavily conditioned by the presence, or the lack, of political
will at the elite level. For one thing, the system's ponderous reliance on
in camera bargaining procedures among national executives minimises the
possibilities for the emergence of a politically organised *Gemeinschaft* at the
popular level. As for the TEU itself, the elites' willingness to compromise
may well diminish the political importance of some of the newly-introduced
democratic reforms to the system such as the principle of subsidiarity (see
chapter 8). From this realist perspective, the possibility of transcending
the current 'managed *Gesellschaft*' by means of furthering the scope and
level of a European *Gemeinschaft* depends decisively upon the political
motivation of national governmental elites, rather than being conditioned
by a genuine commitment to transnational democracy.

Finally, if we are to accept Taylor's prognosis that 'any European
socio-psychological community is more likely to emerge despite rather than
because of the intentions of leaders,'[145] then the persistence of consensus
elite government in the decisional context of the Union clearly highlights
'some of the roadblocks that are in the way'.[146] The predisposition is not to
forge strong identitive links among the constituent *demoi* as a prerequisite
for enhancing the political viability of any larger political entity that aims
to fulfil the democratic functions of government. Rather, it is to satisfy
the central strategic choices of the elite cartel, and to preserve substantive
levels of intergovernmental manoeuvrability in multilateral negotiations.

Against this highly dynamic milieu of interactions which gradually set
the scene for the next millennium, the Union can be best classified as an
unfulfilled democracy: a transnational democratic order in the making
which, at this particular phase of its political evolution, becomes a reflection of its inherent consociational nature. But let us stress once more that
any essential departure from this stage of EU development will most
certainly require the evolution of the presently 'semisovereign' European
demos into something more than merely the numerical aggregate of the
member state *demoi*. It is our contention that this process of democratic
self-transformation is the only possible way to take the Union beyond
executive elite dominance, 'impel the creation of a participatory political
culture and *expectations*,'[147] and bridge the existing gap between the worlds
of intrastate and interstate democracy.

The following table summarises our main points and helps to clarify
the differences between the various models discussed.

Table 7.1 Alternative models of governance

	Federation or federal state	Confederation or union of states	Confederal Consociation
Central actors	Demos	States-national governments	National elites
Central arrangement	Constitution	Pact-contract – international treaty	International treaty
Regime	Constitutional democracy	Democracies	Consensual democracy
Political authority	Central institutions	National governments	Elite cartel
Interaction	Interregional communication (horizontal and vertical)	Interstate co-operation (mainly horizontal)	Inter-elite communication (horizontal)
Decision-making	Majoritarianism/ selective unanimity	Unanimity/ selective majoritarianism	Reversible dissensus
Policy style	Common policies	Co-operation/ co-ordination	Harmonisation/ mutual recognition (common frameworks)
Conflict outcomes	Dynamic 'equilibrium pluralism'	'Conflict pluralism' ('natural liberum veto')	Controlled pluralism (Accommodative mutual veto)
Representation/ system support (legitimacy)	Dual Demos – regional governments	National governments	National elites (grand coalition)
Belief systems	Predominantly compatible	Implicitly compatible	Co-existing and/or accommodative
Society	Amalgamated security community/ *Gemeinschaft*	'Exchange *Gesellschaft*'	'Managed *Gesellschaft*'
Political parties/ interest group organisation	Federations	Transnational associations	Transnational associations

Keeping this discussion in mind, we now turn to the final chapter, and examine the way in which the package agreed at Maastricht has furthered the foundations of democracy in the Union. The rationale behind this endeavour is three-fold: the fact that the extent to which the TEU has actually increased the democratic properties of the system remains in dispute; the evident need to link any discussion of the concept of Confederal Consociation with concrete proposals for redressing the fragmented nature of the European citizen body; and the question of whether it is possible to democratise the Union without submerging the sub-units in a federal state.

Notes on Chapter 7

1   On this type of agreements see Lehmbruch, Gerard, 'A Non-Competitive Pattern of Conflict Management in Liberal Democracies: the Case of Switzerland, Austria and Lebanon', in McRae, Kenneth D. (ed.), *Consociational Democracy: Political Accommodation in Segmented Societies* (Toronto, 1974, McLelland and Stewart), pp 90-7. Steiner cites the following two defining characteristics of this mode of decision-making: that the final compromise reached by the participants is acceptable to all sides; and that it develops from a free bargaining process. See Steiner, Jürg, 'The Consociational Theory and Beyond', *Comparative Politics*, April 1981, p 349.

2   Forsyth, Murray, *Unions of States: The Theory and Practice of Confederation* (Leicester, 1981, Leicester University Press), pp 1-16.

3   Sbragia, Alberta M., 'Thinking about the European Future: The Uses of Comparison', in Sbragia, Alberta M. (ed.), *Euro-Politics: Institutions and Policymaking in the 'New' European Community* (Washington DC, 1992, The Brookings Institution), pp 13 and 257.

4   Christiansen, Thomas, 'European Integration Between Political Science and International Relations Theory: The End of Sovereignty?', EUI Working Paper no 94/4 (San Domenico, 1994, Badia Fiesolana), p 10.

5   On the distinction between these concepts see Forsyth, Murray, *Unions of States*, pp 10-16.

6   For more on this see Chryssochoou, Dimitris N., 'New Challenges to the Study of European Integration: Implications for Theory-Building', *Journal of Common Market Studies*, December 1997, pp 521-42.

7   Wallace, William, 'Theory and Practice in European Integration', in Bulmer, Simon and Scott, Andrew (eds), *Economic and Political Integration in Europe: Internal Dynamics and Global Context* (Oxford, 1994, Basil Blackwell), p 274. Likewise, Adonis has observed: 'It is fashionable to talk of a "democratic deficit", but that is but one aspect of a more chronic malaise: constitutional chaos'. See Adonis, Andrew, 'Subsidiarity: Myth, Reality and the Community's Future', House of Lords Select Committee on the European Commumities, London, June 1990, p 11.

8   *Ibid.* and p 275.

9   Sbragia, Alberta M., 'The European Community: A Balancing Act', *Publius*, Summer 1993, p 24.

10   See, respectively, Kirchner, Emil J., *Decision Making in the European Community: The Council Presidency and European Integration* (Manchester and New York, 1992, Manchester University Press), pp 10-14; Bulmer, Simon and Wessels, Wolfgang, *The European Council: Decision-making in European Politics* (London, 1987, Macmillan), pp 8-11; and Taylor, Paul, *International Organization in the Modern World: The Regional and the Global Process* (London and New York, 1993 Pinter), pp 80-111.

11   McKay, David, 'On the Origins of Political Unions', paper presented at the Second ECSA-World Conference, Brussels, 4-5 May 1994, p 6.

12 Moravcsik, Andrew, 'Preferences and Power in the European Community: A Liberal Intergovernmentalist Approach', *Journal of Common Market Studies*, December 1993, p 507.

13 Puchala, Donald J., 'Of Blind Men, Elephants and International Integration', *Journal of Common Market Studies*, March 1972.

14 Wallace, William, 'Less than a Federation, More than a Regime: the Community as a Political System', in Wallace, Hellen *et al.* (eds), *Policy-Making in the European Community*, Second edn (Chichester, 1983, John Wiley & Sons), p 410.

15 Quoted in *ibid.*, p 406.

16 See Cameron, David, R., 'The 1992 Initiative: Causes and Consequences' in Sbragia, Alberta M. (ed.), *Europolitics*, pp 23-74.

17 Keohane, Robert O., and Hoffmann, Stanley, 'Conclusions: Community Politics and Institutional Change' in Wallace, William (ed.), *The Dynamics of European Integration*, (London and New York, 1990, Pinter), p 282.

18 Scharpf, Fritz W., 'The Joint-Decision Trap: Lessons from German Federalism and European Integration', *Public Administration*, Autumn 1988, p 265.

19 *Ibid.*, p 257 and p 242. Cf Wallace, William, 'Europe as a Confederation: the Community and the Nation-State', *Journal of Common Market Studies*, September-December 1982, p 67; Taylor, Paul, 'Interdependence and Autonomy in the European Communities: The Case of the European Monetary System', *Journal of Common Market Studies*, June 1980, p 373; and Hoffmann, Stanley, 'Obstinate or Obsolete? The Fate of the Nation State in Western Europe', *Daedalus*, Summer 1966, p 910.

20 Groom, A.J.R., 'The European Community: Building Up, Building Down, and Building Across', in Conference Proceedings, 'People's Rights and European Structures', Manressa: Centre Unesco de Catalunya, 1993, p 47.

21 *Ibid.*, p 48.

22 Forsyth, Murray, *Unions of States*, p 1-16.

23 Sharma, B.M. and Choudhry, L.P., *Federal Polity* (London, 1967, Asia Publishing House), pp 11-12. Cf Taylor, Paul, *The Limits of European Integration* (New York, 1983, Columbia University Press), pp 270-5. Likewise, Watts has remarked: 'The difference between the federal and confederal forms lies in the fact that in federal systems, the central institutions are free to exercise responsibilities assigned to them under the constitution in a direct relationship with the electorate, while in confederal systems the central agencies, operating as delegates of the regional governments, are dependent upon them for agreement to common policies'. See Watts, Ronald L., 'Federalism, Regionalism, and Political Integration', in Cameron, David M. (ed.), *Regionalism and Supranationalism: Challenges and Alternatives to the Nation-State in Canada and Europe* (London, 1981, The Institute for Research on Public Policy), p 12.

24 Forsyth, Murray, *Unions of States*, p 16.

25 Dahl, Robert A., *A Preface to Democratic Theory* (Chicago and London, 1956, The University of Chicago Press), p 38.

26 Forsyth, Murray, *Unions of States*, pp 15-16.

27 Forsyth, Murray, 'Towards a New Concept of Confederation', European Commission for Democracy Through Law, Council of Europe, 1994, p 12.

28 Forsyth, Murray, *Unions of States*, p 1.

29 Elazar, Daniel J. *et al.*, *Federal Systems of the World: A Handbook of Federal, Confederal and Autonomy Arrangements*, Second edn (London, 1994, Longman Current Affairs), p xvi. The author defines federation as 'a compound polity compounded of strong constituent entities and a strong general government, each possessing powers delegated to it by the people and empowered to deal directly with the citizenry in the exercise of those powers'.

30 Forsyth, Murray, *Unions of States*, pp 11 and 15-16.

31 Ibid., p 16.

32 Ibid., p 15.

33 von Trietschke, Heinrich, 'State Confederations and Federated States', book III, in Forsyth, Murray *et al.* (eds), *The Theory of International Relations: Selected Texts from Gentili to Treitschke* (London, 1970, Allen and Unwin), p 330 and p 331.

34 Forsyth, Murray, *Unions of States*, p 13.

35 *Ibid.*, pp 13-14.

36 On this idea see Smith, Anthony D., *National Identity* (Harmondsworth, 1991, Penguin), pp 153.

37 Forsyth, *Unions of States*, p 15.

38 *Ibid.* and p 205.

39 Friedrich, Carl J., *Trends of Federalism in Theory and Practice* (London, 1968, Pall Mall Press), pp 11-12. Friedrich defines federation as 'a union of groups, united by one or more common objectives, rooted in common values, interests, or beliefs, but retaining their distinctive group character for other purposes'. See p 177.

40 Forsyth, Murray, 'Federalism and Confederalism', in Bacon, Chris (ed.), *Political Restructuring in Europe: Ethical Perspectives* (London and New York, 1994, Routledge), p 58.

41 Friedrich, Carl J., *Trends of Federalism in Theory and Practice*, p 82.

42 Forsyth, Murray, 'Federalism and Confederalism', pp 57-8.

43 See Barry, Brian, 'Political Accommodation and Consociational Democracy', *British Journal of Political Science*, October 1975, p 478.

44 Daalder, Hans, 'On Building Consociational Nations: The Cases of the Netherlands and Switzerland', *International Social Science Journal*, vol. 23, no 3, 1971, p 358. He elaborates: 'Common affairs were decided *ad hoc* by political procedures that resembled international conferences rather than legitimate national government... There were no organs of the State which could act on the individual and there was no concept of common citizenship'.

45 Vasovic, Vucina, 'Polyarchical or Consociational Democracy?', in Tatu Vanhanan (ed.), *Strategies of Democratization* (Washington, 1992, Crane Russak), p 91. For a brief summary see Gierke, Otto, *Natural Law and the Theory of Society 1500 to 1800* (Cambridge, 1958, Cambridge University Press), pp 70-9.

46 Quoted in Boulle, L.J., *Constitutional Reform and the Apartheid State: Legitimacy, Consociationalism and Control in South Africa* (New York, 1984, St Martin's Press),

note 1, p 66. The definition appears in Apter, David, *The Political Kingdom in Uganda: A Study in Bureaucratic Nationalism* (Princeton NJ, 1961, Princeton University Press), p 24.

47 See *ibid.*, and Sartori, Giovanni, *The Theory of Democracy Revisited* (Chatham NJ, 1987, Chatham House), p 238. Cf Lijphart, Arend, 'Consociational Democracy', *World Politics*, January 1969, pp 207-25.

48 On these concepts see respectively, Lehmbruch, Gerald, 'A Non-Competitive Pattern of Conflict Management in Liberal Democracies'; Church, Clive H., 'The Crisis of Konkordanz Democracy in Switzerland', ECPR Bordeaux Joint Sessions of Workshops, April 1995; and Bluhm, William T., 'Nation-Building: The Case of Austria', *Polity*, vol. 1, 1968, pp 149-77.

49 Stevenson, Garth, *Unfulfilled Union: Canadian Federalism and National Unity*, revised edn (Toronto, 1982, Gage), p 37.

50 See Lijphart, Arend, 'Consociation and Federation: Conceptual and Empirical Links', *Canadian Journal of Political Science*, September 1979, p 500.

51 Boulle, L.J., *Constitutional Reform and the Apartheid State*, p 46. For the original argument see Lijphart, Arend, *The Politics of Accommodation: Pluralism and Democracy in the Netherlands* (Berkeley, 1968, University of California Press). Cf van Schendelen, M.P.C.M., 'The Views of Arend Lijphart and Collected Criticisms', *Acta Politica*, January 1984, pp 19-55 and the bibliography at the end of the volume, pp 161-75.

52 On these concepts see Lustick, Ian, 'Stability in Deeply Divided Societies: Consociationalism Versus Control', *World Politics*, April 1979, pp 325-44. The author considers a society as deeply divided 'if ascriptive ties generate an antagonistic segmentation of society, based on terminal identities with high political salience, sustained over a substantial period of time and a wide variety of issues'. See p 325.

53 On the distinction between Lijphart's consociationalism and the pluralist approach see *ibid.*, p 327.

54 Lijphart, Arend, *Democracy in Plural Societies: A Comparative Exploration* (New Haven, 1977, Yale University Press), pp 25-52.

55 Boulle, L.J., *Constitutional Reform and the Apartheid State*, p 47. Cf Daalder, Haans, 'The Consociational Democracy Theme', *World Politics*, July 1974, pp 604-21.

56 Dahrendorf, Ralf, *Society and Democracy in Germany* (London, 1967, Weidenfeld and Nicolson), p 269. Cf Boulle, L.J., *Constitutional Reform and the Apartheid State*, pp 46-7. This is not to imply, however, that inter-elite accommodation in the grand coalition will be enough without popular support. See Powell, G. Bingham Jr, *Contemporary Democracies: Participation, Stability, and Violence*, (Cambridge MA, 1982, Harvard University Press), p 214. On the leader-follower relationship in consociational systems see Pappalardo, Adriano, 'The Conditions for Consociational Democracy: a Logical and Empirical Critique', *European Journal of Political Research*, December 1981, pp 365-90.

57 According to Sartori, however, in Calhoun's system, 'the veto is an implication rather than a standing principle'. For details see Sartori, Giovanni, *The Theory of Democracy Revisited*, p 239. On the theory of 'concurrent majorities' see Calhoun, John C., *A Disquisition on Government* (New York, 1943, Peter Smith).

58 Lijphart, Arend, 'Consociation and Federation', p 501. Calhoun's basic
    hypothesis is that by giving each minority the right to exercise a veto in the
    process of decision-making, the majority would find it all the more difficult
    to oppress the interests of the minority, thus encouraging intersegmental
    compromise. It would also eliminate the possibilities for the 'tyranny of the
    majority' since each group should consent to the making and execution of
    laws. See Calhoun, John C., *A Disquisition on Government.* For a brief but com-
    prehensive critique on these ideas see Rae, Douglas W., 'The Limits of
    Consensual Decision', *American Political Science Review,* December 1975,
    pp 1270-4.

59 Powell, G. Bingham Jr, *Contemporary Democracies*, p 214.

60 Boulle, L.J., *Constitutional Reform and the Apartheid State*, p 49. On this subject
    see Steiner, Jürgen, 'The Principles of Majority and Proportionality', *British
    Journal of Political Science*, January 1971, pp 63-70.

61 *Ibid.*, p 51. For the related issue of ideological cleavages and political cohe-
    sion see Lorwin, Val R., 'Segmented Pluralism: Ideological Cleavages and
    Political Cohesion in Small European Democracies', *Comparative Politics*,
    January 1971, pp 141-75.

62 *Ibid.* Boulle adds: 'in countries such as Switzerland where the segments are
    territorially concentrated... [segmental autonomy] can be more easily insti-
    tutionalised through a geographic federation'.

63 Lijphart, Arend, 'Consociational Democracy', p 218. For a comprehensive
    critique on Lijphart's theory see Halpern, Sue M., 'The Disorderly Universe
    of Consociational Democracy', *West European Politics* April 1986, pp 181-97.

64 Lijphart, Arend, 'Cultural Diversity and Theories of Political Integration',
    Canadian Journal of Political Science, March 1971, p 9.

65 On this point see Hallowell, John H, *The Moral Foundation of Democracy*,
    (Chicago, 1954, The University of Chicago Press), p 29.

66 Holden, Barry, *Understanding Liberal Democracy* Second edn (London, 1993,
    Harvester Wheatsheaf), p 112.

67 *Ibid.* 'The nature of decision making,' Holden notes, 'is then taken as given,
    democratic theory proper being assumed to provide the necessary analysis'.

68 In the latter types of democracy the existence of a 'two-party system' and of
    a 'homogeneous, secular political culture' facilitates the identification of
    citizens with the institutions of popular control. On this point see Lijphart,
    Arend, 'Typologies of Democratic Systems', in Lijphart, Arend, *Politics in
    Europe* (Englewood Cliffs NJ, 1969, Prentice-Hall), pp 51-2. See also Almond,
    Gabriel A., 'Comparative Political Systems', *Journal of Politics*, August 1956,
    pp 398-9.

69 Hallowell, John H, *The Moral Foundation of Democracy*, p 45. He explains: 'The
    breakdown of democracy comes when... common agreement on fundamental
    principles does not exist'.

70 Kellas, James G., *The Politics of Nationalism and Ethnicity* (London, 1991,
    Macmillan), pp 136. The author examines the validity of consociational
    democracy as an alternative to the classical nationalist idea of 'one nation,
    one state'.

71 Sartori, Giovanni, *The Theory of Democracy Revisited*, p 239.

72 Keohane, Robert O., and Hoffmann, Stanley, 'Conclusions', p 279.

73 See, respectively, Brewin, Christopher, 'The European Community: A Union of States without unity of government', *Journal of Common Market Studies*, vol. 26, no 1, 1987, pp 1-24; Church, Clive H., 'The Not So Model Republic? The Relevance of Swiss Federalism to the European Community', Leicester University Discussion Papers in Federal Studies, No. FS93/4, November 1994, p 15; and Elazar, Daniel J. *et al.*, *Federal Systems of the World*, p xvi.

74 Taylor, Paul, 'Consociationalism and Federalism as Approaches to International Integration', in Groom, A.J.R. and Taylor, Paul (eds), *Frameworks for International Co-operation* (London, 1990, Pinter), pp 172-84.

75 Lijphart, Arend, 'Consociation and Federation', p 506.

76 *Ibid.*, p 500.

77 *Ibid.*

78 Taylor, Paul, *International Organization in the Modern World*, p 88.

79 *Ibid.*, p 89.

80 This does not apply to the allocation of seats in the European Parliament per member state. Instead, there are stong criticisms by the larger states that the current arrangements favour the overrepresentation of the smaller states. On this point see Jacobs, Francis *et al.*, *The European Parliament*, Second edn (Harlow, 1992, Longman Current Affairs), pp 23-4.

81 Taylor, Paul, 'Consociationalism and Federalism as Approaches to International Integration', p 177.

82 *Ibid.*, p 176.

83 For these quotations see respectively, *ibid.* and Graziano, Luigi, 'The Historic Compromise and Consociational Democracy: Toward a "New Democracy"', *International Political Science Review*, vol. 1, no 3, 1980, p 351 (emphasis added).

84 Taylor, Paul, 'Consociationalism and Federalism as Approaches to International Integration', p 177.

85 Lijphart, Arend, 'Cultural Diversity and Theories of Political Integration', p 11.

86 This argument draws on a lecture given by Paul Taylor at The University of Reading, Department of Politics, on 16 May 1995 under the title 'The Principle of Subsidiarity: Theory and Practice'.

87 For a definition of the term see Duchacek, Ivo D., *Comparative Federalism: The Territorial Dimension of Politics* (London, 1970, Holt, Rinehart and Winston), p 20.

88 Taylor, Paul, *International Organization in the Modern World*, p 82.

89 The quotation is taken from Paul Taylor's lecture 'The Principle of Subsidiarity'.

90 Taylor, Paul, *International Organization in the Modern World*, p 108.

91 See Scharpf, Fritz W., 'Community and Policy and Autonomy: Multilevel Policy-Making in the European Union', EUI Working Paper no 94/1 (San Domenico, 1994, Badia Fiesolana), pp 3-5.

92 Sbragia, Alberta M., 'Introduction', in Sbragia, Alberta M. (ed.), *Euro-Politics*, p 13.

93 *Ibid.*

94 *Ibid.*, p 278 and p 279.

95 Scharpf, Fritz W., 'Community and Policy and Autonomy', p 4.

96 Quoted in *ibid.*, p 285, note 71.

97 Sbragia, Alberta M., 'Thinking about the European Future', p 285. Cf Scharpf, Fritz W., 'Community and Policy and Autonomy', p 242-3.

98 Sturm, Ronald and Jeffery, Charlie, 'German Unity, European Integration and the Future of the Federal System: Revival or Permanent Loss of Substance?', in Jeffery, Charlie and Sturm, Ronald (eds), *Federalism, Unification and European Integration*, (London, 1993, Frank Cass), p 165. In addition to these problems of public accountability, the authors identify problems of governmental inefficiency. See pp 166-7.

99 Scharpf, Fritz W., 'Community and Policy and Autonomy', p 3.

100 Wessels, Wolfgang, 'Rationalizing Maastricht: The Search for an Optimal Strategy of the New Europe', *International Affairs*, July 1994, p 456.

101 Kirchner, Emil J., *Decision Making in the European Community*, p 14.

102 Sbragia, Alberta M., 'Thinking about the European Future', pp 288-9.

103 *Ibid.*, p 289.

104 Tsinisizelis, Michael J. and Chryssochoou, Dimitris N., 'From "Gesellschaft" to "Gemeinschaft"? Confederal Consociation and Democracy in the European Union', *Current Politics and Economics of Europe*, vol. 5, no 4, p 5.

105 Peters, B. Guy, 'Bureaucratic Politics and the Institutions of the European Community', in Sbragia, Alberta M. (ed.), *Euro-Politics*, p 121.

106 *Ibid.*, p 111. On the idea of a two-level 'game' between domestic and international politics see Putnam, Robert D., 'Diplomacy and Domestic Politics: the Logic of Two-level Games', *International Organization*, Summer 1988, pp 429-60.

107 For definitions of congruent and incogruent federations see Lijphart, Arend, *Democracies: Patterns of Majoritarian and Consensus Government in Twenty-One Countries* (New Haven and London, 1984, Yale University Press), pp 179-83.

108 Groom, A.J.R., 'The European Community', p 46.

109 Taylor, Paul, 'Consociationalism and Federalism as Approaches to International Integration', p 182.

110 Groom, A.J.R., 'The European Community', p 47.

111 Taylor, Paul, 'Confederalism: The Case of the European Communities', in Groom, A.J.R. and Taylor, Paul (eds), *International Organization: A Conceptual Approach* (London, 1978, Pinter), p 317.

112 I owe this point to Dr Michael Burgess, The University of Hull.

113 Lodge, Juliet, 'Loyalty and the EEC: The Limits of the Functionalist Approach', *Political Studies*, June 1978, p 234

114 Boulle, L.J., *Constitutional Reform and the Apartheid State*, p 33.

115 *Ibid.*, p 31.

116 Chryssochoou, Dimitris N., 'European Union and the Dynamics of Confederal Consociation: Problems and Prospects for a Democratic Future', *Journal of European Integration*, vol. XVIII, nos 2-3, 1995, p 303.

117 *Ibid.*, p 61.

118 *Ibid.*, p 47.

119 Zeigler, Dye, *The Irony of Democracy: An Uncommon Introduction to American Politics*, ninth edn (Belmont, 1993, Washington Publishing Company), p 2. This observation reflects also Dunn's famous phrase on the impossibility of democracy: 'Today, in politics, democracy is the name of what we cannot have – yet cannot cease to want'. See Dunn, John, *Western Political Theory in the Face of the Future* (Cambridge, 1993, Cambridge University Press), p 28.

120 *Ibid.*, p 2.

121 For definitions of these terms see Sartori, Giovanni, *The Theory of Democracy Revisited*, p 234.

122 See Parry, Geraint, *Political Elites* (London, 1969, Allen & Unwin) pp 30-63 and 120-40.

123 For more on the behind-the-scenes activities which led to the signing of the SEA see Taylor, Paul, 'The New Dynamics of EC integration in the 1980s', in Lodge, Juliet (ed.), *The European Community and the Challenge of the Future* (Pinter, 1989, London), pp 3-25.

124 Taylor, Paul, 'Consociationalism and Federalism as Approaches to International Integration', pp 176-7.

125 Vasovic, Vucina, 'Polyarchical or Consociational Democracy?', p 91.

126 *Ibid.*

127 For more on this concept see Bachrach, Peter, *The Theory of Democratic Elitism: A Critique* (London, 1967, The University of London Press).

128 Neunreither, Karlheinz, 'The Syndrome of Democratic Deficit in the European Community', in Parry, Geraint (ed.), *Politics in an Interdependent World: Essays Presented to Ghita Ionescu* (London, 1994, Edward Elgar), p 97.

129 Moravcsik, Andrew, 'Preferences and Power in the European Community', p 518.

130 For more on this point see Riker, William R., *The Theory of Political Coalitions*, (New Haven, 1962, Yale University Press).

131 Holden, Barry, *Understanding Liberal Democracy* second edn, p 112.

132 Barker, Ernest, *Principles of Social and Political Theory*, (Oxford, 1951, Oxford University Press), p 207.

133 The idea of this diagram largely draws upon Beetham's conception of the Democratic Pyramid. See Beetham, David, 'Key Principles and Indices for a Democratic Audit', in Beetham, David (ed.), *Defining and Measuring Democracy* (London, 1994, Sage), p 30.

134 Indeed, turnout in the European electoral process has been constantly decreasing in successive elections, from 61.4% in 1979 to 56.5% in 1994.

135 For a distinction between the 'old' and 'new' intergovernmentalism in EU politics see Lord, Christopher, 'From Intergovernmental to Interparliamentary Union: Democratizing Pastiche Europe', *Contemporary European Affairs*, vol. 4, no 2/3, 1991, pp 229-44.

136 Scharpf, Fritz W., 'The Joint-Decision Trap', p 254.

137 Sbragia, Alberta M, 'Thinking about the European Future', p 275.

138 *Ibid.*, p 263.

139 *Ibid.*, p 262.

140 Taylor, Paul, *International Organization in the Modern World*, p 108.

141 Groom, A.J.R., 'The European Community', p 47.

142 *Ibid.*, p 49.

143 Lijphart, Arend, 'Consociational Democracy', p 222.

144 Taylor, Paul, 'The Politics of the European Communities', p 346.

145 Taylor, Paul, 'Consociationalism and Federalism as approaches to international integration', p 182.

146 *Ibid.*, p 182.

147 Lodge, Juliet, 'Transparency and Democratic Legitimacy', *Journal of Common Market Studies*, September 1994, p 347.

CHAPTER 8

New Dynamics of Democratic Reform

A NOTE ON METHODOLOGY

This final chapter aims to link our previous theoretical discussion to the democratic potential of the Maastricht Treaty and its subsequent revision in Amsterdam. This order of enquiry springs from a general methodological belief that any institutionally-centred analysis should follow, rather than precede, a larger theoretical framework. Not that there always exists a clear-cut dichotomy between the art of theorising European integration and that of projecting its empirical dimension. The mere fact that during the elaboration of the Confederal Consociation theme a number of institutional parameters had to be explored, often by means of employing the language of comparative federalism, is indicative of the difficulties involved in distinguishing between what the present Union looks like and how it actually operates, let alone what kind of polity it might become in the future.

However, consistent with this methodology, we will attempt to build on our previous theoretical findings through the examination of the 'letter' and 'spirit' of the much-debated TEU and, more briefly, the new Treaty of Amsterdam (AMT). In the interests of economy, or rather against those of compulsive constitutional decoding, a rather selective use of the TEU will be made, focusing on its two potentially most important democratic innovations: the new co-decision procedure and the common citizenship provisions. Attention to these issues will be followed by an examination of the principle of subsidiarity and its relation to 'the problem of competence'. Yet, if one subscribes to the view that the TEU can be seen more as an experiment in legalistic or even technocratic graphomania, than in comprehensible treaty-making, then even a limited contextual approach becomes too nebulous a task to fulfil.

A NOT TOO PERFECT INTEGRATIVE BLUEPRINT?

To start with, Art. A TEU states that 'The Union shall be founded on the European Communities, supplemented by the policies and forms of cooperation established in this Treaty'. A first point here might be that the Union provides for a general umbrella under which the pre-established Communities continue to exist as separate legal personalities. It is mainly for this reason that, as in previous chapters, the following discussion will be centred on the European Community. As for the other two pillars complementing this 'temple model' – namely the 'Common Foreign and Security Policy' (CFSP) and 'Cooperation in the Fields of Justice and Home Affairs' (JHA) – by establishing two additional arenas for intergovernmental co-operation, they reveal the limits, or better the selective use, of majority voting in still sensitive policy areas.

In particular, the *locus decidendi* of the new competences 'pooled' to the central institutions in these two sectors rests firmly in the hands of the Council of Ministers assisted, respectively, by the Political Committee and the Co-ordinating Committee, the limited advisory involvement of the European Commission and the European Parliament notwithstanding. As Taylor put it: 'The whole was to be consolidated into a single package of activities linked in systems of common management'.[1] From a theoretical perspective, due to the cautiously designated stages for arriving at common policies and, in the case of the CFSP, joint actions, both sets of procedures operating in these 'pluralist' structures resemble an exercise in transnational regime-formation: a co-operative venture based on a commonly agreed set of principles, norms, rules and procedures, elaborate enough to promote a relatively high degree of horizontal interactions among the participating entities, and elastic enough to be wholly consistent with the pursuit of a fairly wide range of segmental interests in certain fields of transnational life.[2]

According to Bulmer and Scott: 'the two new pillars of the Union constitute an extension of the terrain of inter-state co-operation… a strengthening of the kind of intergovernmental arrangements which exacerbate the democratic deficit'.[3] This is a point further supported in the following areas: the perpetuation of a 'comitology' system which effectively escapes proper parliamentary control;[4] the issue of extending the European Parliament's co-responsibility over compulsory expenditure; the absence of a 'workable' settlement over the European Parliament's 'seat issue' (currently leaving the institution to spread itself over 15 buildings located in three different cities); the unresolved question of a uniform procedure for European elections; issues concerning the clarity, openness and transparency of EU decision-making; and the inadequacy of democratic control over the operations of the envisaged European Central Bank.[5] To complete the puzzle, there are also 17 associated Protocols and 33 Declarations which, albeit not legally binding, serve as possible means of interpreting and implementing parts of the Treaty.

It is noteworthy that according to Art. E TEU the four main institutions of the Union shall exercise their powers 'under the conditions and for the purposes provided for' by the provisions of the Treaty, and that Art. N TEU renders all parts of the Treaty subject to the same revisionary rules. Thus, given the fact that in terms of implementation the Treaty rests on two different sets of legal mechanisms – ie, the 'Community method' and the 'intergovernmental method'[6] – the extent to which it has indeed provided for a 'single institutional framework' – Art. C TEU – is far from self-evident. However, Demaret recognises that 'the dividing line between the two types of mechanisms and between their respective fields of application is, in several instances, less than clear-cut'.[7] Even despite these fairly understandable reservations, it seems that the legal maze of the Maastricht Treaty, especially in terms of institutional coherence and policy co-ordination, has raised more questions than it originally sought to address, proving to be – in spite of the rhetoric on the potential benefits of collective action – 'a source of controversy'.[8] In this context, Wallace has claimed that 'the terms of Maastricht... can be interpreted as easily making efforts to set a ceiling on, even a roll back of, the forces of supranationalism as they can be seen as crossing a new threshold on the route towards a European transnational polity'.[9]

Overall, it is conceivable, at least to some of its students, that the Union, whose three-pillar edifice is presided over by the European Council, courtesy of Art. D TEU, does not possess a legal personality of its own. Rather, as Ress comments: 'it must be considered a new *international organisation sui generis* and thus as a subject of international law'.[10] If by the term 'international organisation' we mean 'a formal, continuous structure established by agreement between members... from two or more sovereign states with the aim of pursuing the common interests of membership,'[11] challenging this view is no easy task. But what makes for the precise nature of the Union's legal personality is arguably for the international lawyers to determine.

Suffice it to stress that the confusion surrounding the 'constitutionality' of this curious hybrid is a perfect illustration of the fact that the question of whether the Union has moved closer to being a 'federal state' or whether it can still be conceived in terms of a 'union of states' remains largely unanswered. Notwithstanding our view that Confederal Consociation provides an exact frontier between these models, and irrespective of whether the Union is 'fragmenting or evolving',[12] let us agree with the drafters of the TEU that its coming into force on 1 November 1993 has signalled a 'new stage in the process of creating an ever closer union among the peoples of Europe'. Whether this stage is one in which, as Art. A TEU states, 'decisions are taken as closely as possible to the citizens,' is evidently in need of further clarification.

What is also remarkable in the new central arrangements is the insistence of the member states to protect their own cultural, political and constitutional features, a point clearly made in Art. F (1) TEU: 'The Union shall respect the national identities of the Member States, whose systems of government are founded on the principles of democracy'. Apart from the latter part of this provision, stressing the universality of democracy within the component polities, the former part is indicative of the need to sustain a pluralistic form of society at the larger level. It implies that any challenge to constituent identities would be both legally and practically unacceptable. At the same time, the search for regional unity through the striking of an uneasy compromise between federal principles, confederal structures and consociational processes implies a series of mutual concessions taken by the states to meet the challenges of joint decision-making, without losing sight of their claims to national autonomy.

Both points seem to substantiate the Confederal Consociation thesis because of the premium it places on preserving satisfactory levels of segmental distinctiveness and civic autonomy within a sensibly arranged framework of mutual governance, and due to its unique blend of consensual mechanisms for accommodating varying degrees of diversity within a nascent, yet highly fragile, political unity. Joining together diverse entities in a close political incorporation that respects their individual integrities, Confederal Consociation challenges the compact (or organic) theory of the polity, without relying entirely on the properties of 'segmented differentiation'. From this stems its greatest merit as a new framework for analysis, but also its strongest concern: to provide equality of status to its members, whilst allowing for a less rigid understanding of statehood so that those members can bear the fruits of their partnership. This has been achieved so far in the Union by applying a mixed system of consensus and majority government, the operational expression of which is close to what Forsyth calls 'unanimity at the base, majority voting in the superstructure'.[13]

To open a small parenthesis here, the political 'fragility' of such an approach to European unity has clearly shown itself not only during the negotiations leading up to the signing of the TEU in February 1992 – a process inaugurated in June 1991 by the Luxembourg 'reference document' on the Union – but more importantly perhaps during its adventurous and prolonged course of ratification, and the subsequent 'opt-outs' secured by the more sceptical members as a *quid pro quo* for giving their final consent to the Treaty.[14] Against the background of an ever-more cynical electorate, any residual touch of optimism from the mid-1980s, a period described by many as a neofunctionalist 'come-back',[15] seemed to have evaporated by the time Germany formally concluded the ratification process on 12 October 1993.[16] Although the Treaty has finally managed to survive the new tides of Euroscepticism, albeit not entirely intact for two of its signatories, a new 'democratic disjunction' became manifest between the wishes of national leaders and popular political sentiments.[17]

In addition to the 'conventional' democratic deficit, this attendant democratic discrepancy was evident in the rejection of the TEU in the first Danish referendum on 2 June 1992 (although nearly 75% of the *Folketing* supported ratification), and in the 49% of the French who voted against the Treaty on 20 September 1992 (despite the fact that only three months earlier a 'Congress' of both legislative Houses produced an overwhelming majority of 87% in favour of ratification).[18] Both incidents, by sharpening the divide between elites and *demos*, have moved the Union closer to a state of 'illegitimacy'. As in past endeavours to reach accommodation on a final text, the TEU – criticised by Wallace as 'a document negotiated in a room without windows'[19] – reflected in a most tenacious way the on-going tussle between those defending the rights of the member states and those projecting an independent legitimacy for the new polity. In Neunreither's words: 'It is a text for insiders, not only in being difficult to read and to digest, but even more because of its paternalistic approach – everything is done *for* the people, not very much *by* the people'.[20]

The lessons to be learned from the Maastricht process, as a case of forging a variety of segmental differences into a single political blueprint, is that unless there is a sufficient area of consensus at the elite level to bridge the tensions arising from a classical interpretation of the principle of self-determination, and a more advanced conception of the practice of co-determination, no viable outcomes can exist. This accords with what most sceptical students of integration have implicitly assumed: over the last decade, the weight of the evidence is that the extension of both its scope and level has exploited to the highest possible degree a crucial property of consensual politics: the capacity to reconcile the challenges of innovation with the need for continuity. The conclusion is that in the Union of the 1990s 'the burden of proof' seems to lie more on federalism rather than on intergovernmentalism as a method of organising the affairs of the polity in terms of convincing leaders and led of its validity both as a *condition* and a *process* of transnational governance.

DEMOCRATIC DYNAMICS AND THE INCEPTION
OF THE FOURTH EUROPE

Although the above description fits neatly with the nature of the Maastricht Treaty, as it does with our consociationalist terminology, a more optimistic interpretation of the facts might lead to the suggestion that its coming into force has signalled the beginning of a new transitional period which might be described best by the term 'nascent *Gemeinschaft*'. From a historical perspective, just as Hallstein's 'First Europe' (1958-1966) (institutional centralisation) was succeeded by Dahrendorf's 'Second Europe' (1969-1974) (a more favourable version of intergovernmentalism) and that by what Taylor calls a 'Third Europe' (1974-1993) (a creative synthesis of the two), so the latter seems to be giving way to a Fourth Europe (1993-today).[21]

This phase, characterised by a conscious striving to redress perhaps the gravest democratic deficiency of the symbiotic model – who should ultimately be accountable to whom – can also be seen as part of a wider evolution towards a politically organised *Gemeinschaft*: a European 'constitutive polity' comprised of citizens capable of being simultaneously conscious of their separate existence as distinctive cultural and political entities and of their collective existence as one European *demos*. At the moment, however, nascent *Gemeinschaft* represents an attempt at distancing current EU practices from the logic of consensus elite government by stressing the democratic potential of the constituent publics.

Put simply, instead of large-scale decisions being mainly the result of agreements reached within the elite cartel, they should be subjected as closely as possible to the conditions of the democratic process. But unless a dialectic encounter of federalism and democracy – the former seen as the territorial twin of the latter[22] – takes place within EU structures, the chances of its citizens going further down the post-Maastricht road will be particularly bleak. In its most elevated form, nascent *Gemeinschaft* aims to turn an 'aggregate of electors' into a politically aware, active and responsible citizenry whose members feel part of a larger purposive unit: a European 'public sphere' through which democratic considerations become more firmly embedded in the civic culture of its members. Hence, nascent *Gemeinschaft* represents both a conceptual position and a point of departure for free people to develop a lively sense of membership within an 'inclusive' political whole.

In attempting now to capture the major stages in the process of transnational *demos*-formation by means of examining the relationship between the structure of the European *demos* and the patterns of elite behaviour, we offer the following typology.

Figure 8.1 A Typology of Transnational *Demos*-Formation

STRUCTURE OF TRANSNATIONAL *DEMOS*

		Fragmented	Cohesive
PATTERNS OF ELITE BEHAVIOUR	Confrontational	Exchange *Gesellschaft* (self-determination)	Nascent *Gemeinschaft* (democratic dynamic)
	Co-operative	Managed *Gesellschaft* (concordance system)	Complete *Gemeinschaft* (political community)

As the above typology illustrates, the possible forms of political organisation that the larger polity may take range from a system of self-determination to a political community. It needs to be said, however, that the transformation of the Union from 'managed *Gesellschaft*' to nascent *Gemeinschaft* is neither automatic nor certain. Much will depend on the outcome of future 'deepening rounds' – ie, along the experience of the 1996/7 IGC (see below) – in terms of transcending the tensions between those states which form a rather sceptical coalition with regard to far-reaching constitutional reforms and those driven by similar federalist aspirations.

Although no straightforward answer exists as to whether the bonds of unity created by Maastricht will prove strong enough to revitalise the forces of integration so as to overcome a number of obstacles that are in the way of a European *Gemeinschaft*, should they succeed, then the whole movement could mark a step forward in the making of a transnational *demos*. To that end, it is essential that a 'communitarian' logic prevails over any consociationalist-inspired tendencies to sustain the elite-dominated character of the system at the expense of the emergence of a European *demos*. In particular, this is crucial for the long-term implications of the 'democratic dynamics' embodied in the TEU for increasing the levels of public awareness of, and citizen identification with, the central institutions, as well as furthering the range and depth of citizen participation in EU decision-making.

Yet, the same basic assumptions underlying the dynamics of transnational *demos*-formation as expressed in the previous typology can be found in the exercise of collapsing the 'hexagon' into a 'diamond'. It is expected that such a move will create direct links of communication between the Union and its citizens as a prerequisite for a more democratic process of integration. The following figure helps to illustrate this point by reference to the dominant role of national governmental elites in the relationship between the central authorities and the member publics.

Figure 8.2 Collapsing the 'hexagon' into a 'diamond'

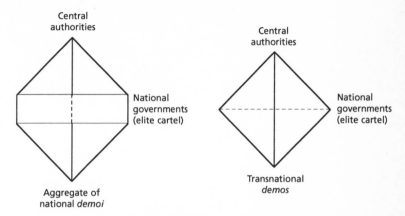

Arguably, the greatest challenge facing the Fourth Europe is neither the preservation by all costs of an informal culture of consensus-building among the segment elites for managing the transnational *Gesellschaft* – a process based on 'the equalisation of the hierarchy of actors'[23] – nor the safeguarding of a neofunctionalist-inspired 'procedural consensus' through which rival groups agree to pursue their interests.[24] Instead, only through the abandonment of the *Gesellschaft*-like qualities of the larger system, and the simultaneous setting up of a more 'communitarian' agenda for investing in the participative potential of citizens can there be a case for bringing about the qualitative transformation of the Union from democracies to democracy.

Inevitably, some may venture to claim that this path to integration will most certainly challenge the 'hard-core' of the member nation-states. They may even argue that the major effects of conscious community-strengthening, possibly accompanied by acts of formal constitutional engineering, might be seen in the light of the existing equilibrium of territorial and non-territorial forces as an apology for confrontational behaviour. Such a development may take the form of various disjointed responses on the part of the segment elites, as to which particular set of institutional reforms might produce an optimal model for EU democracy.

It is exactly in relation to this possible outbreak of an uncontrolled (by the forces of unity) and detrimental (to systemic stability) intersegmental conflict over the selection of the means for democratising the collectivity that, to borrow a phrase, 'the shadows of a turbulent future are visible'.[25] Yet, one should also recognise that these reservations amount to a rather deceptive dilemma between the requirements of democratic government, such as indirect *demos* control and popular legitimacy, and the conditions responsible for the political viability of the Union.

Nearing the end of our preliminary reflections on the integrative corpus created by the TEU, and before focusing on its actual and potential democratic qualities, it is important to stress that the nature of the relationship between the Union and the states, and between the two separate legal bases on which the TEU is based, were liable to amendment by the 1996 review conference, courtesy of Art. N TEU (see below). The following figure aims to capture the range of possibilities open to the interested parties for moving towards a mode *demos*-oriented process of integration.[26]

Figure 8.3 Democracy and European Constitutional Change

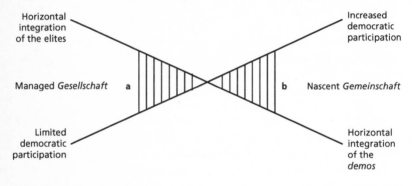

Note
a democracy in input
b democracy in output

As this diagram illustrates, the move from the upper left to the lower right side of the first axis points to the strengthening of the horizontal links among the member publics, as a fundamental prerequisite for the embodiment of a stronger *Gemeinschaft* element at the popular level. As for the process shown by the second axis, it stresses the quality of democratic participation in the integration process. Taken together, these tendencies form part of the wider qualitative leap, in both structural and socio-psychological terms, from *Gesellschaft* to *Gemeinschaft*.

Although the dynamics of 'constitutional' review seem to have escaped Lord Mackenzie-Stuart's characterisation of the TEU as a 'driving-mirror Treaty', in that it writes down *de jure* what has already been achieved *de facto*,[27] in essence, Art. N TEU implies that irrespective of the Treaty's contribution to the academic exercise of theory-building, and its practical impact on joint decision-making, Maastricht cannot be considered the final vocation of the integrative journey. This is a view which gives ample ground for speculative assessments on what the ultimate destination might look like, as well as for the formulation of a 'beyond Maastricht-approach'. Although the latter exercise entails numerous risks for the student of integration, some of which might *in passu* prove to be worth taking, our conclusions will be drawn mainly from the evidence offered by the TEU – and, albeit to a lesser extent, by its partial revision in the 1997 Amsterdam Summit – about the political physiognomy of the Union.

In summary, the central question which underlies our concluding chapter asks whether Maastricht represents a breakthrough in the process of democratising the Union, in terms of addressing and effectively dealing with both dimensions of the democratic deficit, as previously identified in this study: the structural and the socio-psychological. *Grosso modo*, the former was meant to be tackled by the authors of the Treaty mainly through the introduction of a new legislative procedure, granting the European Parliament the right to veto European legislation in certain policy areas. The latter was to be addressed through the establishment of a common European citizenship. Finally, both aspects of the polity's democratic pathology were intended to be affected in a positive way through the application of the principle of subsidiarity.

At best, it was believed that the combined impact of these measures would put an end to the most serious facets of the democratic deficit. At worst, it was expected that these parts of the Treaty, however 'poorly thought out' they may have been,[28] would act as a prelude for further democratic reforms through the operations of the new review conference. In both cases, however, the partisan polemics against the whole project aside, this triptych of democratic innovations represents a welcome, albeit moderate, development in the exercise of transnational democracy-building. It is to the exact effect of these novelties that we now turn.

THE NEW POLITICS OF CO-DECISION

It took the European Parliament twelve years of intensive inter-institutional struggles since its first direct elections, as well as two formal revisions of the original treaties, to secure a final say on European legislation; to be granted an indirect right of legislative initiative; to forge its links with the European peoples through the formal recognition of the right to petition; to codify its powers over the appointment of the President of the

Commission and link the Commission's term of office to its own; to improve the conditions of its involvement in the central judicial process (action for annulment); to rename its transnational political groups into political parties; to appoint – and dismiss at its request – a European Ombudsman; to increase its supervisory powers by setting up temporary committees of inquiry to investigate alleged contraventions or maladministration in the implementation of European law; to be given a right of veto over any future Council decision on a uniform electoral procedure; and to further its legislative impact through the extension of the assent and co-operation procedures.

Although no fewer than 22 variants have been identified in EU decision-making procedures resulting from the TEU,[29] the following three are arguably the most important ones in relation to the European Parliament's legislative involvement: assent, co-operation and co-decision, with the consultation procedure being applied in the remaining 70 areas where unanimity is still formally required in Council.[30] There is a strong feeling that the legislative reforms introduced by the TEU are part of a wider institutional evolution inaugurated by the SEA in July 1987, an important contribution of which was to speed up the passage of European legislation after years of stagnation as a result of the 1966 Luxembourg Accords. Under the new co-decision procedure, and on the basis of a worst-case scenario in the event of a continuous disagreement between the European Parliament and the Council, a legislative act would require at least 15-16 months from the moment the Commission has submitted its proposal to the Council. Under a best-case scenario though, the time periods can be considerably shortened to 3-6 months.[31]

The outcome of the Maastricht negotiations reflected the pressures put upon the member states by domestic and external environments, some favourable and others inimical to 'deepening' integration. But the final arrangements came into being as a result of partial reconciliations among the different interests and aspirations of the states, rather than by pressures generated by 'the birth of some transcendental European entity'.[32] Accordingly, the key to their viability rests on the equal stressing of joint management practices and territorial safeguards or, simply, interdependence and autonomy: the strengthening of the Union and the preservation of the separate constitutional orders of states became two interconnected dynamics of equal weight.

After a long period of confederal preparation, essential principles of federal government, such as the establishment of strong representational links between the *demos*, the states and the central institutions were compromised on the grounds that they were either structurally or politically inappropriate to the collectivity. Fears of impairing the integrity of constituent identities prevailed over federalist-driven prescriptions of power-sharing and acceptance of an elementary 'community of destiny' among the member publics. In essence, the dynamic enmeshing of consensual politics, territorial considerations and contradictory motives questioned the possibility of a more democratic process of union, whilst stressing the limits for the development of a nascent *Gemeinschaft.* In a word, the belief that the 'Union' decided at Maastricht bears the marks of the Community's confederal past seems to hold true.

This is not to belittle the significance of the changes introduced by the TEU, but rather to verify their incrementalist nature, and substantiate our point that a radical break, not to say a 'constitutional revolution', with established rules concerning the dialectics of consensus elite government was too great a step to be taken in the early 1990s. As Weiler put it: 'TEU does not represent a qualitative and transformative structural leap, but proceeds along the well-trodden path of cautious incrementalism'.[33] For neither far-reaching institutional reforms have taken place, nor are there strong federalist elements in the Treaty to justify an immediate threat to the constitutional conditions of national sovereignty. This, in turn, relates to the view that the Union remains in the category of Confederal Consociation. Overall, these partial improvements left the European Parliament short of its original aspirations to become an equal partner in a bicameral European legislature. The following points aim to support this view.

First, the procedure of Art. 189b EC was deliberately left nameless by the negotiators as a clear indication of refusing Parliament's claims for full legislative equality with the Council. As a result, a number of alternative terms have appeared in the literature such as 'negative assent', 'new conciliation' and 'co-decision' procedure, with the EP preferring the latter. Second, the field of application of the new procedure has been restricted to non-conflictual policy areas in the sense that the member states not only felt that their 'vital national interests' were hardly at stake, but also that a general consensus existed among them to see the relevant acts becoming legislation.

As for the implications of majority voting in these areas, Taylor has pointed out that, instead of breaching the sovereignty of states, or even eroding their powers to veto any action of which they disapproved, 'its main effect was to put greater pressure on states to compromise so that a general agreement could be found'.[34] Hence, majority voting became 'a lubricant of the consensus-forming process'.[35] This was particularly the case with Arts. 100a and 100b EC which, all the more so, would no longer serve a purpose after the completion of the Single Market.

A third argument challenges more directly the substance of the co-decision procedure. According to Corbett, the application of Art. 189b EC 'is limited to the approval of general "guidelines" or "programmes", leaving the specific items of legislation to be decided by other procedures'.[36] This sceptical assertion assumes particular weight when considering the areas of research and technological development, trans-European networks and environmental policy, where the Council retains extensive powers on the selection of individual programmes and has the final say on the implementation of the general guidelines.[37] In addition to these problems, a number of democratic inconsistencies arise when examining the 'letter' of the procedure in question.

More specifically, in the absence of an agreement between Parliament and Council in the context of a new Conciliation Committee comprising an equal number of representatives from each – an institution largely inspired from the *Bundestag-Bundesrat* 'mediation committee' – the Council is entitled to act unilaterally on a third reading by adopting a text which will become law unless Parliament rejects it by a majority of its members or fails to respond within six weeks. Our reservation here is twofold. First, the right of veto corresponds to a negative or 'counteractive' power in that it gives Parliament the right to reject legislation, rather than to one capable of contributing something positive to the inter-institutional debate in terms of improving the quality of a specific item of legislation in the course of the procedure. Thus, far from acting in the interests of co-legislative creativity, or even against those of decisional rigidity and inter-institutional deadlock, this particular stage of Art. 189b EC compromises the prospects for a new kind of legislative dialogue favourable to the Council. And second, despite the fact that Parliament's right to 'block' legislation gives it a certain degree of bargaining power *vis-à-vis* the Council, if it fails to produce the majority needed to reject the text, then the Council can still adopt the proposed act by a qualified majority of its members. Here one can also take into account Corbett's point that the European Parliament might prefer from the outset 'a half measure to nothing at all', and that 'it does not wish to be perceived in a negative light as responsible for hold-ups, delays and failures in the legislative procedure'.[38] The latter point is not without wider political implications for the public image of the European Parliament.

There are, however, two other important provisions in Art. 189b EC which differentiate Parliament's position from the co-operation procedure of the SEA: it can now reject the text outright in second reading, without the Council being able to overrule Parliament's decision by unanimity; and any second reading amendments proposed by the European Parliament are now submitted individually to the Council which can either approve them by a qualified majority (if they enjoy the backing of the Commission), or reject them by unanimity (if they lack support by the Commission). The crucial point is that since the amendments accepted by the Commission are not incorporated into the text automatically, their fate rests entirely on the Council's ability to obtain a qualified majority to support them. And since over the last few years the Council has accepted about a half of the European Parliament's amendments in second reading, it is likely that under the new procedure this percentage will fall, increasing the need for conciliations and widening the distance separating the two bodies before they enter into negotiations.[39]

Finally, if we were to judge the new procedure against the European Parliament's claims for full co-decision through its becoming the source of legislative initiative, then it is difficult to refrain from stating that these arrangements leave much to be desired. To start with, Art. 138b(2) EC, in a similar vein with Art. 152 EC, states: 'The European Parliament may, acting by a majority of its members, request the Commission to submit any appropriate proposal on matters on which it considers that a Community act is required for the purpose of implementing this Treaty'. Although the question of whether the response on the part of the Commission is obligatory or not remains open, Ress argues that had it not been obligatory 'the provision would be redundant'.[40]

Prima facie, this represents an indirect recognition that Parliament has indeed gained a right of initiating legislation. However, it does not yet possess any right in the shaping of draft legislation which, even in this case, seems to remain the prerogative of the Commission. And given the absence of *ad hoc* decision-making rules, there are grounds for thinking that the whole issue may lead again to 'Rule by the Court'. In brief, despite Parliament's alleged 'victory' in this area, its actual influence is largely conditioned by the realities of joint decision-making, as well as by the dominant interpretation of the inter-institutional 'rules of the game'.

What conclusion may be drawn from the preceding discussion? Viewed from a realist perspective, our final statement on the subject is that although co-decision was hailed as only a partial solution to the institutional aspects of the democratic deficit,[41] it does imply a certain degree of movement in bringing the European Parliament closer to the *locus decidendi* of the Union, adding a stronger touch of transparency to the system. And since for the first time the directly elected representatives of European citizens are accepted as more or less equal partners with those of national governments in a political discourse of some substance leading to a deliberative outcome, overall, its coming into force can be said to advance the democratic properties of the system.

PERSPECTIVES ON TRANSNATIONAL CITIZENSHIP

Citizenship, a legal prerequisite of democratic participation, is no longer the prerogative of nation-states. Having symbolised for some centuries now a multi-stranded but 'internally-oriented relationship' which people as individuals have with national political institutions,[42] it has finally acquired in the context of the Union a multinational dimension. Whether a direct challenge to the very idea of statehood or a facilitating condition towards European federation, the granting to member states' nationals of the right to be involved in European and municipal (local) elections of other member states signifies that the era of the national state as the only legitimate actor in determining the politics of citizenship belongs to the past. The actual and symbolic significance of this assertion becomes easily established if one considers that in the vast majority of the member states, especially those with a federal or quasi-federal structure, subnational elections are taken very seriously.

Compared with other provisions embodied in the Treaty for addressing the polity's acute legitimation problems, and despite their legal shortcomings, Arts. 8a-e EC carry an undisputed political weight, perhaps with the most far-reaching implications for the emergence of a stronger *Gemeinschaft* element at the popular level. For they set in train the conditions for the development not only of a Deutschian 'socio-psychological community', or even a Haasian-inspired political one, but also the means for the nurturing of a European civic 'we-ness'; a prerequisite for the configuration of a common political identity among the member publics. In this sense, Union citizenship lays and at the same time strengthens the foundations of a nascent *Gemeinschaft* which may ultimately lead to a full-blown European *demos*. As T.H. Marshall has observed, citizenship is above all 'a claim to be treated as full members of the society,'[43] its most celebrated property being equality of political status and participatory opportunities for the members of a political community.

The civic element underpinning this normative definition is that citizenship presupposes the existence of some form of political community accompanied by a set of institutional arrangements that aim to fulfil the participative potential of the *demos* in the exercise of political power, not only via the electoral process, but also through continuous avenues of citizen involvement in the governmental process. This view accords with the more general description of citizenship as 'complete' or 'total' participation in the public affairs of a polity. In brief, citizenship entails an important feature central to the democratic process which might be termed 'civic competence': the institutional capacity of citizens to have access to the realm of political influence.

Although the inclusion/exclusion divide has been examined else-where,[44] it is worth noting that about nine million third-country nationals legally residing in a member state of the Union are excluded from the electoral process.[45] Indeed, Art. 8(1) EC makes it clear that Union citizen-ship derives from national citizenship. As a result, a 'participatory deficit' has emerged for those belonging to this 'other' Europe 'within', pointing towards a 'dissociational-type democracy' where access to democratic participation is even more restricted than it is for European citizens.[46]

The idea of Union citizenship as a feature *par excellence* of nascent *Gemeinschaft* is based on a two-fold assumption: first, that the establishment of a transnational system of political rights can further induce integrative sentiments at the grass-roots, thus motivating greater democratic par-ticipation in EU affairs; and second, that it strengthens the bonds of belonging to an active political community, thus facilitating the process of positive European awareness-formation at the popular level. Symbolic as these may sound at the time, the democratic dynamic embedded in the common citizenship provisions should not be underestimated, all the more so in view of Art. 8e EC which empowers the Council to 'adopt provisions to strengthen or to add to the rights laid down in this Part [Part Two: Citizenship of the Union]'. This explicit reference to potential improvements, although largely intergovernmental in kind, renders the process of large-scale civic engineering – ie, the achievement of higher levels of 'civic competence' for European citizens – an open-ended one. The question, of course, is whether these would simply entail a rearrange-ment of existing political entitlements for the constituent publics or attribute effective 'civic competence' based on the power of a new 'civic contract' between peoples, states and central authorities.

The idea for this proposal stems from the axiom that as in any other polity so in the Union, no public power should be exercised without the prior consent of the citizen. The constitutional conditions and dynamics of the participating states over the last 200 years imply that the distri-bution of competences and responsibilities passes through, rather than goes beyond, the capacity of citizens to determine the political functions of the community to which they belong. In fact, what still remains vital about modern democracy is that all public decisions are taken by the rep-resentatives of the *demos*, for the interests of the *demos* and, ultimately, in the name of the *demos*. This, in turn, is based on the existence of a 'civic contract' between governors and governed. Should an 'arrangement' of this type fail to materialise, the very legitimacy of publicly binding decisions is being challenged and a state of 'illegitimacy' prevails.

At the Union level, the idea of dual citizenship offers an excellent opportunity to incorporate, but not amalgamate, the separate national 'civic contracts' that currently exist in the constituent polities into a transnational 'public sphere' where the consent of citizens for the larger-scale of decisions is organised 'from below': a new horizontally structured 'union of peoples' whose members would be able to participate actively in integration processes. According to Neunreither, this would require the evolution of the 'member-state citizen' from a 'functionalist' or 'fragmented citizen' to an 'indirect' or 'derived' one, and then to an 'interactive citizen'.[47] What is absolutely essential, however, is that the transition from one stage to another should come as a conscious act of civic self-development, that is an exercise in 'political self-identification'.[48] As Herzog has observed: 'European citizenship must proceed from the desire and the capacity of the persons concerned to found an active community seeking to serve common goals... Citizens of the Member States would seek to enrich their identity and ability to act by assuming shared responsibilities'.[49]

Arguably, much will depend upon the 'quality' of future proposals to strengthen Union citizenship and build on the occurrence of a common civic identity. Of such measures, the following are worth mentioning: the detachment of Union citizenship from the 'nationality requirement' and its placing on an independent sphere of civic entitlements; the institutionalisation of citizens' right to information on all EU issues that directly affect them; the drafting of a 'European social public order' based on the principle of solidarity to impose obligations on institutions and corporations;[50] the creation of protective legal mechanisms against any potential infringement of explicitly stated fundamental rights, including all forms of discrimination; the enrichment of the citizens' social and economic rights, especially those relating to free movement, social welfare, working conditions and co-operative management-participation schemes; the codification of the conditions under which consular protection is to be provided for Union citizens in the territory of a third country; and the recognition of electoral rights to legally resident third-country nationals.

In general, it is important that the principle of additionality apply in this context: that the present and future sets of Euro-citizenship rights are established in addition to national citizenship, 'attached', in Close's words, 'to a novel, distinct and... supranational citizenship status'.[51] It is only then that this array of treaty-based entitlements may be taken to symbolise, or even institutionalise, the federal properties of a unique relationship between an emerging citizen body and the central authorities. As Holland claims: 'the conditions and terms of citizenship may have been constrained and limited in scope... [but] an important federal precedent has been established'.[52] He adds: 'The Maastricht reforms began the process of demonstrating the existence of common and shared rights, and the liberal principles of the Single Market were seen to be equally applicable to democratic rights'.[53] Indeed, despite the inclusion of the 'nationality requirement' to entertain member states' fears of a loss of national identity to an emerging European federation, a positive feeling seems to underpin the democratic implications of the new *status civitatis*. As O'Keeffe put it: 'The importance of the TEU citizenship provisions lies not in their content but rather in the promise they hold out for the future. The concept is a dynamic one, capable of being added to or strengthened, but not diminished'.[54]

On the other hand, the Treaty avoided the incorporation of any set of civic entitlements in a formal 'constitutional' document addressed directly to the citizen, thus reflecting the political rationale behind the member states' insistence on a fairly acceptable citizenship package. Similarly, the language used in the TEU implies that there was no intention on the part of national governments to create a 'new political subject' – ie, a potentially sovereign European *demos* – capable of associating itself 'with notions of nation or people or with citizenship of a state'.[55] Instead, as some sceptical commentators put it: 'The texts on citizenship which emerged from Maastricht represented a codification of existing trends in both jurisprudence and legislation which added little to what was already in the pipeline or being practised'.[56]

What these criticisms fail to recognise is the democratic dynamics of Union citizenship, in that the progressive evolution and strengthening of European 'civic competence' depends as much upon legal requirements and judicial procedures as it does upon the actual responses this new citizenship status might receive from those who have acquired it. Accordingly, the prospects of common citizenship lie in the ability of the constituent peoples to make good use of their new rights and broaden their participation in integration processes. To borrow from Dahl: 'important possibilities are yet to be explored'.[57] For the occurrence of Union citizenship implies the fostering of *horizontal* ties among the individuals forming the 'constituent power' of the larger polity.

Indeed, if we recall one of our previous views of democracy – as the highest form of civic association for embracing the participation of the *demos* in the shaping of its political environment – then the implications that Union citizenship generates for the civic quality of European governance assume particular importance. For it points towards a more *demos*-oriented and 'consciousness-raising' process of union, as opposed to an elite-driven one 'governed by opaque procedures of intergovernmental decision making'.[58] These implied effects do not merely concern the position of member publics in the governance of the Union. They also extend at the level of those governmental elites that are firmly involved in joint decision-making. In particular, one may allude to the possibility that a gradual changing of established perceptions about their proper place and role within the regional system will take place, furthering, in Sbragia's words, the transformation of the "'sovereign" Nation-States that created the community or joined it after its creation... into "Member States"'.[59]

The above observation relates to our previous argument on the interplay between the new transnational political culture among Europe's governing elites and the gradual transformation of the principle of 'self-determination' into one of 'co-determination'. This development, now part of a well-consolidated system of governance in which the principle of joint sovereignty has been institutionalised, may be extended at the popular level, acting as an explicit confirmation of the existence of a nascent European *demos*. From this perspective, the political relationship between transnational citizenship, large-scale democratic participation and European 'civic competence' can be best described as a *synergetic* one, involving the simultaneous building of higher levels of political co-determination at both popular and elite levels.

In a larger theoretical framework, the triptych *symbiosis-synergy-osmosis*, as elements directly relating to the basic properties of 'managed *Gesellschaft*', nascent *Gemeinschaft* and complete *Gemeinschaft* respectively, can be also seen as the three stages in the making of a transnational *demos*: the first, describing the current state of union in terms of the relationship between the collectivity and the segments (mutual dependence); the second, pointing to the concurrent development of horizontal links among the constituent publics (cohesive structure) and a strengthening of existing ones among the members of the elite cartel (co-determination); and the third, representing a culmination of these processes and, hence, of earlier phases in a representative and responsible 'union of peoples' (transnational democracy).

In conclusion, the significance of tying the self-image of the elites to the dialectical relationship between Maastricht's citizenship provisions and the process of transnational *demos*-formation is simply that no commonly shared civic identity can come into being unless all major actors in EU politics start thinking about the future of European integration as a process that has to evolve from interaction at the lower level 'upwards', rather than conversely; or, alternatively, that the formation of a European 'constitutive polity' be determined by EU citizens themselves, rather than by the self-interests of executive centred elites. This, however, requires the passage from limited to increased public participation in the affairs of the larger polity, itself a precondition for the transition from 'managed *Gesellschaft*' to nascent *Gemeinschaft*, a transition which can be achieved and maintained only through the development of a transnational civic culture within which large-scale democratic politics can operate.

The above description is not a theoretical transformation derived from a 'pure' political sociological approach and deprived of any empirical implications. Rather, it is a dynamic interactionist activity carried through processes of large-scale community-building and collective identity-formation. This chain of simultaneous interactions, however, should be so structured as to generate and sustain the belief by the composite *demos* of its transnational 'civic competence': its institutional capacity to influence the governance of the larger polity at any particular stage. Otherwise, the drift towards wider 'democratic disjunctions' between the elites and the *demos* will persist. But such activities will have to be supported and complemented by adequate procedural machinery in order to bear fruits. This point brings us to one of the most contentious debates in the history of the Union – whose battle lines have been drawn for some time now – over the allocation of competences between different levels of government through a federal principle of power-sharing: that of subsidiarity.

SUBSIDIARITY IN PRINCIPLE AND PRACTICE

Enshrined in the TEU as a basic guideline for the *vertical* division of (shared) responsibilities between the Union and the states, subsidiarity has opened the way for two separate lines of development: the protection of national autonomy against excessive institutional centralisation; and the extension of transnational legislative authority. Whereas the former favours the thesis of Confederal Consociation, perceiving subsidiarity as a constraint on EU law-making powers, the latter points towards the formation of a more federally definable structure of governance. Whichever tendency is to prevail, much will depend on the dominant interpretation of Art. 3b EC which currently reads thus: 'In areas which do not fall within its exclusive competence, the Community shall take action, in accordance with the principle of subsidiarity, only if and insofar as the objectives of the proposed action cannot be sufficiently achieved by the Member States and can therefore, by reason of the scale or effects of the proposed action, be better achieved by the Community'.

Prima facie, and according to Shaw, subsidiarity appears to create both a 'sufficiency' and an 'effectiveness' criterion: the former suggesting that 'Community institutions must demonstrate that Member State action is not sufficient', and the latter based on the assumption that 'Community action must be better able to achieve the end in view'.[60] Yet, there is also a third criterion embodied in the TEU which, although only indirectly related to the principle, links the previous two with a fundamental aspect of democratic government: decisional closeness in relation to the *demos*. Contextually, this preference for lower level decision-making is reflected in Art. A of the Common Provisions which, after re-affirming the integrative nature of the TEU, provides that decisions should be taken 'as closely as possible to the citizen'.

This criterion fits well with the consociationalist logic of Union governance in the 1990s since, by justifying a potential flow of decision-making competences to subnational units of government, it offers a 'partial offset' to the quest for legislative autonomy within the member states.[61] Further, if one connects this development with the creation of the Committee of the Regions to involve these units in the process of managing EU affairs, albeit (as yet) in a strictly advisory manner, subsidiarity may be seen as a tool for granting a more participatory status to lower level communities.

Under a less optimistic, but more probable, scenario, the principle resembles what Taylor called 'reserved powers' to the constituent governments, indicating that states have once more effectively managed to countervail possible federalising tendencies by means of balancing 'the loss of powers in one realm against the gain or retention of powers in another'.[62] Here, signs of an inverse type of federalism limiting the concentration of law-making power at the central level and favouring its diffusion down to the national level, are difficult to overlook. Put simply, insofar as these signs articulate a presumption of competence to national authorities, inverse federalism remains a useful instrument in analysing the allocation of power within the Union. Procedurally, this means that 'the burden of proof' lies with the Commission, which has to justify that its proposed legislation is compatible with the principle of subsidiarity. In the event of an inter-institutional disagreement, however, the question is still open as to who will finally decide and in what way. In the absence of a clear demarcation of responsibilities between national and European authorities, a solution may be the creation of an *ad hoc* instrument with functions similar to the French *Conseil Constitutionnel* but with a 'mixed' composition – political and judicial – assigned the task of examining the 'constitutionality' of relevant draft legislation; namely, whether it is compatible with the principle of subsidiarity.[63]

A less attractive option, in terms of delaying decisions and causing intersegmental friction, would be the incorporation in the Treaty of a so-called 'challenge mechanism' controlled by a *de facto* 'Congress' of national parliaments, or the establishment of a 'mixed' parliamentary body composed of an equal number of delegates from national parliaments and the European Parliament on the lines of the newly formed Conference of European Affairs Committees (or in French COSAC). An even less likely solution might be the application of a procedure analogous to that depicted by Art. 38 of the Belgian Constitution, commonly known as the 'alarm bell' procedure,[64] enabling the Council, acting by some extended form of majority voting, to initially delay – and if it so desires – prevent the adoption of a proposed measure on the grounds of being incompatible with the principle of subsidiarity. This mechanism 'could even be made binding through its insertion into the rules of procedures of the Council'.[65] In fact, the range of possibilities appears to be considerably wide.

One of the problems associated with the principle in question is that although subsidiarity is far from being a new term in the vocabulary of EU politics, a great deal of ambivalence exists with regard to the criteria of its application. *Inter alia*, the principle appeared in the 1975 Tindemans Report as a means of extending the scope of EC competences; in the 1977 MacDougal Report as a 'bottom-up' approach to fiscal federalism; in the 1984 Draft Treaty on European Union (EUT) prepared by the European Parliament and linked, in Art. 12(2), with cross-frontier dimension effects; in the SEA, albeit not *expressis verbi*, in Art. 130r (4) EC concerning environmental issues; in the 1987 Padoa-Scioppa Report in relation to EC economic intervention; in the 1989 Delors Report on EMU with regard to macroeconomic policy; and in the 1990 Martin Report stressing the tasks which are essential to the political viability of the Union.[66] Unlike, however, the Tindemans Report and the EUT, the Union envisaged by Maastricht is neither 'an entirely new creation', nor is there any provision in the text determining the precise allocation of competences between the Union and the states, nor finally is there any distinction between different types of competences such as exclusive, concurrent (or non-exclusive) and potential (areas which might in the future come within Union competence but which initially remain with the states).[67]

Applied to the TEU, and given, in Weiler's terms, 'the open-textured nature of the provision',[68] it is hardly coincidental that most legal experts have resented its inclusion. Indeed, Lord MacKenzie-Stuart went as far as to describe it as 'gobbledygook' on the grounds that the ECJ will find it next to impossible to apply the principle since questions on the 'effectiveness' criterion will be incapable of judicial resolution.[69] In particular, the difficulty lies in the 'objectivity' of the legal grounds upon which the ECJ would rule that a given task is better achieved at the larger level without being accused of being 'politically' biased against the lower level authorities. Similarly, an independent report concluded that 'there is a risk that, in straying into very obviously political territory, the Court may jeopardise its hard-won credibility'.[70]

All the above amount to 'the problem of competence': the absence of an explicit formal mechanism for allocating responsibilities within the Union, outside the areas that are considered as belonging to its exclusive sphere of activity. According to the ECJ these areas include commercial policy and the protection of the sea, whilst the Commission's broader interpretation includes in this category the four freedoms of movement and the policies that are a corollary to them.[71] It follows that these areas are not subject to the principle of subsidiarity, but are determined by the preemption doctrine: 'once the Community legislates in a field, it occupies that field, thereby precluding Member State action'.[72] Thus, subsidiarity can be used as a rule for the allocation of competences only in cases of concurrence, that is when decision-making responsibility is shared between the Union and the states, or 'when the Community legislated for the first time in a new field'.[73] Finally, in matters unaffected by Community law it is presumed that the states retain exclusive competence. It is in relation to the second set of competences that a number of controversies arise.

More specifically, Toth argues that the distinction between 'exclusive' and 'concurrent' competences is unknown to Community law insofar as one understands concurrent competence as 'a situation in which two different bodies can act with equal authority at the same time'.[74] For the powers that have been conferred on the Union are in principle exclusive and hence there is no room for any concurrent powers on the part of the states.[75] This seems to create more legal problems than it actually solves. One reason for this is that according to Toth's thesis – 'where Community competence begins that of the states ends'[76] – subsidiarity becomes irrelevant at least as the polity's legal basis now stands. As Toth maintains: '[Art. 3b EC] cannot *create* or *confer* competences on the Community. It can only be used to allocate the *exercise* of competences which have already been created by other provisions of the Treaty'.[77] If, on the other hand, Toth's formulation is invalid, then subsidiarity is the decisive, if not formally the sole, criterion – even restricting the so-called 'catch-all' provision of Art. 235 EC – for the delineation of disputed legislative boundaries.

Whichever is the case, it seems appropriate that the powers specifically entrusted to the 'centre' be specified in the Treaty, as the Australian Constitution does; or that a clear mechanism to delegate specific competences to the 'centre' be provided, as is the case of the German *Grundgesetz*; or even that a 'residual clause' be included in a manner similar to the US Constitution. In the first case, Art. 51 stipulates 39 areas which fall within the jurisdiction of the Federal Parliament. In the second case, and according to Art. 72 II, the *Bund* will have the right to legislate if federal legal regulation is needed (a) 'because a matter could not be settled effectively by the legislation of the various *Länder*,' or (b) 'because the regulation of a matter by a *Land* law could affect the interests of other or all *Länder*,' or (c) 'to safeguard the legal or economic unit, and particularly to safeguard the homogeneity of the living conditions beyond the territory of a *Land*'. In the last case, the Tenth Amendment added in 1791 to the US Constitution establishes a presumption favourable to decision-making at the level of government closer to the citizen, providing thus: 'The powers not delegated to the United States by the Constitution, nor prohibited by it to the States, are reserved to the States respectively, or to the people'. This creates a sense of 'constitutive autonomy' on the parts of the states. Similarly, Art. 30 of the *Grundgesetz* states: 'The exercise of governmental powers and the discharge of governmental functions shall be incumbent on the *Lander* in so far as this *Grundgesetz* does not otherwise prescribe or permit'.

In general terms, reflecting upon the federalist experience, the gist of the thesis is that the case for the allocation of competences to the federation has to be proved; otherwise, power rests with the partners to it. Historically, this line of reasoning has been mainly justified on the grounds that the constituent units, in the form of previously independent political entities, have preceded the creation of a federal authority in the form of a state. This approach to the concept, by favouring the diffusion of power to lower levels of government, rather than to the federal level, falls within the logic of 'bottom-up' subsidiarity, in turn derived from the theoretical foundations of European thought on the relationship between the individual, the state and society, as well as on a federalist-inspired division of political authority on the vertical axis.[78] Needless to say that in the case of the Union an ensemble *sui generis* formula of some or even all of the above possibilities should not be excluded. What remains of great importance, however, is for a balance to be struck between national and Union competences. As Taylor put it: 'the optimum distribution would be to have national control in areas that were adjacent to areas of community control. This might be called the principle of *balanced competencies* which should be set alongside *subsidiarity* as a key principle for the governance of the European Union'.[79]

The relevance of the principle of subsidiarity to the democratic deficit is not, perhaps, immediately obvious. It has been justified by Delors with reference to the importance for the individual citizen 'to be able to understand in global terms what belongs to each of the levels of authority,' as well as to 'the clear determination of the citizen's reciprocal responsibilities'.[80] But even under this positive interpretation, equating subsidiarity with responsible government, in terms of indirect *demos* control, and regarding it as a self-standing democratic principle, is rather presumptuous: it is one thing to determine which level of political authority is responsible for the taking of a particular decision (or set of decisions), and quite another to ensure its answerability to the *demos*. Doing so would be to confuse a principle for the functional allocation of shared competences with the quality of popular control over the decisions taken by the designated sphere of government.

The preceding arguments suggest that whereas subsidiarity is primarily concerned with the establishment of operational criteria for the organisation of authority within a multilevel polity, democracy, in its modern form, is about holding those empowered to decide on behalf of the *demos* accountable to those affected by these decisions. Moreover, Adonis has made the point that 'efficiency' rather than 'democracy' criteria are paramount in any discussion of its application.[81] 'Closeness', on the other hand, despite the fact that it has impressed contemporary scholarship on the democratic properties of the principle,[82] is a criterion which is badly in need of further qualification and, possibly, Treaty amendments to have any legal effect on the democratic management of EU affairs. Indeed, whatever the thrust of political rhetoric may be, it is rather naive to believe that the quality of transnational democracy can depend merely upon a preambular clause. Instead, what is urgently needed is for a comprehensive political formula to be fully integrated in the Treaty and to determine the *locus decidendi* in the interests of a balanced mixture of criteria: comparative efficiency, cross-boundary effects, transparency, and the potential of citizen identification with legislative outcomes. Otherwise, as Lodge has warned, the Community will stop short of 'crossing the Rubicon'.[83]

Let us conclude, then, that insofar as substantive structural aspects of the democratic deficit – like those relating to the vertical distribution of competences within the larger polity – reflect its uncrystallised constitutional identity, subsidiarity remains too nebulous a concept to address, let alone resolve, questions of a democratic nature. This is particularly true if one takes into account that, despite the steady growth of its competences since the mid-1980s, its internal 'rules of the game' have not yet produced a clear separation of authority between the Union and the states. The mere fact that in a hybrid polity which is neither a 'federal state' nor a classical 'union of states', its students have hailed the principle as 'the word that saves Maastricht', 'an effective barrier "against the enterprises of ambition"', 'a meaningless or even misleading term in English', or even 'an ugly word but a useful concept',[84] is a clear enough indication to justify a rather cautious approach to the subject. As Steiner has remarked: 'Is it too much to hope that the subsidiarity principle, as well as affording an opportunity to "mediate power distribution" and "diffuse political conflict" will provide a new impetus for the Community to re-order its priorities?'[85] To provide a relatively safe prognosis, if we were to embrace Cass's view of subsidiarity as 'a still-maturing principle of European Community law',[86] our answer might be that, at this stage of the Union's institutional development, it is.

'STIRRED, NOT SHAKEN...' – REFLECTIONS ON THE AMSTERDAM TREATY

It is fair to suggest that what was not formally discussed in the context of the 1996/97 IGC was more important than a number of allegedly controversial issues concerning the 'mechanics' of the revision process. For instance, an essential part of the hidden agenda of the IGC concerned the future role of the component nation-states, their constitutional relationship with an emerging European polity characterised by an expensive jurisdictional competence, and questions relating to the locus of accountability for complex decision-making processes. Similarly, the potentially dramatic consequences of further enlargement on EU institutions, along with the impact of a new 'flexibility clause' on the constitutional integrity and political cohesion of the *acquis communautaire* are good cases in point. Although these issues constitute the *raison d'être* of EU constitutional change, the possibility of the IGC providing the Union with a clearer political physiognomy became distinct even from the early stages of the revision process – ie, in the discussions which took place in the Reflection Group (RG), a body of experts set up by the Corfu European Council in June 1994.

As in the past, a tension became manifest between federalist-inspired reforms and tactical consolidation of pre-existing intergovernmental arrangements. In the end, a balance was sought between collective governance and independent self-rule. The end-product was the preservation of the Union's 'contractual' nature – ie, a unity constituted by states – and the postponement of substantive democratic reforms. According to Wessels's prognosis, the following options were open to the interested parties: (a) implement Maastricht; (b) reform Maastricht; (c) build upon Maastricht; and (d) abort Maastricht.[87] The growing 'democratic disjunction' between the wishes of a fragmented European *demos* and its respective governing elites,[88] an abundance of interrelated problems of (structural) socio-economic adjustment, and the uncertain future of the

(Western) European welfare state, were among the major factors that rendered to the '1996 process' an air of distress.

For the groundwork leading to the IGC, the RG became the dominant forum for interstate communication but not for interstate negotiation, thus reflecting the member states' intention to identify first the various options for further integration and then to negotiate their possible outcomes. The RG presented its findings in the Final Report of December 1995 that was later submitted to the Madrid European Council (an Interim Report was presented a few months earlier).[89] In the meantime, all major EU institutions, as well as the component states individually, submitted their views for the negotiations ahead.[90] The following points attempt to outline these discussions and insinuate some primordial theoretical conclusions.

In the Final Report, the RG defined its own tasks as being (a) the improvement in the workings of the Union, and (b) the expansion of the capabilities of the Union so as to enable it to face both internal and external challenges, including the new waves of enlargement towards the Central and Eastern European countries (CEEC). The Report was structured around three dimensions: flexibility, effectiveness and democracy. Although the former was seen at the time as potentially becoming a major operational principle of Union governance, creating however problems related to the idea of differentiated integration, or even to 'variable geometry' practices, the Report was quick to recognise that this can only be a temporary arrangement. Flexibility becomes all the more important as an organising principle in view of 1999, when the final stage of EMU will commence. If this type of organisation prevails, *ceteris paribus*, a pattern of differentiated participation in integrative schemes would inevitably emerge. Under this scenario, EU members may well find themselves split into different groups according to their particular domestic or other priorities. For instance, areas like social policy, EMU, CFSP and common defence arrangements are easy to link with the flexibility clause, which also entails a strong dose of political pragmatism concerning the hidden agenda of convergence, economic or otherwise. The expected result would be the enhancement of the Union's intergovernmental features and the consolidation of its dominant consociational properties. Although the major dilemma was initially between a pragmatic versus a normative approach,[91] at the final stage of the negotiations, there also emerged the possibility of adopting a 'mixed' approach to European treaty reform. The typology below summarises the alternatives:

Table 8.1 A Typology of European Constitutional Choice

| | APPROACHES | | |
	Pragmatic	Normative	Mixed
PROPERTIES			
End Result	Confederation	Federation	Confederal Consociation
Modus Operandi	Flexibility/ Efficiency	*Demos-*Formation	Controlled Pluralism
Locus of Sovereignty	State Rule	Civic Rule	Consensus Elite Government
Central Arrangement	Constitutions	Constitution	Constitutional Engineering

Moving on to the principle of efficiency, and in conjunction with that of flexibility, it may well accelerate the pace of EU policy-making in various functional areas without any reference to its quality or for that matter to the number of the participating states. But the Final Report did not bother to hint at a single institutional set-up capable of satisfying both conditions. It merely stated that the final outcome of the revision process should preserve the 'single institutional framework' within which the composition of the European Court of Justice, the Commission and the European Parliament will be a constant, whereas that of the Council and the procedures established therein, a variable. The picture was further complicated with the introduction in the Report of issues relating to the democratisation of the Union and the need to bring the latter 'closer to its citizens', although the Report failed to provide a concrete strategy to that end. Instead, it proposed only marginal modifications to existing quasi-democratic arrangements. All in all, the outstanding issues composing the institutional agenda were, *inter alia*, the principles of transparency and subsidiarity, the hierarchy of Community Acts, the comitology phenom-enon, the need for rationalising central decision-making, and the question of enlargement and institutional adjustment. It is to these issues that we now turn.

Increased transparency is vital if the Union wishes to eliminate the chasm between its citizens and the central institutions. The term relates also to a right of information for Union citizens and the need for more simplified EU decision-making. The Commission has stated that, although there have been positive steps in this direction, there is still ample ground for further improvements.[92] Although a number of Council meetings have been held in public – mostly during the Danish Presidency in the first half of 1993 – they have nevertheless dealt with secondary, if not manifestly insignificant matters. With regard to subsidiarity, the majority of members of the RG wished that the relevant treaty provisions should remain unchanged. For its part, the Commission suggested that '[t]he concepts of the directive, of mutual recognition or that of partnership (in the case of regional policy) reflect the principle of subsidiarity'. Whether this statement reveals a misunderstanding of what subsidiarity is all about, or merely a preference for enhancing the Union's legislative competences, it is imperative that a specific body should be set up for the allocation of decision-making competences, as well as for controlling both the sphere of applicability of the principle and its 'constitutionality' in each case separately.

The issue concerning the hierarchy of Community Acts has also been raised during the 1990/91 twin IGCs – a proposal, however, which was rejected at that time on the grounds that it would produce a *de facto* classification of levels of governance and a *de jure* classification of institutions 'top-down'. Yet, Declaration No 16 attached to the TEU proclaims that the IGC 'will examine the degree to which it is possible to revise the classification of the Community Acts so as to arrive at a hierarchy in the various Community Acts'. In defence of this classification, the European Parliament and the Italian government formed an alliance during the previous IGCs, suggesting the following types of Community Acts: (a) Constitutional acts, referring to treaty reform; (b) Organic laws, referring to the functioning of EU institutions; (c) Regular laws, referring to formal EU decision-making processes; and (d) Regulations, referring to policy implementation. Differences between these types reflect mainly the differences in the actual decision-taking mode for each category as the required majorities get lower if one moves down from (a) to (d). There was a slight modification of this proposal in the Interim Report where the classes of acts (d) and (c) are merged into one. The RG did not discuss this issue in any detail, preferring instead to refer the matter to the IGC. It thus became clear that differences among the member states were more or less reproducing those of the previous IGCs.

As for the comitology phenomenon, it refers to developments since the Council decision of 17 December 1987, according to which a strong network of technical committees composed of national representatives within the Council hierarchy was established. This system of 'management committee government' reshaping the content of decisions already made in the context of formal legislative procedures tends to override the formal powers of the European Parliament – ie, those stemming from the co-decision procedure – to the benefit of national governments. Although comitology exacerbates the already problematic relationship between democracy and integration, the RG failed to produce a unified stance on this dainty emission and, as with most other conflict-prone issues, referred the whole matter to the IGC.[93]

The issue of rationalising EU decision-making relates to the composite three-pillar structure created by the TEU: a messy institutional set up where the Union and the states intermingle in a plethora of different legislative procedures, depending on the policy area and the pillar in question. This problem was compounded after the 'Ioannina Compromise' of July 1994, according to which, under certain conditions, the minority veto in the Council is not the normal 23 votes but instead 26. As little doubt exists that Arts. 189c and 189b EC have increased the democratic properties of the Union by bringing the European Parliament closer to the *locus decidendi* in certain policy areas, they represent a unique, albeit federalist-inspired, exercise in inter-institutional power-sharing which is still far from being comprehensive. Hence, the acquisition of new co-decision powers by Parliament is at best a 'partial offset' to the more difficult issues of EU democratisation concerning the social legitimation of the Union as an nascent polity. In theory, the transformation of the Union from a Confederal Consociation to a federal state (or state-like polity based on the properties of federal government) would require a republican system of 'checks and balances' as an interim arrangement on the way to a system of full-blown *demos* control.

Finally, it was suggested that the real task of the 1996/97 IGC was to offer the necessary mechanisms for the smooth accession of CEEC (and possibly others from the Mediterranean region) during the Union's next wave of enlargement. But such a challenging task presents potentially insurmountable problems given the possibility of 27-30 EU members. Flexibility and efficiency support this appendage, as does the final stage of EMU given that, *ceteris paribus*, some member states will not fulfil the convergence criteria spelled out in Maastricht. It is thus expected that a system of 'flexible geometry', this time formally institutionalised, will again be established post-1999. The issue is further complicated since the vast majority of the newcomers are small states which, if added to the existing group of small states in the Union, will upset an already delicate balance in central decision-making. Thus, a new formula for arriving at collective decisions should be so devised as to ensure that in the enlarged Union, neither the larger nor the smaller members will be alienated. In light of the above, Vibert has suggested a system of 'double concurrent majorities' as a means of balancing the interests of small and big states in a Union of 30 members,[94] justified on the grounds that any decision-making arrangement that takes into account either the number of states alone, or the size of their population, will upset the existing balance of power in the Council. Under this system, 'a two thirds majority would require both two thirds of the number of the member states accounting for two thirds of the population'.[95] Whether or not such a proposal will find accommodation remains to be seen, since a decision on this issue has been postponed by EU leaders. What seems certain, however, is that for some countries the emphasis will be on the possibilities of forming an effective minority veto, whilst for others in overcoming a small minority of dissenting states. Confederal Consociation, and its explicit reliance on reversible dissensus practices in joint decision-taking, seems to be currently justifying its analytical validity for the student of European integration.

A similar conclusion is drawn when examining in greater detail the content of the Amsterdam Treaty, signed on 2 October 1997. As *The Economist* colourfully put it, the new Treaty 'produced more of a mouse than a mountain'.[96] Whether a 'reasonable step', or one which is 'lacking ambition', the moderate reforms embedded in the AMT preserve the three-pillar structure of the Union and with it the existence of two separate legal mechanisms. Some areas previously falling in the area of JHA will be gradually transferred to the Community (partial communitarisation) while the Schengen *acquis* is fully incorporated into the Union (with Britain and Ireland having secured an opt out). A new employment chapter is also part of the new Treaty as a job-creating measure, and so is Maastricht's 'Social Chapter'. In the field of the CFSP, the AMT provides, *inter alia*, for a limited extension of qualified majority voting for detailed policy implementation; the appointment of a 'high representative'; the creation of a 'planning unit'; and the use of 'constructive abstention' in joint actions.

It is also agreed that at the first enlargement the big countries will lose their second Commissioner provided that they are compensated through a reweighting of votes in the Council. But, as previously noted, a decision has been deferred until a new IGC is convened, at least one year before EU membership exceeds 20. Qualified majority voting has been extended in the fields of emergency immigration measures, employment (guidelines and incentive measures), customs co-operation, countering fraud, social exclusion, equality of opportunity and treatment of men and women, public health, transparency (general principles, fundamental rights sanctions, outermost regions, and statistics (independent advisory authority on data protection).[97] The now simplified co-decision procedure applies also to citizens' rights, social security for migrant workers, rights of self-employed, cultural measures and, in five years time, to visa procedures and conditions, and visa uniformity rules.[98] The common legislative procedures involving the European Parliament are reduced to three:

co-decision, consultation and assent (the co-operation procedure remains only in the field of EMU). Moreover, a Chapter on Fundamental Rights and Non-discrimination has been inserted in the new Treaty to strengthen the Union's 'human face' and safeguard the protection of human rights.

A new protocol is also enshrined in the AMT in an attempt to define more precisely the criteria for applying the principles of subsidiarity and proportionality. It states: 'In exercising the powers conferred on it, each institution shall ensure that the principle of subsidiarity is complied with,' and 'any action of the Community shall not go beyond any action necessary for the attainment of the objectives of the Treaty'. It is also noted that these principles shall respect the *acquis communautaire* and the institutional balance, whilst taking into account that 'the Union shall provide itself with the means necessary to attain its objectives and carry through its policies'. Still, however, it is the Community that has to justify compliance of proposed legislation to these principles. *Ceteris paribus*, directives should be preferred to regulations and so should framework directives to detailed measures, leaving as much scope for national decisions as possible. The Commission should seek maximum consultation prior to initiating legislation; minimise administrative or financial burdens; and submit an annual report to the other EU institutions on the application of these principles.

Flexibility was finally included in the AMT, albeit precluding the creation of a *Europe à la carte* by introducing strict conditions for its application. In particular, this principle should further the objectives and protect the interests of the Union; respect the principles of the Treaties and the single institutional framework; be used only as a last resort; concern at least a majority of EU members; respect the *acquis communautaire*; not affect the competences, rights, obligations and interests of those members that do not wish to participate therein; remain open to all members states; and be authorised by the Council. It is also stated that the new 'flexible' arrangements will be governed by the same decision-making rules as in the TEU, adjusted accordingly for membership, and that the European Parliament will be regularly informed by the Commission and the Council. But the AMT precludes the member states from initiating flexible arrangements in areas which fall within the exclusive competences of the Community; affect Community policies, actions, or programmes; concern Union citizenship or discriminate between member state nationals; fall outside the limits of the powers conferred upon the Community by the AMT; and constitute discrimination or restrict trade and/or distort competition between member states. Authorisation for such 'flexible' schemes 'shall be granted by the Council, acting by a qualified majority on a proposal by the Commission and after consulting the EP'. Any objection by a member state on grounds of 'important and stated reasons' results in the whole matter being referred to the European Council for a unanimous decision.

Turning to the democratic dynamics of EU constitutional change, the new Treaty, in a manner similar to the TEU, forms part of a wider evolution towards a pluralist structure of governance based on an incipient constitutional system. Bellamy and Castiglione, who conceptualise the Union as a 'mixed commonwealth', go even further to suggest that 'the subjects of the constitution are not homogeneous, but a mixture of political agents sharing in the sovereignty of the polity under different titles'.[99] From this view, the larger system still forms part of a transition stage – ie, a constituent process – which remains relevant to the inception of the Fourth Europe.

Duff's commentary, however, on the shortcomings of the AMT is equally revealing, in that the latter has failed to extend equally the scope of qualified majority voting and co-decision; to introduce judicial review in crucial issues concerning the citizen (like Europol); to extend the Parliament's right of assent to legislation in JHA, to decisions over the Community's 'own resources', and to treaty amendments (Art. N); and to give the Union (as opposed to the Community) legal competence.[100] Whether or not this phase will result in a genuine European 'constitutive polity' is too early to assess (especially since ratification of the AMT is pending). All too often, deterministic approaches to the outcome of treaty revisions have been widely misleading, whilst the nature of the relationship between the region and its sub-units has relied upon the preferred lines of interpretation of the new central arrangements. As for now, the 'new' EU continues to be defined along the lines of a Confederal Consociation, not least because substantive democratic reforms have been largely referred *ad calendas Graecas*. Whatever the winds of further treaty reform may hold for the future, and whether or not the states will direct their efforts to re-discovering 'a sense of process' in the regional system, one thing is certain: European integration in the 1990s is neither about the subordination of states to a higher central authority, nor is it about a linear process towards a federal end. Rather, it is about the preservation of those state qualities that make the segments survive as separate collectivities, whilst engaging themselves in a polity-formation process that transforms their traditional patterns of interaction. The next section builds on this point, by examining the relationship between theory and reform in the larger management system.

REFORMING THEORY AND THEORISING REFORM

It is no secret by now that our view of the Union as a Confederal Consociation, and of the recent treaty reforms as 'partial offsets' to the democratic deficit, can be better classified with those belonging to the sceptical school of integration. Sceptical, however, not in the commonly accepted sense of the word, implying a passionate attitude against an 'ever closer union', but in its original meaning, pointing to the development of both a theoretically and empirically based awareness of the dialectical interaction between the limits and possibilities of integration at a given moment in time. If anything, our examination of the basic properties of managed *Gesellschaft* in relation to those envisaged for a nascent *Gemeinschaft* has been largely conducted through this prism. More importantly, this is a distinction which does justice to those who genuinely believe in the cause of European unity, but are also prepared to recognise the difficulties involved in its achievement. Put simply, being sceptical is not synonymous with being negatively predisposed. For the latter entails the dangers of reaching foregone conclusions on an inherently open-ended process such as European integration.

Whether or not the conceptual lenses employed in this study to project a macroscopic view of the Union, and represented, *inter alia*, by such terms as Confederal Consociation, controlled pluralism, inverse federalism, transnational *demos*-formation, European 'civic competence' and nascent *Gemeinschaft*, may contribute towards a 'conceptual consensus', the point is clearly made that familiarity with theory is a two-way process: it helps to test our analytical tools and appreciate their relevance in real-life situations. Indeed, theorising the European polity and linking together its composite governance structures to established and novel political properties and dynamics offers an opportunity to communicate the main concerns underlying both the study as well as the making of a politically viable Union: the coming together of highly interdependent 'bodies politic' into a larger polycentric arrangement which, although it has fallen short of becoming a supranational state, it has nevertheless evolved into something more than merely a 'system of governments'. Rather, a dynamic system of co-operative states and *demoi* has emerged based on the institutionalisation of joint sovereignty and the practice of political co-determination.

In attempting to sketch some final lines of our understanding of the Union in the late 1990s, the following need to be set out. At the dawn of the new millennium, and against the background of a mounting *crise de confiance* at the grass-roots, the Union finds itself once more in its arduous journey to unification in a state of flux. Although determined to build on the *relance* of integration inaugurated by the SEA in the mid-1980s, its members have lost nothing of their anxiety to preserve the integrity of their polities against the tides of federalism and institutional centralisation. As a result, throughout the 1990s, an increased tension became manifest between democracy and integration: the incorporation of the former into the latter was often taken to imply a straightforward loss of national democratic autonomy to an over-ambitious European Parliament, or the making of a federal Union that would be detrimental to the constitutional properties of states.

This antithesis between 'intergovernmentalists' and 'federalists' has marked its impact on the debate over the future direction of the European polity, demonstrating that the process of uniting distinct culturally defined and politically organised units is neither a smooth nor automatic political exercise; all the more so, if it is product of a predominantly utilitarian, cost-benefit calculus among the dominant governing elites of the component parts. Further, it has shown that it is difficult to maintain the politics of democratic 'deepening' without active citizen support. Indeed, the 'permissive consensus', pinpointed by Lindberg and Scheingold in 1970,[101] cannot generate the necessary public commitment to transnational democracy-building. The ratification of the TEU made it clear that the exclusion of citizens from the governance of the larger polity and, hence, the absence of an effective European 'civic competence', is at the expense of popular fragmentation.

The picture was completed with the ever pertinent divide between elites and *demos*, territorial and non-territorial claims and, finally, technocracy and democracy. This development has alarmingly emphasised the limits of integration in the form of various democratic 'deficits' and 'disjunctions' between governors and governed. If anything, the Maastricht experience – and to a lesser extent that of the 1996/97 IGC leading to the revision of the TEU – has shown that the prospects for developing democracy among democracies have been conditioned 'from above', stemming from a variety of sources aiming to reconcile the defence of territorially-based quests for segmental autonomy with the prospects for furthering the pace of integration. This message appears to have been clearly received by a large section of the European public.

In many respects, the current situation has produced exactly the opposite of what neofunctionalists had hoped to achieve: instead of politicisation – ie, the process of linking the management of integration with the daily lives of European citizens – becoming an additional weapon in the hands of pro-integrationist forces, it is increasingly used by the more sceptical actors, thus making it difficult to mobilise the constituent publics in favour of further integration, and towards a 'complete equilibrium' between different levels of government. Such a development contests the idea that the implied benefits of joint action, or for that matter of commonly performed functions, even when requiring resort to majority rule, would somehow overcome any divisive issues which may arise as European polity-formation proceeds. But this may in turn lead to 'multiple flexible equilibria': a 'condominio... based on variation of both territorial as well as functional constituencies',[102] where the form that the future European polity is allowed to take will determine the outcome of specific functions.

The theoretical thesis underlying this argument is that we are currently witnessing the reversal of the Mitranian logic to international integration: instead of 'form follows function', it is increasingly the case that the structural properties of the system dictate to a great extent both the depth and range of joint integrative schemes. The implications that this new thesis generates for the study of European integration in the 1990s is that the 'scope' (new policy arenas) of integration may well be extended, if not at the expense of its 'level' (ways of management), without significantly either altering the locus of sovereignty, or having a significant impact on the way in which the central institutions exercise political authority. All formal treaty revisions, from the 'policy-generating' SEA, to the 'polity-creating' TEU, and then to the sensibly arranged reform package agreed at Amsterdam, illustrate this point. At the macrotheoretical level, whatever mode of political interaction eventually prevails, Schmitter's view of the Union as 'the most complex polity that human agency... has ever devised', is likely to remain unchallenged, at least in the foreseeable future. Or, as Puchala may have put it, until we know what exactly the 'elephant' is, and towards what it is developing, the 'elusive' European polity will continue, to borrow a phrase, 'to enjoy an enviable reputation in the pantheon of political experiments'.

The question posed today is whether the core-theories of European integration are capable of offering any concrete sense of direction in assessing the relationship between a cluster of democratic polities and the building of a new one. In this context, Hix has clearly made the point that the time is right for students of EU politics 'to challenge the dominance of the international approaches'.[103] Indeed, whereas the older functionalism developed by Mitrany has focused on the role of international functional agencies as a means of establishing a 'working peace system' based on the notion of 'technical self-determination' within an 'a-territorial' policy environment, Haas's neofunctionalism on the dynamics of a pluralistic and self-regulated society of organised interests, functional and political spill-overs, and patterns of elite socialisation, and continental federalism on the importance of large-scale constitution-making, they all aimed at

245

providing answers about 'who governs and how?' – ie, the relationship between national and regional/international dynamics, joint decision rules, who controls the setting of the integrative agenda, how different policies are pursued at different levels of governance, whether the common system is capable of dealing with internal crises and so on. Thus, they have failed to ask, let alone answer, perhaps the single most important question: 'who is governed?' Throughout this study, this largely metatheoretical concern has directed our analytical *foci* to explaining a striking paradox: although the Union represents a firmly enough established collective entity in which traditional notions of democracy are losing their notrmative characteristics, it exhibits a notable potential for democratic self-development.

Indeed, if the process of democratising the collectivity is to be properly linked with the requirements of a nascent *Gemeinschaft*, it need not be merely a reflection of a 'balanced' intergovernmental compromise between the advantages of collective action and the costs of autonomous decision-making. Rather, the move towards the Fourth Europe requires a reversal of roles between those who have traditionally determined EU politics and those who have passively accepted their outcomes. This can only be achieved through the emergence of a European 'civic sphere' that should leave as much scope for democratic participation as possible. This amounts to the making of a transnational *demos* and the corresponding strengthening of European 'civic competence', both based on the institutional capacity of European citizens to direct their democratic claims to, and via, the central institutions, and demand a more *demos*-oriented process of union; flexible enough to accommodate high levels of democratic diversity, yet solid enough to stand firm against the politics of consensus elite government. The timing for the Union to affirm the role of its citizens in its complex governance structures, as the best possible antidote to its democratic deficit, has come. Anything less will be yet another compromised structure achieved by a predominantly elitist operation and detrimental to the interests of the only sovereign political body: the European peoples themselves.

Echoes of this approach to democratic self-transformation were found in Parliament's Committee on Institutional Affairs proposal for a European Constitution based, *inter alia*, on a double democratic legitimacy, respect for national identity, adherence to the rule of law, protection of fundamental rights and, above all, the affirmation of a European political identity.[104] At best, this way forward would guarantee the 'constitutive autonomy' of states, and reflect, in the process of managing the public affairs of the Union, the democratic properties of its constituent polities and *demoi*. At least, the envisaged Constitution would begin by reference to the sovereign peoples of Europe, rather than to the 'High Contracting

Parties'. In both cases, however, it is for European citizens to decide and no one else.

CONCLUSION – OR A BEGINNING?

Having reached the final section of this study, there is little to add to our basic assumptions, arguments and propositions about the transformation of the Union from democracies to democracy. Thus, instead of a conventional conclusion summing up the main points raised so far, it might be better to end (this part of) our theoretical journey by recalling how a foremost scholar of contemporary democratic thought has chosen to draw the final curtain on the democratic vision. Such a conclusion not only remains relevant to the future of transnational democracy and the means for bringing the nascent European *demos* to its full democratic potential, but also represents the greatest wish one might express for the shape of things to come. Indeed, one which should be interpreted as a prelude to new and far-reaching 'democratic beginnings'.

Whatever form it takes, the democracy of our successors will not and cannot be the democracy of our predecessors. Nor should it be. For the limits and possibilities of democracy in a world we can already dimly foresee are certain to be radically unlike the limits and possibilities of democracy in any previous time or place... Yet, the vision of people governing themselves as political equals, and possessing all the resources and institutions necessary to do so, will I believe remain a compelling if always demanding guide in the search for a society in which people may live together in peace, respect each other's intrinsic equality, and jointly seek the best possible life.[105]

Notes on Chapter 8

1   Taylor, Paul, *International Organization in the Modern World: The Regional and the Global Process*, (London and New York, 1993, Pinter), p 99.
2   This formulation draws on Krasner's definition of regime as 'implicit or explicit principles, norms, rules and decision-making procedures around which actors' expectations converge in a given area of international relations'. See Krasner, Stephen, 'Structural Causes and Regime Consequences: Regimes as Intervening Variables', in Krasner, Stephen (ed.), *International Regimes* (Ithaca, 1983, Cornell University Press), p 2.
3   Bulmer, Simon and Scott, Andrew, 'Introduction', in Bulmer, Simon and Scott, Andrew (eds), *Economic and Political Integration in Europe: Internal Dynamics and Global Context* (Oxford, 1994, Basil Blackwell), p 8. For more details see

Stavridis, Stelios, 'The "Second" Democratic Deficit in the European Community: The Process of European Political Co-operation', in Pfetsch Frank R. (ed), *International Relations and Pan-Europe: Theoretical Approaches and Empirical Findings* (Münster, 1993, Lit Verlag), pp 173-94; Anderson, Malcolm, den Boer, Minica and Miller, Gary, 'European Citizenship and Cooperation in Justice and Home Affairs', in Duff, Andrew *et al.* (eds), *Maastricht and Beyond: Building the European Union* (London, 1994, Routledge), pp 104-22.

4 Indeed, comitology procedures, similar to the practice of 'delegated legislation' in national parliaments, may alter the content of European legislation if there is sufficient agreement between the Commission and various technical committees convened under the auspices of the Council, without requiring the approval of the European Parliament. Interviews with Roger Barton and Brandon Donnelly, MEPs, 28/6/1995 and 29/6/1995 respectively.

5 See Shackleton, Michael, 'Democratic Accountability in the European Union', in Brouwer, Frank *et al.* (eds), *Economic Policy and the European Union* (London, 1994, Federal Trust), pp 91-101.

6 Demaret, Paul, 'The Treaty Framework', in O'Keeffe, David and Twomey, Patrick M. (eds), *Legal Issues of the Maastricht Treaty* (London, 1994, Wiley Chancery Law), p 5.

7 *Ibid.* and p 6.

8 Pryce, Roy, 'The Maastricht Treaty and the New Europe', in Duff, Andrew *et al.* (eds), *Maastricht and Beyond*, p 3.

9 Wallace, Helen, 'European Governance in Turbulent Times', *Journal of Common Market Studies*, September 1993, p 294.

10 Quoted in Ress, Georg, 'Democratic Decision-Making in the European Union and the Role of the European Parliament', in Curtin, Deidre and Heukels, Tom (eds), *Institutional Dynamics of European Integration: Essays in Honour of Henry G. Schermers* vol. II (Dordrecht, 1994, Martinus Nijhoff), p 156.

11 Archer, Clive, *International Organizations*, Second edn (London, 1992, Routledge), p 37.

12 Weatherill, Stephen, 'Beyond Preemption? Shared Competence and Constitutional Change in the European Community', in O'Keeffe, David and Twomey, Patrick M. (eds), *Legal Issues of the Maastricht Treaty*, p 32.

13 Forsyth, Murray, 'Towards a New Concept of Confederation', European Commission of Democracy Through Law, Council of Europe, 1994, p 66. He explains: 'Because the union is intended to act, majority decisions by the member states must be permitted in at least some areas... [and] unanimity must apply for decisions amending the original constitutional pact, and for the admission of new member states'.

14 For a brief account on the ratification of the TEU and the implications of the 'special arrangements' secured by Britain and Denmark see Corbett, Richard, 'Convergence and Institutional Development', *Journal of Common Market Studies*, August 1993, pp 27-50. On the Luxembourg Presidency draft see Europe Documents, 'Draft Treaty on the Union', No 1722/1723, July 1991.

15 On this point see Tranholm-Mikkelsen, Jeppe, 'Neo-functionalism: Obstinate or Obsolete? A Reappraisal in the Light of the New Dynamism of the EC', *Millennium*, Spring 1991, pp 1-22.

16 Although the new Treaty was ratified by the *Bundestag* on 2 December 1992 and by the *Bundesrat* fifteen days later, it was not until the German Federal Constitutional Court issued a favourable ruling on the 'constitutionality' of TEU that the ratification process terminated. See BVerfG, EuGRZ, 1993.

17 For details see Stavridis, Stelios, 'Democracy in Europe: East and West', Conference Proceedings on 'People's Rights and European Structures', (Manresa, 1993, Centre Unesco de Catalunya), p 130.

18 *Ibid.*

19 Wallace, Helen, 'European Governance in Turbulent Times', p 296.

20 Neunreither, Karlheinz, 'The syndrom of democratic deficit in the European Community', in Parry, Geraint (ed.), *Politics in an Interdependent World: Essays Presented to Ghita Ionescu* (London, 1994, Edward Elgar), p 96.

21 On the distinction between the 'First Europe' and the 'Second Europe' see Taylor, Paul, *The Limits of European Integration* (New York, 1983, Columbia University Press), pp 62-3. The concept of a 'Third Europe' has been employed by Taylor in one of his European Institutions lectures at the London School of Economics and Political Science, on 21 October 1991. In this context he stated: 'Since 1974 we are not seeing the development of a European federation nor the winning of intergovernmentalism but a creative synthesis or symbiosis of the two'.

22 Duchacek, Ivo, 'Perforated Sovereignties: Towards a Typology of New Actors in International Relations', in Michelmann, Hans J. and Soldatos, Panayotis (eds), *Federalism and International Relations: The Role of Subnational Units*, (Oxford, 1990, Clarendon Press), p 3. He defines federalism as 'a pluralist democracy in which two separate sets of governments, neither being at the mercy of the other, legislate and administrate within their separate yet inter-locked jurisdictions'. See p 4.

23 Taylor, Paul, *The Limits of European Integration*, p 109.

24 *Ibid.*, p 7.

25 Wallace, Helen, 'European Governance in Turbulent Times', p 302.

26 Dimitris N. Chryssochoou, 'Rethinking Democracy in the European Union: The Case for a "Transnational Demos"', in Stavridis, Stelios *et al.* (eds), *New Challenges to the European Union: Policies and Policy-Making* (Aldershot, 1997 Dartmouth), p 82.

27 Quoted in Duff, Andrew, 'The Main Reforms', in Duff, Andrew *et al.* (eds), *Maastricht and Beyond*, p 26.

28 On this point see Wallace, Helen, 'The EC and Western Europe after Maastricht', in Miall, Hugh (ed.), *Redefinind Europe: New Patterns of Conflict and Co-operation* (London, 1994, Pinter), p 19.

29 European Parliament, 'Report on the functioning of the Treaty on European Union with a view to the 1996 Intergovernmental Conference – implemen-tation and development of the Union', Doc. EN/RR/273/273375, p 18.

30 According to the TEU, the assent procedure applies to Arts. 8a, 105(6), 106(5), 130d, 138(3), and Art. O of Title VII; the co-operation procedure to Arts. 2(2), 6, 75, 103(5), 104a, 104b, 108(3), 118a, 125, 127(4), 129d, 130e, 130j, 130k, 130l, 139s(1), and 130w; and the co-decision procedure to Arts, 49, 54, 56, 57(1), 57(2), 66, 100a, 100b, 126, 128(5), 129a(2), 129d, 129(4), and 130i. See also Secretary General of the Council, 'Draft Report of the Council on the Functioning of the Treaty on European Union', 5082/95, Brussels, April 1995, pp 47-8.

31 For further details see European Parliament, 'Report on the First Applications of the Codecision Procedure', DOC EN/DV/235/253629, June 1994; and European Parliament, 'Progress Report for the Second Half of 1994', PE 211.522/rev. 2/ann, March 1995. The latter report reveals that 30 out of 124 proposals for codecision acts have been adopted and that this procedure covers approximately 25% of EC legislative activity. See p 12.

32 Taylor, Paul, *The Limits of European Integration*, p 114.

33 Weiler, Joseph H.H., 'After Maastricht: Community Legitimacy in Post-1992 Europe', in Adams, William J. (ed.), *Singular Europe: Economy and Polity of the European Community after 1992* (Ann Arbor, 1992, University of Michigan Press), p 14.

34 Taylor, Paul, *International Organization in the Modern World*, pp 96-7.

35 Ibid., p 97. Johana R. Maij-Weggen, MEP, finds from her experience in the Council meetings that dissenting member states prefer not to be outvoted but to 'go into consensus'. Interview, 28/06/1995.

36 Corbett, Richard, 'Representing the States', in Duff, Andrew *et al.* (eds), *Maastricht and Beyond*, pp 208-9. This he finds to be yet another expression of the elite-dominated nature of EU decision-making. Interview, 27/06/1995.

37 *Ibid.*, p 209.

38 *Ibid.*

39 *Ibid.*, p 211.

40 Ress, Georg, 'Democratic Decision-Making in the European Union and the Role of the European Parliament', p 169.

41 See Raworth, Philip, 'A Timid Step Forwards: Maastricht and the Democratisation of the European Community', *European Law Review*, February 1994, pp 16-33.

42 Close, Paul, *Citizenship, Europe and Change*, (London, 1995, Macmillan), pp 2-3.

43 Marshall, T.H., *Citizenship and Social Class* (Cambridge, 1950, Cambridge University Press), p 8.

44 For a comprehensive account of the subject see Dahl, Robert A., *Democracy and its Critics* (New Haven and London, 1989, Yale University Press), pp 106-31.

45 Quoted in Geddes, Andrew, 'The Democratic Deficit and the Position of Immigrant and Ethnic Minorities in the European Union', paper presented at the Madrid ECPR Joint Sessions of Workshops, April 1994, p 16. Shaun M. Spiers, MEP, comments that in Britain, this situation excludes no less than 1.5 million of Commonwealth citizens who are not official British and, hence, Union citizens. Interview, 27/06/1995.

46 For more on this type of democracy see *ibid.*, pp 18-21 and pp 28-9.
47 On these concepts see Neureither, Karlheinz, 'Citizens and the Exercise of Power in the European Union: Towards a New Social Contract?', in Rosas, Allan and Antona, Esko (eds), *A Citizens' Europe: In Search of a New Order*, (London, 1995, Sage), p 10. The first category of citizens refers to a situation in which individuals are divided into 'segmented parts'; the second to the acquisition of a European citizenship not through a 'constitutive act' but by means of the 'nationality requirement'; and the third to a citizen 'who on the basis of information possibilities is able and motivated to participate in a dialogue both with other citizens and with those exercising public power'. See p 10 and p 18.
48 *Ibid.*, p 13.
49 European Parliament, 'Report on the functioning of the Treaty on European Union', p 67. Cf Parry, John, *European Citizenship* (London, 1991, European Movement), p 28. He states: 'A European is not a matter of mixing various nationalities into one pudding; it is more a question of fostering the understanding that we share a common destiny'.
50 *Ibid.*, p 68.
51 Close, Paul, *Citizenship, Europe and Change*, p 255. Cf Welsh, Jennifer M., 'A Peoples' Europe? European Citizenship and European Identity', EUI Working Paper no 93/3 (San Domenico, 1993, Badia Fiesolana), p 7.
52 Holland, Martin, *European Integration: From Community to Union* (London, 1994, Pinter), p 154.
53 *Ibid.*
54 O'Keefe, David, 'Union Citizenship', in O'Keefe, David and Twomey, Patrik M. (eds), *Legal Issues of the Maastricht Treaty*, p 106.
55 *Ibid.*, p 91. Cf Closa, Carlos, 'The Concept of Citizenship in the Treaty on European Union', *Common Market Law Review*, vol. 29, 1992, p 1169. Closa concludes: 'The important point is that the decisive entitlement for individuals' decisions on the Union is not citizenship but nationality. It remains to be seen whether the basis of citizenship of the Union provided by the Treaty could evolve in the future to develop a *political subject* for the Union' (emphasis added).
56 Anderson, Malcolm, *et al.*, 'European Citizenship and Cooperation in Justice and Home Affairs' in Duff, Andrew *et al.* (eds), *Maastricht and Beyond*, p 109.
57 Dahl, Robert A., *Democracy and its Critics*, p 338.
58 Anderson, Malcolm, *et al.*, 'European Citizenship and Cooperation in Justice and Home Affairs' in Duff, Andrew *et al.* (eds), *Maastricht and Beyond*, p 106.
59 Sbragia, Alberta M., 'From "Nation-States" to "Member States": The Evolution of the European Community', in Lutzeler, Paul M. (ed.), *Europe after Maastricht: American and European Perspectives* (Providence, Oxford, 1994, Berghahn Books), p 87.
60 Shaw, Josephine, *European Community Law* (London, 1993, Macmillan), p 333.
61 Taylor, Paul, *International Organization in the Modern World*, p 87.
62 *Ibid.*, p 98.

63 See Giscard D'Estaing, V., 'The Principle of Subsidiarity', report drawn up on behalf of the Committee on Institutional Affairs, European Parliament, Doc. EN/RR/98228, October 1990.

64 For details see Ginderachter, J. Van, 'The Belgian Federal Model', Second ECSA-World Conference on 'Federalism, Subsidiarity and Democracy in the European Union', Brussels, May 1994, p 4.

65 Dehousse, Renaud, 'Does Subsidiarity Really Matter?', EUI Working Paper No. 92/93 (San Domenico, 1993, Badia Fiesolana), p 25.

66 For details see Cass, Deborah Z., 'The Word that Saves Maastricht? The Principle of Subsidiarity and the Division of Powers within the European Community', *Common Market Law Review*, vol. 29, 1992, pp 1112-28.

67 Toth, A.G., 'The principle of subsidiarity in the Treaty of Maastricht', *Common Market Law Review* vol. 29, 1992, pp 1090-1.

68 Weiler, Joseph H.H., 'Journey to an Unknown Destination: A Retrospective and Prospective on the European Court of Justice in the Arena of Political Integration', in Bulmer, Simon and Scott, Andrew (eds), *Economic and Political Integration in Europe*, p 152.

69 *The Times*, 11/12/1992.

70 The Centre for Economic Policy Research, 'Making Sense of Subsidiarity: How Much Centralization for Europe?', Monitoring European Integration No 4, Annual Report, London, 1993, p 22.

71 *Ibid.*, p 17 and pp 21-2.

72 Demaret, Paul, 'The Treaty Framework', in O'Keefe, David and Twomey, Patrik M. (eds), *Legal Issues of the Maastricht Treaty*, p 16.

73 Hartley, Trevor C., 'Constitutional and Institutional Aspects of the Maastricht Agreement', *International and Comparative Law Quarterly*, April 1993, p 216.

74 Toth, A.G., 'The principle of subsidiarity and the Treaty of Maastricht', p 1081.

75 *Ibid.*, p 1080.

76 *Ibid.*, p 1081.

77 *Ibid.*, p 1092.

78 For further details see Emiliou, Nicholas, 'Subsidiarity: An Effective Barrier Against "the Enterprises of Ambition"?', *European Law Review*, October 1992, pp 384-7.

79 Taylor, Paul, *The European Union in the 1990s* (Oxford, 1996, Oxford University Press), p 188.

80 Delors, Jacques, 'The Principle of Subsidiarity: Contribution to the Debate', in Proceedings of the Jacques Delors Colloquium, 'Subsidiarity: The Challenge of Change' (Maastricht, 1991, European Institute of Public Administration), p 18.

81 See Adonis, Andrew, 'Subsidiarity: Myth, Reality and the Community's Future', House of Lords Select Committee on the European Communities, London, June 1990.

82 On this point see Neuwahl, Nanette A., 'A Europe Close to the Citizen? The "Trinity Concepts" of Subsidiarity, Transparency and Democracy', Rosas, Allan and Antona, Esko (eds), *A Citizens' Europe*, pp 39-57.

83 See Lodge, Juliet, 'The European Parliament and the Authority-Democracy Crisis', *The Annals of the American Academy of Political and Social Sciences*, January 1994, note 11, p 82.

84 Quoted in Cass, Deborah Z., 'The Word that Saves Maastricht?', p 1107; Emiliou, Nicolas, 'Subsidiarity', p 383; and Adonis, Andrew, 'Subsidiarity', p 15 and p 1.

85 Steiner, Jo, 'Subsidiarity under the Maastricht Treaty', in O'Keefe, David and Twomey, Patrik M. (eds), *Legal Issues of the Maastricht Treaty*, p 64.

86 Cass, Deborah Z., 'The Word that Saves Maastricht?', p 1136.

87 Wessels, Wolfgang, 'The Modern West European State: Democratic Erosion from Above or Below?', in Andersen, Svein S. and Eliassen, Kjell A. (eds), *The European Union: How Democratic Is It?*, (London, 1996, Sage), pp 57-69.

88 On this point see Stavridis, Stelios, 'Democracy in Europe', pp 129-133.

89 See respectively, the Interim Report of the Reflection Group, 24 August 1995, SN 5509/95, and the Final Report of the Reflection Group, 5 December 1995, SN 520 REV.

90 On this issue see Edwards, Geoffrey and Pijpers, Alfred (eds), *The Politics of European Treaty Reform: The 1996 Intergovernmental Conference and Beyond* (London, 1997, Pinter), esp. chapters 10 and 11.

91 See also Tsinisizelis, Michael J. and Chryssochoou, Dimitris N., 'The European Union: Trends in Theory and Reform', in Weale, Albert and Nentwich, Michael (eds), *Political Theory and the European Union: Legitimacy, Constitutional Choice and Citizenship* (London and New York, 1998, Routledge), pp 83-97.

92 European Commission, 'Report on the functioning of the Treaty on European Union', SEC (95) 731 Final, 10 May 1995, Appendix No. 10, p 110.

93 Final Report of the Reflection Group, p 16.

94 Vibert, Frank, *A Core Agenda for the 1996 Inter-Governmental Conference (IGC)* (London, 1995, European Policy Forum), p 54.

95 *Ibid.*

96 *The Economist*, 21 June 1997, p 37.

97 Duff, Andrew (ed.), *The Treaty of Amsterdam: Text and Commentary* (London, 1997, Sweet & Maxwell), pp 152-3.

98 *Ibid.*, p 145.

99 See Bellamy, Richard and Castiglione, Dario, 'Building the Union: The Nature of Sovereignty in the Political Architecture of Europe', *Law and Philosophy*, vol. 16, 1997, pp 421-45. They explain: 'The polycentric polity that is therefore emerging is a definite departure from the nation state, mainly because it implies a dissociation of the traditional elements that come with state sovereignty: a unified system of authority and representation controlling all functions of governance over a given territory'. See p 443.

100 Duff, Andrew (ed.), *The Treaty of Amsterdam*, p xxxvi-ii and p 143.

101 Lindberg, Leon N. and Scheingold, Stuart A., *Europe's Would-Be Polity: Patterns of Change in the European Community* (Englewood Cliffs NJ, 1970, Pretice-Hall), esp. pp 38-63.

102 Schmitter, Philippe C., 'Some alternative futures for the European polity and their implications for European public policy', in Mény, Yves *et al.* (eds), *Adjusting to Europe: the impact of the European Union on national institutions and policies* (London, 1996, Routledge), p 31.
103 Hix, Simon, 'Approaches to the Study of the EC: The Challenge to Comparative Politics', *West European Politics*, January 1994, p 24.
104 See European Parliament, 'Working Document on the Constitution of the European Union', Committee on Institutional Affairs, Doc. EN/DT/234/234285, September 1993; and European Parliament, 'Draft Report on the Constitution of the European Union', Doc. EN/PR/234/234101, September 1993.
105 Dahl, Robert A., *Democracy and its Critics*, pp 340-1.

Bibliography

OFFICIAL DOCUMENTS AND PUBLICATIONS OF THE EUROPEAN UNION

Commission of the European Communities, Bulletin of the European Communities, Supplements 1-1976 and 3-1982

Commission of the European Communities, 'Commission Opinion of 21 October 1990 on the Proposal for Amendment of the Treaty Establishing the European Economic Community with a View to Political Union', Com (90) 600 final, Brussels, October 1990

Commission of the European Communities, 'A Citizen's Europe', DG X, Catalogue No. CC-60-91-773-EN-C, Luxembourg, 1991

Commission of the European Communities, 'The European Community: 1992 and Beyond', DG X, Catalogue No. CC-60-91-385-EN-C, Luxembourg, 1991

Commission of the European Communities, 'European Union', DG X, Catalogue No. CC-74-92-265-EN-C, Luxembourg, 1992

Commission of the European Communities, 'From Single Market to European Union', DG X, Catalogue No. CC-74-92-289-EN-C, Luxembourg, 1992

Commission of the European Communities, 'Strengthening Democracy in the EC', DG X, Catalogue No. CC-77-93-813-EN-C, Luxembourg, 1993

Council of the European Communities, 'The Council of the European Community: An Introduction to its Structures and Activities', General Secretariat, Luxembourg: Office for Official Publications of the European Communities, 1991

D'Estaing, Valerie, 'The Principal of Subsidiarity', report drawn up on behalf of the Committee on Institutional Affairs, European Parliament, Doc. EN-RR-98228, October 1990

Eurobarometer, 20th Anniversary, Trends 1974-1993, May 1994

European Parliament, 'Symposium on European Integration and the Future of Parliaments in Europe', DG for Research & Documentation, October 1975

European Parliament, 'Concepts of Democracy in the European Community', Political Affairs Comittee, DG for Research & Documentation, November 1980

European Parliament, 'Report on Relations between the European Parliament and the National Parliaments', Working Documents, Doc. 1-206/81, May 1981

European Parliament, 'Transfer of Responsibilities and the Democratic Deficit', Political Series No 4, January 1984

European Parliament, 'Report on the Democratic Deficit in the European Community', Institutional Affairs Committee, Session Documents, Series A, Doc. A 2-0276/87, February 1987

European Parliament, 'The Powers of the European Paliament', Political Series No 15, Research and Documentation Papers, February 1989

European Parliament, 'Symposium on the European Parliament in the Community System', 'National Parliaments' Series No 5, DG for Research, March 1989

European Parliament, 'Rome Conference of Parliamentarians: The Future of Europe', Final Communique, November 1990

European Parliament, 'The Principle of Subsidiarity', Committee on Institutional Affairs, Doc. EN/RR/98228, October 1990

European Parliament, '1993 The New Treaties: European Parliament Proposals', Luxembourg: Office for Official Publications of the European Communities, 1991

European Parliament, 'Report on the Results of the Intergovernmental Conferences', Institutional Affairs Comittee, Session Documents, Doc. EN/RR/205517, March 1992

European Parliament, 'Bodies within National Parliaments Specialising in European Community Affairs', 'National Parliaments' Series, Directorate General for Research, March 1992

European Parliament, 'Report on the structure and strategy for the European Union with regard to its enlargement and the creation of a Europe-wide order', Institutional Affairs Committee, Doc. EN/RR/208537, May 1992

European Parliament, 'Report on the Institutional Role of the Council', Session Documents, Institutional Affairs Committee, EN/RR/208536, May 1992

European Parliament, 'Proceedings of the Symposium on the European Community in the Historical Context of its Parliament', September 1992

European Parliament, 'Maastricht', Luxembourg: Office for Official Publications of the European Communities, 1992

European Parliament, 'Working Document on the Constitution of the European Union', Institutional Affairs Committee, Doc. EN/DT/234/234285, September 1993

European Parliament, 'Draft Report on the Constitution of the European Union', Institutional Affairs Committee, Doc. EN/PR/234/234101, September 1993

European Parliament, 'Report on the First Applications of the Codecision Procedure', Conciliation Secretariat, Doc. EN/DV/253629, June 1994

European Parliament, 'Implementation of the Conciliation Procedure (Article 189b EC) in the European Parliament', Conciliation Secretariat, Doc. EN/DV/263/2632627, March 1995

European Parliament, 'Progress Report for the Second Half of 1994', EP Delegations to the Conciliation Committee, Doc. EN/DV/269/268293, March 1995

European Parliament, 'Report on the Functioning of the Treaty on European Union with a View to the 1996 Intergovernmental Conference', Committee on

Institutional Affairs, Doc. EN/RR/273/273345, Doc. EN/RR/273/273683, and Doc. EN/RR/273/27337, May 1995

'European Union', Report by Leo Tindemans to the European Council, *Bulletin of the European Communities*, Supplement 1-1976

Final Report of the Reflection Group, SN 520 Rev, 5 December 1995

Interim Report of the Reflection Group, SN 5509/95, 24 August 1995

Parlement Européen, 'Symposium sur les Relations entre le Droit International Public, le Droit Communuautaire et le Droit Constitutionnel des Etats Membres', Commission Juridique et des droits de Citoyens, PE 213.411/8, Juin 1995

Secretary General of the Council, 'Draft Report of the Council on the Functioning of the Treaty on European Union', 5082/95, Brussels, April 1995

BOOKS

Aberbach, Joel D. *et al.*, *Bureaucrats and Politicians in Western Democracies* (Cambridge MA, 1981, Harvard University Press)

Ackerman, Bruce, *We the People: Foundations* (Cambridge MA, 1991, Harvard University Press)

Acton, H.B. (ed.), *Utilitarianism, Liberty, and Representative Democracy* (London, 1972, Dent & Sons)

Adams, William J. (ed.), *Singular Europe: Economy and Polity of the European Community after 1992* (Ann Arbor, 1992, The University of Michigan Press).

Allum, Percy (ed.), *State and Society in Western Europe*, (Cambridge, 1995, Polity Press).

Andersen, Svein S. and Eliassen, Kjell A. (eds), *Making Policy in Europe* (London, 1993, Sage)

Andersen, Svein S. and Eliassen, Kjell A. (eds), *The European Union: How Democratic Is It?* (London, 1996, Sage)

Apter, David, *The Political Kingdom in Uganda: A Study in Bureaucratic Politics*, (Princeton NJ, 1961, Princeton University Press)

Arblaster, Anthony, *Democracy* (Milton Keynes, 1987, Open University Press)

Archer, Clive, *International Organizations*, Second edn (London, 1992, Routledge)

Archibugi, Daniele and Held, David (eds), *Cosmopolitan Democracy: An Agenda for a New World Order* (Cambridge, 1995, Polity Press)

Bachrach, Peter, *The Theory of Democratic Elitism: A Critique* (London, 1967, The University of London Press)

Bacon, Chris (ed.), *Political Restructuring in Europe: Ethical Perspectives* (London and New York, 1994, Routledge)

Bailey, Sydney D., *United Europe: A Short History of the Idea* (London, 1948, National News-Letter)

Ball, Terrence *et al.* (eds), *Political Innovation and Conceptual Change* (Cambridge, 1989, Cambridge University Press)

Barber, Benjamin, *Strong Democracy: Participatory Politics for a New Age* (Berkeley, 1984, University of California Press)

Barber, James and Reeds, Bruce (eds), *European Community: Vision and Reality* (London, 1973, Croom Helm)

Barker, Ernest, *Principles of Social and Political Theory* (Oxford, 1951, Oxford University Press)

Barrows, Bernard *et al.* (eds), *Federal Solutions to European Issues* (London, 1978 Macmillan)

Barry, Brian, *Sociologists, Economists and Democracy* (Chicago, 1970, The University of Chicago Press)

Bealey, Frank, *Democracy in the Contemporary State*, (Oxford, 1988, Clarendon Press)

Beer, Samuel H., *To Make a Nation: The Rediscovery of American Federalism* (Cambridge MA, 1993, Harvard University Press)

Beetham, David, *The Legitimation of Power* (London, 1991, Macmillan)

Beetham, David (ed.), *Defining and Measuring Democracy* (London, 1994, Sage)

Bell, Wendel and Freeman, Walter E., *Ethnicity and Nation-Building: Comparative International and Historical Perspectives* (London, 1974, Sage)

Beloff, Max (ed.), *The Federalist, or the New Constitution*, Second edn (Oxford, 1987, Basil Blackwell)

Birch, Anthony H., *Nationalism and National Integration* (London, 1989, Unwin Hyman)

Birch, Anthony H., *The Concepts and Theories of Modern Democracy* (London and New York, 1993, Routledge)

Birnbaum, Pierre *et al.* (eds), *Democracy, Consent and Social Justice* (London, 1978, Sage)

Blondel, Jean, *Comparative Legislatures* (Englewood Cliffs NJ, 1973, Prentice-Hall)

Blondel, Jean (ed.), *Governing Together: The Extent and Limits of Joint Decision-Making in Western European Cabinets*, London: St Martin's Press, 1993

Bloom, William, *Personal Identity, National Identity and International Relations*, Cambridge Studies in International Relations, No 9 (Cambridge, 1993, Cambridge University Press)

Bodenheimer, Susane J., *Political Union: A Microcosm of European Politics* (Leyden, 1967, A.W. Sijthoff)

Bobbio, Norberto, *The Future of Democracy: A Defence of the Rules of the Game* (Cambridge, 1987, Polity Press)

Bogdanor, Vernon (ed.), *Representatives of the People? Parliamentarians and Constituents in Western Europe* (Gower, 1985, Policy Studies Institute)

Bosco, Andrea (ed.), *The Federal Idea: The History of Federalism from Enlightenment to 1945*, Vol. I (London and New York, 1991, Lothian Foundation Press)

Bosco, Andrea (ed.), *The Federal Idea: The History of Federalism Since 1945*, Vol. II (London and New York, 1992, Lothian Foundation Press)

Boulle, L.J., *Constitutional Reform and the Apartheid State: Legitimacy, Consociationalism and Control in South Africa* (New York, 1984, St Martin's Press)

Bowie, Robert R., and Carl J. Friedrich (eds), *Studies in Federalism* (Boston and Toronto, 1954, Little, Brown and Company)

Brailsford, H.N., *The Federal Idea* (London, 1939, Federal Union)

Brinkley, Douglas and Hackett, Clifford (eds), *Jean Monnet: The Path to European Unity* (London, 1991, Macmillan)

Brouwer, Frank, *et. al.* (eds), *Economic Policy and the European Union* (London, 1994, Federal Trust)

Brugmans, Henry, *L'idée Européenne: 1918-1965* (Bruges, 1965, De Tempel)

Bryce, James, *Modern Democracies* (New York, 1921, Macmillan)

Bulmer, Simon and Wessels, Wolfgang, *The European Council: Decision-Making in European Politics* (London, 1988, Macmillan)

Bulmer, Simon and Scott, Andrew (eds), *Economic and Political Integration in Europe: Internal Dynamics and Global Context* (Oxford, 1994, Basil Blackwell)

Burgess, Michael, *Federalism and Federation in Western Europe* (London, 1986, Croom Helm)

Burgess, Michael, *Federalism and European Union: Political Ideas, Influences and Strategies in the European Community, 1972-1987* (London and New York, 1989, Routledge)

Burgess, Michael and Gagnon, Alan-G (eds), *Comparative Federalism and Federation: Competing Traditions and Future Directions* (New York, 1993, Harvester Weatsheaf)

Calhoun, John C., *A Disquisition on Government* (New York, 1943, Peter Smith)

Cameron, David (ed.), *Regionalism and Supranationalism: Challenges and Alternatives to the Nation-State in Canada and Europe* (London, 1981, The Institute for Research on Public Policy)

Cappelletti, Mario *et al.*, *Integration Through Law*, Vol. 1, Book 1 (Berlin and New York, 1986, Walter de Gruyer)

Close, Paul, *Citizenship, Europe and Change* (London, 1995, Macmillan)

Cohen, Carl, *Democracy* (Athens GA, 1971, The University of Georgia Press)

Conlan, Timothy, *New Federalism* (Washington DC, 1988, The Brookings Institution)

Crick, Bernard, *The Reform of Parliament* (London, 1964, Weidenfeld and Nicolson)

Crozier, Michael *et al.*, *The Crisis of Democracy* (New York, 1975, New York University Press)

Curtin, Deirdre and Heukels, Tom (eds), *Institutional Dynamics of European Integration: Essays in Honour of Henry G. Schermers* (Dortrecht, 1994, Martinus Nijhoff)

Dahl, Robert A., *A Preface to Democratic Theory* (Chicago and London, 1956, University of Chicago Press)

Dahl, Robert A., *Polyarchy: Participation and Opposition* (New Haven, 1971, Yale University Press)

Dahl, Robert A., *Dilemmas of Pluralist Democracy: Autonomy vs. Control* (New Haven and London, 1982, Yale University Press)

Dahl, Robert A., *Democracy and its Critics* (New Haven and London, 1989, Yale University Press)

Dahrendorf, Ralf, *Society and Democracy in Germany* (London, 1967, Weidenfeld and Nicolson)

Dahrendorf, Ralf *et. al.*, *Whose Europe? Competing Visions for 1992*, (London, 1989, Institute of Economic Affairs)

Day, Patricia and Klein, Rudolf, *Accountabilities: Five Public Services* (London, 1987, Tavistock)

Deutsch, Karl *et al.*, *Political Community and the North Atlantic Area* (Princeton NJ, 1957, Princeton University Press)

Deutsch, Karl and Foltz, William J. (eds), *Nation-Building* (New York, 1966, Atherton Press)

Deutsch, Karl, *The Analysis of International Relations* (Englewood Cliffs NJ, 1971, Prentice-Hall)

Dewey, John, *The Public and its Problems* (New York, 1927, Holt)

Dinan, Desmond, *An Ever Closer Union? An Introduction to the European Community* (London, 1994, Macmillan)

Duchacek, Ivo D., *Comparative Federalism: The Territorial Dimension of Politics* (London, 1970, Holt, Rinehart and Winston)

Duff, Andrew *et al.* (eds), *Maastricht and Beyond: Building the European Union* (London, 1994, Routledge)

Duff, Andrew (ed.), The Treaty of Amsterdam: Text and Commentary (London, 1997, Sweet & Maxwell)

Duncan, Graeme (ed.), *Democratic Theory and Practice* (Cambridge, 1994, Cambridge University Press)

Dunn, John (ed.), *Democracy: the Unfinished Journey, 508 BC to 1993* (Oxford, 1992, Oxford University Press)

Dunn, John, *Western Political Theory in the Face of the Future* (Cambridge, 1993 Cambridge University Press)

Edwards, Geoffrey and Pijpers, Alfred (eds), *The Politics of European Treaty Reform: The 1996 Intergovernmental Conference and Beyond* (London, 1997, Pinter)

Elazar, Daniel J. (ed.), *Federalism and Political Integration* (Ramat Gan, 1979, Turtledove)

Elazar, Daniel J., *Exploring Federalism* (Tuscaloosa, 1987, The University of Alabama Press)

Elazar, Daniel J. *et al.*, *Federal Systems of the World: A Handbook of Federal, Confederal and Autonomy Arrangements*, Second edn (London, 1994, Longman Current Affairs)

Etzioni, Amitai, *The Spirit of Community: The Reinvention of American Society* (New York, 1993, Simon and Shuster)

Eulau, Heinz (ed.), *Political Behaviour* (Glencloe IL, 1956, The Free Press)

Eulau, Heinz and Whalke John C. (eds), *The Politics of Representation* (London and Beverly Hills, 1978, Sage)

Forsyth, Murray *et al.* (eds), *The Theory of International Relations: Selected Texts From Gentili to Treitschke* (London, 1970, Allen & Unwin)

Forsyth, Murray, *Unions of States: The Theory and Practice of Confederation* (Leicester, 1981, Leicester University Press)

Fremantle, Anne (ed.), *The Papal Encycliasticals in their Historical Context* (London, 1963, Mentor Omega)

Friedrich, Carl J., *Trends of Federalism in Theory and Practice* (London, 1968, Pall Mall Press)

García, Soledad (ed.), *European Identity and the Search for Legitimacy* (London, 1993, Pinter)

Garner, John W., *Building Community* (Washington, 1991, Independent Sector)

Gierke, Otto, *Natural Law and the Theory of Society 1500 to 1800* (Cambridge, 1958, Cambridge University Press)

Gould, Carol C., *Rethinking Democracy* (Cambridge, 1993, Cambridge University Press)

de Grazia, Sebastian, *The Political Community: A Study of Anomie* (Chicago and London, 1969, The University of Chicago Press)

Green, Philip, *Retrieving Democracy: In Search of Civic Equality* (London, 1985, Methuen)

Groom, A.J.R. and Taylor, Paul (eds), *International Organization: A Conceptual Approach* (London, 1978, Pinter)

Groom, A.J.R. and Taylor, Paul (eds), *Frameworks for International Co-operation* (London, 1990, Pinter)

Haas, Ernst B., *The Uniting of Europe: Political, Social and Economic Forces 1950-1957*, (London, 1958, Stevens & Sons)

Haas, Ernst B., *Beyond the Nation-State: Functionalism and International Organization*, (Stanford, 1964, Stanford University Press)

Hallowell, John H., *The Moral Foundation of Democracy* (Chicago IL, 1954, University of Chicago Press)

Hallstein, Walter, *Europe in the Making* (London, 1972, Allen & Unwin)

Hampshire-Monk, I. (ed.), *The Political Theory of Edmund Burke* (London, 1987, Longman)

Harrison, Reginald J., *Europe in Question: Theories of Regional International Integration*, (London, 1974, Allen & Unwin)

Held, David, *Models of Democracy*, (Cambridge, 1987, Polity Press)

Held, David (ed.), *Political Theory Today*, (Cambridge, 1991, Polity Press)

Held, David (ed.), *Prospects for Democracy*, (Cambridge, 1993, Polity Press)

Herman, Valentine and Lodge, Juliet, *The European Parliament and the European Community* (London, 1978, Macmillan)

Herman, Valentine and Schendelen, Rinus van (eds), *The European Parliament and the National Parliaments* (Westmead, 1979, Saxon House)

Hill, Stephen (ed.), *Visions of Europe: Summing up the political choices* (London, 1993, Duckworth)

Hirst, Paul, *Associative Democracy: New Forms of Economic and Social Governance*, (Cambridge, 1993, Polity Press)

Hobbes, Thomas, *Leviathan* (Harmondsworth, 1968, Penguin)

Hogan, Williard N., *Representative Government and European Integration* (Lincoln, 1967, The University of Nebraska Press)

Holden, Barry, *Understanding Liberal Democracy*, Second edn (London, 1993, Harvester Wheatsheaft)

Holland, Martin, *European Integration: From Community to Union* (London, 1994, Pinter)

Hutchinson, John and Smith, Anthony D. (eds), *Nationalism* (Oxford, 1994, Oxford University Press)

Ionescu, Ghita (ed.), *The New Politics of European Integration* (London, 1972, Macmillan)

Jacobs, Francis *et al.*, *The European Parliament*, Second. edn (Harlow, 1992, Longman Current Affairs)

Jeffery, Charlie and Sturm, Ronald (eds), *Federalism, Unification and European Integration* (London, 1993, Frank Cass)

Jones, Roy E., *Principles of Foreign Policy: The Civil State and its World Settings* (Oxford, 1979, Martin Robertson)

Kamenka, Eugene, *Bureaucracy* (Oxford, 1989, Basil Blackwell)

Kellas, James G., *The Politics of Nationalism and Ethnicity* (London, 1991, Macmillan)

Keohane, Robert O. and Nye, Joseph S. (eds), *Transnational Relations and World Politics* (Cambridge MA, 1981, Harvard University Press)

Keohane, Robert O. and Hoffmann, Stanley (eds), *The New European Community: Decisionmaking and Institutional Change* (Boulder, 1991, Westview Press)

King, Preston, *Federalism and Federation* (London and Canberra, 1982, Croom Helm)

Kirchner, Emil J., *Decision Making in the European Community: The Council Presidency and European Integration* (Manchester and New York, 1992, Manchester University Press)

Kitzinger, Uwe, *The European Common Market and Community* (London, 1967, Routledge)

Köchler, Hans (ed.), *The Crisis of Representative Democracy* (Frankfurt, 1987, Verlag Peter Lang)

Krasner, Stephen (ed.), *International Regimes* (Ithaca, 1983, Cornell University Press)

Kuper, Leo and Smith, M.G. (eds), *Pluralism in Africa* (Berkeley, 1971, University of California Press)

Laffan, Brigid, *Integration and Co-operation in Europe* (London and New York, 1992, Routledge)

Lasok, Dominik and Soldatos, Panayotis (eds), *The European Community in Action* (Brussels, 1981, Brylond)

Lehman, Edward W., *The Viable Polity* (Philadelphia, 1992, Temple University Press)

Levi, Lucio (ed.), *Altiero Spinelli and Federalism in Europe and in the World* (Milano, 1990, Franco Angeli)

Lijphart, Arend, *The Politics of Accommodation: Pluralism and Democracy in the Netherlands* (Berkeley, 1968, University of California Press)

Lijphart, Arend, *Democracy in Plural Societies: A Competitive Exploration* (New Haven, 1977, Yale University Press)

Lijphart, Arend, *Democracies: Patterns of Majoritarian and Consensus Government in Twenty-One Countries* (New Haven and London, 1984, Yale University Press)

Lijphart, Arend and Grofman, Bernard (eds), *Choosing an Electoral System: Issues and Alternatives* (New York, 1984, Praeger)

Lindberg, Leon N., *The Political Dynamics of European Economic Integration* (Stanford, 1963, Stanford University Press)

Lindberg, Leon N. and Scheingold, Stuart A., *Europe's Would-Be Polity: Patterns of Change in the European Community* (Englewood Cliffs NJ, 1970, Prentice-Hall)

Lindsay, Kenneth, *European Assemblies: The Experimental Period 1949-1959* (London, 1960, Stevens & Sons)

Lipset, Seymour M., *Political Man: The Social Bases of Politics* (London, 1983, Heinemann)

Lively, Jack, *Democracy* (Oxford, 1975, Basil Blackwell)

Lively, Jack and Parry, Geraint (eds), *Democracy, Consent and Social Justice* (London, 1978, Sage)

Lodge, Juliet (ed.), *The European Community and the Challenge of the Future* (London, 1989, Pinter)

Lodge, Juliet (ed.), *The European Community and the Challenge of the Future*, Second edn (London, 1993, Pinter)

Loewenberg, Gerhard (ed.), *Modern Parliaments: Change or Decline?* (Chicago, 1971, Aldine-Atherton)

Loewenstein, Karl, *Political Power and the Governmental Process* (Chicago, 1957, University of Chicago Press)

Lucas, John R., *Democracy and Participation* (Harmondsworth, 1976, Penguin)

Lutzeler, Paul M. (ed.), *Europe After Maastricht: American and European Perspectives*, (Providence Oxford, 1994, Berghahn Books)

MacIver, R.M., *Community: A Sociological Study*, (London, 1936, Macmillan)

Macmahon, Arthur W. (ed.), *Federalism: Mature and Emergent* (New York, 1955, Garden City)

Macridis, Roy C. and Brown, Bernard E. (eds), *Comparative Politics: Notes and Readings*, Third edn (Homewood, 1968, Dorsey Press)

George E. Marcus and Russell L. Hanson (eds), *Reconsidering the Democratic Public* (Pennsylvania, 1993, The Pennsylvania State University Press)

Marshall, Geoffrey (ed.), *Ministerial Responsibility* (Oxford, 1989, Oxford University Press)

Marshall, T.H., *Citizenship and Social Class* (Cambridge, 1950, Cambridge University Press)

Martin, David, *Europe: An Ever Closer Union* (Nottingham, 1991, Spokesman)

Mayne, Richard *et al.*, *Federal Union: The Pioneers*, (London, 1990, Macmillan)

Mayo, H.B., *An Introduction to Democratic Theory* (New York, 1960, Oxford University Press)

McKeon, Richard (ed.), *Democracy in a World of Tensions* (Paris, 1951, Unesco)

McRae, Kenneth (ed.), *Consociational Democracy: Political Accommodation in Segmented Societies* (Toronto, 1974, McLelland and Stewart)

McWhinney, Edward, *Federal Constitution-Making for a Multinational World* (Leyden, 1966, A.W. Sijthoff)

Mény, Yves *et al.* (eds), *Adjusting to Europe: the impact of the European Union on national institutions and policies* (London, 1996, Routledge)

Mezey, Michael, *Comparative Legislatures* (Durham NC, 1979, Duke University Press)

Miall, Hugh (ed.), *Redefining Europe: New Patterns of Conflict and Co-operation* (London, 1994, Pinter)

Michelmann, Hans and Soldatos, Panayotis (eds), *Federalism and International Relations: The Role of Subnational Units* (Oxford, 1990, Clarendon Press)

Michelmann, Hans and Soldatos, Panayotis (eds), *European Integration: Theories and Approaches* (University Press of America, 1994, Lanham)

Mitchell, Austin, *Government by Party* (London,1966, Whitecombe and Tombs)

Michels, Robert, *Political Parties* (Glencoe IL, 1915, Free Press)

Milward, Alan S. *et al.*, *The Frontier of National Sovereignty: History and Theory 1945-1992* (London and New York, 1993, Routledge)

Mill, James, *An Essay on Government* (New York, 1937, Cambridge University Press)

Mitrany, David, *A Working Peace System* (Chicago, 1966, Quadrangle Books)

Mitrany, David, *The Functional Theory of Politics* (London, 1976, Martin Robertson)

Monnet, Jean, *Memoirs* (New York, 1978, Doubleday and Co.)

Mouffe, Chantal (ed.), *Dimensions of Radical Democracy* (London and New York, 1992, Verso)

Mouffe, Chantal, *The Return of the Political* (London and New York, 1993, Verso)

Nicol, William and Salmon, Trevor, *Understanding the New European Community* (New York, 1994, Harvester Weatsheaf)

Norton, Philip (ed.), *Legislatures* (Oxford, 1970, Oxford University Press)

Nugent, Neil, *The Government and Politics of the European Community*, Second ed.n (London, 1991, Macmillan)

O'Keeffe, David and Twomey, Patrick M. (eds), *Legal Issues of the Maastricht Treaty*, (London, 1994, Wiley Chancery Law)

Paine, Thomas, *Rights of Man* (Harmondsworth, 1984, Penguin)

Parry, John, *European Citizenship* (London, 1991, European Movement)

Parry, Geraint, *Political Elites* (London, 1969, Allen & Unwin)

Parry, Geraint and Moran, Michael (eds), *Democracy and Democratization* (London and New York, 1994, Routledge)

Parry, Geraint (ed.), *Politics in an Interdependent World: Essays Presented to Guita Ionescu* (London, 1994, Edwar Eldgar)

Pateman, Carole, *Participation and Democratic Theory* (Cambridge, 1970, Cambridge University Press)

Pennock, Ronald and Chapman, John W. (eds), *Representation*, Nomos X (New York, 1968, Atherton Press)

Channing-Pearce, Melvin (ed.), *Federal Union: A Symposium* (London, 1991, Lothian Foundation Press)

Pentland, Charles, *International Theory and European Integration* (London, 1973, Faber)

Pfetsch, Frank R. (ed.), *International Relations and Pan-Europe: Theoretical Approaches and Empirical Findings* (Münster, 1993, Lit Verlag)

Pickles, Dorothy, *Democracy* (London, 1970, Methuen & Co.)

Pinder, John, *European Community: The Building of a Union* (Oxford, 1991, Oxford University Press)

Plamenatz, John, *The English Utilitarians*, Second. edn (Oxford, 1958, Basil Blackwell)

Plamenatz, John, *Democracy and Illusion* (London, 1978, Longman)

Plant, Raymond, *Community and Ideology: An Essay in Applied Social Philosophy*, (London and Boston, 1974, Routledge and Kegan Paul)

Poplin, Dennis E., *Communities: A Survey of Theories and Methods of Research* (London, 1979, Macmillan)

Powell, G. Bingham, Jr, *Contemporary Democracies: Participation, Stability, and Violence* (Cambridge MA, 1982, Harvard University Press)

Pryce, Roy, *The Dynamics of European Union* (London, 1987, Croom Helm)

Raphael, D.D., *Problems of Political Philosophy*, revised edn (London, 1976, Macmillan)

Rees, G. Wyn (ed.), *International Politics in Europe* (London and New York, 1993, Routledge)

Reis, Hans (ed.), *Kant's Political Writings* (Cambridge, 1970, Cambridge University Press)

Riker, William R., *The Theory of Political Coalitions* (New Haven, 1962, Yale University Press)

Ringrose, Marjorie and Lehrner, Adams J. (eds), *Reinventing the Nation* (Buckingham, 1993, Open University Press)

Robins, Lionel, *The Economic Causes of War* (London, 1939, Jonathan Cape)

Rosas, Allan and Antona, Esko (eds), *A Citizens' Europe: In Search of a New Order* (London, 1995, Sage)

Ross, Alf, *Why Democracy?* (Cambridge MA, 1952, Harvard University Press)

Rousseau, Jean Jacques, *The Social Contract* (Harmondsworth, 1968, Penguin)

Sartori, Giovanni, *The Theory of Democracy Revisited* (Chatham NJ, 1987, Chatham House, 1987)

Sbragia, Alberta M. (ed.), *Euro-Politics: Institutions and Policymaking in the 'New' European Community* (Washington DC, 1992, The Brookings Institution)

Schattschneider, Elmer E., *The Semisovereign People: A Realist's View of Democracy in America* (New York, 1960, Rinehart and Wilson)

Schattschneider, Elmer E., *Two Hundred Million Americans in Search of a Government* (New York, 1969, Holt, Rinehart and Wilson)

Schmitt, Carl, *The Crisis of Parliamentary Democracy* (Cambridge MA, 1988, MIT Press)

Schwartz, Nancy L., *The Blue Guitar: Political Representation and Community* (Chicago and London, 1988, The University of Chicago Press)

Schumpeter, Joseph A., *Capitalism, Socialism and Democracy* (London, 1994, Routledge)

Sharma, B.M. and Choudhry, L. P., *Federal Polity* (London, 1967, Asia Publishing House)

Shaw, Josephine, *European Community Law* (London, 1993, Macmillan)

Shepherd, Robert J., *Public Opinion and European Integration* (Farnborough, 1975, Saxon House)

Shonfield, Andrew, *Europe: Journey to an Unknown Destination* (London, 1973, Allen Lane)

Smith, Anthony D., *National Identity* (Harmondsworth, 1991, Penguin)

Smith, Gordon, *Politics in Western Europe*, Fifth edn (Aldershot, 1990, Dartmouth)

Snyder, Louis L., *The Dynamics of Nationalism: Readings in its Meaning and Development*, (Princeton NJ, 1954, Van Nostrand Company)

Snyder, Louis L., *Encyclopaedia of Nationalism* (New York, 1990, Paragon House)

Sørensen, Georg, *Democracy and Democratization* (Boulder, 1992, Westview Press)

Spinelli, Altiero and Rossi, Ernesto, *Il Manifesto di Ventotene* (Pavia, 1944)

Stavridis, Stelios *et al.* (eds), *New Challenges to the European Union: Policies and Policy-Making* (Aldershot, 1997, Dartmouth)

Stevenson, Garth, *Unfulfilled Union: Canadian Federalism and National Unity*, revised edn (Toronto, 1982, Gage)

Taylor, Paul, *The Limits of European Integration* (New York, 1983, Columbia University Press)

Taylor, Paul, *International Organization in the Modern World: The Regional and the Global Process* (London and New York, 1993, Pinter)

Taylor, Paul, *The European Union in the 1990s* (Oxford, 1996, Oxford University Press)

Tinder, Glenn, *Community: Reflections on a Tragic Ideal* (Baton Rouge and London, 1980, Louisiana State University Press)

Tivey, Leonard (ed.), *The Nation-State: the formation of modern politics* (Oxford, 1981, Martin Robertson)

Tönnies, Ferdinant, *Community and Association* (London, 1974, Routledge and Kegan Paul)

Vanhanen, Tatu, *The Process of Democratization: A Comparative Study of 147 States, 1980-88* (London, 1990, Crane Russak)

Vanhanen, Tatu (ed.), *Strategies of Democratization* (Washington DC, 1991, Crane Russak)

Vile, M.J.C., *The Structure of American Federalism* (London and New York, 1962, Oxford University Press)

Vile, M.J.C., *Constitutionalism and the Separation of Powers* (Oxford, 1967, Clarendon Press)

Wallace, Helen *et al.* (eds), *Policy-Making in the European Community*, Second edn (Chichester, 1983, John Wiley & Sons)

Wallace, William (ed.), *The Dynamics of European Integration* (London and New York, 1990, Pinter)

Wallace, William, *The Transformation of Western Europe* (London, 1990, Royal Institute of International Affairs)

Wallace, William, *Regional Integration: The West European Experience* (Washington DC, 1994, The Brookings Institution Press)

Weale, Albert and Nentwich, Michael (eds), *Political Theory and the European Union: Legitimacy Constitutional Choice and Citizenship* (London and New York, 1998, Routledge)

Wheare, Kenneth C., *Federal Government*, Second edn (London, 1953, Oxford University Press)

Wheare, Kenneth C., *Legislatures*, Second. edn (New York and Toronto, 1968, Oxford University Press)

Wright, Tony, *Citizens and Subjects: An essay on British politics* (London and New York, 1994, Routledge)

Zeigler, Dye, *The Irony of Democracy: An Uncommon Introduction to American Politics*, Ninth edn (Belmont, 1993, Washington Publishing Company)

Zetterholm, Staffan (ed.), *National Cultures and European Integration* (Oxford and Providence, 1994, BERG)

Zolo, Danilo, *Democracy and Complexity: A Realist Approach* (Cambridge, 1992, Polity Press)

ARTICLES

Almond, Gabriel A., 'Comparative Political Systems', *Journal of Politics*, August 1956, pp 391-409

Averyt, William F., 'Eurogroups, Clientela and the European Community', *International Organization*, Autumn 1977, pp 949-72

Barry, Brian, 'Political Accommodation and Consociational Democracy', *British Journal of Political Science*, October 1975, pp 477-505

Bellamy, Richard amd Castiglione, Dario, 'Building the Union: The Nature of Sovereignty in the Political Architecture of Europe', *Law and Philosophy*, Vol. 16, 1997, pp 421-45

Bluhm, W.T., 'Nation-Building: The Case of Austria', *Polity*, Vol. 1, 1968, pp 149-77

Bogdanor, Vernon, 'The Future of the European Community: Two Models of Democracy', *Government and Opposition*, Spring 1986, pp 161-76

Bogdanor, Vernon, 'The June 1989 European Elections and the Institutions of the Community', *Government and Opposition*, Spring 1989, pp 199-214

Bogdanor, Vernon, 'Direct Elections, Representative Democracy and European Integration', *Electoral Studies*, December 1989, pp 205-16

Bogdanor, Vernon and Woodcock, Geoffrey, 'The European Community and Sovereignty', *Parliamentary Affairs*, October 1991, pp 481-92

Bowler, Shaun and Farrell, David M., 'Legislator Shrinking and Voter Monitoring: Impacts of European Parliament Electoral Systems upon Legislator-Voter Relationships', *Journal of Common Market Studies*, March 1993, pp 45-69

Boyce, Brigitte, 'The Democratic Deficit of the European Community', *Parliamentary Affairs*, Vol. 46, No 4, 1993, pp 458-77

Bracher, Karl D., 'Problems of Parliamentary Democracy in Europe', *Daedalus*, Winter 1964, pp 179-98

Brewin, Chistopher, 'The European Community: A Union of States without unity of government', *Journal of Common Market Studies*, September 1987, pp 1-23

Burgess, Michael, 'Federal Ideas in the European Community: Altiero Spinelli and European Union', *Government and Opposition*, Summer 1984, pp 339-47

Cass, Deborah Z., 'The Word that Saves Maastricht? The Principle of Subsidiarity and the Division of Powers in the European Community', *Common Market Law Review*, Vol. 29, 1992, pp 1107-36

Chiti-Batelli, Andrea, 'Functional Federalism', *Common Cause*, April 1950, pp 472-7

Chryssochoou, Dimitris N., 'Democracy and Symbiosis in the European Union: Towards a Confederal Consociation?', *West European Politics*, October 1994, pp 1-14

Chryssochoou, Dimitris N., 'European Union and the Dynamics of Confederal Consociation: Problems and Prospects for a Democratic Future', *Journal of European Integration*, Vol. XVIII, Nos 2-3, 1995, pp 279-305

Chryssochoou, Dimitris N., 'Europe's Could-Be Demos: Recasting the Debate', *West European Politics*, October 1996, pp 787-801

Chryssochoou, Dimitris N., 'New Challenges to the Study of European Integration: Implications for Theory-Building', *Journal of Common Market Studies*, December 1997, pp 521-542

Closa, Carlos, 'The Concept of Citizenship in the Treaty on European Union', *Common Market Law Review*, Vol. 29, pp 1137-69

Connor, Walker, 'Nation-Building or Nation-Destroying?', *World Politics*, April 1971, pp 319-55

Connor, Walker, 'A Nation is a Nation, is a State, is an Ethnic Group, is... ' *Ethnic and Racial Studies*, October 1978, pp 379-88

Corbett, Richard, 'Convergence and Institutional Development', *Journal of Common Market Studies*, August 1993, pp 27-50

Daalder, Hans, 'On building consociational nations: the cases of the Netherlands and Switzerland', *International Social Science Journal*, Vol. 23, No 3, 1971, pp 355-70

Daalder, Hans, 'The Consociational Democracy Theme', *World Politics*, July 1974, pp 604-21

Emiliou, Nicholas, 'Subsidiarity: An Effective Barrier Against "the Enterprises of Ambition"?', *European Law Review*, October 1992, pp 384-407

Featherstone, Kevin, 'Jean Monnet and the "Democratic Deficit" in the European Union', *Journal of Common Market Studies*, June 1994, pp 149-70

Frears, John, 'The French Parliament: Loyal Workhorse, Poor Watchdog', *West European Politics*, July 1990, pp 32-51

Fukuyama, Francis, 'The End of History', *National Interest*, Summer 1989, pp 3-18

Graziano, Luigi, 'The Historic Compromise and Consociational Democracy: Toward a "New Democracy?"', *International Political Science Review*, Vol. 1, No 3, 1980, pp 345-69

Grosser, Alfred, 'The Evolution of European Parliaments', *Daedalus*, Winter 1964, pp 153-78

Haas, Ernst B., 'The Study of Regional Integration: Reflections on the Joy and Anguish of Pretheorizing', *International Organization*, Autumn 1970, pp 607-46

Halpern, Sue M., 'The Disorderly Universe of Consociational Democracy', *West European Politics*, April 1986, pp 181-97

Hartley, Trevor C., 'Constitutional and Institutional Aspects of the Maastricht Agreement', *International and Comparative Law Quarterly*, April 1993, pp 213-37

Hayward, Jack (ed.), 'Special Issue on The Crisis of Representation in Europe', *West European Politics*, July 1995

Hirst, Paul, 'Representative Democracy and its Limits', *Political Quarterly*, April-June 1988, pp 190-205

Hix, Simon, 'Approaches to the Study of the EC: The Challenge to Comparative Politics', *West European Politics*, January 1994, pp 1-30

Hoffmann, Stanley, 'Obstinate or Obsolete? The fate of the nation state in Western Europe', *Daedalus*, Summer 1966, pp 862-915

Hoffmann, Stanley, 'Reflections on the Nation-State in Western Europe', *Journal of Common Market Studies*, September-December 1982, pp 21-37.

Kaiser, Ronn D., 'Toward the Copernican Phase of Regional Integration Theory', *Journal of Common Market Studies*, March 1972, pp 207-32

Kirchner, Emil J. and Williams, Karen, 'The Legal, Political and Institutional Implications of the Isoglucose Judgements', *Journal of Common Market Studies*, December 1983, pp 173-90

Klepsch Egon A., 'The Democratic Dimension of European Integration', *Government and Opposition*, Autumn 1992, pp 407-13

Langeheine, Bernd and Weinstoch, Ulrich, 'Graduated Integration: A Modest Path Towards Progress', *Journal of Common Market Studies*, March 1985, pp 185-97

Lijphart, Arend, 'Consociational Democracy', *World Politics*, January 1969, pp 207-25

Lijphart, Arend, 'Cultural Diversity and Theories of Political Integration', *Canadian Journal of Political Science*, March 1971, pp 1-14

Lijphart, Arend, 'Consociation and Federation: Conceptual and Empirical Links', *Canadian Journal of Political Science*, September 1979, pp 499-515

Lipset, Seymour M., 'The Centrality of Political Culture', *Journal of Democracy*, Fall 1989, pp 80-3

Lodge, Juliet, 'Loyalty and the EEC: The Limits of the Functionalist Approach', *Political Studies*, June 1978, pp 232-48

Lodge, Juliet, 'European Union and the "Democratic Deficit"', *Social Sciences Review*, March 1991, pp 149-153

Lodge, Juliet, 'The European Parliament and the Authority-Democracy Crisis', *The Annals of the American Academy of Political and Social Sciences*, January 1994, pp 69-83

Lodge, Juliet, 'Transparency and Democratic Legitimacy', *Journal of Common Market Studies*, September 1994, pp 343-68

Lord, Christopher, 'From Intergovernmental to Interparliamentary Union: Democratizing Pastiche Europe', *Contemporary European Affairs*, Vol. 4, Nos 2/3, 1991, pp 229-44

Lorwin, Val R., 'Segmented Pluralism: Ideological Cleavages and Political Cohesion in the Smaller European Democracies', *Comparative Politics*, January 1971, pp 141-175

Lustick, Ian, 'Stability in Deeply Divided Societies: Consociationalism versus Control', *World Politics*, April 1979, pp 325-44

Mayne, Richard, 'The Role of Jean Monnet', *Government and Opposition*, April-July 1967, pp 349-71

Mitrany, David, 'Functional Federalism', *Common Cause*, November 1950, pp 196-9

Moravcsik, Andrew, 'Preferences and Power in the European Community: A Liberal Intergovernmentalist Approach', *Journal of Common Market Studies*, December 1993, pp 473-524

Morris Jones, W.H., 'In Defence of Apathy', *Political Studies*, February 1954, pp 25-37

Neunreither, Karlheinz, 'The Democratic Deficit of the European Union: Towards Closer Cooperation between the European Parliament and the National Parliaments', *Government and Opposition*, Summer 1994, pp 299-314

Norton, Philip, 'Parliaments: A Framework for Analysis', *West European Politics*, July 1990, pp 1-9

Norton, Philip, 'Parliament in the United Kingdom: Balancing Effectiveness and Consent?', *West European Politics*, July 1990, pp 10-31

Norton, Philip, 'Legislatures in Perspective', *West European Politics*, July 1990, pp 143-52

Norton, Philip (ed.), 'Special Issue on National Parliaments and the European Union', *The Journal of Legislative Studies*, Vol. 1. No 3, 1995.

Papalardo, Adriano, 'The Conditions for Consociational Democracy: a Logical and Empirical Critique', *European Journal of Political Research*, December 1981, pp 365-90

Pinder, John, 'Positive integration and negative integration', *The World Today*, March 1968, pp 88-110

Pinder, John, 'European Community and nation-state: a case for a neo-federalism?', *International Affairs*, January 1986, pp 41-54

Plumb, Lord, 'Building a democratic community: the role of the European Parliament', *The World Today*, July 1989, pp 112-7.

Puchala, Donald J., 'Of Blind Men, Elephants and International Integration', *Journal of Common Market Studies*, March 1972, pp 267-84

Putman, Robert D., 'Diplomacy and domestic politics: the logic of two-levels game', *International Organization*, Summer 1988, pp 429-60

Raworth, Philip, 'A Timid Step Forwards: Maastricht and the Democratisation of the European Community', *European Law Review*, February 1994, pp 16-33

Rae, Douglas W., 'The Limits of Consensual Decision', *American Political Science Review*, December 1975, pp 1270-4

Saalfeld, Thomas, 'The West German Bundestag after 40 Years: The Role of Parliament in a "Party Democracy"', *West European Politics*, July 1990, pp 68-89

Sartori, Giovanni, 'Electoral Studies and Democratic Theory: A Continental View', *Political Studies*, February 1958, pp 9-15.

Sbragia, Alberta M., 'The European Community: A Balancing Act', *Publius*, Summer 1993, pp 23-38

Scharpf, Fritz W., 'The Joint-Decision Trap: Lessons from German Federalism and European Integration', *Public Administration*, Autumn 1988, pp 239-78

van Scendelen, M.P.C.M., 'The views of Arend Lijphart and collected criticisms', *Acta Politica*, January 1984, pp 19-55

Schmitter, Philippe C. and Karl, Terry L., 'What Democracy is... and is not', *Journal of Democracy*, Summer 1991, pp 75-88

Slater, Martin, 'Political Elites, Popular Indifference and Community Building', *Journal of Common Market Studies*, September-December 1982, pp 69-87

Smith, Anthony D., 'National identity and the idea of European unity', *International Affairs*, January 1992, pp 55-76

Spinelli, Altiero, 'European Union and the Resistance', *Government and Opposition*, April-July 1967, pp 321-29

Stavridis, Stelios, 'The Forgotten Question of the European Parliament's Current Lack of Legitimacy', *The Oxford International Review*, Spring 1992, pp 27-29

Steiner, Jürgen, 'The Principles of Majority and Proportionality', *British Journal of Political Science*, January 1971, pp 63-70

Steiner, Jürgen, 'The Consociational Theory and Beyond', *Comparative Politics*, April 1981, pp 339-54

Taylor, Paul, 'The Concept of Community and the European Integration Process', *Journal of Common Market Studies*, December 1968, pp 83-101

Taylor, Paul, 'The Politics of the European Communities: The Confederal Phase', *World Politics*, April 1975, pp 336-60

Taylor, Paul, 'Interdependence and Autonomy in the European Communities: The Case of the European Monetary System', *Journal of Common Market Studies*, June 1980, pp 370-87

Taylor, Paul, 'The European Community and the state: theories, assumptions and propositions', *Review of International Studies*, April 1991, pp 109-25

Toth, A.G, 'The Principle of Subsidiarity in the Maastricht Treaty', *Common Market Law Review*, Vol. 29, 1992, pp 1079-1105

Tranholm-Mikkelsen, Jeppe, 'Neo-functionalism: Obstinate or Obsolete? A Reappraisal in the Light of the New Dynamism of the EC', *Millennium*, Spring 1991, pp 1-22

Tsinisizelis, Michael J. and Chryssochoou, Dimitris N., 'From "Gesellschaft" to "Gemeinschaft"? Confederal Consociation and Democracy in the European Union', *Current Politics and Economics of Europe*, Vol. 5, No 4, 1995, pp 1-33

Wallace, Helen, 'European Governance in Turbulent Times', *Journal of Common Market Studies*, June 1994, pp 293-303

Wallace, William, 'Europe as a Confederation: the Community and the Nation-State', *Journal of Common Market Studies*, September-December 1982, pp 57-68

Wessels, Wolfgang, 'Rationalizing Maastricht: the search for an optimal strategy of the new Europe', *International Affairs*, July 1994, pp 445-57.

Williams, Shirley, 'Sovereignty and Accountability in the European Community', *Political Quarterly*, July 1990, pp 299-317

OTHER CONTRIBUTIONS

Adonis, Andrew, 'Subsidiarity: Myth, Reality and the Community's Future', House of Lords Select Committee on the European Communities, London, 1990

Bogdanor, Vernon, 'Democratizing the Community', London: Federal Trust, 1990

Bolick, Clint, 'European Federalism: Lessons from America', Occasional Paper No 93, London: The Institute of Economic Affairs, 1994

Bosco, Andrea, 'What is Federalism? Towards a General Theory of Federalism', Second ECSA-World Conference on 'Federalism, Subsidiarity and Democracy in the European Union', Brussels, May 1994

Centre for Economic Policy Research, 'Making Sense of Subsidiarity: How Much Centralization for Europe?', Monitoring European Integration No 4, Annual Report, London, 1993

Church, Clive H., 'The Not So Model Republic? The Relevance of Swiss Federalism to the European Community', Leicester University Discussion Papers in Federal Studies, No FS93/4, November 1994

Church, Clive H., 'The Crisis of Konkordanz Democracy in Switzerland', Bordeaux ECPR Joint Sessions of Workshops, April 1995

Christiansen, Thomas, 'European Integration Between Political Science and International Relations Theory: The End of Sovereignty?', EUI Working Paper No 94/4, San Domenico: Badia Fiesolana, 1994

Dehousse, Ronald, 'Does Subsidiarity Really Matter?', EUI Working Paper No 92/93, San Domenico: Badia Fiesolana, 1993

Delors, Jacques, 'The Principle of Subsidiarity: Contribution to the Debate', in Proceedings of the Jacques Delors Colloquium, 'Subsidiarity: The Challenge of Change', Maastricht: European Institute of Public Administration, 1991

Dunn, Bill N., 'Why the public should be worried about the EEC's democratic deficit', European Democratic Group, Discussion Paper, EPPE, 1988

Geddes, Andrew, 'The Democratic Deficit and the Position of Immigrant and Ethnic Minorities in the European Union', Madrid ECPR Joint Sessions of Workshops, April 1994

Ginderachter, J. Van, 'The Belgian Federal Model', Second ECSA-World Conference on 'Federalism, Subsidiarity and Democracy in the European Union', Brussels, May 1994

Groom, A.J.R., 'The European Community: building up, building down and building across', in Conference Proceedings, 'People's Rights and European Structures', Manresa: Centre Unesco de Catalunya, September 1993, pp 45-50

Forsyth, Murray, 'Towards a New Concept of Confederation', European Commission of Democracy Through Law', Council of Europe, 1994

Held, David, 'Democracy and the New International Order', London: Institute for Public Policy Research, October 1993

Lodge, Juliet, 'The Democratic Deficit and the European Parliament', Fabian Society, Discussion Paper No 4, January 1991

Martin, David, 'European Union and the Democratic Deficit', John Wheatley Centre, June 1990

McKay, David, 'On the Origins of Political Unions', Second ECSA-World Conference on 'Federalism, Subsidiarity and Democracy in the European Union', Brussels, May 1994

Scharpf, Fritz W., 'Community Policy and Autonomy: Multilevel Policy-Making in the European Union', EUI Working Papers No 94/1, San Domenico: Badia Fiesolana, 1994

Shackleton, Michael, 'The Internal Legitimacy Crisis of the European Union', Occasional Paper 1, Europa Institute, The University of Edinburgh, 1994

Stavridis, Stelios, 'Democratic Principles and Foreign Policy: The Case of European Political Cooperation', unpublished PhD dissertation, University of London, London School of Economics and Political Science, 1991

Stavridis, Stelios, 'Democracy in Europe: East and West', in Conference Proceedings, 'People's Rights and European Structures', Manresa: Centre Unesco de Catalunya, September 1993, pp 129-33

Teasdale, Anthony and Huxham, Quentin, 'National Parliaments and the European Parliament: How to improve democratic accountability in the European Community', London: A Bow Group Memorandum, April 1991

Vibert, Frank, *A Core Agenda for the 1996 Inter-Governmental Conference (IGC)* (London, 1995, European Policy Forum)

Welsh, Jennifer M., 'A Peoples' Europe? European Citizenship and European Identity', EUI Working Paper No 93/3, San Domenico: Badia Fiesolana, 1993

Welsh, Michael, 'Accountability and the European Institutions: The Complementary Roles of Westminster and Strasbourg', London: Tory Reform Group, 1990

Williams, Raymond, 'Democracy and Parliament', London: A Socialist Pamphlet, 1982

Index